Financial Service Organizations

Cases in Strategic Management

Richard D. Crawford
New Vision Financial, Inc.

William W. Sihler
Darden School, University of Virginia

HarperCollinsCollegePublishers

Sponsoring Editor: Kirsten Sandberg
Cover Design: Wendy Fredericks
Production Manager: Hilda Koparanian
Printer and Binder: Malloy Lithographing, Inc.
Cover Printer: Malloy Lithographing, Inc.

Library of Congress Cataloging-in-Publication Data

Crawford, Richard
Financial service organizations : cases in strategic management / Richard D. Crawford, William W. Sihler.
p. cm.
ISBN 0-673-46995-6
1. Financial services industry--Management--Case studies.
I. Sihler, William W. II. Title.
HG174.C73 1994
332.1'068--dc20 93-21378
CIP

93 94 95 96 9 8 7 6 5 4 3 2 1

Contents

PREFACE

Purpose and Structure of the Book

This collection of cases was prepared to accompany a text in courses dealing with the financial industry and money and banking. They provide a managerial perspective to add to the conceptual frameworks of a text. The cases also can be used by themselves in an advanced elective with a strategic, policy-level orientation rather than an operations thrust. The cases also offer material to enrich section or lab discussion periods by presenting students with concrete decisions that managers have to make.

Cases in the first three sections of the book address the most basic issues of where the organization should be going and how it should get there. The first section includes an *Introduction* that briefly describes the major players in the financial service industry, the changes that are taking place, and the options that are available to the financial service organizations. Case 1, the short *Unidentified Financial Institutions* case, tests the students' understanding by asking them to identify the type of institution using operating and balance sheet ratios.

The cases in the second section address interest rate and portfolio structure decisions (Case 2), provide an introduction to securitization (Case 3), and raise the issue of how securities trading will be conducted in the future (Case 4).

The third section contains cases that introduce strategic issues taken from a broad spectrum of the financial service industry: credit cards (Case 5) to global finance (Case 15), credit unions (Case 9) to investment banking (Cases 6, 11, and 12), large and small banks (Cases 7 and 8), and insurance companies (Case 10). A wide variety of strategies are discussed:

- how to get into an industry;
- what new role an existing institution can adopt to replace its old one;
- the development of new products to meet competitive challenges (Cases 13 and 14).

The cases in the final section deal with the micro issues of asset allocation. The *National Bank of Los Angeles* (Case 16) is a bridge between the earlier and the final sections. It raises the cost of capital question for a financial institution and the implications for an asset-allocation strategy. Cases 17-22 represent typical types of risk-asset decisions that financial service organizations make and that are usually discussed in texts dealing with these institutions. Cases 17 and 18 illustrate the challenges of underwriting equity and debt issues. Case 19 is a short-term lending analysis; Case 20 is a long-term loan decision. Case 21 is a prospective loan to an information services organization, typical of a loan without heavy asset backing. Case 22 is a commercial real estate loan.

The last two cases look at managerial issues associated with the new world of derivative products (Case 23) and options (Case 24).

The financial service industry has changed so rapidly in the last 30 years, and continues to change so rapidly, that illustrative and case material can quickly go out of date. We have tried to avoid including stale issues in this collection. In some instances, such as the *First Boston* case dealing with the departure of Messrs. Wasserstein and Perella in 1988, the particular incident may have taken place some years ago, but the issues raised are still very current and undecided. Current news reports show that the debate on the proper structure of an investment banking firm is still hotly contested. Likewise, the issue of how to structure an organization to compete globally, raised in the *Credit Suisse* case, has not been settled.

In other cases where the outcome is known, such as the *Discover Card* case, it is important to take the perspective of the decision makers at the time. Once this analysis has been completed, it is appropriate to speculate on whether the outcome could have been foreseen versus the effect of later developments.

Case Analysis

These cases are not expanded problems of the type included in many textbooks—they have been written with the goal of making them as brief as possible. Nevertheless, they provide sufficient information about the contemporary competitive environment that the reader is given a sense of the issues facing the managers at the time. Industry detail has been included in the *Introduction* and compressed into exhibits rather than elaborated in the case text. Students should not have to do further research to prepare the case, although information included in the basic texts will often have useful additional data.

These are not "trick" cases, hiding a rabbit for the lucky analyst to pull out of a hat. The solutions to many of them remain controversial—to many, there is still no right answer. All of the cases are drawn from real situations, although some have been disguised or altered to protect confidential information.

Because not all students will be familiar with the way to analyze this type of case, here are a few hints for how to get started. Above all, don't get lost in the thickets of detail until you have some general understanding of the situation. What are the big issues? Who are the major players? What are their strengths and weaknesses? Answering these questions may require digging in the numbers, but digging with an objective is much more productive than random spadework.

A Generalized Approach

The analysis of these cases, like the analysis of any of life's unstructured challenges, has four basic elements:

1. *Problem identification and verification.* What is *really* going on in the situation? Often, the individuals in the case will state the problem(s) as they see it. That is a good starting point, but sometimes the individuals do not see the proper problem. Look carefully to determine whether the players understand what game they are in and how to play it. You will sometimes conclude that the real problem is something quite different—which creates the problem (if you were in the situation yourself) of how to communicate that insight to those involved.

Effective problem identification and evaluation require you to think carefully about the environment in which the problems have arisen. Many frameworks for strategic thinking have been developed to help you with this task, all of which have relevant insights. Is the business growing or declining? What does it take to succeed in its market? What are the organization's strengths and weaknesses? Are they the right ones? How can they be strengthened (or obtained)? Who are the suppliers? Who are the customers? Who calls the tune? Who dances when ordered to?

You also may need to think about the individual participant's perspective—who will win and who will lose. How might an individual's personal position affect that individual's identification of a problem and support of a solution?

2. *Development of alternative resolutions.* The case may suggest alternatives for you to consider. These are useful starting points, but the wise analyst also will ask if there are better ideas. The search for alternatives is particularly important if you decide that the important problems are not the ones identified by the individuals in the situation.

3. *Evaluation of the alternatives.* It is easy to upset your boss by reporting that you have dismissed the boss's suggested alternative without analysis because you have a better idea. For that reason, first analyzing whatever alternatives are suggested in the case is the order of the day. Then, as the problems with those alternatives are clearer (which should contribute to the generation of new suggestions), you can return to the second stage to come up with better alternatives. The benefits of the new alternatives can be compared with the initial suggestions in the case, which you can consider your boss's ideas.

4. *Selection of the most effective alternative.* Very seldom will the selected alternative remedy all the problems raised, and very frequently the alternative will introduce problems of its own. The solution is usually the alternative that creates the greatest good net of the problems it also creates or does not solve. It is very important (in real life as on examinations) to present a balanced picture in justifying the alternative(s) you recommend.

At some point, because these are real business problems, you need to give thought to implementing or selling the idea to the decision makers and others involved. It is in this area that the most complex ethical questions arise. You may know there are disadvantages to a solution, but how do you explain (or even sell) the solution to those who may be adversely affected? Many components of the financial service industry, which used to offer virtually lifetime employment, have been forced to shrink their staff. For others, expansion into new niches means that new skills have to be developed. Can this be accomplished with the existing employees? These problems often have painful human dimensions. To save the jobs of some, jobs of others have to be eliminated. These difficult issues have to be addressed; frequently the more directly they are addressed, the better the resolution will be.

Acknowledgements

Major support for these cases came from the Darden Graduate School of Business Administration, University of Virginia, and the Darden Graduate School Foundation. Dean John W. Rosenblum provided the released time and funds to gather and write the material. Editorial and secretarial assistance were provided by the Darden School staff, most recently by June Simms. Special thanks are due to Professor Charles O. Meiburg for his support. Research assistance was provided by William Epstein, Kirsten Peterson, and David N. Webb. Material was adapted from student reports written by Jed W. Becksted, Philip E. Haydon, Richard R. Hollington III, Rosemary Basile King, and William C. McGahan. Many of the corporate executives who helped develop these cases wish to remain anonymous, but we are delighted to express our appreciation to C.M. Baker, Frank E. Baxter, Barbara Chu, Lucinda M. Cochrane, Philip H. Davidson, Jack Donaldson, Michael D. Easterly, Richard Gridley, W. Gibson Harris II, Richard R. Hollington Jr., Paul H. Hunn, Allen D. Meadows, Reid Nagle, Richard Pike, Mark A. Seigel, Samuel C. Tallman Jr., Jerald Wigdortz, and Philip L. Zimmerman for their help. We owe a great debt to these individuals, but errors must be charged to our account.

Clip art used in the graphics is copyright by New Vision Technologies, Inc. and used under the terms of its licensing agreement. Bitstream typefaces were used with Facelift for WordPerfect to compose the book. The base body text is Charter set at 11 points with exhibits scaled to make them convenient for the student to use. The heads and subheads are in Zurich bold and bold italics 11 points. The titles and chapter heads are in Clarendon 13 points.

Richard D. Crawford
William W. Sihler
Charlottesville, Virginia

INTRODUCTION TO THE FINANCIAL SERVICES INDUSTRY

This survey provides an overview of the financial services industry's strategic environment. The main components of the financial services industry are commercial banks, thrifts, insurance companies, pension funds, and mutual funds. There are many other players, such as credit unions and investment firms of all types. Historically, the financial services industry in the United States was dominated by depository institutions. At the turn of the century, commercial banks and thrifts held about 85 percent of the financial assets in the portfolios of financial services companies. Insurance companies held most of the rest. Since 1900, this dominance has steadily eroded as nondepository financial services companies expanded their share of the total revenues, assets, and income of the financial services industry. This erosion has accelerated in the last 20 years because of two interrelated factors: the securitization of depository institution loans and the increasing participation of nondepository financial services companies in the traditional activities of depository institutions.

By 1990, only 40 percent of the financial assets held by financial services companies remained at depository institutions. Depository institutions and insurance companies combined held only 55 percent. By the year 2000, depository institutions' share could drop to a mere 30 percent, and the combined assets of depository institution and insurance company assets could be less than 45 percent of all financial service assets.*

This survey is organized in three parts. The first part reviews general trends that are affecting the financial services industry as a whole and relates them to developments that are occurring in the nondepository financial services sector. The second part consists of a brief description of the major segments that make up the nondepository financial services industry. The third part discusses the basic aspects of financial service organization strategic management.

---

*The emergence of the nondepository financial services industry as a major force in the American system was first pointed out in a study by Cleveland A. Christophe titled *Competition in Financial Services*, published by Citicorp in 1974. Subsequent to that analysis, the Federal Reserve Bank of Chicago in 1983 published a report titled *Competition in Financial Services: The Impact of Nonbank Entry* by Harvey Rosenblum and Diane Siegel. This report expanded on the Citicorp study in defining the changing characteristics of the industry and the new dominant players. Since the publication of the Federal Reserve Bank of Chicago study, a great deal has been written about the growth of the financial services industry outside of the depository institution and insurance arenas.

Part 1: An Overview of the Financial Services Industry

Historical Evolution of Financial Services

Banking and insurance have played a role in the economy since the beginning of recorded history. A medium of exchange exists among the most technologically primitive peoples, and a store of value (usually in the form of precious metals—gold and silver) has existed since ancient times. The Chinese made coins as early as 2250 B.C., and the Greeks introduced coins to the West in 625 B.C. The Babylonians insured ships in 3000 B.C. The role of financial intermediaries both to invest society's excess production and to insure against future risks dates to medieval times in Europe. Flemish and Italian bankers (of which the most famous were the Medici) financed wars and trading as far back as the 12th Century. The most famous insurance entity of all, Lloyds of London, traces its origin back to the 17th Century.

With the advent of the Industrial Revolution in England in the 18th Century, financial services grew in scope and complexity. The increased productivity generated surplus to invest. The increasing need for large-scale investment that accompanied industrialization created a demand for newer, larger, and more sophisticated financial intermediaries. The rapid industrialization of the 19th Century saw the rise of financial powerhouses, such as the Rothschilds in Europe and J.P. Morgan and Company in the United States, which played major roles in gathering the savings generated in the industrial age and investing it in new major enterprises such as the building of the Suez Canal (the Rothschilds) and the formation of the U.S. Steel Company (J. P. Morgan and Company).

Accompanying the rise of major financial organizations in the 19th Century was the development of new legal instruments and new techniques in finance. Many of the standard products of the banking and insurance business, ranging from the corporate bond to life insurance, were developed during the industrialization of the 19th Century.

In the 20th Century, the rise of mass consumer societies in Western Europe, North America, and Japan engendered further development of financial services. New products, such as the consumer installment loan and the credit card, were introduced. New types of financial services enterprises, such as retail securities brokers like Merrill Lynch, emerged. During the 20th Century, government's role in financial services also grew. A range of institutions, from the Federal Reserve System and the Federal Deposit Insurance Corporation to the Securities and Exchange Commission, were established in the United States. Similar government institutions developed in other advanced industrial countries. The 20th Century also saw the development of international governmental financial institutions, such as the International Monetary Fund and the World Bank, in response to the increased globalization of commercial activity.

Today, in the United States, there are thousands of financial services companies offering an incredibly complex variety of financial products governed by a maze of governmental regulation and governmental regulatory bodies at the local, state, and Federal level. For the future, the financial services sector of the economy should continue to develop rapidly with new organization forms, services, and industry structure emerging by the beginning of the 21st Century.

Trends in the Financial Services Industry

The financial services industry can be divided into six major categories:

- Commercial banks
- Thrifts
- Insurance companies
- Pension funds
- Mutual funds
- Specialized financial services companies.

Specialized financial services companies, the subject of a later part of this note, can be further divided into six sub-industry categories:

- Government-sponsored enterprises (GSEs)
- Finance companies
- Mortgage banking companies
- Securities firms
- Investment advisory firms
- Miscellaneous financial services companies.

The specialized financial services industry is large by almost any measure: numbers of companies, revenues, assets, and employment. The industry has experienced varied profitability during the 1980s, but on average it was much more profitable than institutions belonging to the first three major categories of the financial services industry: thrifts, commercial banks, and insurance. Some segments of the specialized financial services industry, such as brokerage and investment advisory, routinely experience returns on equity of 20 to 40 percent. In contrast, the thrift industry has been losing money, and the commercial banking industry enjoys only a 5 percent average return. Two major types of financial service organizations, mutual and pension funds, do not report profits as institutions because their earnings are passed directly to the beneficiaries.

Two of the most significant developments in the financial markets in the last 20 years have been the overall growth of financial assets, both domestically and globally, and the emergence of the institutional investor as the dominant force in financial markets. Since 1969, the world's total volume of stocks, bonds, and cash outstanding has grown from $2 trillion to $22 trillion. Financial assets in the United States have grown approximately 900 percent since 1969. Financial assets outside the United States grew almost 2,000 percent in the same period. Financial assets held outside the United States have grown from 33 percent of total world financial assets in 1969 to 55 percent in 1991—$12 trillion of the $22 trillion now reside in non-U.S. markets. At the same time that world financial assets have been growing, ownership of the world's stocks and bonds has shifted toward institutions and away from individual investors.

The staggering growth of institutional investors, particularly of pension funds and mutual funds, the two most important categories, has had a major impact on American financial markets and the ownership of American businesses. In the United States today, pension funds, mutual funds, educational endowments, and charitable foundations own more than 50 percent of common stock outstanding (more than $2 trillion worth). Comparable figures were 40 percent in 1980 and 15 percent in 1950. Institutional investors own an even larger share of the fixed-income securities. The existence of a growing pool of institutional money with a strong appetite for fixed income securities has made possible the securitization revolution, which will be described later in this survey.

Institutions may trade securities frequently as a way to improve both the return and liquidity of their portfolios. Because of the growth of institutional investors, today more than 70 percent of all outstanding shares changes hands during a year, compared to about 20 percent in the 1970s. Institutions account for 80 percent of this trading. Daily trading on the New York Stock Exchange averages over 150 million shares, more than ten times the daily average in 1974 and 100 times the daily average in the early 1950s. The majority of shares trade in large blocks. Half the daily trading volume takes place in blocks of shares of 10,000 or more. The average transaction on the New York Stock Exchange exceeds 2,000 shares, nearly six times what it was in 1974. Trading volume is even higher in the bond market, with daily trading averaging $100 billion, a rate that means the entire U.S. government debt changes hands ten times a year.

The growth of the institutional investment community and the increased volume of activity in the financial markets benefit most types of specialized financial services companies, from finance companies to mortgage banking companies to securities brokers and investment advisors. The finance companies benefit from a broader market in which to raise funds because pension funds and mutual funds are the principal purchasers of commercial paper and intermediate-term debt, the finance companies' primary sources of funds. Mortgage companies benefit because the growth of pension funds and mutual funds provides a ready market for the mortgages they originate, particularly when these mortgages are packaged and sold as securities. Securities firms benefit because they are at the center of the trading and underwriting activities in the vastly expanded financial markets. And investment advisors benefit because they reap investment management fees from the growing pool of assets belonging to the pension funds and mutual funds.

A variety of other forces is also reshaping the financial services industry and contributing to the growth of the specialized financial services companies. Included in these forces are technology, demographics, and government policy. Acting separately and together, these forces are creating competitive advantages for specialized financial services companies and are speeding their growth relative to depository institutions and insurance companies.

Technology and Financial Services

The single most important force reshaping the financial services landscape is technology. Computer and communications technology is changing the economics of the financial services industry and making winners of companies with economies of scale in areas such as consumer banking and of companies serving specialized market niches such as institutional brokerage. As computer and communications technology evolves rapidly in the 1990s, it will continue to reshape the financial services industry and provide surprising success stories. Companies with large fixed investments in existing computer systems or large office networks may be leapfrogged by more nimble competitors that can take advantage of technological change to improve productivity and lower costs. This has already occurred in the credit card area. Nondepository companies, such as AT&T and Sears, Roebuck, have leveraged existing customer relationships and processing capability to create a large base of credit card relationships.

Within the area of technology, a major force reshaping the financial services industry is the securitization of loans. Loan securitization is the combination of a group of loans in a form that allows the group to be sold to the public as one or more securities. The ultimate security may take a variety of forms, but it is usually a debt instrument. The growth of loan securitization has arisen as a direct result of the dramatic improvements in computer processing power required to make the myriad calculations involved in the securitization process.

Securitization of Loans

Basic Structure

The key element of loan securitization is the separation of the credit risk of the securities to be sold from the credit risk associated with the corporation or financial institution originating the loans. Investors buy a share of a pool of assets rather than depositing funds with or otherwise lending money to an intermediary to invest for them. Buyers of securitized loans therefore look to the cash flow from the loans (plus any credit enhancement features) to support the debt service of the resulting securities rather than to the credit quality of the corporation or financial institution originating the loans.

When a financial institution, such as a bank or thrift, originates and holds a loan in its own portfolio, it is involved as the only intermediary. It connects the ultimate source and user of funds (that is, the bank depositor and the bank borrower). When a financial institution originates a loan and securitizes it, many intermediaries are involved in the process. Securities firms underwrite, distribute, and trade the securities involved; investment advisors manage the pension funds or mutual funds that buy the securities; and specialized insurance entities (frequently government-sponsored enterprises like Freddie Mac and Fannie Mae) insure the securities or the assets that underlie the securities.

History

Securitization of loans made by banks and other financial institutions began in 1970 when the Government National Mortgage Association (Ginnie Mae) offered investors the opportunity to buy a security representing an interest in a pool of FHA and VA mortgages. The volume of mortgage-backed securities outstanding grew rapidly during the 15 years after the initial Ginnie Mae issue. By 1985, mortgage-backed securities represented the second largest pool of securities outstanding after U.S. government securities. Between 1981 and 1986, the percentage of new mortgage originations that were securitized rose from less than 20 percent to approximately 70 percent. Since 1986, the percentage of new mortgages securitized has ranged between two-thirds and three-quarters of all new mortgages issued each year. At the end of 1991, there were $1.2 trillion in mortgage-backed securities outstanding, accounting for 40 percent of the $3 trillion in residential mortgages. In 1991, the annual volume of new mortgage-backed securities issued was $250 billion, almost five times the volume five years earlier.

Until 1985, securitization of loans involved principally residential mortgages. The market for securitized "loans" expanded dramatically when Sperry Rand offered participations in a group of computer leases through its investment banker, First Boston. With this successful offering of securitized nonmortgage assets and a subsequent successful offering of securitized automobile loan receivables by Marine Midland Bank, the securitization of nonmortgage assets (also called asset-backed securities or ABSs) took off. By the end of 1991, a wide array of automobile lenders issued automobile-receivables-backed securities, and the annual volume of new automobile loan ABSs reached $19 billion. Credit card ABSs, first publicly offered in 1987, became the largest sector of the nonmortgage ABS market; $20.8 billion in credit card securities were underwritten in 1991.

By the end of 1991, asset securitization had become the single most important activity of Wall Street. Total underwriting volume of ABSs reached a record $299 billion, almost double the volume of 1990. ABS underwriting accounted for over half of all volume in a record year for securities underwriting of all types. It exceeded the combined total of a record $76 billion in new equity issues and a record $208 billion in new long-term debt issues.

Implications

Overall, loan securitization is driving a massive restructuring of the American financial system, giving a much broader role to nondepository, noninsurance financial institutions. Securitization allows financial institutions such as finance companies and mortgage bankers to originate increased volumes of assets because they do not have to hold them in portfolio. This freedom allows them to compete more aggressively for loan originations with banks and thrifts, which have access to insured deposits.

Government-sponsored enterprises like Fannie Mae and Freddie Mac, finance companies like General Electric Credit, and mortgage banking companies like Countrywide and Lomas and Nettleton benefit from their ability to originate a growing volume of new assets. Securities firms benefit from the huge volume of fees generated by their packaging activities. Investment advisory firms benefit from the growing volume of assets requiring asset management services.

Securitization also curtails the role depository institutions play as major holders of financial assets and transfers much of that role to pension funds and mutual funds. This change from depository institutions to pension funds and mutual funds as the primary holder of financial assets in the financial system will be significant for many other constituents of the financial services industry. Specialized financial services companies that are the originators, packagers, placers, and managers of the assets of pension funds and mutual funds will increasingly play the central role in the financial system.

Demographics and Financial Services

A major force reshaping the financial services landscape is demographics. The United States is now experiencing a rise in the median and average age of the American population. The increase in the average age of Americans helps certain categories of financial services firms and hurts others because of effect of the "consumer-financial-product life cycle." Consumers purchase different types of financial services at different stages of their lives.

People are most likely to borrow in their younger years when they first enter the work force and are buying their homes and consumer durables such as furniture and automobiles. People under age 35 tend to use credit products, such as auto loans, credit card loans, and mortgage loans, and products such as life insurance. In their middle years, when they have higher incomes, they begin to save to accumulate financial assets to finance their children's education and provide income for retirement. Over age 35, people purchase savings products, such as stocks, bonds, and mutual funds, and insurance products, such as health and liability insurance. In their older, retirement years, people are often neither extreme borrowers or savers; they live off the income generated by their earlier savings.

Obviously, people under 35 buy stocks and bonds and health and liability insurance and older people seek auto loans, use credit cards, and buy life insurance. As a person ages, however, the general trend is to move from borrowing to savings and from life insurance (to protect a young family) to health and liability insurance (to protect oneself and one's assets).

As America ages over the next 20 years, reflecting the movement of the baby boomers into their middle-age years, the savings rate in the United States should rise dramatically and reach more than 10 percent of disposable personal income. The purchases of financial services will mirror the shift in the consumer-financial-product life cycle. The volume of consumer credit products and life insurance should slacken, and the volume of savings products should grow. Because the purveyors of consumer credit products and life insurance products are principally depository institutions and life insurance companies, these institutions face flat demand and will be adversely affected by the aging of America. The purveyors of today's popular savings products are principally securities brokers and investment advisors. These financial institutions will be positively affected by the rising median age of Americans.

Demographics, like technology, will thus adversely affect traditional depository and insurance institutions while helping those providing specialized financial services.

Regulation and Financial Services

Adding to the turbulence in the financial services industry is the shifting regulatory policy at both the state and federal level. Historically, the financial services industry has been one of the most regulated industries in the United States, with both state and federal oversight. For example, every state has an extensive web of regulation for both banking and insurance activities. Often, these regulations reflect conditions that no longer exist.

Because specialized financial services firms are not as thoroughly regulated as depository institutions and insurance companies, they have a competitive advantage. As the financial services environment evolves because of changing technology and demographics, specialized financial services companies will have more flexibility to adapt because of their lower regulatory constraints and burdens. They are not subject to mandated expenses that banks face, such as insurance fees and expenses created by the Community Reinvestment Act. They will not have to pay for the cost of their failed brethren the way banks, thrifts, and even insurance companies will. Over time, the differences in the regulatory burden should guarantee higher profits for specialized financial services companies than for traditional banks and thrifts.

Part 2: Components of the Financial Services Industry

Depository Institutions

In the United States at the end of the 1980s, depository institutions fell into two basic categories: commercial banks and thrifts. Both types of institutions were licensed to accept deposits from the public in the form of checking accounts, savings accounts, certificates of deposit, and similar instruments. The two types of institutions differed, however, in the type of investments they were licensed to make and the regulatory framework surrounding them. Together, commercial banks and thrifts held $4 trillion of deposits, the largest share of the economy's financial assets. Commercial banks accounted for about three-quarters of deposits ($3 trillion) and thrifts for about one-quarter ($1 trillion). There were approximately 11,900 commercial banks in the United States and 2,500 thrifts.

New lending powers granted to the thrifts in the early 1980s and changing strategic directions for commercial banks have blurred the distinctions between the two types of institutions. Historically, thrifts focused on residential mortgage lending, and commercial banks focused on lending to commercial borrowers. Today, with thrifts having powers to make commercial loans and construction loans and banks aggressively expanding into residential mortgage lending, banks and thrifts are increasingly similar. Industry experts expect the distinctions between the two types of institutions to disappear by the end of the century with the development of a universal depository institution charter and common regulatory framework.* By that time, depository institutions should become national, broad-based financial services companies offering a complete range of financial services, from consumer loans and retail securities brokerage to underwriting corporate securities, and providing comprehensive financing packages (debt and equity) to businesses. There will still be room for many specialized entities playing a variety of niche roles.

Despite their importance, the pressures on depository institutions are evident in the reduction in their numbers. The thrift segment has been particularly hard hit. From 1960 to the beginning of 1993, the number of thrifts dropped from 6,835 to 2,529. By the end of the century, there may be fewer than 500 thrifts left, and the distinctions between thrifts and banks will probably have disappeared.

The absolute number of banks has not dropped as rapidly as the number of thrifts, but consolidation is occurring rapidly there as well. This trend reflects the reality of nationwide banking and the continued concentration of banking assets. In 1990, there were about 12,000 independent banking organizations in the United States. Because of multiple ownership, the true figure was closer to 8,500 banks and bank groups, a substantial drop from the post-depression peak of over 14,000. Through a combination of failures and merger, the total could decline to between 1,500 and 3,000 by the year 2000.

Commercial bank assets in September 1991 were structured as shown in Table 1.

Table 1
Bank Assets as of September 1991
(dollars in billions)

Asset Class	Amount	Percent
Loans	$ 2,252	66
Federal government securities	498	15
Other securities	159	4
Other assets	514	15
Total	$ 3,423	100

Source: Federal Reserve Board

*Predictions of industry rationalization have long been foiled by a complex structure of industry-legislative relationships and a regulatory system that tends to protect the status quo. This prediction may suffer the same fate.

Insurance Institutions

Insurance institutions fall into two major categories: life and health insurance companies and property-casualty insurance companies. Life and health insurance companies (as their name implies) provide individual and group life insurance, health insurance, and annuity products to their customer base. Annuities are now the fastest growing life-insurance product, followed by health insurance. Property-casualty insurance protects against loss or damage to property owned by the insured and against liability to others for injury, damage, or destruction of their person or property.

Life and health insurance companies are the larger of the two major categories, with combined assets of almost three times the size of property-casualty assets ($1,551 billion in assets for life insurance companies versus $501 billion in assets for property-casualty companies in 1991). Annual life insurance premium volume is approximately 76 percent higher than property-casualty premiums ($264 billion in 1991 versus $180 billion).

Though the two major types of insurance companies differ in size, the more important differences are in operating characteristics, which require different approaches to the investment markets. Because property-casualty companies pay out the bulk of their premiums in claims in the year the premiums are earned, and often even pay out more in claims than premiums earned, property-casualty companies emphasize liquidity in their investment policies. Property-casualty companies invest the bulk of their assets in shorter term, safe, lower yield assets. Life and health companies, by contrast, pay out the bulk of current premiums in future years because of the long-term nature of life insurance and annuity products. Consequently, life and health companies are more long-term investors than property-casualty companies. They can accept higher risk assets for the higher yield they provide.

The distinction in the types of assets the two types of companies invest in can be seen in the percentage distribution of their assets. Table 2 shows a comparative breakdown of the assets of the two types of companies at the end of 1990.

Table 2
Asset Distribution of Insurance Company Investments, 1990

Asset Category	Life Insurance Companies	Property-Casualty Companies
Cash & gov't securities	17.4%	23.0%
Municipal bonds	—	37.0
Other bonds	40.2	18.5
Stocks	10.6	18.5
Mortgages	17.1	—
Policy loans	4.3	—
Other assets	10.4	3.0
Total	100.0%	100.0%

Source: Standard and Poor's *Industry Survey*, January 1993

Pension Funds

Pension funds are a relative new entry to the financial institution scene. The first private pension plan was founded in the United States in 1875 by American Express, but the industry developed only in the 20th Century. Since World War II, pension funds have grown very rapidly, becoming major actors in the capital markets scene. In 1950, there were 2,000 pension plans in the United States with $17 billion in assets covering 25 percent of the U.S. work force. By 1974, when the Employee Retirement Income Security Act (ERISA) was signed into law, the number of pension plans had grown to 50,000 with total assets of $200 billion covering 50 percent of the work force.

In the 17 years following ERISA, total pension fund assets increased almost 15 times, reaching $2.9 trillion in 1991, about equal to the total assets in the commercial banking system. Between 1950 and 1991, pension assets grew at six times the growth rate for GNP. During their rapid growth in the 1980s, pension fund assets grew at an annual compounded rate of 12.5 percent. In the United States, corporate, union, and government pension funds held about half of the pension-fund assets and were major forces in the intermediate and long-term investment markets.

Pension funds now own approximately 40 percent of the equity capital of U.S. companies and more than two-thirds of the equity capital of the 1,000 largest businesses. Pension funds had thus become the primary suppliers of equity capital in the United States in addition to being major sources of debt financing. By the year 2000, pension funds will be even more significant in the overall investment environment. By then, pension funds may hold at least two-thirds of the share capital of all U.S. businesses, excepting the smallest firms.

By the end of 1991, there were more than 37,000 corporate, union, and government pension funds in the United States. Table 3 shows the distribution of asset holdings by the major types of pension funds at the end of 1990.

Table 3
Asset Class Breakdowns for Major Institutional Fund Categories, 1990

	Institutional Fund Categories		
Asset Class	Corporate	Union	Government
Cash equivalents	7.2%	9.5%	7.3%
Bonds	22.2	43.8	36.3
Guaranteed investment contracts	12.3	5.2	0.7
Mortgages	1.3	3.4	10.0
Stocks	42.1	31.5	38.6
Real estate equity	3.6	3.3	4.2
Other	11.3	3.3	2.9
Total	100.0%	100.0%	100.0%

Source: *Money Market Directory*, Money Market Directories, Inc., Charlottesville, VA, 1991.

There are two major types of pension plans: defined-benefit pension plans and defined-contribution pension plans. Defined-benefit pension plans promise specified benefits, typically a monthly retirement pension. The size of the pension typically is a function of preretirement compensation and years of service. Defined-contribution plans periodically pay to the pension trustee a specific amount for each participant. The payment is usually defined as a percentage of compensation. The ultimate retirement benefits depend on the amount contributed and on the skill of the investment manager rather than on any predetermined formula. Pension plans for which tax deductions are allowed to the employer must meet many tests, and the contributions are not related to the company's profits. Profit-sharing plans also exist and can be structured very much like defined-contribution pension plans.

Until the adoption of ERISA in 1974, pension fund regulation emphasized conservative, income-oriented investments under the "prudent man" rule. With the adoption of ERISA, which considered risk in the total portfolio rather than in individual investments, pension funds could begin to diversify into nontraditional assets such as real estate, international securities, and venture capital.

Mutual Funds

The growth of mutual funds since the end of World War II has been even more dramatic than the growth of pension funds. In 1945, total assets of mutual funds in the United States equaled $1 billion. By 1970, mutual fund assets had grown to $50 billion. By 1990, the assets of mutual funds had mushroomed to $1 trillion, and one in four Americans owned shares of mutual funds. In the 15 years between 1976 and 1991, mutual fund assets grew at a compounded annual rate of 25 percent.

This growth reflects households' shifting from depository institutions to mutual funds as their financial intermediary of choice. In 1982, households channeled $151.5 billion of discretionary investment flows into banks and thrifts and $38.6 billion into mutual funds. By 1991, this pattern had been completely reversed: $184.4 billion of household discretionary investments went into mutual funds, but only $10.6 billion flowed into banks and thrifts. Mutual fund growth should continue strongly in the 1990s, although at a lower rate. Current projections for long-term mutual fund growth rates in the 1990s is in the 13 percent to 14 percent range.

A major factor in the growth of mutual funds in the 1980s was the success of money-market mutual funds (MMF). First offered in 1974, MMFs experienced phenomenal growth in the 1980s, which reflected their attractiveness to savers as an alternative to bank deposits. In the ten-year period between 1980 and 1990, the assets of MMFs rose from $74 billion to $422 billion, an increase of 470 percent.

MMFs offer higher interest rates but similar liquidity to bank deposits, although they are not insured by an implicit U.S. government guarantee. The investor can obtain safety, however, by selecting funds that only invested in U.S. government short-term securities. In some cases, a fund of this type might even be safer than a large bank certificate of deposit. In addition, MMFs increasingly offer the same convenience as bank accounts, such as a check-writing feature. The MMFs also can be structured to deliver a yield free of federal and state income taxes. As a result, money funds began to replace commercial banks in many of their traditional functions. They raised funds from the liquid resources of individuals and invested them in government and high-quality short-term corporate debt (through the purchase of commercial paper).

The MMFs thus operate in 1992 in much the way commercial banks did in 1950 but without the need for substantial stockholder capital, deposit insurance, regulatory expenses, and social costs. These cost advantages allowed the MMFs to capture much of the traditional low-risk, low-margin business of the commercial banking system.

Specialized Financial Services

In addition to the major segments of the financial services industry, there are several large, important but more narrowly focused institutions. This section will describe the most significant types of these companies.

Government Sponsored Enterprises

Congress chartered the Government Sponsored Enterprises (GSEs) to serve specialized niches in the financial system that Congress concluded were not adequately served by purely private-sector financial institutions. GSEs have a long history. The oldest GSE, the Farm Credit System, was founded in 1916, when the federal government established the Federal Land Banks and related cooperative associations. These institutions were to provide credit to the agriculture sector. The second oldest GSE, the Federal Home Loan Bank System, was established in 1932 to provide funding to the thrift industry.

GSEs are authorized to issue debt with most of the characteristics of federal agency securities. They are governed by boards that often include government-appointed directors, have debt that is implicitly guaranteed by the federal government, and are usually supported by lines of credit to the U.S. Treasury. Their federal charters allow them to operate nationally and override some state laws and taxes. Although they are creatures of the federal government, GSEs are privately owned; their equity was raised through stock sold to individuals and private institutions. They are not governed by federal civil service and procurement laws. They are profit-making operations that do not depend on regular federal appropriations.

There are six GSEs. Some are publicly owned companies and some are privately held, often by financial institutions in the special niche market that these institutions are expected to serve. Of the current GSEs, the Federal National Mortgage Association (Fannie Mae), the Federal Home Loan Mortgage Corporation (Freddie Mac), and the Student Loan Marketing Association (Sallie Mae) have sold stock to the public. These three institutions have been among the most rapidly growing financial institutions in America. In the five-year period between 1986 and 1991, all three of these institutions more than doubled their net income, with similar high growth rates in assets and total revenues. Fannie Mae's growth in net income was particularly spectacular: net income grew from $105 million in 1986 to $1.4 billion in 1991. In the 1990s, these GSEs should have continued growth, although at a slower rate.

Finance Companies

Finance companies were originally established to provide financing to consumers and businesses that were not adequately served by traditional depository institutions. Many of these companies provide credit to consumers not considered credit worthy or attractive to depository institutions and to small businesses insufficiently capitalized to attract commercial bank financing.

Finance companies fall into three categories, although many companies operate in more than one segment:

- Consumer finance companies, also known as small-loan or direct-loan companies, lend money to individuals according to the terms of the small-loan laws of each state.
- Sales finance companies, also called acceptance companies, purchase retail and wholesale paper from automobile and other consumer and capital goods dealers.

- Commercial finance companies make loans to manufacturers and wholesalers secured by accounts receivables, inventories, and equipment.

The assets of the finance company industry are evenly split between consumer lending and commercial finance lending. Overall, the total assets of the finance company industry are equal to about one-tenth of the assets of the depository system. Some companies are independently owned. Some are subsidiaries of companies engaged in other lines of business.

Unlike the commercial banks with which they compete, finance companies do not take in deposits. They fund themselves through commercial paper, bank loans, and intermediate and long-term bonds. Finance companies typically enjoy high credit ratings and can borrow at the lowest market rates. This ability enables them to make loans at rates not much higher than bank rates despite the finance companies' lack of access to low-cost consumer deposits. Although their customers usually do not qualify for bank credit, the specialized credit expertise and loan workout skills of finance companies can keep their default rates low. Because of their dependence on money-market sources for funding, finance companies are usually very interest-rate sensitive, with changes in interest rates inversely affecting their profits.

■ *Consumer finance* consists of making and investing in residential real estate–secured loans to individuals, making secured and unsecured installment loans to individuals, purchasing consumer retail installment debt, investing in credit card receivables, financing manufactured housing purchases, and providing other consumer financial services.

A good example of a typical traditional consumer finance company is Beneficial Corporation. Beneficial competes through high-quality personal service provided by a branch office network (894 offices throughout the United States at the end of 1991). It typically gets new customers through sales finance customers to whom it provides credit, or it buys accounts from local vendors such as furniture or appliance dealers. Beneficial then contacts these customers through telephone and mail solicitations to offer other products, including home equity loans and loans for such purposes as bill consolidation, home improvement, or college education.

■ *Commercial finance* consists of the purchase of time sales obligations and leases, direct leases, and secured direct loans to companies. The most important activity of commercial finance is asset-based lending. Asset-based lending is a form of commercial lending in which the assets of a company are used to secure the company's debt. In the broadest sense, all secured loans can be classified as asset-based loans. However, the financial community has defined asset-based lending to include only those loans in which the lender looks first to collateral, rather than to cash flow, for repayment. This collateral may include accounts receivable, inventory, machinery and equipment, or real estate, either alone or packaged in various combinations (for example, receivables and inventory; receivables and machinery).

The higher amount of policing or monitoring required to ensure the existence, value, and integrity of the collateral for an asset-based loan is a further distinction between asset-based loans and other secured loans. From the time the loan is made until it is paid off, the commercial finance company is an active participant in the management of the loan. It focuses on maintaining the integrity of the collateral securing the loan. Collections, for example, are often sent directly to the commercial finance company and credited to the loan. Banks rarely police a loan as thoroughly.

It is this monitoring and the constant collateral appraisal process that differentiates asset-based loans from other secured commercial loans. It also explains why asset-based financing is an expensive form of lending. Commercial finance companies price asset-based loans at prime plus 3 to 4 (or more) percent to cover cost of supervision and help given to customers. In contrast, banks charge less (prime plus 1.75 percent to 2.25 percent) because they have lower labor costs associated with loans and because they often enjoy other revenue from the client.

■ *Captive finance companies* are financial subsidiaries of publicly held companies that are engaged in some line of business other than finance. Three examples of major captive finance companies that have followed the route of expanding from financing the parent's products into a broad-based financial services company are General Electric Credit Corporation, Ford Financial Services, and General Motors Acceptance Corp. At the end of 1991, all three of these financial companies had assets of more than $100 billion, which would have placed each of them among the five largest banks.

Typically, captive finance companies are established to provide financing for the parent company's products and later often branch out into other lines of business that have nothing to do with financing the parent's products. When this occurs, the captive finance companies typically seek the most profitable niches in the financial services marketplace, being driven by direct profitability rather than the profitability of their parents' lines of business.

Unlike their nonfinancial parents, captive finance subsidiaries are usually highly leveraged like other financial companies. Because they cannot take deposits, captive finance companies rely on the commercial paper and bond markets for their funding requirements in the same fashion as independent finance companies. Although captive finance subsidiaries stand on their own financially, they frequently receive subordinated loans from their parent companies as a way of improving their equity positions for borrowing purposes. In addition, the markets believe that the parents have both a moral and practical obligation to support their finance subsidiaries. Failure to do so would undermine market confidence in the parent, although this has occasionally happened. This parental obligation usually results in the finance company's rating being set by the parent's financial position. A captive with a strong parent may have lower funding costs than an independent finance company with an identical portfolio and balance sheet.

Founded in 1959, Ford Motor Credit Co. is a good example of the diversification of captive finance companies today. It first entered direct consumer lending in 1966. Since then it has steadily extended its direct consumer finance operations through a combination of internal expansion and selected acquisitions. Nationwide Savings (the nation's second largest thrift) was acquired in 1985, United States Leasing International in 1987, and The Associates (one of the nation's largest independent consumer finance companies) in 1989. In addition to its traditional auto loans and through its various subsidiaries, the Ford Financial Services Group today is in a range of financial services from group credit life and home mortgages to transportation equipment leasing. Ford's financial services division is a major contributor to Ford's profits. In 1990, 89 percent of Ford's net income was provided by its finance division.

Credit cards are a market in which captive finance companies are proving to be formidable competitors to the banks. Several captive finance companies have successfully entered the credit card market in recent years. One example is Sears, Roebuck. In the five years following Sears' introduction of the Discover card, Sears became one of the leading credit card issuers with over 33 million credit cards outstanding. Another instance has been AT&T Credit's launch of the Universal Card, a combination calling and Visa/MasterCard. The public's enthusiastic response has put AT&T among the five largest credit card issuers. There are also several independent and captive finance companies that offer Visa or MasterCard, including Ford, General Electric, and Household International. By 1995, five of the top ten credit card issuers are expected to be non-banks, representing about 50 percent of all charges made on credit cards.

Accelerating the growth of captive finance companies' credit card business has been the securitization of credit card receivables. This practice has allowed them to reduce the capital required to carry the receivables and maximize the economies of scale many of them enjoy in the transaction processing area. Credit cards are a classic example of an area in which technology is changing the dynamics of the financial services arena to the benefit of the specialized financial services companies.

The outlook for the finance company industry is similar in many ways to the outlook for the commercial banking industry. Although the finance industry does not suffer from the same regulatory restrictions that the banking industry does (restrictions that have aggravated the overcapacity of the banking industry), the same technological and demographic trends affect it. Technology is improving the productivity of finance companies and giving increasing advantages to large companies that can achieve economies of scale. The shift from a consumption to an investment-oriented economy in the 1990s also will hurt consumer finance companies because consumer borrowing will slacken. A counter trend will help commercial finance companies as small business borrowing grows. Small businesses, a primary market for commercial finance companies, have been growing rapidly in recent years and will continue increasing their share of the economy as larger companies contract.

Mortgage Banking Companies

Mortgage banking companies specialize in the origination and sale of residential and commercial mortgages. They then service the monthly payments, keep related records, and act as escrow agent to disperse funds for taxes and insurance. A mortgage banker's income derives from origination and servicing fees, interest on escrow balances, profits on the resale of loans, and the spread between mortgage yields and the interest paid on borrowings while mortgages are held for resale. To protect against negative spreads or mortgages that cannot be resold, mortgage bankers use purchase commitments from secondary purchasers such as Fannie Mae.

Mortgage bankers have benefited from the demise of the thrift industry. Their share of the servicing market has grown because of reduced competition. In addition, it has grown as mortgage bankers have purchased the servicing portfolios of failed thrifts. Between 1980 and 1991, mortgage bankers' share of the mortgage servicing market grew from 19.8 percent to 38.5 percent. Most of this gain came at the expense of the thrifts, whose share of the servicing market dropped from 44.2 percent in 1980 to 24.5 percent in 1991.

Although most of the glamour of the mortgage banking industry is concentrated in the origination process, with its highly paid loan production personnel, from a business profitability standpoint the real action is in mortgage servicing. The industry loses money on originations and makes money on servicing, and there are significant economies of scale in servicing. This fact is fueling a gradual consolidation of the mortgage banking business. Nonetheless, the industry remains very fragmented, with no player having more than a 3 percent share of the national market.

Mortgage banking is very interest-rate sensitive. When interest rates decline, mortgage originations grow both as a result of increased home sales and as a result of refinancing of existing mortgages at lower rates. When interest rates rise, mortgage originations are likely to drop sharply as home sales decrease and refinancing dries up. In 1991, falling interest rates created a boom for mortgage bankers as refinancings reached record levels: more than 35 percent of an estimated $550 billion in mortgage originations resulted from refinancings. Although the demographics suggest that home-sale markets will be slow for the remainder of the 1990s, mortgage banking companies should benefit from a continuing volume of refinancings that will result if long-term interest rates remain low.

Ironically, the success of the mortgage banking industry has led to a surge in initial public offerings of mortgage banking companies despite the consolidation trend. In the 1980s, thrifts and commercial banks saw mortgage banking as an attractive way to increase fee income and profits without adding assets. They therefore bought or set up mortgage banking firms. In the 1990s, depository institutions have spun off their mortgage bankers to generate capital to support their commercial banking assets.

Securities and Brokerage Firms

The securities industry has traditionally consisted of three types of organizations: investment banks performing underwriting and M&A advisory services; brokers arranging the buying and selling of securities; and exchanges providing a place to conduct transactions and a vehicle for setting price.

Securities and brokerage firms provide liquidity in the markets, including trading out of their own accounts as market makers. They help raise money through the underwriting of public securities offerings. They finance customer transactions, both in the purchase and repurchase of securities and in the provision of bridge loans to assist in corporate acquisitions. They also may provide security analysis and portfolio management, services that will be discussed in a later section. Finally, they have been highly profitable in recent years acting as agents, advisors, and sometimes partners in corporate acquisitions and restructurings.

The 8,000 firms performing these functions come in all sizes and product-line configurations. Some firms specialize regionally or by limiting themselves to one or two of these services. Others are full-service brokerage houses having anywhere from only one main office to hundreds of branch offices across the country and overseas.

Despite the large number of registered securities firms in the United States, the industry is actually highly concentrated, the result of a consolidation that took place after 1974 when fixed commissions were eliminated. In the late 1970s, many small brokerage firms merged in a process caused by economies-of-scale technology just as banking is now being consolidated by similar forces. Today, the ten largest securities firms account for approximately 60 percent of the industry's revenues, and the 25 largest account for almost 80 percent. Because the securities industry is already consolidated, its profitability in the 1990s will not be depressed the way that the banking industry's profitability is predicted to be.

The 1980s was thus a period of high growth but also of consolidation for the securities industry. From 1982 to 1986, total employment in the securities industry grew 64 percent compared to a 19 percent growth in the insurance industry and a 5 percent growth in commercial banking. Returns in the securities industry were excellent. This, along with expansion into new or underdeveloped markets, including junk bonds and merchant banking, attracted new capital to the industry.

Part of this capital came from large companies like General Electric Co., Prudential Insurance Company, and Sears, Roebuck & Co. These firms bought or developed their own securities subsidiaries to take advantage of returns that were often much higher than their traditional business sectors. (This development was similar to the expansion of the captive finance subsidiaries.) The five-fold increase in equity capital in the first six years of the 1980s flattened and eventually began to push down returns on equity in the industry.

The stock market collapse in October 1987 accelerated the decline in returns for most securities firms. Significant reductions in equity trading volume and merger and acquisition activity, along with escalating costs, reduced securities firms' return on equity sharply during the 1987-1990 period. In response to the falloff in profits, the securities industry drastically reduced its work force, cutting jobs by 70,000, one-fifth of the precrash total.

Since then, companies have brought costs under control and improved operating margins. Much of this improvement has resulted from the development of new and inexpensive computer technology that can be used to set up central processing units capable of supporting very large volumes of transactions. This, in turn, has encouraged the reduction of costs through economies of scale created by mergers and by smaller companies purchasing back-office support from bigger players. The increased efficiency of support functions is of growing importance in the newly competitive environment that includes threats from banks, which are constantly pushing at the legal barriers separating commercial and investment banking.

Securities firms' profitability revived in 1991 as a result of increased activity in the equity markets, the growing volume of securitization, and the more efficient cost structure resulting from the cutbacks of the late 1980s. Markets rose to postcrash levels. The new issues markets absorbed a record level of activity, principally from established companies taking advantage of the high price-earnings ratios of most stocks to raise cheap equity capital. Most Wall Street firms posted record earnings in 1991 as a result of the flood of new equity and securitized loan issues that boosted underwriting fees.

In 1992, low interest rates and an improved economy together with the growing securitization trend have led to an increasingly healthy securities industry. In fact, the industry will probably mirror Merrill Lynch, which took a $470 million restructuring charge in the fourth quarter of 1989 but expects another record earnings year in 1992.

Investment Banks

Investment banks derive their name from their traditional functions: locating and collecting funds for clients that need capital to finance new projects. Investment banks are best known for their ability to underwrite and distribute common stock and new corporate, government, and municipal debt issues; arrange private placements; provide funds management and real estate advice; and act as advisors in the mergers and acquisition business and in other corporate services. Investment banks usually participate in most financial markets, including the money and capital markets, spot and futures markets, foreign exchange markets, real estate markets, commodities markets, and many secondary markets. In addition, as the capital markets are becoming closely linked across national borders, firms such as Morgan Stanley, First Boston, and Goldman, Sachs are becoming global in their orientation. Investment banks generate most of their revenues from the difference or spread between what they pay for the securities they underwrite or trade in and what they sell those securities for.

The classic underwriting and corporate finance functions of the investment banking business are going through a period of upheaval and change. Commercial banks and insurance companies have begun competing in some segments of the business, such as the underwriting of revenue bonds, Eurodollar syndications, and commercial paper, as well as acting as merger and acquisition advisors. These institutions, attracted by the reputed profitability of investment banking in contrast with their own businesses, are eager to expand their initial incursions into investment banking. Commercial banks, in particular, are expected to be more significant participants in the future if Glass-Steagall restrictions are further relaxed.

Profits from underwriting depend upon the number of new issues in the money and capital markets. The growth of shelf-registrations, which allow companies to decide to issue securities on short notice, has changed the way investment bankers act as underwriters, reduced underwriting spreads (thereby reducing revenue), and helped concentrate the industry into larger firms.

The sources of income for investment banking firms also vary as a function of cost containment, interest rates, market conditions, the volume of trading activity, and merger and acquisition fees earned. For example, many investment banks generate income from trading and from negotiating large block trades of outstanding securities among institutional investors and in redistributing those blocks more widely through secondary offerings. The largest volume of all securities trading on the secondary market is on the over-the-counter market by dealers on a negotiated basis. Profits in this area depend more on trading volume than on underwriting activity.

Brokerage Firms

Brokerage firms generate revenues from:

- Commissions on agency activities
- Spreads on market-making activities
- Fees for various activities and services
- Margin and position interest and dividends.

On the retail side, securities and brokerage firms historically serviced primarily wealthy retail clients by selling them stocks and bonds. In recent years, securities and brokerage firms have broadened their retail client base to include large numbers of investors of modest means and have substantially enlarged their product offerings to retail investors. Today, the typical brokerage firm's products include traditional stocks and bonds as well as commodities, options, mutual funds, bank certificates of deposit, and a variety of limited partnerships. In addition, the types of customer accounts have been broadened to include asset management accounts that combine holdings of stocks and bonds with a money market fund that provides check writing and credit card features.

Stock-market trading, although still a vital part of brokerage firm profitability, is shrinking as a source of income for the nation's top securities firms. The giant institutions that do most of the trading, such as bank trust departments and pension funds, have pushed commissions down to about five cents a share on average. At the same time, deficit-laden governments and cash-hungry corporations have continued to raise huge sums of capital via bonds and other fixed-income securities. Furthermore, institutions are trading these securities at a more rapid rate, a function of interest-rate volatility and new quantitative techniques in risk-return analysis. As a result, bond trading has become a major source of revenue for the brokerage houses, emerging as a prince after several years as the frog of the industry.

Investment Advisors

Investment advisors are firms that provide investment advice for a fee. Investment advisors must register with the Securities and Exchange Commission and abide by the rules of the Investment Advisors Act of 1940. Investment advisory firms usually specialize in a particular type of investment—for example, emerging growth stocks, international stocks, mutual funds, or commodities. Some services only offer advice through a newsletter or publications, others will manage a client's money. Investment advisory firms that manage money include two major types of firms: firms that manage mutual funds and firms that directly manage client assets. Investment management companies generate fees for services as their primary revenue source. Fees are generally a function of the quantity of assets under management, although occasionally the advisor receives a bonus if the returns on the portfolio are significantly above the market's. Annual fees range from 0.25 percent to 2.5 percent of assets.

The 1980s was the golden age of the investment advisory business. Reflecting a dramatic increase in the amount of pension fund dollars as a result of the ERISA legislation of 1974 and a quadrupling of the amount of money in mutual funds during the decade, the number of investment advisors registered with the SEC more than tripled. By 1991, the number reached 18,000, a figure exceeding the number of banks and thrifts combined.

The funds investment advisors manage have become massive. The total amount of institutional money managed in 1991 exceeded $5 trillion, an amount just shy of the combined assets of commercial banks, thrifts, and insurance companies. Significantly, the pool of institutionally managed money has been growing at a much faster rate than the assets of the traditional depository and insurance institutions.

The golden age of investment management is shown by the profitability of the investment management industry as well as by its growth. Overall industry statistics are not available because the majority of investment managers are privately held or operate as subsidiaries of financial institutions. Where data are available, however, they show very high profitability for the investment management industry, reflecting the large volume of financial assets on which management fees are earned and the minimal capital required by the business (perhaps less than 1 percent of assets under management). Although increasing competition may affect profitability in the 1990s, continued industry growth should offset the negative impact of competition.

The dramatic growth of institutional money being managed has led to some very large investment management organizations. There are more than 100 investment management organizations each managing more than $10 billion in assets. In fact, there are far more investment management organizations with portfolios exceeding $10 billion than there are banks with $10 billion in assets. The ten largest investment management firms manage a combined total of $800 billion in assets.

Investment advisors of all types should continue to thrive in the 1990s. Changing U.S. demographics, particularly the aging of the baby boomers, is a leading reason for the continued optimistic outlook for investment advisory services. Baby boomers, now in their late thirties and early forties, should begin to increase their savings levels dramatically in the 1990s as they put funds aside for their children's education and their own retirement. A higher level of savings will push interest levels lower and stimulate new investment while increasing the value of existing investments. Pension and mutual fund assets are expected to continue to grow as the preferred intermediaries for investment of this growing savings pools. In particular, mutual funds, currently worth more than $1 trillion, should benefit from this savings explosion.

Although the general market environment will be favorable for investment advisors, the overall business environment for investment advisors may be more challenging in the 1990s than it was in the 1980s. The investment advisory industry is now in transition from a business driven by investment performance to one requiring a broader base of business skills. In the 1990s, marketing and client service skills will gain in importance as individuals obtain greater control over their retirement assets and savings. This change is required by employers that hope to reduce potential litigation about pension management by leaving investment decisions to the individual employee or retiree. The change also shifts some administrative costs from the company to the pension fund.

The profitability of the asset management industry will come under increasing pressure as service demands rise and fees do not, though by most standards the investment advisory industry should remain very profitable. Low-cost producers increasingly will be able to exploit this advantage to enlarge their already substantial share of the pension and mutual fund business. Though the business will continue to be fragmented compared to the securities industry, strong customer ties, lower costs, consistently excellent investment performance, and specialized expertise will ensure strong profitability for those players with these advantages. Ultimately, the most significant competitive advantage will be a strong consumer franchise.

Increasing pressures from banks trying to expand their investment advisory business will add to the challenges of the industry in the 1990s. Banks have traditionally been in the investment advisory business through their trust departments and in recent years have been expanding aggressively into the mutual fund business. Although Glass-Steagall restrictions continue to prevent them from underwriting mutual funds, banks can still act as investment advisors and manage and sell funds. Currently, over 80 percent of the largest commercial banks sponsor their own funds.

Miscellaneous Financial Services Companies

Miscellaneous financial services companies include a variety of specialized financial services companies that do not fit into any of the other general categories of specialized financial services companies. A representative company is American Express. Because of the diversity of its financial services (consumer lending, securities brokerage, and investment management), it cannot be clearly classified in any of the more precise definitions. SafeCard Services, which provides specialized services to the credit card industry such as a credit card loss notification service that is marketed to consumers through the major credit cards, is another company in this group. Another example is INVG Mortgage Securities Corp, a real-estate trust that specializes in investing in mortgage-backed securities. These special firms will not be discussed, although they are interesting, because their total significance is not as great as the major segments that have been reviewed in this survey.

Part 3: Financial Service Organization Strategic Management

Since about 1960, the financial services industry has been undergoing dramatic changes. Hardly a month goes by without the introduction of new sophisticated products and services. Competition is also becoming more intense among industry segments that formerly were constrained by regulatory barriers. Fluctuations in both interest rates and the financial markets have heightened the uncertainty in which financial institutions operate. Compounding the problem is the fact that both competition and uncertainty are relatively new concepts to the financial services industry, at least since the 1930s.

Given this environment, each financial institution must formulate a strategy that will allow it to cope with change, particularly technological change, economic change, social and demographic change, and regulatory change. Furthermore, the strategy chosen must permit the institution to add value to its clients and create value for its owners. Simply stated, unless a financial institution can meet (or better) competitors' prices for comparable benefits or provide distinctive benefits that offset a higher price, the future of that institution will be in doubt. Unlike 35 years ago, today's financial institutions operate in a classic Darwinian situation: only the strongest and most adaptable will survive.

In formulating a strategy that will both add value and cope with change, an institution's management should ask itself:

- What are the customers' needs and how can the institution create value for those customers?
- How can it differentiate itself from its competitors?
- What will the effect be of technological changes on its strategy?
- Will the strategy chosen be responsive to the changing regulatory environment?

Technology has turned most of the products financial institutions provide into commodities. As a result, financial institutions must change the way they package and present their products to their customers. Both the products and the delivery of those products must focus on meeting customers' needs.

Technology has been both a blessing and a curse to the financial services industry—a blessing because it encourages the development of new products and the provision of old products more efficiently; a curse because it has created overcapacity. Technology has also allowed old products to be unbundled, thereby proliferating new and complex products. Because technology is evolving, the product life cycle of these new products can be very short. Consequently, a financial institution that survives will both formulate and implement a strategy that allows it to be responsive to short product life cycles and to cope with the overcapacity often associated with major changes. Yet, the failure of a new product also can be disastrous. The profound impact of technology can be easily seen in the credit securitization area.

Unfortunately, many institutions, particularly community and local banks, are either resisting or barely aware of the technology. As technology continues both to add to overcapacity and to decrease costs for those institutions of a scale to use the latest technological advances, institutions resisting technology or unable to afford it will be forced out. Finally, technology will continue to reshape strategies in the future—a successful strategy today may not be a successful strategy tomorrow!

Certain segments of the financial services industry are prohibited by law from engaging in certain activities. Creative management, supported by solid legal work, sympathetic regulators, and court decisions, has been remarkably successful in reducing these barriers. The regulatory environment will probably continue to change as much in the 1990s as it did in the 1980s. Nevertheless, anticipated opportunities, such as repeal of Glass-Steagall barriers, may never occur.

Most institutions do not appreciate how different other parts of the financial industry are from their own. Many of them will therefore find it harder to provide new functions than they expect. Underwriting securities and selling mutual funds are different than commercial or retail banking. Selling insurance is different than selling common stocks, bonds, or mutual funds.

Successful Financial Services Strategies: The Banking Industry as an Example

In this section, several strategies that have allowed banks to differentiate themselves, add value to their customers, and adapt to change will be discussed to illustrate the types of options available.

Broadly speaking, banks compete for three types of customers: consumers, small businesses, and corporate clients. Strategies for success differ among the three segments. For example, a corporate-banking strategy may require the bank initially to make loans to select clients even at a loss to build a client base. As the bank builds its client base, it gets a wealth of information about each client which allows it to develop profitable fee-based service relationships. If offered by a large bank, these additional services might encompass investment and merchant banking, securities trading and brokerage, foreign exchange and money market activities, and securities trust and custodial services.

A consumer banking strategy, on the other hand, does not provide the high margins that the corporate investment banking services can command. Rather, consumer banks compete in a low-margin environment by developing economies of scale and by adding on services. As a result of this environment, a financial institution pursuing a consumer banking strategy must market its services (such as money orders, checking accounts, mortgages, credit cards) to the masses. It must either have the ability to handle the scale itself or become a subcontractor, a local outlet for another institution that has developed the systems.

In the past, it was possible to target all three segments. Fewer and fewer banks, however, now attempt to cater to all three segments. For example, in the early 1980s, Bankers Trust sold its entire retail activity. Bankers Trust, as well as many other money center banks, had found that competition had eroded its profitability. Consequently, its ability to cross-subsidize weak businesses with profits from strong businesses was decreasing. As a result, Bankers Trust changed its strategy and successfully repositioned itself to a product line in which management believed the bank could compete more effectively.

In addition to deciding whether a financial institution wants to serve consumers, small businesses, or corporate clients, management also must decide what products it will offer and where it will offer those products. In essence, the strategy chosen must address such questions as: What products? Where? To whom? Customers' needs can be met three ways: first, by creating value through distribution systems that are tailored to the customer; second, by creating product value by adding information that emphasizes product attributes; and third, by emphasizing quality of service and prompt, error-free delivery.

In addressing distribution system challenges, banks will continue to move away from fixed-site delivery locations (branches) to distribution systems that deliver products to convenient locations (perhaps the home, office, supermarket, mall) via cable TV, telephones, automated teller machines (ATMs), and the mail. In formulating a strategy, banks must be alert to the inevitable growth of electronic delivery systems within their operating environment. The phenomenal growth of ATMs is one piece of evidence that customers want universal access to their accounts. Initially introduced to save labor, the ATMs have proven so acceptable to customers that many banks levy fees for ATM transactions that are higher than fees for the same transaction across the counter.

The information component of banking is important for several reasons. First, consumers usually appear to try to limit the unanticipated consequences of their decisions. Consequently, consumers want to be informed. Second, consumers are willing to pay for information that creates value. Consumers' willingness to pay for value-added information is clear in the explosive growth of the American Express Gold Card and the Merrill Lynch Cash Management Account (CMA). By providing year-end summaries, by tying checking with stock purchases, and by providing additional information or services, these services have been able to command a price premium. As an information provider, the bank that designs its products for specific customers or that focuses on explaining product attributes will have an information advantage that will enhance the bank's ability to differentiate its products.

With respect to the third component, quality service and prompt, error-free delivery, institutions must recognize that today's customers are different from the customers of yesterday. Today's customers are more cost conscious and feisty. Today's customers are strategic shoppers who are willing to fight for what they want. Because the costs to move relationships from one institution to another are minimal, today's customers can easily switch institutions if they are not satisfied with the service they receive. Those institutions not willing to accommodate these customers will lose them.

The extent to which a financial institution can differentiate itself from its competitors is an important element of strategic formulation. As competition continues to increase, it is becoming more apparent that institutions will need to refine this segmentation approach.

Products and distribution systems will have to be designed for ever more narrow and discrete segments (such as affluent, private banking, small business, middle-corporate banking) to provide distinctive value. This market segmentation approach is one of the most successful ways an institution can differentiate itself, adding value to itself and to its customers.

For example, many analysts question the viability of small, community banks. Others, however, believe community banks are strategically positioned. In spite of these opposing views, all parties agree on one point: it is hard to generalize about community banks because they are as diverse as the communities they serve. Lowell Bryan, of McKinsey & Company, suggests that community banks can be very successful. As a lender, a community bank has a competitive advantage because it has a closer rapport with its customers. Its officers can know and understand customers' needs better and learn of them sooner than a large, remote money center or regional bank could. A community bank probably also has strong relationships with the key decision makers in the community, who may be among its owners. Furthermore, a community bank can often be effective in delivering specialized products to specific, local customers.

In developing a strategy, the community bank should consider several points. First, what services should it offer? All too often, small banks try to offer too many services to which they add too little value at too great a cost. Second, what type of customer should it focus on: consumers, small businesses, or perhaps both? A consumer focus will probably require more branches in good locations; a small business focus may not. Third, should it specialize? Fourth, can it operate in a niche that will be ignored by larger banks because the niche does not allow for economies of scale?

In his book *Breaking up the Bank*, Bryan argues that the most successful community banks will be those that disaggregate. In other words, a community bank that picks a niche strategy of serving just depositors or just borrowers may be more successful than the community bank that attempts to serve both depositors and borrowers. Because the basic skills required to be a depository bank are sufficiently different from the skills necessary to be a lending bank, economies of scale for a small bank can be obtained by specializing in one of the two functions. The provision of individualized service to either function is expensive, however. To obtain the profit necessary for the best community banks to survive, the banking industry concentration needs to proceed further.

Considering the competitive advantages that super-regional banks enjoy over small regional banks, it is likely that consolidation of regional banks will continue. However, consolidation itself limits future consolidations. Consequently, the time will soon come when super-regionals will no longer succeed by outperforming small institutions. Instead, they will be forced to compete against other super-regionals, money center banks, and nontraditional institutions such as American Express, Sears, and GE Financial Services. Studies by McKinsey and Company have suggested that the size necessary to be efficient increases dramatically as an institution changes strategy, such as moving from the community level to the regional level. A highly profitable community bank can turn itself into a highly unprofitable regional bank. This outcome is another reflection of the advantage a strong niche position provides and which can be lost through careless expansion.

In addition to facing the same competitive environment that super-regionals face, money center banks must currently wrestle with significant loan losses to developing countries, costly infrastructures designed to serve a corporate base that will no longer pay for it, and competitive pressures from investment banks. In spite of this environment, money center banks have enormous strengths—two of which include a powerful regional presence and a customer base that consists of large clients.

To become more competitive, many super-regional and money center banks are converting their integrated bank holding companies into several decentralized businesses. By pushing profit and loss responsibilities down through the organization, unprofitable products and services will be detected. As decentralization has occurred, an important insight into what future strategies must entail has been uncovered—disaggregation.

Disaggregation, "breaking up the bank," does not mean that large banks will not play important roles in a wide variety of banking activities. Disaggregation does imply, however, that banks must recognize that different skills are required for success in each of the basic roles of classic banking: deposit taking, credit-risk taking, and interest-risk taking. Consequently, banks must be restructured around these areas. In the restructuring process, management must remember that deposit taking is driven not just by paper-based processing but also by electronic and consumer retailing; that credit-risk taking is being driven more and more by asset securitization; and that interest-risk taking is being driven by market-linked, technology-based products, such as swaps, futures, and forwards.

Characteristics of Future Financial Institutions

Overall, the long-term trends in the financial services industry are clear. Specialized financial services companies should continue to expand and to show higher average profitability than the traditional depository and insurance companies. The higher profitability of specialized financial services reflects the changing structure of the financial system as a result of technology and demographics.

Although some companies in the depository and insurance company arena are busily trying to evolve into broad-based financial services companies with the help of increasingly favorable regulation, most depository institutions and insurance companies are sticking to their basic businesses, with lackluster results. This reality and the changing nature of the financial system provide significant opportunities for a few specialized financial services companies that are in the forefront of this change. These firms should show above average returns and growth in the 1990s.

As we approach the 21st Century, it is likely that the financial services industry will see change continue as it has in the past 15 years. Rather than ATMs and fixed-site delivery systems, telephone, mail, and cable TV will be the most likely delivery systems. Current products such as securitization of assets will be replaced by other products not yet conceived to meet consumer requirements and opportunities provided by technology.

As the 1990s proceed, there will be:

- further consolidation of traditional banks;
- a blurring of functions among banks, credit card companies, consumer finance companies, industrial finance firms, and other financial service companies;
- an unprecedented sophistication among consumers;
- the disaggregation of financial service companies.

Regardless of where the industry is ten years from now, the surviving participants will be those that anticipate and act on the basic trends in the society.

The essence of financial service is information: who has what, who wants what, who owes what, whose record is good, who is paying to whom (or not paying and why), and what developments are occurring (or likely to occur and how likely) to alter these facts. Institutions having, organizing, and using the most information on consumers, businesses, and governments and controlling electronic delivery systems may come to dominate the financial services industry in the future.

Information is so important to the financial services industry that the industry itself can be considered a subset of the information industry. This relationship was highlighted by the successful entry of American Telephone & Telegraph into the credit-card business with its Universal Card. (A few years earlier AT&T abandoned plans to allow telephone subscribers to overpay their telephone bills and earn interest on the balance because of opposition from the financial service industry.) Communications companies could become the most formidable non-bank financial service competitors before the end of the 1990s because of their control of the electronic delivery system. The folding of the financial services industry into the information industry will increasingly transform the strategic landscape for traditional financial services organizations.

Notes

Case 1: UNIDENTIFIED FINANCIAL INSTITUTIONS (1991)

The structure of the financial statements of a financial service organization reflects the functions the organization serves in the segment of the financial marketplace in which it operates. Thus, statements even for firms that are operating within the same segment may differ significantly depending on the individual strategies the institutions are following. Measures of profitability and asset utilization provide information to supplement insights offered by a ratio analysis of balance sheets and income statements.

Exhibit 1 presents financial statements in ratio form (as of the fiscal year ending in 1991) and selected operating and asset use ratios for eleven financial service organizations. Each organization represents a major segment of the financial industry. Match the institution with the financial data you think most representative of its type, which are listed below:

1. International wholesale commercial bank
2. Regional commercial bank
3. Retail commercial bank
4. Credit union
5. Savings and loan company (minor activities in insurance)
6. Consumer finance company
7. Mutual life insurance company
8. Property and casualty insurance company (with a small life insurance subsidiary)
9. Mortgage banking company (with a savings-and-loan subsidiary)
10. Wholesale investment bank (known for its trading skills)
11. Retail investment bank

Exhibit 1
UNIDENTIFIED FINANCIAL INSTITUTIONS (1991)

Company	A	B	C	D	E	F	G	H	I	J	K
ASSETS											
Cash & equivalent	1.7%	1.2%	8.4%	0.5%	12.5%	4.8%	n.a.	6.1%	1.6%	0.4%	0.7%
ST investments	0.8	1.2	7.9	49.3	26.4	0.0	7.1	18.6	23.7	3.3	32.8
ST loans	0.6	83.5	34.6	0.0	38.3	27.3	8.5	16.8	50.5	0.0	33.4
LT loans & leases	0.0	0.0	17.5	0.0	0.0	0.0	0.0	21.3	0.0	0.0	0.0
LT investments	79.7	5.3	9.7	0.0	9.9	26.6	45.2	21.4	2.5	51.8	7.6
Mortgages & real estate	12.7	0.0	16.8	21.9	0.0	37.7	21.0	0.0	19.4	16.0	3.3
Property, plant & equipt.	1.5	2.2	1.7	3.9	8.9	1.9	1.4	2.1	1.5	1.1	1.0
Other assets	3.1	6.5	3.4	24.4	4.0	1.7	16.8	13.7	0.7	27.5	21.2
Total assets	100.0%	100.0%	100.0%	100.0%	100.0%	100.0%	100.0%	100.0%	100.0%	100.0%	100.0%
➤Assets per employee ($millions)	$4.59	$1.23	$1.60	$1.15	$0.17	$1.68	$2.69	$7.77	$2.06	$0.67	$10.92
LIABILITIES AND EQUITY											
Demand deposits	4.9%	0.0%	23.5%	0.0%	0.0%	12.7%	0.0%	4.2%	12.5%	0.0%	0.0%
Time deposits	78.0	0.0	50.7	19.1	0.0	75.9	0.0	31.6	33.3	0.0	0.0
ST debt	1.7	22.2	8.8	54.7	1.1	1.5	0.0	2.7	8.8	3.9	41.5
Other ST oblig.	7.1	6.4	1.0	0.0	61.0	0.0	0.0	40.0	1.7	0.0	32.8
A/C pay & accls	2.7	4.1	n.a.	1.5	8.8	n.a.	3.8	8.6	0.0	0.0	7.4
LT debt	0.0	50.6	5.3	1.9	0.0	0.0	0.3	5.2	0.0	0.0	7.3
Other LT liabs.	0.0	4.3	3.6	7.6	1.6	0.9	91.2	2.0	16.0	74.2	7.0
Total liabs.	94.4%	87.5%	92.9%	84.8%	72.5%	91.0%	95.4%	94.1%	72.3%	78.1%	95.9%
Pref. stock	0.0	1.2	0.0	3.4	0.0	0.0	0.0	0.5	0.0	0.0	0.7
Cap. stk. & paid-in cap.	1.6	2.6	2.5	7.8	8.6	4.1	0.0	1.5	22.7	3.8	0.4
Retained earnings	4.0	8.8	4.6	4.1	19.0	4.9	4.6	3.9	5.0	18.1	3.0
Total equity	5.6%	12.5%	7.1%	15.2%	27.5%	9.0%	4.6%	5.9%	27.7%	21.9%	4.1%
Total liab. & OE	100.0%	100.0%	100.0%	100.0%	100.0%	100.0%	100.0%	100.0%	100.0%	100.0%	100.0%
FINANCIAL RATIOS											
Return on tot. revs. (TR)	5.4%	8.2%	9.3%	10.6%	8.7%	11.4%	9.9%	10.8%	12.7%	6.4%	5.5%
Int. & div. inc./TR	95.5	82.0	78.4	40.4	9.8	89.8	33.6	75.5	94.0	13.2	63.9
Commission & fees/TR	2.2	0.0	17.0	6.7	51.1	8.0	0.0	11.3	0.0	0.0	2.3
Interest expense/TR	67.8	37.8	36.0	35.1	0.6	50.0	n.a.	61.1	56.9	0.0	61.4
Salaries & benefits/TR	6.8	15.6	20.5	23.6	62.5	15.9	n.a.	14.0	15.0	n.a.	15.0
Return on assets	0.5	1.5	1.1	2.0	4.2	1.1	2.3	1.1	1.2	3.1	0.5
Total revenues/Assets	9.7	18.1	11.4	18.6	48.1	9.5	22.8	10.0	9.4	48.6	9.4
Deposits/Assets	82.9	0.0	74.2	19.1	0.0	88.7	0.0	35.7	45.8	0.0	0.0
Equity/Assets	5.6	12.5	7.1	15.3	27.5	9.0	4.6	5.9	27.7	21.9	4.1
Return on equity	9.3	11.8	14.9	12.9	15.3	12.0	49.1	18.4	4.3	14.1	12.6
Price-earnings ratio	8.3×	9.8×	9.5×	13.4×	11.9×	9.4×	n.a.	9.6×	n.a.	7.5×	7.6×
Market value/Book value	0.8×	1.3×	1.4×	0.9×	1.4×	1.2×	n.a.	1.8×	n.a.	1.1×	1.0×
Beta	1.30	1.30	1.05	1.40	1.45	n.a.	n.a.	1.10	n.a.	0.85	1.35

Case 2: QUIGLEY BANK CORP.

Paul Cunningham, chief operating officer of Quigley Bank Corp., set aside his copy of the 19x5 first quarter earnings report. The time had come to set policy for the bank's investment portfolio. Prudent management of this portfolio while interest rates were declining had enabled the bank to flourish despite massive loan write-offs. It had also brought Quigley Bank Corp. closer to its goal of an 18 percent return on equity. Within the last quarter, however, interest rates had started to increase, and Mr. Cunningham wondered how he should manage the bank's portfolio in the face of rising interest rates.

Bank History

Established in 1929, Quigley Bank Corp. was a bank holding company headquartered in St. Louis, Missouri. At year-end 19x4 the bank had assets of over $28 billion and more than 140 offices in Missouri, Kansas, Iowa, Minnesota, Montana, and North and South Dakota. Quigley Bank Corp. provided financial services to individuals and institutions throughout this economically diversified seven-state region. Products included a broad range of commercial banking and corporate services, consumer loans and depository functions, but limited foreign operations. Exhibits 1a and 1b provide recent financial information for Quigley Bank Corp.

The publicly stated goal of the board of Quigley Bank Corp. was to provide an 18 percent return on equity to its shareholders; however, the competitive nature of the industry and Quigley's market area had made attaining that goal increasingly difficult. Quigley was located in surplus-deposit states, generating substantially more deposits than Quigley could lend to high quality borrowers in the region. This inhibited growth and profitability. Accordingly, seven years earlier, the bank had embarked on an aggressive lending program to create and acquire new types of assets and assets from other regions. Quigley subsequently had experienced one of the most rapid loan growth rates among large banks in the country. During the following four years, the bank experienced compound annual growth in commercial loans and deposits of 20 and 14 percent, respectively. The bank's ratio of loans to deposits increased from 75 to 90 percent.

Contrary to expectations, however, rapid growth did not improve profitability. In Quigley Bank Corp.'s rush to increase its asset base, credit quality standards had apparently been relaxed, and the bank was subsequently plagued by a rash of troubled loans and write-offs. During this four-year period of asset growth, net charge offs increased at a compound annual growth rate of 21 percent. Additions to loan loss reserves caused returns on assets and equity to decrease, with return on assets declining from 0.92 to 0.63 percent and ROE declining from 15 to 12 percent.

At year-end 19x2, management was faced with a nonperforming assets ratio of 1.93 percent and a nonperforming loan ratio of 2.84 percent. Management was also concerned about the chance of a recession. (Exhibit 2 summarizes recent leading economic indicators.) Faced with poor credit quality on the books and expectations of deteriorating credit quality of potential loans, management began to rethink its growth strategy and look for alternate ways to increase earnings.

Investment Strategy

Interest rates had been falling in recent years, with short-term rates falling faster than long-term rates. Expecting a continuation of this trend, the financial managers of the bank investigated the possibility of purchasing long-term Treasuries and financing them with short-term borrowing. In this way, the decline in long-term rates would increase the market value of the bonds. The bank could take advantage of declining short-term rates to roll over the financing of the bonds and maintain attractive interest rate spreads. In addition, as the yield curve grew steeper, the spread offered by this strategy increased, making the benefits even greater. Management saw Treasuries as a way to secure relatively high returns, good capital gains growth, and low credit risk in a questionable economic environment. In addition, any one-time gains from the sale of these instruments could be transferred directly to loan-loss reserves without being taxed, thereby providing tax-free additions to the bank's primary capital ratio.

Management decided to proceed with this investment strategy and rapidly increased the bank's holdings of long-term Treasuries. The bank's investment strategy was to acquire and dispose of Treasuries to achieve substantial capital gains while maintaining an adequate interest rate spread. The investment portfolio grew by $2.8 billion and $2.4 billion during 19x3 and 19x4, respectively, as shown in Exhibit 3. The continuing decline in interest rates increased the market value of the portfolio as well. Exhibit 4 provides a summary of market interest rates during 19x0 through 19x4, and Exhibit 5 outlines the market value of the bank's portfolio during 19x2 through 19x4.

Through careful disposition at a profit of certain investment instruments, the bank covered substantial additions to loan loss reserves during 19x2 through 19x4. During 19x4 alone, Quigley Bank Corp. disposed of over $3.5 billion in investment securities for a profit of $417 million, partially offsetting a record $507 million addition to loan loss reserves. Exhibits 6 and 7 provide loan loss reserve and nonperforming asset information for 19x2 through 19x4.

The bank's net interest income increased during this period, even in the face of declining gross interest margins. (Exhibits 8 and 9 display analyses of interest income for 19x2 through 19x4.) Mr. Cunningham was pleased by the bank's performance and often quoted the information provided in Table 1 as evidence of the bank's intelligent investment strategy.

Table 1
Treasury Investment Portfolio Activity
(dollars in millions)

	19x3	19x4
Investment portfolio premium over book	$183	$ 57
Investment portfolio interest income	369	588
Investment portfolio capital gains	15	417
Additions to loan loss reserves	180	507
Return on equity	15%	16%

Current Situation

During the first quarter of 19x5, interest rates began to rise, as shown in Exhibit 10. The bank received total investment income of $156 million during the quarter and sold a portion of its portfolio for a capital gain of $9.5 million. Rising interest rates, however, meant that the market value of the bank's investment portfolio would begin to deteriorate, thereby precluding any future capital gains. Bank management was not overly concerned, however, because any market value losses would be on paper only and would not be recognized unless the investment instruments were sold.

A more pressing concern was the chance that interest rate spreads would decline, which could harm earnings. During the first quarter of 19x5, all rates were increasing, with long-term rates rising more quickly than short-term rates. (Exhibit 11 presents the average spread between long-term and short-term rates during 19x4 and through the first quarter of 19x5.) This was attractive for new investments in long-term bonds. The rapid increase in short-term rates, however, meant that the source of financing for the bank's existing long-term investment portfolio was becoming increasingly expensive and that the spread was shrinking. (Exhibit 12 presents Mr. Cunningham's estimate of the impact of changing interest rates on the value of the bank's investment portfolio. The effect on reported income would be different, however, depending on whether the change in value was the result of a spread change or a change in the value of the principal.)

Bank and economic analysts were in general agreement that interest rates would increase steadily through the end of 19x6, although there was some disagreement about how quickly they would increase. Exhibit 13 presents interest rate forecasts by 35 industry analysts as of March 19x5.

Alternative Actions

Mr. Cunningham had identified three alternatives in April 19x5. If he assumed that the increase in interest rates was short-lived, his best alternative would be simply to hold his position. Subsequent rate decreases would restore the market value of the portfolio, and the bank could then sell off a portion of the portfolio to recover any losses on the spread incurred during the period of rising rates.

On the other hand, if he thought this were a permanent rise in rates, his best alternative would be to sell off a portion of the bank's investment portfolio immediately. If Mr. Cunningham chose the latter alternative, the bank would be forced to record capital losses at the time of sale but would avoid future losses on the spread.

A third alternative he considered was to hedge against future interest rate increases by selling Treasury bill futures on the open market. This alternative would enable him to protect the bank's equity position in the event of rate increases; however, it also would preclude the bank from enjoying any of the benefits of subsequent rate decreases.

Financial futures contracts consisted of agreements between sellers and buyers to trade U.S. government–backed instruments (such as Treasury bills, notes, or bonds) at some specified future date, at prices agreed upon when the contracts were executed but not paid until delivery of the financial instrument. A typical contract had a face value of $100,000 and a maturity of 13 weeks.

Investors could enter into different types of hedging strategies depending on their expectations of how the interest rate environment would change. For example, hedges could be bought to cover equal movements in the short-term and long-term interest rates or for a total inversion of the yield curve. Mr. Cunningham was attracted to this vehicle because he believed that the sale of financial futures would enable Quigley Bank Corp. to protect its equity position in the face of rising interest rates while also maintaining flexibility in its investment strategy.

At the expiration of a given futures contract, Mr. Cunningham could deliver a financial instrument from the bank's existing portfolio to cover the obligation. In an environment of rising interest rates, the price previously agreed to in the futures contract would be higher than spot prices at the date of delivery. Quigley Bank Corp. would therefore receive a higher sales price than available on the spot market, a profit that would exactly offset the decline in the market value of the investment held in its portfolio. The futures contract, however, would not prevent the bank from experiencing losses on the spread between its long-term, fixed-rate investments and the short-term borrowing used to finance the investment portfolio if the yield curve flattened out.

If, on the other hand, Mr. Cunningham wished to keep the existing portfolio, anticipating falling interest rates, he could purchase a financial instrument on the open market to cover the contract obligation. Again, in an environment of rising interest rates, spot prices would be lower than the price agreed to in the futures contract, and Quigley Bank Corp. could therefore profit by purchasing a financial instrument at a lower spot price and using that instrument to cover the contract obligation. If the portfolio were hedged correctly, the present value of this profit also would offset the present value of losses on the comparable instrument in the portfolio.

Should interest rates fall before the expiration of the futures contract, the bank would be locked into the sales price specified in the contract and would therefore not be able to benefit from the increased market value of the investment. Again, however, a properly hedged portfolio would accrue sufficient gain on the asset saved to cover losses incurred through fulfillment of the futures contract.

Theoretically, therefore, a portfolio that was properly hedged with futures contracts would enable Quigley Bank Corp. to maintain the equity value of its investment portfolio. Unfortunately, however, that meant minimizing both the downside *and* the upside potential of the portfolio. In addition, the bank would still be in a position of having to forecast the most likely type of movement in the interest rate environment to hedge the portfolio accurately.

Mr. Cunningham was considering hedging the portfolio against equal movements in the short-term and long-term interest rates, changes that, in a worst-case scenario, might reduce the bank's net interest margin by as much as 15 basis points. In addition, transaction costs would be incurred in pursuing such a hedging strategy. Brokerage fees were typically $8 per contract for large traders.

Conclusion

Mr. Cunningham knew that his decisions about the bank's investment portfolio would have far-reaching implications for the bank's future earnings growth and capital ratios. His skill at predicting interest rates in the past had enabled Quigley Bank Corp. to increase its profitability during a period of massive loan write-offs. He wondered whether he would have equal success at predicting rates in the future and what strategy the bank should pursue given alternative interest rate scenarios.

He also wondered whether it would be prudent for the bank to continue to rely on interest rate arbitrage for earnings. Recent improvements in the nation's economic indicators and last year's improvement in the bank's nonperforming ratios made him more inclined to reemphasize the bank's traditional lending activities.

Exhibit 1a

QUIGLEY BANK CORP.

Statements of Financial Condition
(dollar figures in millions)

	19x2	19x3	19x4	1Q 19x5
Assets				
Cash and due from banks	$ 987	$ 1,241	$ 1,141	$ 1,038
Interest-bearing deposits with banks	2,428	1,534	1,438	2,442
Investment securities	2,867	5,696	8,079	8,600
Trading account securities	312	363	716	487
Fed. funds sold and sec. purchased under agreements to resell	998	752	239	356
Loans	13,456	14,633	15,095	14,087
Reserve for loan losses	173	229	353	353
Unearned discount	125	149	102	101
Net loans	$ 13,158	$ 14,255	$ 14,640	$ 13,633
Bank premises and equipment	238	209	228	218
Interest receivable	294	293	269	323
Customers' liabilities on acceptances	819	638	785	802
Other assets	337	503	477	486
Total assets	$ 22,438	$ 25,484	$ 28,012	$ 28,385
Liabilities and Shareholders' Equity				
Deposits				
Domestic				
Non-interest bearing	$ 2,852	$ 3,331	$ 3,469	$ 3,033
Interest-bearing	9,628	10,757	11,079	10,784
Total domestic deposits	$ 12,480	$ 14,088	$ 14,548	$ 13,817
Foreign interest-bearing	2,302	1,951	1,713	2,551
Total deposits	$ 14,782	$ 16,039	$ 16,261	$ 16,368
Federal funds purchased	1,418	1,749	1,634	1,473
Securities sold under agreement to repurchase	2,414	2,923	4,710	5,400
Other short-term funds borrowed	883	1,279	1,634	1,310
Long-term debt	572	801	983	989
LT debt qualifying as primary capital	0	250	236	232
Acceptances outstanding	819	638	785	802
Other liabilities	438	565	352	352
Total liabilities	$ 21,326	$ 24,244	$ 26,595	$ 26,926
Shareholders' equity				
Preferred stock (par value $1.00/share)	100	100	100	100
Common stock (par value $1.25/share)	39	39	78	79
Capital surplus	61	70	50	57
Retained earnings	998	1,111	1,256	1,290
Treasury stock	86	80	67	67
Total shareholders' equity	$ 1,112	$ 1,240	$ 1,417	$ 1,459
Total Liabilities and Shareholders' Equity	$ 22,438	$ 25,484	$ 28,012	$ 28,385
Common shares outstanding (net of Treasury stock)*27,279,952	27,833,841	57,906,646	58,370,774	

*In November 19x4 the Board approved a two-for-one stock split in the form of a 100 percent stock dividend to shareholders of record on December 3, 19x4.

Exhibit 1b

QUIGLEY BANK CORP.

Statements of Income and Expenses
(dollar figures in millions)

	19x2	19x3	19x4	1Q 19x5
Interest Income				
Loans, including fees	$1,443.5	$1,493.0	$1,408.5	$ 317.6
Investment securities				
Taxable	238.0	316.5	504.5	138.1
Exempt	62.0	52.6	83.7	17.9
Total income from investments	$ 300.0	$ 369.1	$ 588.2	$ 156.0
Trading account	35.1	22.7	41.4	14.8
Federal funds sold and resale agreements	107.7	83.0	47.6	9.6
Deposits with banks	246.5	226.7	107.4	27.5
Total Interest Income	$2,132.8	$2,194.5	$2,193.1	$ 525.5
Interest Expense				
Deposits	1,092.9	1,039.2	917.3	208.4
Fed funds purchased & repurchase agreements	396.9	364.2	427.4	106.3
Other short-term funds borrowed	66.8	73.6	73.8	23.6
Long-term debt	52.8	77.5	88.2	21.0
Total Interest Expense	$1,609.4	$1,554.5	$1,506.7	$ 359.3
Net Interest Income	523.4	640.0	686.4	166.2
Provision for Loan Losses	135.4	179.7	507.0	35.0
Net Interest Income after Provision	$ 388.0	$ 460.3	$ 179.4	$ 131.2
Noninterest Income				
Trust income	55.8	65.0	75.2	21.1
Service charges on deposit accounts	36.0	40.0	45.3	12.6
Data processing fees	15.3	15.2	12.7	5.3
Trading account profits and commissions	13.4	24.2	21.2	(3.4)
Investment securities gains (losses)	(6.9)	15.1	417.0	9.5
Other	103.9	152.7	165.7	47.1
Total Noninterest Income	$ 217.5	$ 312.2	$ 737.1	$ 92.2
Noninterest Expense				
Salaries	209.7	236.9	271.5	69.0
Employee benefits	47.1	51.9	43.0	12.5
Net occupancy expense	32.3	42.3	52.3	13.8
Furniture and equipment	39.5	43.8	43.8	11.2
Other real estate	8.0	11.4	48.1	3.0
Loss on disposal of subsidiary	0.0	0.0	34.0	0.0
Other	154.4	191.2	246.5	39.6
Total Noninterest Expense	$ 491.0	$ 577.5	$ 739.2	$ 149.1
Income Before Taxes	114.5	195.0	177.3	74.3
Income Taxes (Credit)	(16.6)	28.2	(25.6)	16.9
Net Income	$ 131.1	$ 166.8	$ 202.9	$ 57.4
Dividends on Preferred Stock	10.1	8.8	6.7	1.6
Net Income Applicable to Common Stock	$ 121.0	$ 158.0	$ 196.2	$ 55.8
Dividends on Common Stock	$42.7	$44.1	$51.9	
Return on assets	0.6%	0.7%	0.7%	
Return on common equity	12.0%	14.6%	16.0%	
Primary capital ratio	5.7%	6.7%	7.1%	

Exhibit 2

QUIGLEY BANK CORP.

Economic Indicators

	19x0	19x1	19x2	19x3
Percent change in:				
Real GNP	–2.5%	3.6%	6.8%	3.4%
Consumption—durables	4.5%	2.1%	1.7%	1.0%
Investment—fixed nonresidential	7.1%	–1.2%	–0.9%	–0.2%
Housing starts	–2.6%	59.7%	2.5%	–0.6%
Commercial bank loans	6.9%	8.7%	17.6%	10.5%
Consumer price index	3.8%	3.8%	3.9%	3.8%

Exhibit 3

QUIGLEY BANK CORP.

Investment Securities Portfolio:
Maturity and Yield Information
(dollar figures are in millions)

Carrying Value and Yield by Maturity Date as of December 31, 19x3

	Within 1 Year		1-5 Years		5-10 Years		Over 10 Years		Total	
	Amount	Yield	Amount	Yield	Amount	Yield	Amount	Yield	Amount	Yield
US Treasury	$569	8.95%	$1,607	9.80%	$748	10.62%	$865	11.17%	$3,789	10.15%
US agencies	31	11.50	133	12.35	6	10.45	147	9.41	316	10.87
State & political	675	12.86	224	10.62	330	11.28	230	15.18	1,458	12.52
Other	32	8.39	5	10.37	1	8.74	96	5.69	134	6.51
Total	$1,306	11.02%	$1,968	10.07%	$1,086	10.82%	$1,338	11.27%	$5,696	10.71%

Carrying Value and Yield by Maturity Date as of December 31, 19x4

	Within 1 Yr		1-5 Yrs		5-10 Yrs		Over 10 Yrs		Total	
	Amount	Yield	Amount	Yield	Amount	Yield	Amount	Yield	Amount	Yield
US Treasury	$539	9.16%	$1,951	7.02%	$1,829	7.28%	$624	7.51%	$4,944	7.41%
US agencies	60	10.70	84	12.29	2	10.15	765	9.58	911	9.91
State & political	129	10.13	221	10.62	312	11.76	446	14.14	1,108	12.30
Other	32	7.51	522	7.59	9	8.72	554	6.97	1,116	7.29
Total	$759	9.38%	$2,778	7.57%	$2,152	7.94%	$2,389	9.29%	$8,079	8.35%

Average Maturities

	19x2	19x3	19x4
U.S. Treasury	7 years, 1 month	7 years, 1 month	6 years, 10 months
U.S. agencies	17 years, 7 months	12 years, 1 month	17 years, 7 months
State & Political	7 years, 4 months	5 years, 7 months	11 years, 6 months

Exhibit 4
QUIGLEY BANK CORP.
Monthly Market Interest Rates

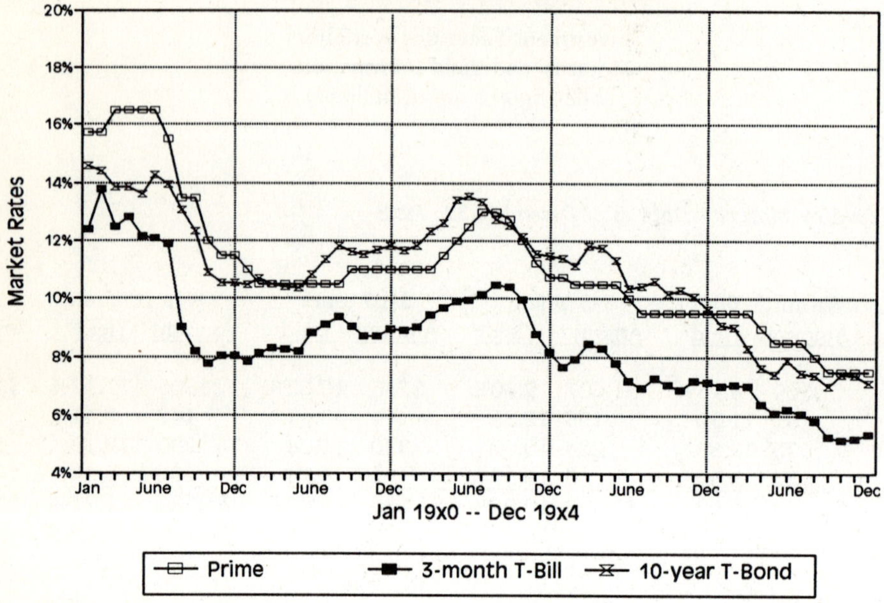

Exhibit 5

QUIGLEY BANK CORP.

Investment Securities Portfolio: Summary Information
(dollar figures in millions)

	19x2		19x3		19x4	
	Carrying Amount	Mkt Value	Carrying Amount	Mkt Value	Carrying Amount	Mkt Value
US Treasury	$1,713	$1,719	$3,789	$4,016	$4,944	$4,974
US agencies	190	174	316	320	911	938
State & political	887	763	1,458	1,409	1,108	1,108
Other	76	76	133	134	1,116	1,116
Total	$2,866	$2,732	$5,696	$5,879	$8,079	$8,136

Exhibit 6
QUIGLEY BANK CORP.
Summary of Loan Loss Reserves and Loan Charge Offs
(dollar figures in millions)

	19x2	19x3	19x4
Balance at beginning of period:			
Domestic	$111.6	$165.0	$219.1
Foreign	6.9	8.0	10.1
	$118.5	$173.0	$229.2
Charge Offs:			
Domestic			
Commercial and financial	$ 47.6	$ 70.0	$219.4
Agricultural	30.3	54.4	76.5
Real estate—mortgage	2.8	4.4	15.9
Real estate—construction	0.9	2.1	64.8
Consumer	8.1	9.6	14.7
Lease funding	0.2	0.4	3.2
Foreign	2.1	2.0	31.8
Gross charge offs	$ 92.0	$142.9	$426.3
Recoveries:			
Domestic			
Commercial and financial	$ 6.7	$ 13.1	$ 19.9
Agricultural	1.2	4.0	13.5
Real estate—mortgage	0.2	0.1	2.6
Real estate—construction	0.5	0.3	1.6
Consumer	1.9	1.9	3.0
Lease funding	0.0	0.0	0.1
Foreign	0.6	0.0	1.1
Gross recoveries	$ 11.1	$ 19.4	$ 41.8
Net Charge Offs	$ 80.9	$123.5	$384.5
Provision charged to operations:			
Domestic	132.8	175.6	476.6
Foreign	2.6	4.1	30.4
	$135.4	$179.7	$507.0
Other			1.7
Balance at end of period:			
Domestic	165.0	219.1	343.6
Foreign	8.0	10.1	9.8
	$173.0	$229.2	$353.4
Reserve as a percentage of period-end loans	1.30%	1.58%	2.36%
Ratio of net charge offs during period to average loans outstanding	0.69%	0.91%	2.63%

Exhibit 7

QUIGLEY BANK CORP.

Summary of Nonperforming Assets
(dollar figures in millions)

	19x2	19x3	19x4
Nonaccrual loans:			
Domestic	$316.4	$436.5	$429.2
Foreign	38.7	45.2	0.6
	$355.1	$481.7	$429.8
Restructured loans:			
Domestic	$ 23.1	$ 36.9	$ 11.7
Foreign	0.0	0.0	0.0
	$ 23.1	$ 36.9	$ 11.7
Nonperforming loans:			
Domestic	$339.5	$473.4	$440.9
Foreign	38.7	45.2	0.6
	$378.2	$518.6	$441.5
Other real estate:			
Domestic	$ 55.9	$ 79.6	$ 72.6
Foreign	0.0	0.0	0.0
	$ 55.9	$ 79.6	$ 72.6
Nonperforming assets:			
Domestic	$395.4	$553.0	$513.5
Foreign	38.7	45.2	0.6
	$434.1	$598.2	$514.1
Accruing loans 90 days or more past due:			
Domestic	$ 47.3	$ 47.7	$ 34.1
Foreign	0.5	3.3	3.7
	$ 47.8	$ 51.0	$ 37.8
Nonperforming loans to total loans	2.84%	3.58%	2.94%
Nonperforming assets to total assets	1.93%	2.35%	1.81%
Net interest lost	$ 50.4	$ 54.2	$ 64.0

Exhibit 8

QUIGLEY BANK CORP.

Effect of Interest Rate Changes on Net Income
(dollar figures in millions)

	19x2 compared with 19x3			19x3 compared with 19x4		
	Volume	Yield/ Rate	Total	Volume	Yield/ Rate	Total
Increase (decrease) in:						
Interest income:						
Domestic loans	$ 217.8	$(142.6)	$ 75.2	$ 107.4	$(154.3)	$ (46.9)
Foreign loans	(2.0)	(2.6)	(4.6)	(0.6)	(13.4)	(14.0)
Taxable investment securities	89.9	(5.8)	84.1	231.5	(49.0)	182.5
Nontaxable investment securities	(26.1)	(1.4)	(27.5)	59.6	7.4	67.0
Federal funds sold and resale agreements	(5.4)	(19.4)	(24.8)	(26.5)	(8.9)	(35.4)
Other	21.9	(58.3)	(36.4)	(57.9)	(39.9)	(97.8)
Total	$ 296.1	$(230.1)	$ 66.0	$ 313.5	$(258.1)	$ 55.4
Interest expense:						
Savings deposits	$ 27.5	$ (62.9)	$ (35.4)	$ 4.6	$ (65.3)	$ (60.7)
Foreign time deposits	18.3	(39.4)	(21.1)	(35.3)	(35.5)	(70.8)
Other domestic time deposits	62.9	(60.1)	2.8	50.2	(40.5)	9.7
Short-term borrowings	70.5	(96.4)	(25.9)	122.5	(59.1)	63.4
Long-term debt	29.3	(4.6)	24.7	32.8	(22.2)	10.6
Total	$ 208.5	$(263.4)	$ (54.9)	$ 174.8	$(222.6)	$ (47.8)
Increase in net interest income	$ 87.6	$ 33.3	$ 120.9	$ 138.7	$ (35.5)	$ 103.2

Exhibit 9

QUIGLEY BANK CORP.

Analysis of Net and Gross Interest Margins
(dollar figures in millions)

	19x2	19x3	19x4
Net interest income (taxable equivalent basis)	$ 654	$ 775	$ 878
Average balances of earning assets supported by:			
Interest-bearing liabilities	$16,447	$18,915	$21,412
Noninterest-bearing liabilities	2,195	2,415	2,963
Total earning assets	$18,642	$21,330	$24,375
Average yields and weighted average rates			
Earning asset yield	12.14%	10.92%	9.78%
Rate paid on interest-bearing liabilities	9.79%	8.22%	7.04%
Gross interest margin	2.35%	2.70%	2.74%
Contribution to net interest margin from earning assets financed by:			
Interest-bearing liabilities	2.07%	2.39%	2.41%
Noninterest-bearing liabilities	1.44%	1.24%	1.19%
Net interest margin	3.51%	3.63%	3.60%

Exhibit 10
QUIGLEY BANK CORP.
Weekly Market Interest Rates

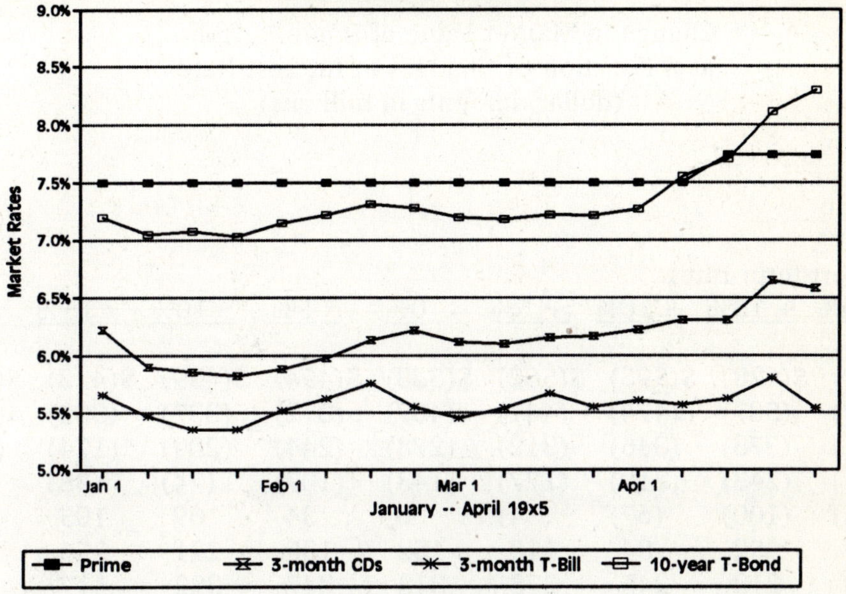

Exhibit 11
QUIGLEY BANK CORP.
Long-term/Short-term Treasury Spread

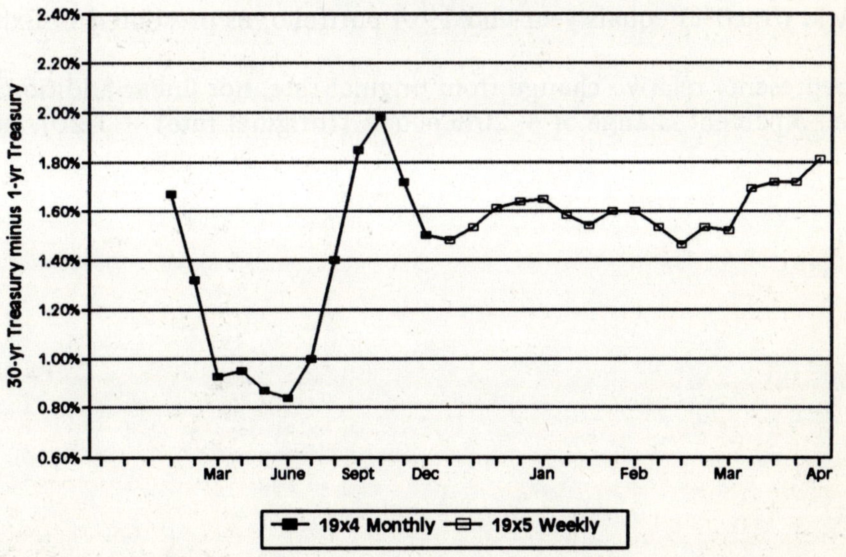

Exhibit 12

QUIGLEY BANK CORP.

Change in Market Value of Bond Portfolio
as a Function of Changes in Interest Rates
(dollar amounts in millions)

Percent change* in:

	Short-term rates								
Long-term rates	+ 20%	+ 15%	+ 10%	+ 5%	0%	- 5%	- 10%	- 15%	- 20%
+ 20%	$(660)	$(628)	$(595)	$(562)	$(528)	$(494)	$(459)	$(423)	$(387)
+ 15%	(539)	(507)	(474)	(441)	(407)	(372)	(337)	(302)	(266)
+ 10%	(411)	(378)	(346)	(312)	(278)	(244)	(209)	(174)	(138)
+ 5%	(275)	(243)	(210)	(177)	(143)	(109)	(74)	(38)	(2)
0%	(132)	(100)	(67)	(34)	0	34	69	105	141
- 5%	19	52	84	118	152	186	221	256	292
- 10%	180	212	245	278	312	347	382	417	453
- 15%	351	383	416	449	483	517	552	588	624
- 20%	533	565	598	631	665	699	734	770	806

Note: Base scenario (0%,0%) equals year-end 19x4 portfolio, as presented in Exhibit 3.

*Percent change represents relative change from original rate, not linear addition or subtraction of basis points, i.e., a percent change of + 20% equals [(original rate) × 1.20], not [(original rate) + .20].

Exhibit 13

QUIGLEY BANK CORP.

Analyst Forecasts of Market Interest Rates as of March 19x5

Forecasts for December 19x5:

	3-mo T-Bills	10-yr T-Bonds
T. Rowe Price	6.63%	9.00%
Manufacturer's Hanover	6.00	9.10
Dean Witter	5.20	7.80
Shearson Lehman	6.15	8.95
Merrill Lynch	6.50	9.00
35 analysts:		
Average	5.91%	8.45%
Std. deviation	0.50	0.66
Low estimate	4.25	5.88
High estimate	6.63	9.40

Forecasts for June 19x6:

	3-mo T-Bills	10-yr T-Bonds
T. Rowe Price	7.00%	9.25%
Manufacturer's Hanover	7.00	9.50
Dean Witter	5.50	7.50
Shearson Lehman	6.35	9.20
Merrill Lynch	6.67	9.30
35 analysts:		
Average	6.19%	8.57%
Std. deviation	0.69	0.88
Low estimate	5.25	6.25
High estimate	7.50	10.30

Notes

Case 3: CARS
(Certificates for Automobile Receivables)

In the late fall of 1988, Mr. Jerald Wigdortz, managing director of Salomon Brothers, Inc. with responsibility for developing new securitized products, was reviewing the history of securitized automobile loan receivables. It was an impressive record. In the two and one-half years since May 1985, when the first issue of securitized automobile loans was offered, 47 public issues of automobile receivables-backed securities had been completed for a total of $17.6 billion in new financing. In addition, substantial private placements of automobile receivables-backed securities had also been made. Issuers had included General Motors Acceptance Corporation, Ford Motor Credit, Chrysler Finance Company, and Nissan Motor Acceptance Corporation as well as major financial institutions such as Bank of America, Marine Midland Bank, and First National Bank of Boston. Mr. Wigdortz realized that securitization of automobile receivables had opened a new chapter in financing with asset-based securities (ABS). (Appendix A contains a glossary of common securitization terms.)

Loan Securitization or Structured Finance

Loan securitization, or structured securitized credit, was a hybrid form of financing that combined features of two well-developed systems: the traditional credit system and the securities system. Securitization could take place without credit securitization. For example, bankers acceptances were a form of securitization that did not involve the literal conversion of loans into securities. Loan securitization occurred when a group of loans held by a financial institution was combined in a form that enabled debt instruments to be created from the loans. Debt securities differed from loans made by banks in that the debt was issued—that is, the debt instruments were sold to the public at large and usually could be traded among investors until they were redeemed by the issuer according to the terms of the original issue.

A key element and benefit of loan or credit securitization was the separation of the credit risk of the securities being purchased from the credit risk associated with the corporation or financial institution originating the loans. Buyers of the securitized loans looked to the cash flow from the loans (plus any credit enhancement features) to cover expected losses and support the debt service of the securities. They did not rely on the credit quality of the corporation or financial institution originating the loans (unless there was specific credit support from the originating institution).

During the 1980s, borrowing that traditionally flowed through the credit system had been increasingly migrating to the securities markets. This occurred because securities were inherently a more efficient, cost-effective method of borrowing.

The cost-effectiveness came from three advantages that securities offered to the source of funds, the end investors. First, securities were liquid and tradable. Loans were illiquid; there was only a very limited secondary market for most loans. Second, debt securities were rated by credit agencies; loans were not. Large classes of investors, including individuals and pension funds, had little ability or desire to assess or cope with credit risk. By investing in rated securities, these groups avoided the dangers and expense of dealing with credit risk, assessing credit worthiness, and working out problem loans to avoid large losses. Third, prudence and often regulation permitted financial intermediaries to loan only a portion of the funds they raised. The balance was used to maintain a highly liquid portfolio to meet liability reductions. The earnings on the loans had to cover the cost of carrying the prudential reserves; directly issued securities did not because reserves were not required.

Historically, investors accepted lower returns as compensation for the greater liquidity and credit transparency of securities over loans. Thus, borrowers who raised money using securities had lower financing costs as long as the costs of issuing the securities were less than the savings on interest. Loan securitization took advantage of the cost differential between loans and securities. This cost differential could both pay for the cost of securitization and provide a profit to the securitizing institution.

In addition to the reduction in required reserves and the profit potential offered by securitization, financial institutions received another benefit from securitizing their assets. Loans that were securitized reduced the overall balance sheet of the originating institution. The total capital the institution required was thus lowered and its return on equity thereby potentially improved for a given level of profits.

Credit securitization was a carefully structured process consisting of five parts: origination, structuring, credit enhancement, placement and trading, and servicing. Exhibit 2 displays the process by which a typical CARS issue would be created.

■*Origination*. Securitization began when a company originated primary assets and assembled them into a pool. If the assets had a fixed maturity, they could be sold as specific receivables. A pool also could be created from earmarked accounts (e.g., credit card accounts) whose balances revolved over time.

■*Structuring*. Typically, the originator then sold the pool of assets to a special purpose vehicle (SPV) set up for the transaction. The nature of the SPV, which could be a trust, a special limited partnership, or a special purpose corporation, determined the tax and accounting structure of the transaction. The SPV also would be designed to accommodate the necessary operational details such as the payment structure of the notes (which could be complex and in multiple series) and protection against bankruptcy risk.

■*Credit Enhancement.* To receive an investment-grade credit rating necessary to make the transaction attractive to investors, some type of credit enhancement arrangement was usually necessary. The SPV first obtained insurance to guarantee against a portion of potential losses on its assets. The guarantee would typically take the form of a "first loss guarantee"* (often in the form of a "spread account") from the originator of the primary asset. The originator also would get a "wrap guarantee" (similar to a reinsurance contract in the property-casualty business) from an insurance company for a multiple of expected losses.

■*Placement and Trading.* The SPV (or a third party, usually the underwriter) then issued notes, which typically were very highly rated. These notes were usually bought by institutional investors such as mutual funds or pension funds.

■*Servicing.* The underlying assets could then be serviced either by a third party for a fee or by the originator. In either case, the originator would retain the spread between the yield on the assets and the interest paid to the investors, net of credit enhancement and other fees. Exhibit 2 compares the traditional commercial bank lending with the new system of asset securitization.

The History of Loan Securitization

Securitization of loans made by banks and other financial institutions began in 1970. The recently created Government National Mortgage Association (GNMA) offered to investors interests in pools of FHA and VA mortgages through the sale of a defined security. During the 15 years after GNMA's initial mortgage-backed security was issued, the market for mortgage-backed securities grew rapidly. By 1985, mortgage-backed securities represented the second largest pool of securities outstanding after U.S. government securities. A total of $334 billion of mortgage-backed securities were outstanding from the three leading issuers: the Government National Mortgage Association (Ginny Mae), the Federal Home Loan Mortgage Corporation (Freddie Mac), and the Federal National Mortgage Association (Fanny Mae).

By the end of 1986, about $600 billion in mortgage-backed securities was outstanding. It was estimated that volume had grown by 25 to 30 percent during 1987 to a total of approximately $750 billion.

Mortgage-backed securities were originally issued only by government-related entities. By 1987, however, private issuers were becoming increasingly important. During 1987, new mortgage-backed securities issues (both public and private) represented about two-thirds of all mortgage originations in that year. There were over 360 privately sponsored new issues in 1987, or 1.5 every business day, for an annual volume of $70 billion.

---

*See the glossary in Appendix A for definitions of technical terms.

Until 1985, securitization of loans was confined principally to residential mortgages. The market for securitized loans then changed dramatically. The first public securitized transaction of nonmortgage assets occurred in March 1985, when Sperry Rand Corporation and its investment banker, First Boston, offered participations in a group of computer leases. Following the success of this offering, in May 1985 Marine Midland Bank and Salomon Brothers demonstrated that nonmortgage assets could be securitized. They issued $60 million of automobile loan receivables.

Securitization of nonmortgage assets has been dominated by automobile and credit-card receivables. Automobile loans were the largest segment of the market. Between the first public offering of automobile loans in 1985 and the fall of 1988, there had been 62 issues with total initial balances approximating $21 billion. General Motors Acceptance Corporation (GMAC), responsible for over half of the total, issued 58 percent and 85 percent of all automobile loan ABS in 1985 and 1986, respectively. During 1987, GMAC sharply decreased its ABS issuance; however, a broader group of participants entered the market, including commercial banks and the finance subsidiaries of other automobile manufacturers.

Credit-card ABS, first publicly offered in 1987, had rapidly become the second largest sector of the nonmortgage market. Issue volume was $2.5 billion in 1987 and $5.2 billion in the first nine months of 1988. Commercial banks and thrifts had been the primary originators of credit-card ABS backed by MasterCard or VISA receivables. In June 1988, Sears, Roebuck introduced the first public ABS supported by retail credit-card receivables. Montgomery Ward and J.C. Penney followed with issues backed by their card receivables. ABS supported by other forms of collateral, such as manufactured housing contracts, unsecured consumer loans, loans on boats and recreational vehicles, airplane leases, unsecured personal loans, life insurance policy-holder loans, and trade receivables, accounted for about 18 percent of the total volume in the first nine months of 1988. This represented a significant increase from 9 percent in 1987.

By the end of 1987, securitization of nonmortgage assets had reached an annual level of $10 billion, and the volume was growing. However, despite the rapid growth of asset-backed securities from 1985-1987, the market was still in its infancy. A large volume of loans were potentially capable of being securitized. Exhibits 3, 4, and 5 provide data on the potential of securitization and the largest issuers of ABS.

The Structure of Asset-Backed Securities

Most of the nonmortgage ABS used the structures developed by automobile loan ABS because automobile loans were comparatively short-term (three to five years) compared to residential mortgage securities. Securities backed by loans made to individuals for purchase of automobiles or light trucks were normally called certificates for automobile receivables or CARS. The securities structures utilized by various forms of CARS were all intended to maximize the advantages associated with automobile loans.

Auto loans were self-amortizing, with monthly payments and two-year to five-year maturities. Most loans had fixed finance rates—also known as annual percentage rates (APRs)—and financed purchases of new vehicles. Three interest accrual methods were commonly used on auto loans, but the interest accrual method was of little concern to CARS investors. They always received their full share of interest calculated on an actuarial basis.

Auto loans could be classified as either "direct" or "indirect." Direct loans were made directly by the lending institution; indirect loans were originated by automobile dealers and sold to the ultimate lender. The lender might have recourse to the dealer on an indirect loan, but the trend was toward nonrecourse arrangements. Indirect loans with recourse had experienced fewer credit losses than nonrecourse loans, but this record reflected dealers' absorption of losses rather than an inherently better borrower profile. The prospectuses of CARS issues often noted whether the collateral consisted of direct or indirect loans and what percentage of the indirect loans had dealer recourse. CARS had mainly been backed by indirect loans.

Virtually all automobile loans were "due-on-sale"—that is, sale or trade-in of the vehicle would result in a prepayment. Turnover resulting from sales and trade-ins was by far the major cause of prepayments. Other reasons included voluntary repayment and refinancing. Voluntary repayments occurred when consumers paid off their loans to own their vehicles free and clear. Refinancing was rare in the auto loan market because loans on used cars had higher APRs and shorter terms—hence higher monthly payments—than loans on new cars. Events such as repossession and the destruction of the vehicle also would result in prepayments of auto loans because insurance or credit enhancement would cause the balance of the loans to be paid.

Three classes of CARS structures dominated the industry up to the fall of 1988. The first was a "pass-through" format similar to GNMA, FHLMC, and FNMA mortgage pass-through securities. In this type of transaction, auto receivables were sold to a grantor trust, which then sold pass-through certificates to investors. The certificates represented undivided interests in the auto loan assets. The simplest pass-through structure used collateral with higher APRs than the security coupon, and principal and interest were paid monthly (usually on the fifteenth of the month with a 14-day interest-free delay, like GNMAs). In this case, all principal received, together with interest at the pass-through rate, was paid to security holders. The spread between the average loan rate and the security coupon was used to pay servicing fees (primarily to the issuer), guarantee fees, and other expenses of the grantor trust.

Alternatively, CARS could be sold using a "pay-through" structure similar to those of cash-flow bonds. Collateralized Mortgage Obligations (CMOs), for which excess cash flows were "passed through" to bondholders, followed a similar procedure. In general, the value of pay-through CARS was supported by the cash flows rather than by the par or market value of the collateral. The principal amount of CARS issued against a given set of assets was determined so that the debt service could be supported by *scheduled* principal and interest payments on the loans. Payment of principal and interest to security holders was not dependent on prepayments, although prepayments altered the yield and average life of the certificates. Issues with pay-through structures normally had some degree of overcollateralization, which might increase over time.

The third class of structure was a "fixed-payment"* CARS security. The simplest form of this transaction used incentive-rate loans with low APRs but larger principal due than sold as collateral. The issue could then be structured assuming no prepayments would be made. A guaranteed investment contract (GIC) at a rate above the APRs of the loans would be obtained to ensure that the fixed debt service schedule could be maintained regardless of prepayments. (Unanticipated repayments would not reduce the return on assets if the spare funds could be redeployed at the same or a better rate.) A further elaboration structured the issue in tranches or classes with different maturities and rates, a form used with CMOs. Some classes would receive repayment early; others would draw interest at a higher rate on their full balance for some time before repayment began. (Exhibit 6 diagrams a more complex than typical CARS structure.) Fixed-payment CARS were more attractive to investors than issues with uncertain prepayment rates. Consequently, they usually traded at smaller yield spreads above Treasuries than other types of CARS issues.

A typical CARS security paid principal and interest monthly and had a final maturity of three to five years with a projected weighted-average life of one to three years. Most issues had "cleanup call" provisions stipulating that the CARS could be called at par after the principal balance had been paid down to a specified percentage—usually 5 percent—of the original amount. This optional redemption had little impact on investors.

All CARS issues, public and private, had featured some sort of credit enhancement, which protected the investor against credit losses on the collateral. The protection usually took a form analogous to a "pool policy" on pools of mortgages. It covered losses up to a fixed percentage, typically 5 to 10 percent, of the pool balance.

Credit protection could be provided by an issuer guaranty, insurance, a letter of credit, or a combination of these. (Third-party credit enhancement could enable a CARS issue to have a higher rating than the issuer.) The form of credit enhancement depended on the issuer. Banks, which were governed by regulatory accounting, relied on third-party credit enhancement because recourse financings by banks were treated as debt and were subject to capital requirements. Finance companies or non-bank issuers could provide their own guaranty, but entities rated lower than AA could usually get a better execution by using third-party credit enhancement. Debt covenants prohibiting recourse transactions also could be a factor in deciding whether to seek third-party credit enhancement.

---

*Sometimes this form of CARS was called a pay-through because a fixed payment CARS security was essentially a special form of pay-through security. In this form, unlike other pay-through securities, only the residual value of the final bullet payment was uncertain. This was frequently returned to the grantor of the SPV.

An alternative to third-party credit enhancement was a senior/junior securities issue. Two classes of securities would be created for a SPV. The senior class would have contractual fixed payments. The junior class payments would be the balance of cash in the SPV. The senior class of securities was sold in the market, and the junior class held by the loan originator. The junior class could also be sold to the market but at a higher yield to the investor as a reflection of the greater uncertainty. The multiple-class form was actively used by companies selling credit-card receivables.

In addition to the credit enhancement devices, investors were protected from losses in several ways. Most issues required that delinquent payments be advanced by the servicer or guarantor. Theft and the destruction of a vehicle were covered by insurance policies on the individual loans. Death of the borrower could be covered by credit life insurance. Some losses on indirect loans could be covered through dealer recourse. The pool policy covered the remainder of the losses up through the specified limits of the policy.

Although auto borrowers rarely refinanced, there was some uncertainty about exactly how fast a CARS issue (without a fixed-payment schedule) would prepay. Because auto loans had such short maturities, however, scheduled amortizations were a much larger component of a CARS security's cash flow than for mortgage securities. As a result, wide swings in prepayment rates had only a minor effect on the investment properties (yield, weighted-average life, and duration) of CARS.

Because they were backed by amortizing assets, CARS were often associated with mortgage pass-throughs. Given their short maturities, however, they were more appropriately compared to shorter-term investment alternatives—bullet instruments like corporate ones. CARS had consistently offered substantial yield premiums relative to comparable corporate debt.

The Advantages and Disadvantages of Asset Securitization

Asset securitization offered many advantages to financial institutions. Broadly, the advantages included reduced capital requirements resulting from a reduced asset base, access to cheaper funding, and greater control of risk. Asset securitization provided financial institutions with increased flexibility for loan portfolio management and risk management: financial institutions now had the option either of keeping loans in inventory or of selling them. Securitizing assets gave the manager of a financial institution control of when and how much risk the institution absorbed because the manager could eliminate interest rate risk and credit risk by selling loans. Similarly, by selling assets, institutions could reduce the cost of required reserves and FDIC insurance.

Probably the greatest advantage of asset securitization was the opportunity it presented financial institutions to improve their return on assets and on equity by reducing the required asset size and equity size for a given level of profits. Financial institutions could generate fees for originating and servicing loans without having the requirement to keep the loans in their own portfolio. By securitizing loans, financial institutions could keep their asset size and capital requirements below what had been required for a given volume of loan origination.

Although asset securitization provided many benefits to lenders, there were some disadvantages. The disadvantages included reduced use of financial institutions as intermediaries, weakened loan portfolios from the selling of the best loans, and increased competition because institutions could originate far more loans than they were required to hold.

New Uses

As Mr. Wigdortz thought about the CARS structure and the various types of asset-backed securities being offered in the marketplace, he wondered what new types of asset-backed securities were possible and how large the overall asset-backed securities market might become. He also wondered what the overall impact of loan securitization might be on various types of financial institutions.

Exhibit 1
CARS
Typical CARS Deal Process

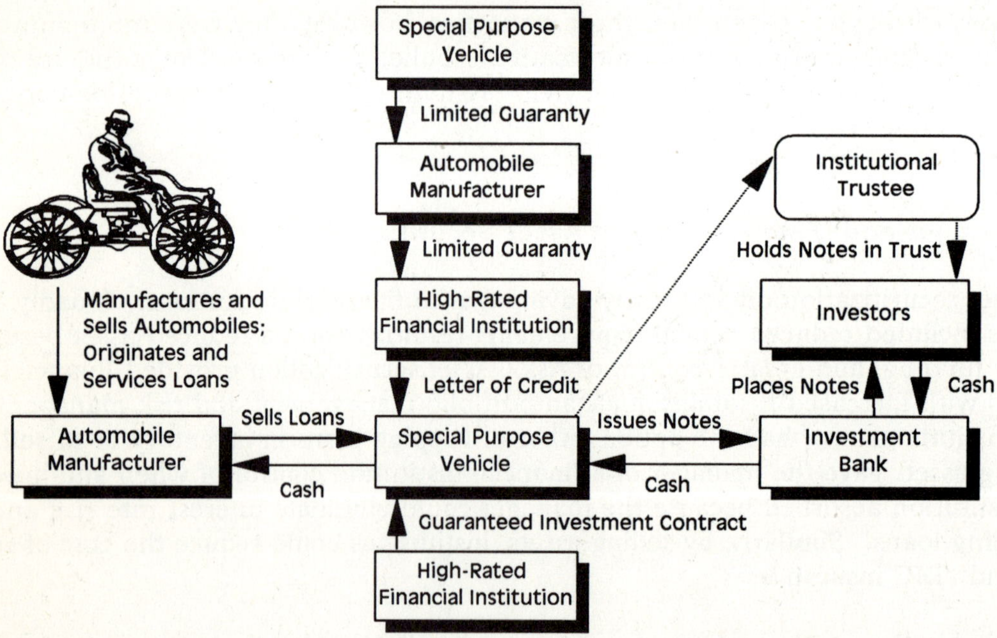

Exhibit 2
CARS
Comparison of Traditional Bank Intermediation with Asset Securitization

Traditional Bank Intermediation

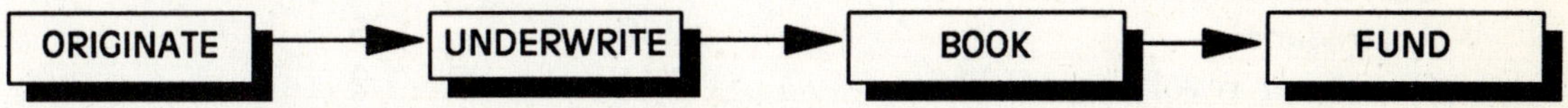

Asset Securitization

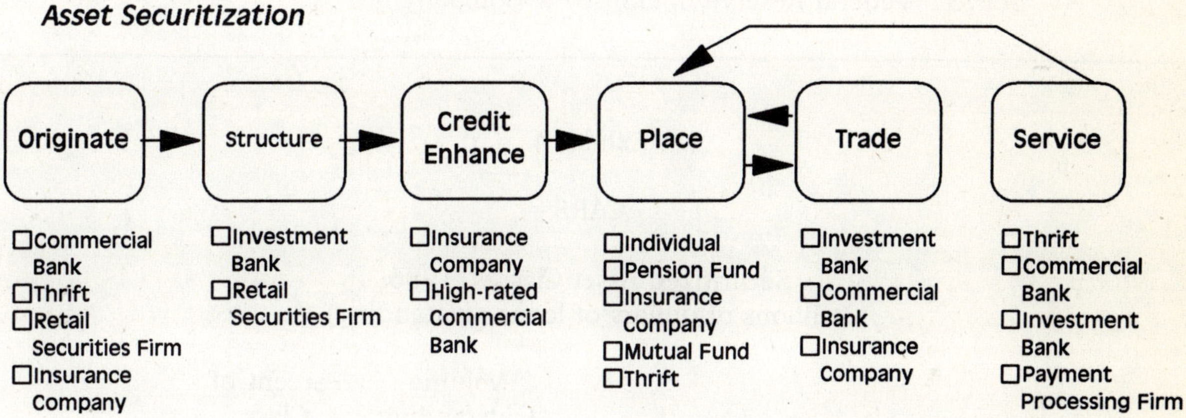

Exhibit 3

CARS

Amount of Credit Securitized, 1987
(billions of dollars in outstanding securities)

Loan Category	Total Loans	Percent Securitized
Home mortgages	$ 1,936	37%
Commercial real estate	649	1
Auto loans	260	5
Consumer revolving credit	144	2

Source: Federal Reserve, McKinsey & Company.

Exhibit 4

CARS

Securitized Asset Classes, 1986
(trillions of dollars of loans outstanding)

	Volume Outstanding	Percent of Class
Consumer Loans		
Mortgages	$1.2	63%
Installment	0.4	21
Other	0.5	16
Total	$1.9	100%
Commercial Loans		
Mortgages	0.5	24%
Trade receivables	0.7	33
Bank loans	0.6	29
Other	0.3	14
Total	$2.1	100%
Total Assets	$4.0	

Source: McKinsey & Company.

Exhibit 5

CARS

Largest Asset-Backed Securities Issuers as of October, 1988*
(dollars in millions)

	Amount Outstanding	Number of Issues
Automobile Loan ABS		
General Motors Acceptance Corporation	$11,430	17
Chrysler Corporation	2,521	4
Marine Midland Bank	1,357	4
Empire of America	1,311	5
Western Financial Savings	892	7
Credit Card ABS		
First Chicago Nat'l Bank	$ 2,100	4
Maryland National Bank	1,500	3
Sears, Roebuck	1,000	2
Bank of America	700	2
Manufacturers Hanover	475	1

*Does not include mortgage-backed securities issues or issuers.

Source: Merrill Lynch.

Exhibit 6
CARS
Typical Payment Flows for CARS Issues

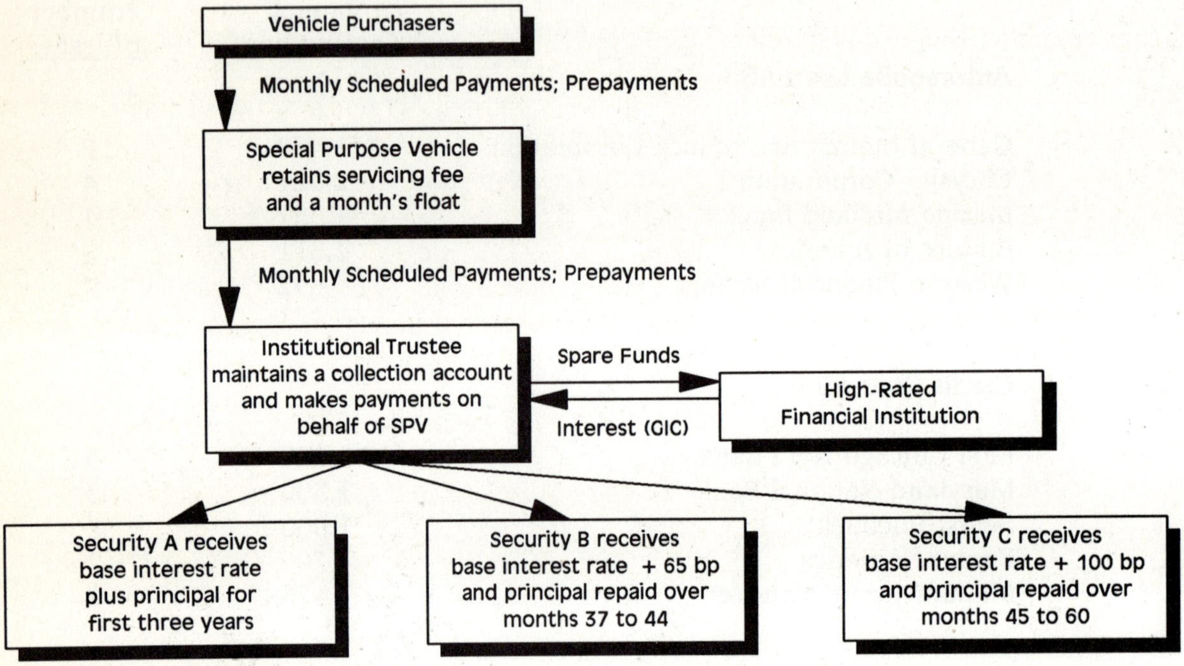

Appendix A

CARS

Glossary of Securitization Terms

Amortization The periodic payment of a debt principal installments together with interest, rather than interest-only payments. The principal payments may be equal each period or the total payments may be equal and contain differing amounts of interest and principal over the life of the loan.

Collateralized Mortgage Obligation ("CMO") A bond structured with varying maturities (tranches) secured by mortgage cash flows.

Conventional Mortgage-Backed Bonds A bond or other debt instrument that is backed by a pool of conventional mortgages and for which the cash flow of the mortgages serves as the source of repayment.

Coupon Strips Cutting off or "stripping" the scheduled interest payments on a bond or mortgage to be sold separately. Stripping, then, separates one instrument into two distinct financial instruments.

First Loss Guarantee A guarantee (usually from the originator of the assets) to reimburse a special purpose vehicle or loan pool for losses incurred on loans up to a specific limit (usually 5 to 10 percent of the total value of the loans). This reimbursement is paid first before other sources of credit enhancement are tapped to make up losses in the loan pool.

GNMA (Ginnie Mae) Government National Mortgage Association.

GNMA-Backed Bond A "mortgage-backed bond" using GNMA Certificates as the collateral rather than the individual mortgages.

GNMA Certificates (Also GNMA Securities) A "fully modified pass-through" mortgage-backed certificate issued by a mortgage banking company on which timely payment of principal and interest is guaranteed by GNMA (backed by the "full faith and credit" of the United States). The mortgage pools underlying a certificate consist of FHA or VA mortgages of similar maturities and with the same interest rate. The "pools" are in multiples of about $1,000,000 in principal amount.

Modified Pass-Through A variation of the "pass-through security" which guarantees and pays to the investor the scheduled monthly principal and interest payment, irrespective of what amounts are collected from the pool mortgages.

Mortgage-Backed Securities (MBS) Certificates issued by governmental and private issuers evidencing undivided interests in the equitable ownership of FHA, VA, and conventional mortgage loans.

Nonrecourse Loan A loan not allowing for a deficiency judgment. The lender's only recourse in the event of default is the collateral. The borrower is not personally liable.

Overcollateralization Sufficient loans must be placed into a collateral pool so their discounted value is sufficient to cover the bond, plus a reserve. Overcollateralization is usually defined as a percentage of the bond, such as 110 percent, of which 10 percent is the reserve overcollateralized amount.

Partially Modified Pass-Through A variation of the "pass-through security" which guarantees, to a limit, that monthly principal and interest payments will be made to the investor, even if not collected from the mortgage pool.

Pass-Through Security A form of "asset-backed bond" which is secured by a mortgage pool and for which the payment features closely resemble that of a "modified pass-through security." The bond is fully amortizing with scheduled principal and interest payments that closely track the scheduled collections on the collateral mortgage pool.

Pay-Through Security See Modified Pass-Through.

Pool All mortgages that secure an individual issue of either GNMA securities, PCs, or MBs.

Pool Insurance Pool insurance represents various forms of insurance that provide investors with additional safety.

Proceeds Account An account into which proceeds received from the payment of the principal and interest on collateral securing a bond are deposited.

Recourse The right of the holder of a note secured by a mortgage or deed of trust to look personally to the borrower or endorser for payment, not just to the property.

Spread Account A spread account is a device to enhance the credit status of asset-backed securities. For instance, an originating bank might sell assets yielding 12 percent to a SPV, which would then issue 7 percent asset-backed securities. The 5 percent spread (the difference between the 12 percent yield on the assets and the 7 percent yield on the securities), less a servicing fee, would be accumulated in the spread account, which is simply a type of escrow account, up to a stated level. After the spread account achieved the stated level, any excess spread would be immediately paid to the originating bank. The funds in the spread account would provide credit support for the asset-backed securities. After those securities were completely paid off, the funds remaining in the spread account would revert to the originating bank.

Stated Maturity The date specified as the fixed date on which the final installment of the principal of a bond is due and payable.

Straight Bond A form of a mortgage-backed bond that is secured by a mortgage pool. The instrument is similar to corporate bonds, with scheduled periodic interest payments. Principal repayment is usually at the end of the bond term.

Straight Pass-Through A variation of the "pass-through security" which pays principal and interest, as and when collected from the pool, to the investors.

Tranche Bond principal amount having a stated priority as to repayment of principal from the collections of principal on the pool of mortgages of a collateralized mortgage obligation. Offering different tranches helps investors to time the maturity of their investments.

Wrap Guarantee A wrap guarantee is a guarantee to reimburse a special purpose vehicle or loan pool for losses incurred on loans after the specific limit of a first loan guarantee (see earlier definition) has been exhausted. As with a first loss guarantee, there is a specific limit to the losses that will be covered by the guarantee. The size of the losses that will be reimbursed is a matter of negotiation with the insurance company providing the guarantee. The size of loss that is sought to be covered is usually determined by the bond-rating agencies' requirements for credit enhancement to support a AAA bond rating for the special purpose vehicles bonds.

Yield The return to an investor on a debt instrument expressed as interest. The yield calculates the effect of the "coupon rate" (or stated interest rate), the points (or loan price), and the expected actual life of the mortgage.

Yield Curve A graph of yields and maturities of securities that are similar in most respects (especially risk) except maturity.

Notes

Case 4: JEFFERIES GROUP, INC.

In early 1992, several articles appeared in the financial press questioning the prospects of the New York Stock Exchange (NYSE). For example, the February 1992 issue of *Institutional Investor* contained a story titled, "Will Bill Donaldson [chairman of the NYSE] go the way of Gorbachev?". "It will take more than pulpit-thumping and a glasnost management style to prevent the New York Stock Exchange from disintegrating," the story began. It pointed out that pressures on the NYSE included high costs, the desire of institutional customers for more liquidity, the block-traders' wish for the NYSE specialists* to have larger capital, the interest of some regional brokers in making markets in NYSE-listed securities, and the resistance to change of the NYSE specialists. The specialists considered the open-auction trading system their best (or only) hope for survival.

In the face of these conflicting demands, the NYSE was losing its market share to other domestic and foreign exchanges, to the NASDAQ (over-the-counter) trading system, and to computerized trading arrangements. Daily trading volume on the NYSE was currently averaging 180 million shares. This was a significant increase from the average of 157 million in 1990 but still below the peak of 186 million in 1987. Volume in early 1992 was exceeding the levels of 1991. Despite the increased volume, however, in 1991 the NYSE accounted for only 59 percent of the stock dollar volume traded, a decline from 76 percent ten years earlier.

The Jefferies Group had introduced one of the computerized trading systems. Mr. Frank E. Baxter, Jefferies' president, thought the current controversy provided an appropriate occasion to review the company's strategy. "I'm not sure we have a strategy except not to have a strategy," he reflected. "We have to be opportunistic, alert to a niche in which we can successfully compete to serve our customers' needs. I can't predict the future, and neither can anyone else. When we detect that our customers need a service or a better service, Jefferies has to decide whether it is within our competencies to develop and deliver it. We've got to be strong on tactics."

---

*A specialist on a stock exchange is responsible for balancing the supply and demand for the securities to which the specialist has been assigned in order that price changes would normally be small and orderly. The specialist accomplishes this by maintaining an inventory position and buying and selling from it when buyers or sellers are temporarily absent from the market, adjusting the price in small increments depending on whether there is buying or selling pressure.

History of Jefferies Group, Inc.

Jefferies, a publicly held financial service firm, developed from Jefferies & Company, which remained the largest component of the Group. Jefferies & Company was founded in San Francisco in 1962 by Boyd Jefferies. Mr. Jefferies was one of the first to identify the need for brokers who specialized in efficiently arranging large transactions in thinly traded stock. Jefferies built a reputation for quietly handling large trades among institutions away from the exchanges, the so-called "third market." Unfortunately, some of Mr. Jefferies' activities violated securities regulations. He pleaded guilty in 1987 to two technical violations and left the firm, subsequently selling his shares.

Mr. Baxter had been in charge of the London office before he returned to the United States to become chief operating officer, a position he had held for a year when Mr. Jefferies' problems developed. Mr. Baxter was elected president. Neither he nor any of the other managers were involved in Mr. Jefferies' situation. They were able to convince clients of this, which was essential to maintaining the firm's viability.

Mr. Jefferies' personal situation coincided with the stock market decline in 1987, presenting a major challenge for the new management team. Despite these difficulties, however, Jefferies Group reported a profit in 1987, unlike many other firms. Profits fluctuated widely over the following years, as shown in Exhibit 1 (which provides income statement data and summary financial information for the period 1986-1991). By the end of 1991, the firm's situation had stabilized, earnings had recovered, and the equity position was strong despite the repurchase of 1.4 million shares of common stock out of the six million shares outstanding. (Balance sheets for 1989-1991 are presented as Exhibits 2.) At the end of 1991, the number of employees had grown to about 500.

Jefferies' mission had always been to:

> Provide all the services professional investors and issuers need to effectively and efficiently implement their strategies.

To implement this mission, Jefferies' objective was to provide professional investors with the means to trade in any market at any time through the most appropriate mechanism. In addition, for those wishing to raise capital, Jefferies would develop and sell innovative market instruments. "It's a people business," Mr. Baxter had often reminded his associates. "Our customers do business with us because of relationships, quality, and integrity. We have to keep in touch with them. The particular medium is transitory. We've got to be alert for new value-added skills and services we can provide our customers." The newly developed competence in convertibles and warrants, for example, had been undertaken on the recommendation of a trader who detected this need among his customers. The customers frequently complained that the dealers in the convertible and warrant markets were too often holding on to the good deals for their own portfolios or for their special clients.

Jefferies Business Structure

In early 1992, Jefferies was divided into six activities, whose revenues over the 1989-1991 period are detailed in Exhibit 3:

- Equities
- Investment Technology Group
- Corporate Finance
- Taxable Fixed Income (Investment and Noninvestment Grade)
- Convertible Securities and Warrants
- Fixed Income Investment Research

Each business was expected to support itself and could use internal or external business resources as its managers saw fit. Mr. Baxter said that this structure did not upset the customers because most of them were similarly specialized. A firm might get multiple calls from Jefferies' traders, but the individual traders at that firm would not get multiple calls. The problem was to be sure that Jefferies' traders shared appropriately among themselves any information they obtained.

Equities Division

The Equities Division's task was to provide 1,600 institutional customers with superior execution of their buy and sell decisions in listed, over-the-counter, and international equities, options, and futures. The division was staffed by 200 account executives and traders at eight locations in the United States and offices in London, England and in Hong Kong. The offices in New York and Los Angeles (2) were the largest and of approximately equal size. Boston, Chicago, and Dallas were about half the size of the largest offices. Atlanta, San Francisco, and London were about a quarter of the size of the largest offices. All but one of Jefferies' offices were connected by a voice and graphic communication system that permitted use of "open outcry" within the firm and immediate access to any domestic exchange.

Jefferies also operated four specialist posts at the Pacific Stock Exchange and two at the Boston Stock Exchange. In addition, because of the rules of certain stock exchanges, such as the NYSE, Jefferies utilized the services of a closely related correspondent to act as its broker on these exchanges.

According to a recent report, Jefferies ranked 12th out of 40 brokers studied for execution quality on listed securities and held a market share of 3.9 percent. The company held a 4.4 percent market share in the over-the-counter markets and was ranked 8th out of 30 brokers studied for execution skills in this business. Jefferies made a market in 204 over-the-counter equity securities and 107 American Depository Receipts.

Contrary to his earlier expectations, Mr. Baxter observed the international component of Jefferies' business growing rapidly as domestic money managers developed international capabilities. Jefferies was therefore adding sales strength in London and integrating the international equity and convertible trading groups. The plan now was to develop an international business in trading illiquid names of every country rather than only those issued in the United States.

He still doubted that 24-hour trading by the exchanges would be the success some were expecting it to be. He believed that traders preferred to use trading systems such as Jefferies' or Reuters'* (which was available 24 hours a day). Transactions on private exchanges were less expensive and more confidential than those executed on a public exchange.

The division maintained detailed records of its customers' trades and investment interests, which could be instantaneously accessed by account executives with orders to execute. Measuring the success of the execution was difficult because of movements in the market between the time the order was placed and the execution was completed. Nevertheless, Jefferies measured the difference between the execution price and the price at the time the order was given, the difference between the execution price and the volume-weighted-average price for the day, and the difference between the execution price and the volatility price, which reflected the size of the order. Management believed that on average Jefferies could execute orders at a favorable 15-basis-point difference from the price at the time the order was placed. The spread over the volume-weighted average was less conclusive, but the spread over the volatility price averaged at least 100 basis points.

Even a small improvement in efficiency could help move a portfolio manager's performance significantly higher. The performance spread between the median and the first-quartile managers was approximately 100 basis points. Hence, an annualized savings of 15 or 20 basis points in transaction costs could be a significant competitive advantage to the manager.

Maintaining its reputation occasionally required Jefferies to engage in principal transactions for its own account to accommodate customers in transactions that could not be completed immediately on an agency basis. In addition, the company derived a significant portion of its revenues from interest on deposits collateralizing borrowed stock required to compensate for "fails-to-deliver" and on borrowed stock required for stock loans, hedging activities, short sales, and for customers. Interest was also derived from margin accounts maintained for a few substantial individual and corporate clients.

Investment Technology Group

Because of its early commitment to improving the execution of its clients' transactions, Jefferies was a pioneer in the development and implementation of electronically aided trading services. These were the responsibility of the Investment Technology Group.

---

*The after-hours volume on Reuters' Instinet Crossing Network had been averaging about 800,000 shares daily in last 1990 and early 1991. Volume spiked to 1.6 million in March 1991, but it had declined thereafter.

Its first product was a joint venture, the Portfolio System for Institutional Trading ("POSIT"), a computerized system that allowed institutions to trade passively among themselves at very low commission rates. Investors using POSIT entered a list of stocks they wished to buy or sell. Twice each day, the POSIT system automatically compared buy and sell orders and matched corresponding orders at a price midway between the last bid and offered price. The status of the transactions was immediately available to the institutions placing the orders, but both parties to a transaction maintained complete confidentiality. If no transaction took place, no one else but the initiating party knew. Unsuccessful or partly filled orders could be placed again or withdrawn to be placed through conventional channels. By 1992, four years after the system had been introduced in 1987, a large percentage of trades placed on the system were being matched. Volume was averaging three million shares daily and occasionally hit seven million shares a day. (A similar system had recently been developed for the European marketplace.)

A second product was introduced in 1990, "QuantEx." This was an "expert" software system that allowed investors automatically to generate buy and sell actions based on parameters established by each customer for its account. As the stock market moved, QuantEx indicated appropriate orders based on the customers' specifications and executed them through POSIT or through Jefferies' direct lines to the appropriate exchange.

Investment Banking

The Corporate Finance Department was a new division, largely staffed with former employees of the Los Angeles' office of Drexel Burnham Lambert. The department offered mid-sized to large, growing corporations a full range of advisory services as well as debt and equity financing. Activity had been at the level of $250 million a month in recent months. Finance specialists worked with clients to meet immediate and long-term financing goals. Products included private placements and public offerings, refinancing and recapitalizations, and mergers and acquisitions. Clients generally required funding in the range of between $10 million and $250 million. Mr. Baxter observed that a major challenge was to bring these companies together with the supply of capital held by pension funds. This would provide money to fund growth to borrowing companies and a better return to the investors.

Securities Trading

The Taxable Fixed Income Department and the traders dealing in convertible securities, warrants, options, financial futures, and similar products (United States and international) were major factors in their respective markets. The Taxable Fixed Income group, which had been started in 1989, specialized in trading and making a market in over 300 noninvestment grade debt issues. Jefferies believed it was one of the top three firms participating in this segment of the market. The company's traders also provided price information to more than 50 percent of all less-than-investment-grade portfolios, amounting to approximately $100 billion in total assets, so that the value of the portfolios could be calculated periodically.

This product line required Jefferies to take positions. Management was willing to take this risk because it believed its traders had better than average insights into the market.

(Exhibit 4 shows Jefferies' securities' position at December 31 of 1990 and 1991.) The company monitored its risk by maintaining preestablished levels that were not to be exceeded.

Because of its global trading network, Jefferies had also become a major trader of United States and international convertible securities and warrants. Using a highly disciplined, value-based approach, account executives and traders assisted clients in identifying attractive investments in these instruments and then executed their trades with customary discretion. This trading ability was also used to place new issues in the market.

Investment Research

The research activity concentrated in servicing portfolio managers investing in less-than-investment-grade securities. Nevertheless, the standard package of research products (i.e., economic outlook for the market, technical analyses, and fundamental analyses) were prepared for this segment. A daily market letter was faxed to clients that subscribed for this service. Jefferies was also the exclusive distribution agent for Zimbalist, Smith Research. A monthly, *The Money Analyst*, was also produced.

Strategic Issues

Although Mr. Baxter believed that the professional staff enjoyed a high *esprit de corp* and a very low turnover, the personal relationships that developed between account executives and key accounts could adversely affect the relationship if an account executive left. Jefferies' management was also very thin, in part because of the firm's action-orientation, low-overhead philosophy and in part because of the dislocations associated with Mr. Jefferies' departure. Furthermore, what type of management would be required to guide the firm into the directions that had been emerging? The higher technology systems and the development of more aggressive trading (as opposed to agency) products required different types of personnel.

Mr. Baxter also wondered if 1,600 clients were too many.

Competition came from Reuters' "Instinet" and from other firms that maintained active trading departments. Instinet allowed buyers and sellers to negotiate prices directly with one another electronically. Reuters also had a "Crossing Network" that allowed big investors to swap large blocks of stock at the day's closing price. Reuters was a formidable competitor, with a daily volume of three million shares (about 4.4 percent of the NYSE volume). Mr. Baxter thought Reuters' approach was fundamentally different from the one Jefferies was developing.

Existing rules prohibited member firms of the NYSE from participating in transactions in the capacity of principal and, in certain cases, even as agent for off-exchange transactions in listed securities. Member firms were allowed to execute other third-market transactions for their customers, although typically they did not. Because these firms were major competitors of Jefferies, which was not bound by these restrictions and practices, a change in these rules could adversely affect Jefferies business. As the NYSE lost market share, the probability of a change in the rules increased.

Despite the rules, some NYSE-member firms were aggressively making markets in over-the-counter securities and purchasing and operating specialist posts on regional exchanges. Morgan Stanley & Co. had even developed its own electronic-trading system, which was handling 500,000 trades a day. The Arizona Stock Exchange, recently opened under the guidance of a former analyst at Kidder, Peabody, was billed as a fully electronic daily auction.

The largest third-market specialist was Bernard Madoff Investment Securities, a NASDAQ dealer, who accounted for volume equivalent to 5 percent of the NYSE volume in NYSE-listed securities. Madoff, like many specialists on regional exchanges, actually paid brokerage firms a cent or two for each order the market-maker was given.

Major investment banks maintained large trading functions, but Mr. Baxter argued that their purpose was different than Jefferies'. Jefferies was in business to capture the commissions. Many other firms were interested primarily in capturing the informational content of the deal flow to make money by taking positions for their own portfolios. The commissions were a minor portion of the reward. "We sell liquidity," Mr. Baxter commented. "They buy information. This isn't our loss-leader to get into some other business activity with the client." On the other hand, NYSE specialists complained that member firms that crossed trades internally were tempted to treat customers preferentially. An anonymous specialist complained to the *Institutional Investor** that an investment bank whose trades on one security the specialist had lost claimed to make more trading that one stock internally than it paid the specialist to execute trades on all other transactions.

Mr. Baxter doubted the value of being publicly owned. "It's an advantage to be able to use the stock for acquisitions when the price-earnings ratio is high," he said, "and the outside directors keep an eye on things. We could get outside directors anyway, and there is some expense associated with public ownership." Jefferies had bought back stock periodically when the market price of the stock was available at less than book value. In addition, the company had repurchased the shares owned by Mr. Jefferies.

As a registered broker-dealer doing business with the public, Jefferies was subject to the Securities and Exchange Commission's minimum capital requirements. Aggregate indebtedness could not exceed 15 times adjusted net capital nor could adjusted net capital be less than 2 percent of aggregate debit balances (primarily receivables from customers and other broker-dealers). At the end of 1991, Jefferies exceeded these requirements by $47 million.

**Institutional Investor*, February 1992, p. 31.

Industry Conditions

According to a *Value Line* analysis of November 1991, the securities brokerage business was having its best year in 1991 since 1987. Trading was the dominant market driver, and the high degree of market volatility created opportunities for the trader to make money. Industry net profit, return on equity, and price-earnings ratios are shown in Table 1.

Table 1
Selected Financial Data for the Securities Brokerage Industry

Year	1988	1989	1990	1991
Net profit (millions)	$971	$1,029	$924	$2,171
Return on equity	9.2%	8.7%	7.7%	15.3%
Price-earnings ratio	10.2×	12.8×	12.5×	7.3×

Exhibit 1
JEFFERIES GROUP, INC.
Income Statement and Selected Financial Information
Years Ending December 31, 1986-1991
(dollars in thousands except per-share figures)

	1986		1987		1988		1989		1990		1991	
Consolidated Statement of Earnings												
Revenues												
Commissions	$104,954	66.2%	$101,759	69.0%	$79,048	54.7%	$87,151	66.7%	$82,098	48.8%	$84,339	43.0%
Principal	21,713	13.7	24,456	16.6	40,615	28.1	20,251	15.5	43,417	25.8	69,972	35.7
Investment banking	903	0.6	1,053	0.7	2,122	1.5	1,940	1.5	8,936	5.3	16,745	8.5
Interest	29,843	18.8	18,758	12.7	15,910	11.0	20,874	16.0	32,975	19.6	23,939	12.2
Other	1,235	0.8	1,422	1.0	6,938	4.8	411	0.3	661	0.4	955	0.5
Total revenues	$158,648	100.0%	$147,448	100.0%	$144,633	100.0%	$130,627	100.0%	$168,087	100.0%	$195,950	100.0%
Expenses												
Compensation and benefits	63,746	40.2	61,431	41.7	56,747	39.2	59,771	45.8	75,408	44.9	92,294	47.1
Floor brokerage and clearing fees	14,175	8.9	14,635	9.9	11,590	8.0	12,927	9.9	12,142	7.2	11,593	5.9
Telecom. and data processing	9,695	6.1	12,273	8.3	12,814	8.9	12,094	9.3	13,839	8.2	16,034	8.2
Interest	21,930	13.8	11,967	8.1	8,499	5.9	12,727	9.7	23,825	14.2	15,959	8.1
Occupancy and equipt. rental	5,426	3.4	5,783	3.9	5,598	3.9	6,610	5.1	7,755	4.6	12,767	6.5
Other	17,856	11.3	29,747	20.2	21,249	14.7	19,604	15.0	22,936	13.6	29,458	15.0
Total expenses	$132,828	83.7%	$135,836	92.1%	$116,497	80.5%	$123,733	94.7%	$155,905	92.8%	$178,105	90.9%
Earnings before income taxes	$ 25,820	16.3%	$ 11,612	7.9%	$ 28,136	19.5%	$ 6,894	5.3%	$ 12,182	7.2%	$ 17,845	9.1%
Income taxes	12,109	7.6	5,461	3.7	12,150	8.4	3,235	2.5	5,459	3.2	7,975	4.1
Net earnings	$ 13,711	8.6%	$ 6,151	4.2%	$ 15,986	11.1%	$ 3,659	2.8%	$ 6,723	4.0%	$ 9,870	5.0%
Per share												
Primary earnings	$1.70		$0.79		$2.17		$0.58		$1.11		$1.74	
Fully diluted earnings	1.55		0.79		1.96		0.58		1.10		1.57	
Dividends	—		—		.20		.20		.20		.20	
Weighted average shares (000)												
Primary	8,077		7,773		7,651		6,315		6,073		5,686	
Fully diluted	10,279		9,204		9,204		6,315		7,907		7,520	
Selected Financial Information												
Selected balance sheet data												
Total assets	$551,515	100.0%	$261,163	100.0%	$288,961	100.0%	$343,379	100.0%	$602,186	100.0%	$528,984	100.0%
Convertible subordinated debt	45,970	8.3	40,291	15.4	40,032	13.9	40,147	11.7	40,288	6.7	40,428	7.6
Total stockholders' equity	83,968	15.2	85,625	32.8	85,046	29.4	80,901	23.6	86,370	14.3	78,085	14.8
Book value per share	10.68		11.56		12.75		13.27		14.53		17.05	
Shares outstanding, end of year (000)	7,859		7,410		6,669		6,098		5,944		4,579	
Return on assets		4.7%		4.4%		9.7%		2.0%		2.0%		3.4%
Return on equity		30.7		13.6		33.1		8.5		14.1		22.9
Growth in revenues				-7.1%		-1.9%		-9.7%		28.7%		16.6%
Growth in earnings				-55.1		159.9		-77.1		83.7		46.8
Growth in earnings per share				-53.5		174.7		-73.3		91.4		56.8
Market price												
High	$17.25		$15.875		$12.75		$14.75		$13.25		$15.25	
Low	9.75		7.75		9.00		10.75		9.25		10.125	

Exhibit 2

JEFFERIES GROUP, INC.

Balance Sheets as of December 31, 1989-1991
(thousands of dollars)

	1989	1990	1991
Assets			
Cash and equivalents	$ 8,613	$ 5,663	$ 5,936
Receivable from brokers & dealers	85,168	284,795	288,077
Reverse repurchase agreement	–	–	10,000
Rec. from cust., officers, & directors	106,617	192,582	116,854
Securities owned	118,592	86,691	67,853
Premises and equipment	8,048	11,103	12,939
Exchange memberships at cost	131	131	131
Other assets	16,210	21,221	27,194
Total assets	$343,379	$602,186	$528,984
Liabilities and Stockholders' Equity			
Liabilities			
Secured bank loans	$ 42,834	$ 27,262	$ 5,686
Payable to brokers and dealers	6,777	176,563	176,542
Repurchase agreements	–	75,000	–
Payable to customers	80,787	111,611	134,735
Securities sold, not yet purchased	70,882	49,112	46,199
Accrued expenses & other liabilities	21,051	35,980	47,309
Total current liabilities	$222,331	$475,528	$410,471
Convertible subordinated debt	40,147	40,288	40,428
Total liabilities	$262,478	$515,816	$450,899
Stockholders' Equity			
Common stock and paid-in capital	24,853	25,462	26,068
Retained earnings	86,909	92,423	101,178
Less:			
Treasury stock	(26,294)	(28,679)	(47,860)
Deferred compensation	(4,539)	(2,759)	(1,301)
Additional minimum pension liability	(28)	(77)	–
Net stockholders' equity	$ 80,901	$ 86,370	$ 78,085
Total liabilities & stockholders' equity	$343,379	$602,186	$528,984

Exhibit 3

JEFFERIES GROUP, INC.

Sources of Revenues for the Years Ending
December 31, 1989-1991
(dollar figures in thousands)

	1989		1990		1991	
Commissions						
Listed	$ 71,033	54.4%	$ 63,927	38.0%	$ 59,944	30.6%
POSIT/QuantEx	3,309	2.5	8,584	5.1	14,255	7.3
Convertible bonds	7,224	5.5	4,711	2.8	5,368	2.7
International	5,585	4.3	4,876	2.9	4,772	2.4
Total	$ 87,151	66.7%	$ 82,098	48.8%	$ 84,339	43.0%
Principal transactions						
Taxable fixed income	(176)	–0.1	21,754	12.9	32,107	16.4
Over-the-counter	20,796	15.9	18,336	10.9	23,579	12.0
International convertibles	—	0.0	1,180	0.7	7,367	3.8
Arbitrage	(987)	–0.8	2,747	1.6	4,209	2.1
International	3,386	2.6	737	0.4	3,284	1.7
Specialist posts	1,829	1.4	1,622	1.0	2,098	1.1
Convertible bonds	(1,540)	–1.2	(2,720)	–1.6	(126)	–0.1
Corporate bonds	1,362	1.0	1,770	1.1	(1,173)	–0.6
Listed securities	(4,419)	–3.4	(2,009)	–1.2	(1,373)	–0.7
Total	$ 20,251	15.5%	$ 43,417	25.8%	$ 69,972	35.7%
Investment banking	1,940	1.5	8,936	5.3	16,745	8.5
Interest	20,874	16.0	32,975	19.6	23,939	12.2
Other	411	0.3	661	0.4	955	0.5
Total	$130,627	100.0%	$168,087	100.0%	$195,950	100.0%

Exhibit 4

JEFFERIES GROUP, INC.

Securities Position, December 31, 1990 and 1991
(thousands of dollars)

	1990		1991	
	Owned	Short*	Owned	Short*
U.S. Government & agency obligations	$ 2,037	$ –	$ 1,944	$ –
Corporate debt securities	12,268	4,867	16,556	4,437
Corporate equity securities	35,835	32,027	29,970	34,041
High-yield securities	36,305	12,120	19,249	7,598
Options	246	98	134	123
Total	$86,691	$49,112	$67,853	$46,199

*Securities sold, not yet purchased

Case 5: DISCOVER CARD

In December 1988, Jane Adams, a security analyst for Darden Securities, Inc., was reviewing her current research report on Sears, Roebuck and Co. Recently, in the face of continuing poor earnings and threats of a raid on the company, Sears had announced a corporate restructuring. The Sears Tower in Chicago and the Coldwell Banker commercial real-estate activity would be sold, 10 percent of the common stock would be repurchased, and a major discounting strategy would be introduced for the merchandise division. Ms. Adams was wondering whether to change her research report, which had been especially negative on Sears' prospects. In particular, she wondered whether Sears' prospects in the insurance and financial-service area (which accounted for 42.5 percent of Sears' sales and 57.4 percent of its profits in 1987) were strong enough, if coupled with a potential modest turnaround in its merchandise division, to merit upgrading her recommendation.

The History of Sears, Roebuck and Co.

Sears, Roebuck and Co. was one of the giants of American business history. Founded in 1886, Sears grew with a growing, changing America by developing new ways to distribute goods. To reach the American farmer in the Midwest and West, Sears pioneered the mail-order catalog, which enabled farmers to buy almost anything they might need without a trip to the city. As America shifted during the post-World War II years from being a nation of farmers to a nation of suburbanites with automobiles, Sears pioneered in building vast suburban stores and shopping malls that enabled suburbanites to buy everything they needed, from barbecues to lingerie, at one location.

In the process of developing new and innovative ways to distribute goods, Sears grew to be the world's largest retailer. By 1972, Sears was at the height of its dominance of the American retailing environment. The 3,500 Sears stores around the country included 900 large, full-line stores; over half the households in the United States had a Sears' credit card; and two-thirds of Americans shopped at Sears at least once in every three-month period. Sears was so large, relative to the overall economy in 1972, that it accounted for over 1 percent of the U.S. gross national product.

Then, in the years following 1972, Sears entered a period of great turmoil. Corporate profits from retailing stagnated or declined for five straight years; interest expenses doubled because of monetary inflation; the company's image was shaken by lawsuits, government investigations, and adverse publicity; workers were laid off for the first time since World War II; and the stock price dropped from $61 in 1972 to $24 in 1977.

Out of the internal soul-searching that accompanied Sears' problems in its basic business, senior management created a new strategy to restore the growth and profitability of the company. This strategy called for developing a major new market for the company by riding emerging economic and social trends in the same way that its mail-order catalogs and suburban stores had served emerging economic and social trends in earlier eras.

The major new market on which Sears chose to focus was consumer financial services. Internal planning studies had identified this as a large and growing market in which Sears had significant competitive advantages derived from its existing financial-service activities. The company also could capitalize on changes management expected to occur in the market's structure. Sears' existing financial-service businesses included a major consumer insurance activity, Allstate Insurance, and the largest proprietary credit-card operation in the United States. Exhibits 1 through 8 provide historical and financial information on Sears and its Dean Witter Financial Services Group, which was assigned responsibility for implementing Sears' financial-services strategy after its acquisition by Sears in 1981.

Sears' Financial-Services Strategy

Sears' financial-services strategy was based on two major premises. The first was that the consumer financial-services industry, which in the early 1980s was growing rapidly but was extremely fragmented, was entering a period of consolidation. High-fixed, low-variable-cost automation would create an industry dominated by very large, efficient, low-cost producers. The second major premise was that Sears had a clear opportunity to capitalize on the trends in consumer financial services because of its large existing customer base, particularly for its credit-card and insurance services; because of its nationwide network of stores and offices; and because of its massive data-processing capability and large credit-card-processing capability. The belief was that Sears could cross-sell a wide range of consumer financial services to its existing customer base. Thus, a whole system of services could be tied together by efficient computer systems that would give Sears economies of scale.

The first major step Sears took to expand into the consumer financial services area was to make two large acquisitions. On October 8, 1981, Sears announced the acquisitions of Dean Witter Reynolds, a major securities firm, and Coldwell Banker, the largest full-service real-estate firm in the United States. These two companies, along with Sears' existing Allstate Insurance and its proprietary credit card, were the foundation on which Sears planned to develop its full range of consumer financial services.

Sears believed it could duplicate its previous success with Allstate Insurance in the consumer insurance industry. Allstate Insurance booths were located in most Sears stores, and Allstate profits were the primary source of Sears' earnings during the late 1970s and early 1980s. Management now decided also to provide its customers with a full range of financial services: consumer banking, retail securities brokerage, residential real-estate brokerage, and mortgage lending.

Sears' first attempt to cross-sell financial-services was the Sears Financial Center. Sales booths representing the newly acquired Dean Witter and Coldwell Bankers subsidiaries were added to its existing in-store Allstate booths to sell real-estate brokerage services and securities brokerage services in the same way that Allstate sold insurance. Introduced in 1983 and expanded to 312 Sears stores in 1983 and 1984, the Sears Financial Centers proved a disappointment: they failed to generate the business expected and were not profitable.

In addition, Sears' failure to tie together its various financial services through the Sears Financial Centers led senior management to look for an alternative to link the various elements of the financial-services activities. After intensive in-house planning, it decided that the integrating element would be a new, general-purpose credit card, which could be used to finance purchases, make loans, and take deposits, and which could be tied to retail securities' accounts.

The Credit-Card Industry

Although travel and entertainment cards (such as American Express) had long existed, and some banks (such as Signet Bank's predecessors) had issued general-purpose cards, the credit-card industry in the United States got a major boost in 1961 when Bank of America introduced the BankAmericard (later sold to a bank cooperative and renamed VISA). Since then, credit cards have become a central feature of American life and a major segment of the financial-services industry.

In 1988, 70 percent of all U.S. consumers had one or more major credit cards (VISA, MasterCard, American Express, or Discover), and 76 percent of all U.S. consumers had one or more credit cards of some kind (major credit cards or special-purpose cards such as those issued by oil companies and department stores). Total major credit cards outstanding at the end of 1988 exceeded 250 million, which included 107 million VISA Cards, 87 million MasterCards, 30 million American Express Cards, and 26 million Discover Cards. Acceptance of credit cards by merchants and service establishments was so widespread as to be almost universal. Worldwide, 6.5 million locations accepted VISA and MasterCard, and 2.2 million accepted American Express. Annual charges on credit cards were estimated at about $300 billion. Exhibits 9 through 13 provide detailed data on the credit-card industry.

The vast majority of credit cards outstanding were bank or bank-related cards, which had several common features. First, the credit-card holder had a prearranged line of credit with the bank that issued the card. Credit was extended when the credit-card holder bought something and signed (or approved) a sales draft at a participating retail outlet. The retail merchant presented the sales draft to the bank for reimbursement, less a merchant's discount.

The merchants' discounts ranged from nothing to 6 percent or more based on:

- the retail outlet's volume of credit-card trade;
- the average size of each credit-card sale;
- the amount of compensating balances kept at the bank;
- some combination of the preceding factors.

If the credit was presented for payment at the merchant's bank (which might not be the bank that issued the credit card), the merchant's bank would keep part of the merchant's discount for handling the transaction and routing it to the bank that had issued the card. Finally, the issuing bank presented the sales draft to the credit-card holder for payment.

The second common feature was that the credit-card holder could pay for the draft in full within a grace period (for example, 30 days) and not be charged interest on the outstanding balance or pay some minimum amount each month on an installment basis with interest being charged on the outstanding balance. Banks depended on interest income earned on these credit balances as the major source of income from their credit-card operations. Some also charged an annual fee (for example, $30) for the privilege of having a credit card.

The final feature was the plastic credit card itself, which served special purposes. First, it identified the customer to the merchant. Second, it was used to transfer account information to the sales draft by use of an imprinting machine. And third, the card might be encoded with a magnetic strip or computer chip that provided additional information about the cardholder's financial condition. The cards with the computer chips were called "smart cards."

About 40 percent of the credit-card debt outstanding was created for convenience. The cardholder used the credit card instead of cash or checks and paid the amount owed in full when billed, thereby avoiding interest charges.

Three types of credit-card plans were available to banks. In the first type of plan, one principal bank issued the credit card, maintained accounts, billed and collected credit, and assumed most of the other functions associated with credit cards. In the second type of plan, one bank acted as a limited agent for the principal bank. The principal bank issued the card, carried the bulk of the credit, and performed the functions described in the first plan. The functions of the agent bank were to establish merchant accounts and accept merchant sales drafts; it received a commission on the business it generated without incurring the costs of a credit-card operation. The limited-agent bank might have its own name and logo on the card. Cardholders assumed that the card was issued and managed by the agent bank, which was not true.

In the third plan, a bank became affiliated with one of the major travel-and-entertainment card (T&E) plans such as American Express. A T&E card was not a credit card. Cardholders had to pay the amount owed when billed; they did not have the option of making small payments over time. Banks affiliating with T&E cards did not set up a credit-card system but offered T&E cardholders an optional line of credit. The cardholder could pay the T&E-card bill through the bank and borrow directly from the bank against a preestablished line of credit.

In this plan, the bank became involved with the transactions only if the cardholder decided to pay the bill in installments or used the line of credit.

The Discover Card

Introduced in the fall of 1985, the Discover Card was planned as the integrating element in Sears' overall consumer-financial-services thrust. Through Discover, management planned to avoid restrictions on nationwide deposit taking and the cost of building a nationwide network to take deposits and make loans. By combining traditional credit-card features with those of an automatic-teller-machine (ATM) card, Sears hoped to get its customers nationally to bank with its subsidiary, Greenwood Trust Company in Greenwood, Delaware. The expectation was that customers would bank by mail with Greenwood and use ATMs to draw out cash from checking accounts, savings accounts, and lines of credit tied to the Discover Card, as well as to purchase certificates of deposit and contribute to individual retirement accounts. Facilities in 800 Sears stores and a network of 5,428 ATMs provided the support for the Discover initiative.

When Sears rolled out its Discover marketing efforts in the fall of 1985 and the spring of 1986, it had ambitious goals. It planned to offer the card to 26 million Sears cardholders with the intent of getting 10 million of them to sign up. To induce prospects to accept and use the Discover Card, Sears offered several benefits:

- no annual fee (most bank cards charged $15 to $30 per year);
- rebates up to 1 percent on the purchase price of an item, to apply to a Discover balance or to add to a Discover savings account (the rebate would be paid annually at a rate that increased with use; charges of $3,000 annually were required to reach the 1-percent rebate level).

To achieve its ambitious goals to sign up cardholders, Sears had to persuade merchants and various service providers (such as airlines and restaurants) to accept the card. To encourage their affiliation, Sears offered substantially lower charges than usual for processing credit-card invoices (1.5 percent of invoice face amount versus 2 to 3 percent for VISA and MasterCard and up to 5 percent for American Express). Discover was also paying the merchants very promptly, often within two days.

In the first two years of marketing the Discover Card, Sears seemed to have made significant progress toward its penetration goals, but it was incurring a substantial cost. By February 1988, 22 million Discover Cards had been issued, and 16 percent of all households carried Discover Cards. In addition, 720,000 merchants, airlines, hotels, and restaurants had been signed up to accept the Discover Card. During these two years, however, Sears had lost $400 million pretax on the card. For 1988, the expectation was that the card would have a small profit or at least break even. The goal was to attain at least one million businesses accepting Discover by mid-1989, with receivables at or above $7 billion and profits of above $70 million.

Despite its tremendous investment and the rapid growth of Discover, Sears was still an "also-ran" in the increasingly competitive credit-card business. The large credit-card market was going through a consolidation that was shrinking margins and leading to an industry dominated by a few big issuers such as Citicorp, First Chicago, Maryland National Bank, Banc One, and BankAmerica, which were highly efficient at processing transactions.

Toward the end of its third year of operation (1988), Discover Card's promise appeared to be showing up. By November 1988, Discover had shown a small profit for two straight quarters, the number of cards outstanding was 26 million, 19 percent of households in the United States had a Discover Card (versus 20 percent with an American Express Card), and full 1988 revenue estimates were $1 billion. In addition, Sears had begun to experiment with charging an annual fee for the use of the card.

The long-term horizon for Discover was increasingly promising. Sears estimated that 40 million Discover Cards would be outstanding within five years, with annual revenues in the area of $2 to $3 billion. Securities analysts estimated that stabilized profits on this level of revenues could reach $200 to $300 million.

The Review

As Ms. Adams reviewed her recommendation on Sears, she wrestled with the primary question: Could Sears generate significant increased profits from its financial-services activities? In addition, was Sears' strategy toward financial services sound, and would Sears' huge expenditure on the Discover Card ultimately pay off?

Exhibit 1

DISCOVER CARD

Chronology of Sears' Expansion into Financial Services

October 8, 1981	Sears announces acquisition of Dean Witter Reynolds and Coldwell Banker.
1983	Sears opens first Sears Financial Centers.
April 24, 1985	The Discover Card, a new combination credit and financial-services card, is unveiled in Atlanta by Sears President Edward A. Brennan.
August 31, 1985	C. Wesley Poulson, 55, founder of Coldwell Banker, retires as chairman and chief executive officer of the Coldwell Banker Real Estate Group.
January 1, 1986	After 39 years of service, Edward R. Telling retires as chairman and chief executive officer of Sears, Roebuck and Co. He is replaced by Edward A. Brennan, 51. Sears begins second century in business.
September 1, 1986	Robert M. "Stretch" Gardiner retires as chairman and chief executive officer of the Dean Witter Financial-Services Group. He is replaced by Philip J. Purcell, former Sears vice president for planning and architect of Sears' financial-services strategy.
November 1988	Edward Brennan, Sears chairman, announces corporate restructuring.

Exhibit 2

DISCOVER CARD

Sears, Roebuck and Co.
Financial Highlights
(millions of dollars except per-share figures)

	1980	1981	1982	1983	1984	1985	1986	1987
Total assets	$28,218	$34,406	$36,541	$46,176	$57,073	$66,417	$65,995	$74,991
Shareholder equity	7,665	8,269	8,812	9,787	10,911	11,794	13,047	13,588
Revenues	25,161	27,357	30,020	35,883	38,928	40,715	44,281	48,440
Net income	610	650	861	1,342	1,455	1,303	1,351	1,649
Dividends	429	429	476	537	631	639	648	756
Earnings per share	$1.93	$2.06	$2.46	$3.80	$4.05	$3.53	$3.62	$4.35
Market price, year-end	$15⅜	$16⅛	$30⅛	$37⅛	$31¾	$39	$39¾	33½
Price/earnings ratio (based on high-low prices)	10-8×	10-7×	13-6×	12-7×	10-7×	12-9×	14-10×	14-7×

Exhibit 3

DISCOVER CARD

Dean Witter Financial-Services Group
Key Five-Year Statistics
(millions of dollars)

	1983	1984	1985	1986	1987
Balance Sheet					
Assets					
Securities-related	$ 7,298	$12,760	$18,720	$12,600	$13,952
Consumer banking	5,155	6,408	7,253	8,639	10,622
Total	$12,453	$19,168	$25,973	$21,239	$24,574
Income Statement					
Revenues					
Securities-related	$ 1,544	$ 1,845	$ 2,031	$ 2,563	$ 2,747
Consumer banking	564	651	826	852	1,248
Total	$ 2,108	$ 2,496	$ 2,857	$ 3,415	$ 3,995
Income before income taxes, equity in net income of unconsolidated companies, and minority interest					
Securities-related	$ 138	$ (94)	$ (3)	$ 154	$ 148
Consumer banking	52	24	21	(212)	(115)
Total	$ 190	$ (70)	$ 18	$ (58)	$ 33
Net income					
Securities-related	$ 69	$ (45)	$ —	$ 80	$ 76
Consumer banking	31	12	13	(117)	(75)
Total	$ 100	$ (33)	$ 13	$ (37)	$ 1

Exhibit 4

DISCOVER CARD

Dean Witter Financial-Services Group
Statements of Financial Position, December 31, 1986 and 1987
(millions of dollars)

	1986	1987
Assets		
Cash and invested cash	$ 934.8	$ 929.8
Securities purchased under agreements to resell	5,228.7	6,400.0
Mortgages, other loans, and investments	5,131.1	4,398.9
Discover Card receivables	1,271.9	3,705.9
Receivable from clients and others, collateralized	3,275.6	3,570.6
Securities, at market value	2,565.0	2,513.1
Consumer-finance notes	1,246.0	1,517.5
Other assets	1,585.8	1,538.6
Total assets	$21,238.9	$24,574.4
Liabilities and Capital		
Deposits and advances from Federal Home Loan Bank	$ 6,648.1	$ 7,222.4
Securities sold under agreements to repurchase	5,887.9	6,817.2
Borrowings	3,037.3	3,356.2
Payable to clients and others	2,845.3	3,120.9
Securities sold but not yet purchased, at market value	477.2	1,532.2
Other liabilities	1,094.4	875.2
Total liabilities	$19,990.2	$22,924.1
Capital	1,248.7	1,650.3
Total liabilities and capital	$21,238.9	$24,574.4

Exhibit 5

DISCOVER CARD

Dean Witter Financial-Services Group
Statements of Income, Years Ended December 31, 1985-87
(millions of dollars)

	1985	1986	1987
Income			
Interest	$1,566.9	$1,699.4	$2,023.9
Commissions	507.1	757.6	763.0
Trading	225.8	275.7	279.2
Investment banking	264.4	255.8	274.8
Other operating revenues	292.4	426.8	653.9
Total revenues	$2,856.6	$3,415.3	$3,994.8
Costs and expenses			
Interest	1,324.0	1,400.3	1,511.4
Personnel	870.1	1,155.2	1,271.4
Other operating costs and expenses	644.1	940.9	1,273.9
Total costs and expenses	$2,838.2	$3,496.4	$4,056.7
Operating income (loss)	$ 18.4	$ (81.1)	$ (61.9)
Gain on sale of savings branches	–	22.9	94.9
Income (loss) before income taxes	$ 18.4	$ (58.2)	$ 33.0
Income taxes (benefit)	5.3	(21.2)	31.8
Group income (loss)	$ 13.1	$ (37.0)	$ 1.2

Exhibit 6

DISCOVER CARD

Dean Witter Financial-Services Group
Financial Summary of **Securities Operations**
Years Ended December 31, 1985-87
(millions of dollars)

	1985	1986	1987
Income			
Interest	$ 858.2	$ 938.1	$ 986.4
Commissions	507.1	757.6	763.0
Trading	225.8	275.7	279.2
Investment banking	264.4	255.8	274.8
Other	175.5	335.5	443.5
Total revenues	$2,031.0	$2,562.7	$2,746.9
Expense			
Personnel	766.7	987.9	1,072.7
Interest	763.7	844.6	877.3
Other	503.5	576.3	648.5
Total expenses	$2,033.9	$2,408.8	$2,598.5
Operating income (loss)	$ (2.9)	$ 153.9	$ 148.4
Income taxes (benefit)	(3.1)	74.4	72.6
Net income	$ 0.2	$ 79.5	$ 75.8

Exhibit 7

DISCOVER CARD

Dean Witter Financial-Services Group
Financial Summary of **Consumer Banking Operations**
Years Ended December 31, 1985-87
(dollars in millions)

	1985	1986	1987
Interest revenue	$ 708.7	$ 761.3	$1,037.5
Interest expense	560.3	555.7	634.1
Net interest income	$ 148.4	$ 205.6	$ 403.4
Provision for loan losses	15.6	55.3	213.5
Net credit income	$ 132.8	$ 150.3	$ 189.9
Net income (loss)	$ 12.9	$(116.5)	$ (74.6)
Volume:			
Discover Card	$ 24.2	$1,755.1	$ 6,004.0
Real-estate loans	3,129.5	4,775.2	4,064.9
Auto, home-equity, and other loans	847.5	1,069.6	1,303.9
Residential-mortgage-servicing portfolio	6,035.4	8,601.6	10,663.7
Discover Card (thousands):			
Cardholders	378	11,372	22,056
Merchant outlets	150	527	726

Exhibit 8

DISCOVER CARD

Sears Merchandise Group
Credit-Card Statistics, 1985-87
(dollars in millions)

	1985	1986	1987
Customer receivables balances at Dec. 31	$11,539.3	$11,714.3	$13,227.1
Balances sold at Dec. 31	2,361.5	2,247.3	831.5
Average account balance	495.0	497.0	515.0
Finance-charge revenues	2,097.8	2,068.5	2,010.8
Credit sales as percentage of gross sales	62.0%	60.6%	58.6%
Yield on receivables	17.7	17.6	17.4
Provision for uncollectible accounts	$224.2	$349.8	$291.3
Ratio to credit sales	1.35%	2.08%	1.75%
Ratio of net charged-off accounts to credit sales	1.24	1.62	1.69
Percentage of accounts delinquent three or more months to total	1.18	1.26	1.02
Interest expense	$872.8	$819.0	$776.5
Credit income	$293.5	$253.2	$263.1
Ratio, credit income to credit sales	1.8%	1.5%	1.6%

Exhibit 9

DISCOVER CARD

Percentage of U.S. Households with Specific Major Charge Cards, November 1988

VISA	53%
MasterCard	44
American Express	20
Discover	19

Source: *American Banker* survey of 1,007 households.

Exhibit 10

DISCOVER CARD

Number of Credit Cards Individuals Held in December 1988

Number of Cards	Percentage of Population
None	26%
1–3	37
4–6	21
7 or more	13
Don't know	3

Source: Maritz Marketing Research, Ameripoll, nationally representative of 1,000 adults.

Exhibit 11

DISCOVER CARD

Estimated Market Share of Major Credit Cards of
Total Dollar Volume Charged on Major Credit Cards in 1988
(billions of dollars)

Card	Charge Volume	Market Share
VISA	$115.0	43.2%
MasterCard	75.1	28.2
American Express	59.9	22.5
Discover	11.2	4.2
Diner's Club	5.0	1.9
	$266.2	100.0%

Source: Sanford C. Bernstein and Company, Inc.

Exhibit 12

DISCOVER CARD

Ten Largest U.S. Bank Credit-Card Issuers, at End of 1988,
Ranked by Number of Active Accounts

	No. of Active Accounts* (millions)	Dollar Volume (billions)	Millions of Cards Outstanding	
			MasterCard	VISA
Citibank	14.2	$27.0	10.1	15.2
Bank of America	4.9	8.7	1.3	6.0
Chase Manhattan	4.7	6.3	2.2	6.7
First Chicago	4.6	9.2	2.5	6.9
Maryland National Bank	2.2	6.8	3.5	1.4
Bank of New York	1.6	3.4	3.0	0.4
Manufacturers Hanover	1.6	3.0	3.5	2.5
Wells Fargo	1.5	2.4	2.4	0.9
Chemical Bank	1.3	2.3	1.6	1.0
Banc One (Ohio)	1.2	1.5	0.8	1.9

*Average number of statements mailed monthly.

Source: The Nilson Report.

Exhibit 13

DISCOVER CARD

Credit-Card Portfolio Growth, 1986-87
(dollar figures in millions)

Rank	Bank Holding Company	Card Assets as of December 31 1986	Card Assets as of December 31 1987	Assets Securitized During 1987	Percentage Increase, Including Securitization 12/86 to 12/87	New Assets Added, Including Securitized
1	Citicorp	$15,319	$17,747	–	16%	$2,428
2	Chase	5,449	6,345	–	16	896
3	Bank of America	6,065	5,121	$ 700	(4)	(244)
4	First Chicago	3,504	4,036	800	38	1,332
5	Sears (Discover)	1,004	3,136	–	212	2,132
6	Wells Fargo	2,816	2,670	–	(5)	(146)
7	Mfg. Hanover	2,029	2,611	–	29	582
8	First Interstate	2,409	2,335	–	(3)	(74)
9	Maryland National	1,706	2,223	500	60	1,017
10	Bank of New York	824	2,103	–	155	1,279
11	Security Pacific	1,432	1,843	–	29	411
12	Amex (Optima)	405	1,671	–	313	1,266
13	Chemical	1,314	1,598	–	22	284
14	Marine Midland	1,447	1,359	–	(6)	(88)
15	Banc One	1,112	1,273	–	14	161
	Top 15 Total	$46,835	$56,071	$2,000	24%	$11,236

Source: *American Banker*, Nilson Report.

Notes

Case 6: GENERAL ELECTRIC FINANCIAL SERVICES, INC.

In early April 1989, Jim Jones, a second-year student at the Darden Graduate Business School, University of Virginia, was deciding which job to accept. He had just received an offer to join the corporate finance staff of Kidder, Peabody, Inc., a major securities firm.* Mr. Jones was excited about his offer because his goal in entering graduate business school had been to become an investment banker. He was also apprehensive, however, because he knew there had been predictions of a significant downturn in business for Wall Street and that his potential employer, Kidder, Peabody, had recently experienced a variety of disturbing problems. Adding to Mr. Jones' apprehension about Kidder was its ownership by the General Electric Company through its financial subsidiary, General Electric Financial Services, Incorporated. In recent months, the financial press had reported that General Electric was dissatisfied with the performance of Kidder and might make major changes.

General Electric Financial Services, Inc.

General Electric Financial Services, Inc. (GEFS), a subsidiary of General Electric Company, held the ownership of three organizations that, together with their affiliates and other investments, constituted General Electric Company's principal financial services activities. GEFS was one of the most diversified participants in the global financial services market, having almost $75 billion in assets and operating 17 different financial and asset management businesses. (Historical financial statements for GEFS are shown in Exhibits 1, 2, and 3. Exhibit 4 shows GEFS's relative position compared to other non-bank finance companies.) GEFS owned all the common stock of General Electric Capital Corporation (GECC) and of Employers Reinsurance Corporation (ERC). It owned 80 percent of Kidder, Peabody Group Inc.; the other 20 percent was held by or on behalf of certain Kidder, Peabody officers.

GECC, which had $42 billion in earning assets, was a major supplier of capital and financial expertise to U.S. business. Its activities included time sales; revolving credit and inventory financing for retail merchants (major appliances, television sets, furniture and other home furnishings, and personal computers); automobile leasing and automobile inventory financing; home and recreation vehicle financing (principally time sales and dealer inventory financing of mobile homes); commercial and industrial loans and equipment sales financing

---

*Mr. Jones also had offers from a regional investment bank and a major commercial bank's investment banking function.

This case was written from publicly available information.

provided through leases, time sales, and loans; leasing services for third-party investors; and commercial and residential real estate financing. Acquisition of Montgomery Ward and Company's credit operations in June 1988 added to GECC's credit card operations. GECC was also an equity investor in certain other service and financial services organizations and participated in leveraged buyouts. Although leasing had been a major factor in GECC's growth in recent years, GECC had changed its investment portfolio to place greater emphasis on asset ownership, management, and operation. Most products financed by GECC were manufactured by companies other than GE.

The insurance activities of GEFS were conducted mainly by ERC, a multiple-line property and casualty reinsurer that wrote all lines of reinsurance other than title and annuities. ERC, with $4 billion as assets, was the second largest property and casualty reinsurer in the United States and fourth largest in the world. It reinsured property and casualty risks written by more than 1,000 domestic and foreign insurers and augmented its foreign business through subsidiaries located in the United Kingdom and, since January 1988, in Denmark. Other subsidiaries wrote property and casualty reinsurance through brokers and provided reinsurance brokerage services. ERC itself also directly wrote certain specialty lines of insurance, principally excess workers' compensation for self-insurers, libel and allied torts, and errors and omissions coverage for insurance agents and brokers. It was licensed in all states of the United States, the District of Columbia, certain provinces of Canada, and in other jurisdictions. ERC's business was subject to regulation by various insurance regulatory agencies. Additional but less significant insurance activities of GEFS included certain GECC affiliates that provided private mortgage insurance, life reinsurance, and, for GECC customers, credit life and certain types of property/casualty insurance.

The investment banking and securities activities of GEFS were conducted principally through Kidder, Peabody, a major investment banking and securities firm. Kidder had been acquired by GEFS in 1986 as a way by which GEFS could both enter the securities business and expand its overall financial service activities.

GEFS had shown continuous growth in revenues in the five-year period 1983-1988. This growth had come both from internal growth of existing businesses and from acquisitions. New acquisitions in 1988 included FGIC Corporation, an insurer of municipal bonds, Foremost Mortgage Insurance of Wisconsin, and the private label credit card business of the Montgomery Ward Credit Corporation (six million active customers). Through its various subsidiaries, GECC authorized more than three million consumer purchases each week. Existing businesses showed strong internal growth, with full-service leasing being one of GE capital's fastest growing areas. Leasing products included auto leasing; trailer and space leasing; the leasing of more than 47,000 railcars; Genstar Container Corporation, the world's largest lessor of shipping containers; Polaris Aircraft Leasing, the world's largest lessor of commercial jet aircraft; and a truck leasing business with more than $1.5 billion in assets and 55,000 vehicles.

Despite its strong growth and profitability, GEFS was apparently placed by security analysts in the same category as money center banks because of the nature of its customers and the types of financing provided. Consequently, it was accorded an earnings multiple similar to that of money center banks when analysts computed GE's overall earnings multiple. GE management considered this valuation incorrect because it believed GECC had superior management to that of the money center banks. GE expected GEFS to continue to show superior growth and profitability in the 1990s compared to other financial institutions because of its management strength and culture.

GE had long been recognized as one of the best managed companies in the United States, with impressive depth of management, and as a leader in management innovation. Of particular interest for GE's future in the 1990s was GE chairman Welch's efforts to refine the GE culture to make the company operate like "a big company and small company simultaneously." Underlying Mr. Welch's effort was his belief that GE had to shift from a command-and-control organization, in which large corporate staffs and stiff planning processes existed to oversee decentralized enterprises, to an information-based organization. This new structure would require knowledge specialists to dominate and information to flow as efficiently as possible throughout and to the top of the organization. As part of his refinement of GE's culture, Mr. Welch was trying to reduce the layers of management, increase the span of managerial control, and make his managers think more entrepreneurially. He was putting special emphasis on increasing participatory management.

Kidder, Peabody, Inc.

In June 1986, for $600 million, General Electric acquired 80 percent of Kidder, Peabody, Inc., one of the 15 largest securities firms in the United States. It was one of the oldest on Wall Street, with a history dating back to the Civil War. Kidder's principal businesses included securities underwriting; sales and trading of equity and fixed income securities; financial futures activities; advisory services for mergers, acquisitions, and other corporate finance matters; merchant banking; research services; and asset management. These services were provided in the United States and abroad to domestic and foreign business entities, governments, government agencies, and individual and institutional investors. Kidder was a member of the principal domestic securities and commodities exchanges and was a primary dealer (authorized to deal directly with the Federal Reserve money desk) in United States government securities.

Because of the combination of Kidder's high quality staff and GE's capital and financial strength, Kidder's acquisition by GE was favorably received by the market. Industry analysts speculated that Kidder now had a chance to become one of the top five securities firms in the United States and one of the top two or three leading investment banks (together with Goldman, Sachs & Company and Salomon Brothers, Inc.). This expectation had not yet materialized. Exhibits 5 and 6 show financial information on Kidder, Peabody and its position in the securities industry.

In November 1986, Kidder's star merger strategist, Martin Siegel, was implicated in the Ivan Boesky insider-trading scandal. To settle the implications of this and other matters, GE in spring of 1987 agreed to pay the Securities and Exchange Commission $25.3 million in penalties. Kidder chairman Ralph D. DeNuzio was replaced by GE director and Midwestern industrialist Silas S. Cathcart.

To avoid the chance of further securities violations, Mr. Cathcart installed new management controls. The staff increased to provide the controls, and additional people were hired to expand Kidder's business using GE's capital resources. The initial result was a rapid increase in Kidder's expenses. These expenses, coupled with a downturn in Kidder's business as a result of the October 1987 stock market crash and the one-time costs of the SEC settlement, resulted in a major swing in profits for Kidder in 1987. From a record high of $81 million in profits in 1986, Kidder reported a $28 million loss in 1987.

The losses in 1987 stimulated GE's management to exert greater influence on Kidder's operations. By the end of 1987, Kidder had cut employment by 1,500 people, 20 percent of company staff. Profits rebounded in 1988 to $46 million, but mutual dissatisfaction and disenchantment between Kidder's management and its GE parent were reported to be growing. This disillusionment came to a head in January 1989 when GE selected Michael Carpenter, a 41-year-old GE strategic planner, as Kidder's new CEO. Kidder's president and 20-year Kidder veteran, Max Chapman (age 45), immediately resigned. Soon after, three other senior executives resigned, including the head of investment banking, amid predictions that many additional Kidder executives would resign in June 1989 when their three-year noncompete contracts with GE expired.

As a result of the selection of Mr. Carpenter as CEO and the subsequent resignation of key Kidder executives, Wall Street began predicting that Kidder's existence as an independent unit would soon be ended. Kidder would be folded into GE Capital with the Kidder name kept for specialized marketing purposes. The impact of such an integration on Kidder's various lines of business was unclear, but there were serious questions whether GE's structured, controlled environment would fit with Kidder's freewheeling, entrepreneurial activities. The bearish sentiment on Kidder was not shared by Mr. Carpenter, who had stated he believed Kidder could thrive in the 1990s by combining its traditional entrepreneurship with GE's discipline.

The Investment Banking Industry

The first investment banking house in the United States was founded by Thomas A. Biddle in Philadelphia in 1764. In the 19th Century, others joining the transition from selling goods to selling credit included Alexander Brown and Company in Baltimore, Lehman Brothers, Goldman, Sachs and Company, and Kuhn Loeb in New York.

Investment banks derived their name from their traditional functions: locating and collecting funds for clients that needed capital to finance new projects. The securities industry traditionally consisted of three types of organizations: investment banks performing the service surrounding a public offering of securities; brokers arranging the buying and selling of securities; and exchanges providing a place to conduct transactions and a vehicle for setting price. Investment banks could be classified into two categories: originating firms and distributing firms. Originating firms were the major players in the development of securities offerings. Distributing firms came together in syndication, under the guidance of an originating firm, to guarantee the purchase and to sell the securities of an issuer. Brokerage involved bringing together buyers and sellers, facilitating trades through maintaining a marketplace, and assuring that the trade was complete.

The investment banking community was best known for its ability to underwrite and distribute common stock and new corporate, government, and municipal debt issues; arrange private placements; provide funds management and real estate investment advice; and act as marriage brokers and advisers in the merger and acquisition business and in other corporate services in the United States and abroad. Investment banking was becoming more internationally oriented, causing firms such as Goldman, Sachs, Morgan Stanley, and First Boston to become global in nature.

Many of these investment banking firms also provided brokerage services both to institutional and to retail clients. Investment bankers were often called securities dealers. They usually participated in most financial markets, including the money and capital markets, spot and futures markets, foreign exchange markets, real estate markets, commodities markets, and most secondary markets.

The classic underwriting and corporate finance functions of the investment banking business were going through a period of upheaval and change. Commercial banks and insurance companies had begun competing in some segments of the business, such as the underwriting of revenue bonds, Eurodollar syndications, and commercial paper, as well as acting as merger and acquisition advisers. These institutions, attracted by the reputed high profitability of investment banking in contrast with their own businesses, were eager to expand their incursion into investment banking. Commercial banks, in particular, were expected to be more significant participants in the future of investment banking when Glass-Steagall restrictions were relaxed.

Furthermore, within the industry, a consolidation of large financial resources among a few large investment bankers was taking place. (Exhibit 7 shows the leading underwriters in the U.S. for 1985, 1986, and 1987.) Historically, many investment banking firms had specialized in one or more products, such as institutional brokerage, research, retail brokerage, or the financing of corporations, government agencies, and state and local governments. Some firms focused on a particular geographic region, while others specialized in a particular industry, such as energy, insurance, or banking. Although many securities firms offered both investment banking and broker services, by the early 1980s only a dozen firms were providing broker services nationwide. About two dozen firms operated corporate finance departments that could underwrite and distribute sizable new issues for corporations. Regional firms had combined many smaller units into larger regional groups that competed vigorously for business in their regions.

Brokerage firms generated revenues from commissions on agency activities, spreads on market-making activities, fees for various activities and services, and margin and position interest and dividends. Although investment banks made considerable income by underwriting in the primary market, they also generated income from trading and from negotiating large block trades of outstanding securities among institutional investors and in redistributing those blocks more widely through secondary offerings. The largest volume of all security trading on the secondary market was on the over-the-counter market by dealers on a negotiated basis. Profits from underwriting depended upon the number of new issues in the money and capital markets. The growth of shelf-registrations, however, reduced the need for investment bankers to act as underwriters, which had reduced the underwriting spreads available to investment bankers.

The sources of income for investment banking firms varied alsó as a function of cost containment, interest rates, and market conditions; the volume of trading activity; and merger and acquisition fees earned. Profits were volatile and could vary dramatically from year to year. (Exhibit 8 shows revenue sources for investment banks for selected years from 1973 to 1986.)

Stock market trading, while still a vital part of brokerage firms' profitability, was shrinking as a source of income for the nation's top securities firms. (This can be seen in Exhibit 9 in the slower growth of commission revenue than total revenue.) The giant institutions that did most of the trading, such as bank trust departments and pension funds, had pushed commissions down to about five cents a share on the average. Simultaneously, deficit-laden governments and cash-hungry corporations had continued to raise huge sums of capital via bonds and other fixed-income securities. Institutions had begun trading these securities at more rapid rates, a function of interest-rate volatility and new quantitative techniques in risk-return analysis. Thus, bond trading had become one of the most important sources of revenue for the brokerage industry. However, when interest rates were stable, there was less institutional bond trading, which adversely affected brokerage firm revenues. The volatility of the industry is suggested by the price of a seat on the New York Stock Exchange, shown for the 1972-1988 period in Exhibit 10.

In 1985 and 1986, the American securities industry was highly profitable, following a poor year in 1984. Although the fortunes of retail-oriented brokerage firms had fluctuated with the movement of stock prices and the number of shares traded, investment banks in general averaged after-tax returns on equity capital of close to 30 percent in the 1979-1986 period. A number of select "wholesale" firms had been remarkably profitable, earning pretax returns of 80 percent or more. (Exhibit 11 charts pretax return on equity for major types of firms. Exhibit 12 provides additional profitability information for the years 1986 and 1987.) Some analysts had predicted that increasing competition would shave these profits, as had happened to institutional brokerage commission rates and underwriting spreads.

The securities industry in 1987-1988 did in fact experience reduced revenues and profits, and many Wall Street firms had announced large layoffs in an effort to eliminate unprofitable business lines, reduce high overhead, and curtail large trading losses that revealed meager management controls. The problems were caused in part by plunging bond and stock-market prices and volumes. Competitive pressures also squeezed the profit margins of once-successful businesses, such as public finance and money market instruments.

Mr. Jones' Decision

Mr. Jones' interviewing had not been limited to Kidder, Peabody. He had interviewed with a wide range of financial institutions, including a variety of commercial banks and investment banks. He had not received offers from other major investment banks and was not expecting to receive any. He had received an offer to join the merger and acquisition (M&A) department of a small regional investment bank. He also had an offer from the Capital Markets Group of the Chase Manhattan Bank in their M&A group. Since the interviewing season was over, Mr. Jones did not expect to receive any other investment banking offers.

As he thought about the three investment banking offers, Mr. Jones wondered which represented the best career opportunity. He knew each company had benefits and disadvantages. In particular, he wondered which company would thrive in the investment banking world of the 1990s.

Exhibit 1

GENERAL ELECTRIC FINANCIAL SERVICES, INC.

Statement of Earnings
For the Years Ended December 31, 1986-1988
(millions)

	1986	1987	1988
Revenues			
GEFS earned income from operations	$5,986	$8,225	$10,655
Effect of change in tax-rate assumptions for leveraged leases	(172)	–	–
Total revenues	$5,814	$8,225	$10,655
Costs and expenses			
Interest and other financial charges	2,063	3,277	4,177
Insurance policyholder losses and benefits	1,439	1,560	1,501
Provision for losses on financing receivables	558	290	434
Other costs and expenses	1,805	2,440	3,484
Unusual expenses, including provisions for business restructuring	–	91	–
Minority interest in net earnings (loss) of consolidated affiliates	10	(5)	32
Total costs and expenses	5,875	7,653	9,628
Earnings (loss) before income taxes, extraordinary item and cumulative effect of accounting changes	(61)	572	1,027
(Provision) credit for income taxes	173	(20)	(239)
Effect of change in tax-rate assumptions for leveraged leases	392	–	–
Earnings before extraordinary item and cumulative effect of accounting changes	504	552	788
Extraordinary item	–	(62)	–
Cumulative effect to January 1, 1987, of accounting changes: initial application of Statement of Financial Accounting Standards No. 96—"Accounting for Income Taxes"	–	518	–
Net earnings	$ 504	$1,008	$ 788

Exhibit 2

GENERAL ELECTRIC FINANCIAL SERVICES, INC.

Statement of Financial Position at December 31, 1987-1988
(in millions)

	1987	1988
Assets		
Cash	$ 709	$ 633
Marketable securities carried at cost	4,495	5,430
Marketable securities carried at market	4,000	5,089
Securities purchased under agreements to resell	12,889	13,811
GEFS financing receivables (investment in time sales, loans and financing leases)—net	27,931	35,939
Other GEFS receivables	4,641	4,806
Property, plant, and equipment (including equipment leased to others)—net	3,718	4,251
Intangible assets	1,318	1,568
All other assets	1,705	3,418
Total assets	$61,406	$74,945
Liabilities and Equity		
Short-term borrowing	$22,848	$28,731
Accounts payable	3,329	4,132
Securities sold under agreements to repurchase	13,187	13,864
Securities sold but not yet purchased, at market	1,407	2,088
Long-term borrowing	8,037	10,862
Reserves of insurance affiliates	3,549	4,177
All other liabilities	1,237	1,505
Deferred income taxes	3,720	4,014
Total liabilities	$57,314	$69,373
Minority interest in equity of consolidated affiliates	112	753
Common stock	1	1
Other capital	1,328	1,379
Retained earnings	2,651	3,439
Total share owners' equity	$ 3,980	$ 4,819
Total liabilities and equity	$61,406	$74,945

Exhibit 3

GENERAL ELECTRIC FINANCIAL SERVICES, INC.

Selected Historical Statistics
(dollars in millions)

	1984	1985	1986	1987	1988
Revenues					
Financing	$ 2,093	$ 2,469	$ 2,594	$ 3,507	$ 5,827
Insurance	831	1,329	2,017	2,206	2,469
Securities Broker-Dealer	—	—	1,176	2,491	2,316
All other	9	7	27	21	43
Total GEFS Revenues	$ 2,933	$ 3,805	$ 5,814	$ 8,225	$10,655
Operating Profit					
Financing	$ 444	$ 501	$ (99)	$ 636	$ 899
Insurance	3	45	123	172	325
Securities Broker-Dealer	—	—	83	(23)	64
All other	(93)	(122)	(168)	(213)	(261)
Total GEFS Operating Profit	$ 354	$ 424	$ (61)	$ 572	$ 1,027
Earnings before extraordinary loss and cumulative effect of accounting change	$ 329	$ 413	$ 504	$ 552	$ 788
Net earnings	329	413	504	1,008	788
Shareowners' equity	1,874	2,302	2,994	3,980	4,819
Earned on average shareowners' equity	19.1%	19.9%	19.7%	18.0%	18.0%
Borrowing from others	$13,402	$16,393	$23,397	$30,885	$39,593
Ratio of debt to equity (GE Capital)	7.97:1	7.89:1	7.83:1	7.98:1	7.67:1
Earning assets of financing businesses	$17,054	$20,169	$25,169	$32,423	$42,173
Insurance premiums written	$ 637	$ 1,092	$ 1,704	$ 1,729	$ 1,809

Exhibit 4

GENERAL ELECTRIC FINANCIAL SERVICES, INC.

Top Largest Domestic Non-Commercial-Bank–related Finance Companies
in the United States Ranked by Size of Capital Funds
(December 31, 1985 or Nearest Fiscal Year-End)

Rank	Company	Total Capital Funds (millions)
1.	General Motors Acceptance Corp., Detroit, MI	$6,563
2.	Ford Motor Credit Company, Dearborn, MI	3,269
3.	Chrysler Financial Corporation, Troy, MI	2,790
4.	General Electric Credit Corp., Stamford, CT	2,253
5.	Sears Roebuck Acceptance Corp., Wilmington, DE	2,200
6.	C.I.T. Financial Corp., Livingston, NJ	1,592
7.	Associates Corp. of North America, Dallas, TX	1,372
8.	Household Financial Services, Prospect Heights, IL	1,371
9.	ITT Financial Corp., St. Louis, MO	1,277
10.	Avco Financial Services, Inc., Newport Beach, CA	1,167

Exhibit 5

GENERAL ELECTRIC FINANCIAL SERVICES, INC.

Kidder, Peabody Group, Inc.
Consolidated Statement of Financial Condition
December 28, 1987
(millions)

Assets	
Cash	$ 31
Cash and securities segregated under Federal and other regulations	42
Deposits with clearing organizations and others	2
Receivable from brokers and dealers	1,667
Securities purchased under agreements to resell (at contract value, plus accrued interest)	12,889
Receivable from customers	1,072
Securities owned by the Company—at market value:	
U.S. Government and Federal agency	1,822
Corporate stocks, bonds, foreign, and other	1,412
State and municipal	426
Fixed Assets (less allowance for depreciation and amortization of $79,039)	116
Other	238
Total	$19,717
Liabilities and Stockholders' Equity	
Short-term liabilities	
Short-term loans	$ 1,712
Payable to brokers and dealers	1,328
Securities sold under agreements to repurchase (at contract value, plus accrued interest)	13,187
Payable to customers	706
Securities sold but not yet purchased (primarily U.S. Government obligations)—at market value	1,407
Other	618
Total short-term liabilities	$18,958
Subordinated borrowing	337
Total liabilities	$19,295
Stockholders' equity	422
Total liabilities and stockholders' equity	$19,717

Exhibit 6
GENERAL ELECTRIC FINANCIAL SERVICES, INC.
List of the 25 Brokerage Firms Ranked by 1987 Capital

Firm	Owner	Capital ($ millions)	Offices No.	Offices Rank	Employees No.	Employees Rank	Regist. Reps. No.	Regist. Reps. Rank
1. Shearson Lehman*	American Express	4,584	710	2	40,000	1	11,750	2
2. Salomon Brothers	Public	3,133	11	81	4,868	15	1,021	13
3. Merrill Lynch	Public	2,904	531	4	37,500	2	13,300	1
4. Goldman, Sachs*	Private	2,402	19	63	7,213	8	646	18
5. Drexel Group Inc.	Private	2,185	54	18	10,500	6	1,840	11
6. First Boston	Credit Suisse	1,486	13	71	5,535	13	97	96
7. PaineWebber Group	Public	1,438	290	7	12,900	5	4,350	5
8. Dean Witter	Sears, Roebuck	1,345	668	3	17,982	3	7,758	3
9. Bear, Stearns & Co.	Public	1,320	13	71	6,120	12	2,106	10
10. Prudential-Bache	Prudential Ins.	1,264	340	6	16,772	4	6,082	4
11. E.F. Hutton*	Shearson	1,114	NR	–	NR	–	NR	–
12. Morgan Stanley	Public	1,097	4	–	6,532	11	484	27
13. Smith Barney	Primerica	952	105	10	6,800	9	2,400	7
14. Donaldson, Lufkin & Jenrette Securities	Equitable Ins.	849	15	68	3,075	17	425	35
15. Kidder, Peabody	General Electric	676	72	12	7,385	7	2,178	9
16. The Bank of Tokyo Trust Co.	Bank of Tokyo	376	NR	–	NR	–	NR	–
17. First Options	Continental Bank	368	4	–	883	45	NR	–
18. Kemper Financial	Kemper Corp.	332	1	–	960	42	62	–
19. Thomson McKinnon	Prudential-Bache	305	181	8	5,198	14	2,311	8
20. J.P. Morgan Securities Inc.	J.P. Morgan Bank	266	4	–	577	66	100	95
21. Oppenheimer & Co.	Mercantile House Holdings, plc	247	9	93	2,300	18	654	16
22. A.G. Edwards	Public	243	341	5	6,771	10	3,250	6
23. Van Kampen Merritt	Xerox	241	10	84	395	88	20	–
24. Spear, Leeds & Kellogg	Private	238	8	95	851	47	NR	–
25. Dillon, Read & Co.	Travellers Inc.	223	4	–	661	56	136	66
Total, top 25 firms		29,588	3,417	–	201,778	–	61,020	–

*All data are as of 1/1/88 except for Goldman, Sachs' capital (11/28/87) and Shearson Lehman Brothers (12/31/87), at which time Shearson and E.F. Hutton were still separate legal entities. The capital is therefore shown separately although all other data for the combination is consolidated into Shearson Lehman figures.

Source: Securities Industry Association

Exhibit 7

GENERAL ELECTRIC FINANCIAL SERVICES, INC.

Leading Underwriters for U.S. Issuers
(billions)

Manager	Total Amount Managed 1985	1986	1987
Salomon Brothers	$34.2	$53.6	$40.8
First Boston	25.7	47.0	32.6
Morgan Stanley	12.7	33.2	31.8
Merrill Lynch	17.6	31.4	31.8
Goldman, Sachs	19.9	31.0	29.2
Drexel Burnham Lambert	13.3	30.0	21.2
Shearson Lehman	10.3	19.9	20.0
Kidder, Peabody	3.9	10.5	10.0

Exhibit 8

GENERAL ELECTRIC FINANCIAL SERVICES, INC.

Revenue Sources of Investment Banks

Activity	Percent of Total Revenues 1973	1983	1985	1986
Commissions	56%	28%	21%	21%
Trading and investing	8	26	28	27
Underwriting	9	12	11	12
Margin lending	13	7	7	6
Commodities	4	3	3	2
Other*	10	24	30	32
Total	100%	100%	100%	100%

*Fees for mutual fund sales, investment advice and counsel, service charges, custodian fees, dividends, and interest on term investments, and miscellaneous other income.
Source: NYSE Fact Books

Exhibit 9
GENERAL ELECTRIC FINANCIAL SERVICES, INC.
Revenue, Expenses, and Profit of
New York Stock Exchange Member Firms, 1975-1986

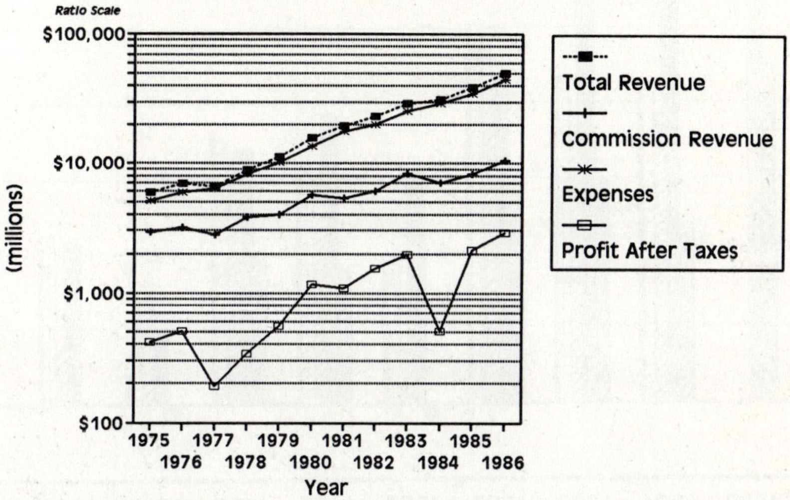

Exhibit 10
GENERAL ELECTRIC FINANCIAL SERVICES, INC.
Price of a Seat on the New York Stock Exchange

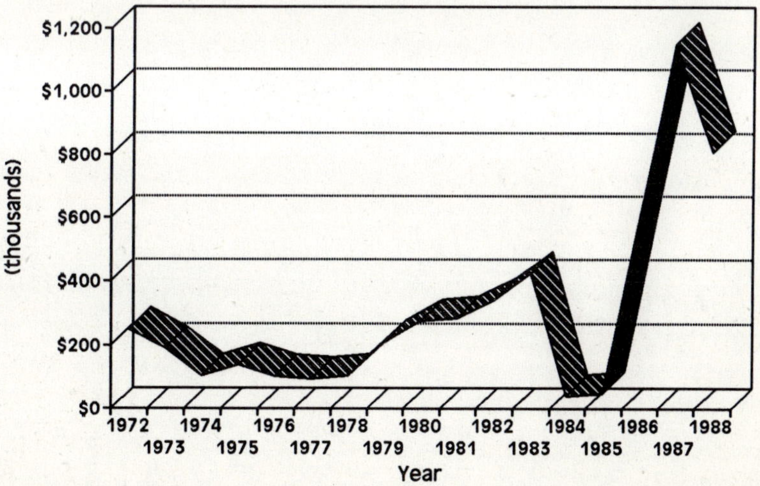

Exhibit 11
GENERAL ELECTRIC FINANCIAL SERVICES, INC.
Brokerage Firms' Pretax Return on Equity, 1980-1988

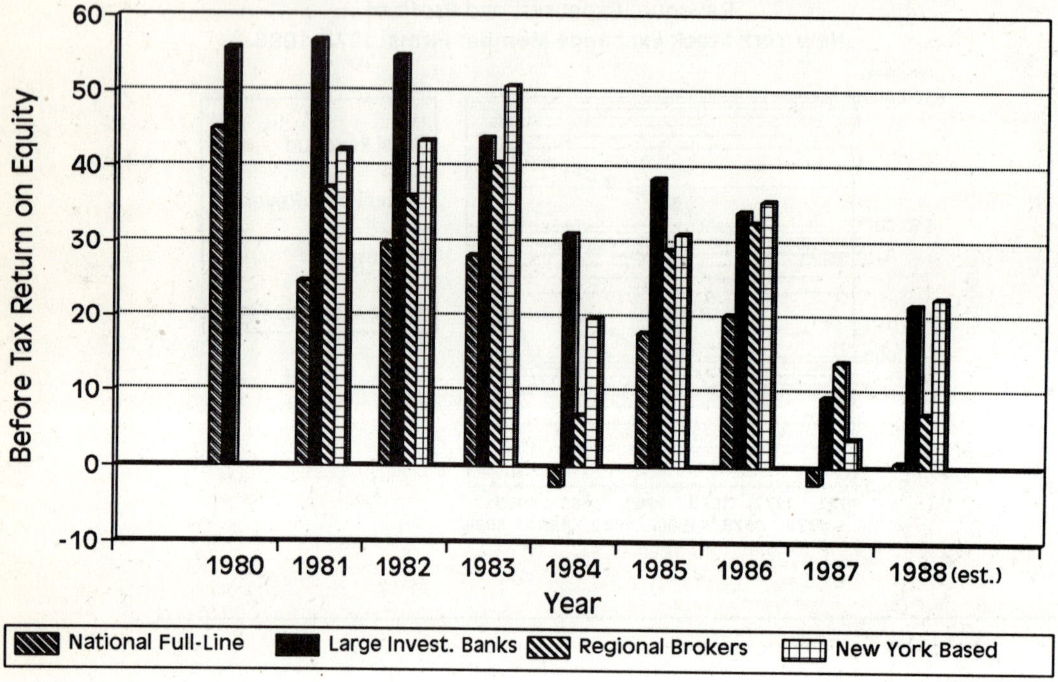

Source: Securities Industry Association

Exhibit 12

GENERAL ELECTRIC FINANCIAL SERVICES, INC.

Performance of Major Types of Securities Firms
(dollars in millions)

Market Segment	Gross Revenues 1986	Gross Revenues 1987	Net Income Before Taxes 1986	Net Income Before Taxes 1987	Profit Margin* 1986	Profit Margin* 1987	Return on Equity* 1986	Return on Equity* 1987
NYSE members								
Large investment banking houses	$15,260	$14,774	$2,067	$ 693	13.5%	4.7%	33.1%	9.2%
National full-line firms	21,897	21,683	1,519	(193)	6.9	(0.9)	19.8	(2.1)
New York-based firms	3,839	4,539	618	98	16.1	2.2	34.5	3.7
Small New York based firms	493	727	90	2	18.3	0.3	28.3	0.4
Large New York based firms	3,346	3,809	528	95	15.8	2.5	35.8	4.9
NYSE regional firms	4,967	4,961	546	273	11.0	5.5	31.6	13.9
Small NYSE regional firms	489	485	41	(14)	8.4	(2.9)	26.7	(8.9)
Medium NYSE regional firms	1,479	1,434	148	69	10.0	4.7	26.3	10.2
Large NYSE regional firms	2,999	3,041	356	220	11.9	7.2	35.3	19.0
Discounters	894	1,230	140	106	15.7	8.6	46.0	18.0
Commission-introducing	700	899	155	166	22.1	18.4	42.1	36.0
All others	2,525	2,727	466	31	18.5	1.1	26.1	1.5
Total securities industry	50,082	50,811	5,512	1,173	11.0	2.3	33.3	11.4

*Before taxes
Source: Securities Industry Association

Notes

Case 7: GREAT WESTERN BANK

Allen Meadows, vice president of corporate planning for Great Western Bank, sat back to reflect on the acquisition candidate he had just reviewed. It was an unusual candidate because it had a large amount of capital, unlike most thrift organizations in the spring of 1989. Mr. Meadows wondered how to allow for possible synergies with Great Western (such as new markets and operations efficiencies) into the analysis and how to incorporate the acquisition's value as a source of new equity capital for Great Western (which was already strongly capitalized). This would be a major acquisition for Great Western, although Great Western had many acquisition opportunities because of its size and strong capital position. The poor condition of the thrift industry in 1989 had resulted in hundreds of thrifts being put on the market for potential buyers.

Great Western Bank

Great Western Bank, with $33 billion in assets, was the third largest thrift organization in the United States at the end of 1988. It delivered its services through a network of over 880 offices in 29 states. Its financial strength was unusual among the more than 3,000 thrifts in the United States. With substantially more capital than required by regulatory guidelines and because of its continuing profitability, Great Western was highly regarded by the rating agencies and investment banking community. Its bonds were rated A, and its capability to raise significant levels of additional capital either in the form of debt or equity was unquestioned. Exhibits 1 and 2 present Great Western's financial statements for 1988.

Great Western's management believed that the key to being a successful survivor in the expected consolidation of the financial services industry was distinctive competence in selected market niches. Therefore, Great Western's strategy called for it to concentrate its resources on selected market segments in which it could be a very strong or the strongest player and in which it could achieve a competitive edge through low costs derived from economies-of-scale efficiencies. Great Western's four core businesses (real estate finance, mortgage banking, retail banking, and consumer finance), had all been selected because management believed the bank could achieve the competitive edge necessary for success. Great Western also focused its corporate resources geographically. Although it had offices in many states, over 90 percent of Great Western's activities were located in five key states: California, Arizona, Washington, Florida, and New York. California alone accounted for 75 percent of the bank's business.

The Financial Services Environment

The financial services environment facing Great Western in 1989 was one of rapid change, increasing competition, and growing risk. Forecasts for the 1990s called for dramatic consolidation of the depository industry and the evolution into nationwide banking. Great Western's home state of California would be open to all U.S. depository institutions in 1991. At the same time, accelerating securitization of a wide range of bank loans, including mortgages, auto loans, and credit card receivables, was changing the industry's economics and dynamics. Increasing competition and growing overcapacity in the industry was shrinking margins on most financial services products. The growing risks of the business were clear from the problems of the thrift industry, which were staple front-page news in the winter of 1988 and spring of 1989.

The problems of the thrift industry had reached crisis proportions in the winter of 1988-1989. One third of the nation's 3,000 thrifts were either insolvent or on the brink of insolvency. Newly elected President Bush had proposed a major overhaul of the regulatory environment for thrifts to deal with the growing problems. Included in the plan were higher deposit insurance premiums for thrifts, shift of thrift supervision from the Federal Home Loan Bank Board to the Federal Deposit Insurance Corporation, and higher capital requirements for thrifts to bring them in line with banking requirements. Because of the high estimated cost of President Bush's plan to the Treasury (estimated at over $100 billion) and the opposition of the thrift and banking industries to parts of the plan, the ultimate outcome of the Bush proposals and the future shape of the regulatory environment were uncertain.

Compounding the dynamic and uncertain nature of the financial services environment were the demographic changes occurring in Great Western's consumer markets. An aging population was shifting basic borrowing and savings patterns.

Great Western's Acquisition Criteria

Great Western used a four-step process to determine whether a proposed acquisition was acceptable. This process depended partly on the size of the candidate. The larger the acquisition, the stricter the requirement that it pass all steps in process.

The first step in the Great Western process was to determine whether the proposed acquisition had a good strategic fit with Great Western. To qualify on this dimension, an acquisition should fit into one of Great Western's core businesses; should add value to those core businesses through its customer base, facilities, geographic reach, or other benefits; and should offer synergies for Great Western's other core businesses. Great Western was very conservative in making this analysis, emphasizing the uncertain environment and the need to avoid undue risk while maximizing unrealized value.

The second step was to determine whether the proposed acquisition was an economically viable, financially acceptable business. Great Western defined this criterion as a high-quality balance sheet with real net worth and real earnings, calculated according to generally accepted accounting principles.

The third step in the process was to assess the quality of the management of the proposed acquisition. The basic questions that were asked at this stage were whether it was currently well managed and whether the existing management would stay with the organization if needed.

The fourth and final step was to determine whether the proposed price for the acquisition was reasonable. A reasonable asking price was defined as one consistent with or lower than market asking prices for similar acquisitions. The price was also required to provide Great Western with a net benefit for the value it would create in the acquisition.

The Proposed Acquisition

The proposed acquisition was Atlantic Savings Bank (ASB), a $1.6-billion-asset FDIC-insured state-chartered savings bank headquartered in Boston, Massachusetts, with 13 branches in Massachusetts and Connecticut. An almost generic FDIC-insured Northeastern savings bank, ASB was typical of a group that shared a common financial profile of high net worth, solid but unleveraged earnings (high return on assets, low return on equity), limited origination capacity, securities-heavy earning-asset portfolios, good asset quality, and notably low funding costs because of high percentages of core deposits.

ASB was established in Boston in 1901 as the Beacon Hill Savings Bank. Its first acquisition occurred 78 years later with the purchase of $211-million-asset Faculty & Students Savings Bank, a four-branch institution located in nearby Cambridge. Since 1983, ASB had followed the well-thumbed recipe favored by analysts and regulators: originate adjustable-rate mortgages (ARM) and shorter-term interest-sensitive loans; sell older fixed-rate mortgages (FRM) and originate new FRMs only for sale; renew focus on asset quality; control costs stringently; and issue common stock to the public to raise capital. The bank's management chose to limit growth of certificates of deposit (CDs) as other New England banks fought a rate war but actively sought acquisitions. In 1986, ASB acquired four branches in affluent Connecticut through a supervisory-assisted purchase of the $409-million-asset Atlantic Savings Bank of Hartford. Following the acquisition, ASB assumed its present name.

On November 28, 1986, the ASB fell into step with similar institutions that were raising capital to meet the opportunities of deregulation. The bank converted from a mutual structure to a stock form of ownership and issued 12,025,000 shares at $10.75 per share. The $118.4 million in net proceeds provided the capital needed to carry out a restructuring plan adopted in 1983, raising equity from an adequate 4 percent of assets to more than 14 percent of assets. The stock offering also allowed ASB's management to obtain an equity stake in the institution. Management held less than 1 percent of ASB's outstanding stock, but it also held options for an additional 1.7 percent. (Recent ASB financial statements are provided in Exhibits 3 and 4.)

ASB, aided by a favorable rate environment, had followed its plan closely. As of June 30, 1988, ARMs and short-term loans made up only $220.8 million or 25 percent of total loans, but the one-year negative asset-liability gap had fallen from nearly 40 percent in 1985 to 10.17 percent. In addition, nonperforming assets were equal to only 0.67 percent of assets, general and administrative (G&A) expenses were a very low 1.44 percent of assets, and stockholders' equity was 14.4 percent of assets.

ASB reported net income of $30.0 million in 1986, $26.1 million in 1987, and $17.6 million through the third quarter of 1988. The bank's last red ink had occurred in 1984, before the Atlantic Savings Bank of Hartford acquisition in 1986, when it had lost $4.6 million.

Where the quality of earnings of many thrifts was suspect because of nonrecurring sources of income (especially loan and securities sales), ASB's quality of earnings suffered slightly from an overdependence on net interest income. Net interest income provided substantially all of ASB's earnings. In 1987, for example, pretax core earnings, excluding a $4.7 million loss on securities sales, a $6.0 million loan-sale gain, and $1.0 million in real estate income, were $39.6 million or 94 percent of pretax income, equivalent to 2.55 percent of pretax ROA. Through September 30, 1988, pretax core earnings were $27.5 million, 96 percent of total pretax income. Only $1.4 million came from recurring noninterest sources such as loan fees, service charges, and servicing income. ASB's noninterest income (excluding gains on the sale of loans and securities) was only 0.09 percent of assets through the third quarter. The U.S. thrift average was 0.52 percent, and the California average was 0.60 percent.

Successful dependence on net interest income required either a consistently favorable rate climate or especially astute asset/liability management. ASB had benefited from falling rates since 1984, and management had also significantly reduced the bank's rate risk. Although ASB's 10 percent negative one-year gap was moderate by the standards of most thrifts, the bank's dependence on net interest income tended to exacerbate the impact of rising rates on profits.

ASB's primary spread had increased from 1.99 percent in 1985 to 3.07 percent in 1986 and 3.29 percent in 1987. Although the bank's earning-asset yield was stable over the three-year period, declining only 23 basis points (bp) from 9.47 percent to 9.24 percent, cost of funds fell 153 bp from 7.48 percent to 5.95 percent. The rapid fall in the cost of funds was due to the general decline in rates and the replacement of more expensive CDs with interest-free equity funding. During the three-year period, management let deposits decrease 4.4 percent per year despite a moderate increase in assets of 7.7 percent. Equity filled the funding gap. Aided by loan-and-securities sales gains and net-operating-loss carry-forwards, ASB's ROE averaged 18.95 percent over the period. Because the bank was internally funding its modest growth, equity actually increased from 14.1 percent of assets in 1986 to 14.6 percent of assets as of September 30, 1988.

ASB's G&A expense was 1.34 percent of average assets through the end of the third quarter of 1988, down from 1.44 percent in 1987. End-of-year expenses increased the bank's final ratio, but ASB was known for running a lean operation. Analysts with Keefe, Bruyette, a firm specializing in bank analysis, had observed that the bank maximized the abilities of its existing employees to the point where the bank "could be vulnerable to the loss of key personnel." ASB's high net interest income and low G&A expense produced a very high coverage ratio. The bank's net interest income was 236 percent of G&A expense through June 30, 1988, compared to the 134 percent average of its New England savings bank competitors.

ASB was a niche player in the New England market. It emphasized lending on middle-market income-producing real estate, typically nonluxury apartment buildings and commercial buildings too small to attract major lenders. (The composition of the gross loan portfolio is summarized in Exhibit 5.) Management had emphasized loans of this type since the equity issue to obtain higher yields and greater rate sensitivity. In 1987, the bank originated $235.0 million in income-producing property loans, 66 percent of total originations of $355.7 million. The second largest component of 1987 originations was $91.5 million in 1–4 family mortgages, 25.7 percent of total originations. Cooperative, commercial, and a variety of consumer loans (such as student, passbook, and home improvement) composed the remainder of the loan portfolio. About 89 percent of loans originated in 1987 were adjustable rate or repriced within one to five years. ASB also purchased $287.3 million in mortgage-backed securities and whole loans in 1987.

Originations in 1988 totaled only $106.6 million through September, compared with $281.3 million in the same period of 1987. Management attributed the decline to higher interest rates and reduced loan demand. ASB, however, was not a high-volume originator in the best of markets. In 1987, a record year for the bank, originations were equal to only 49 percent of the small $718.9 million beginning loan portfolio.

Commercial real estate and multifamily loans had been the fastest growing major loan categories since 1985, increasing by 123 percent and 96.6 percent, compared to a 27.9 percent increase in 1–4 family loans. Conservative lending had enabled ASB to avoid major loan quality problems. Using FDIC classifications, nonperforming assets equaled only $10.9 million or 0.67 percent of total assets as of June 30, 1988, up slightly from $9.3 million or 0.57 percent of assets at year-end 1987 but still well below the industry average. Nonaccrual loans (past due 90 days) increased 40 percent from $6.9 million to $9.7 million over the first nine months of 1988.

Historically, few of ASB's loans had resulted in foreclosures. The bank's strict underwriting standards tended to reduce borrower defaults. For example, the average loan-to-value ratio on ASB's 1987 1–4 family originations was 52 percent. The average loan-to-value ratio was 56 percent for income-producing property loans, and cash flow coverage of debt service was at least 125 percent. Considering the overall quality of ASB's loan portfolio, its $1.3 million loans loss reserve, equal to 11.9 percent of nonperforming assets, appeared adequate. ASB's earning assets included a diversified collection of $584.4 million in securities comprising 35.9 percent of total assets as of September 30, 1988. (Portfolio details as of June 1988 are shown in Exhibit 6.) Real estate owned through foreclosure was only $865,000 (.05 percent of assets as of June 30, 1988) virtually unchanged from $868,000 at year-end 1987.

Like other New England savings banks, ASB benefited from a large, stable low-cost core deposit base. Core deposits (regular savings, checking, and money market accounts) were $668.9 million, 56.7 percent of the total $1.2 billion in deposits as of September 30, 1988. A remarkable $443.7 million (37.6 percent of total deposits) consisted of passbook or statement savings accounts. ASB relied less than many banks on CDs, which totaled only $502.5 million (43.3 percent of total deposits), than on core deposits for funding. As a result, only $667.7 million ($502.5 million in CDs and $165.3 million in borrowings), 56.6 percent of ASB's total interest-bearing liabilities, was subject to significant market-driven changes in interest rates.

The vast majority of ASB's CDs, $394.2 million (77.6 percent of total CDs as of June 30, 1988), were concentrated in the one-year-or-less category. Average rates were low: 7.13 percent for the one-year-or-less category and 7.97 percent for the next largest category, $89.2 million with terms of one to three years. Jumbo CDs* accounted for only 2.49 percent of total CDs, and brokered CDs were equal to less than 1 percent. ASB's 13 branches averaged $90.7 million in deposits per branch, low by New England savings bank standards but well above the industry average. It maintained respectable deposit market shares in the Boston metropolitan (2.0 percent) and Hartford (1.2 percent) markets.

Since 1985, management had reduced ASB's negative one-year gap from 40 percent to 10.17 percent as of June 30, 1988. Long-term fixed-assets had been sold when possible, including $96.0 million in corporate bonds with an average maturity of 16 years and $59.3 million in fixed-rate loans with an average maturity of 15 years in 1987. Management replaced securities and loans sold with adjustable rate and short-term loans, 89 percent of total 1987 originations. Even so, ARM and short-term loans still totaled only $220.8 million, or 25 percent of total loans (13.4 percent of assets), as of June 30, 1988.

The interest-free equity funding ASB's public offering, however, was the primary factor in the bank's improving gap. These funds immediately supported a higher volume of net interest-earning assets (an average of $190.9 million through September 30, 1988) relative to interest-bearing liabilities. As previously mentioned, management also was able to allow selected short-term deposits to run off while booking more adjustable-rate assets. The reduction in interest rate risk was shown by declining earnings variability. Based on asset/liability repricing data ASB supplied the FDIC, a uniform 1 percent change in rates would decrease the bank's net income by roughly 5 percent.

ASB's stockholder's equity totaled $238.2 million as of September 30, 1988, an impressive 14.6 percent of assets. Tangible equity was not much lower at $224.0 million, or 13.8 percent of assets, after subtracting $14.2 million in goodwill resulting from the Atlantic Savings Bank of Hartford acquisition. A peculiarity of ASB's goodwill was the 15-year amortization period mandated by the FDIC. ASB's overcapitalization had produced low returns

---

*Jumbo CDs were certificates of deposit greater than $100,000 and therefore not subject to the rate restrictions of Regulation Q. These funds were often placed with banks by money brokers seeking the highest yield.

on equity. Annualized ROE through the third quarter equaled only 10.07 percent, which was perhaps reflected in the price of the common stock trading at a 11 to 12 percent discount from book value.

The Recommendation

Mr. Meadows wondered what he should recommend to Great Western's senior management about the proposed acquisition of Atlantic Savings. ASB appeared to offer a solid foothold in the New England market and represented a natural expansion of Great Western's activities in the northeast. The bank had strong core earnings, a low G&A ratio, few nonperforming assets, stable low-cost core deposits, comparatively low interest rate risk, high net worth and a capable management. It lacked, however, stable, recurring sources of noninterest income. It had few nonperforming assets but also maintained a large portfolio of underwater assets with subpar yields supported by its low cost of funds. The bank's high net worth was also underleveraged, partly as a result of anemic origination capacity. Finally, Mr. Meadows suspected that other New England savings banks might be available.

Mr. Meadows wondered what value he should place on Atlantic's excess capital. Should he view the acquisition as a way of raising additional capital when cheaper alternatives were available for Great Western? He expected to pay 1.2 times the book value for Atlantic, but Great Western could raise new equity capital directly at a 4 percent underwriting discount from the current market price of $16.50 a share. As he thought about his decision, Mr. Meadows knew he would have to make a recommendation either to proceed with the acquisition on specific terms or to pass on the opportunity. He also knew he would have to explain the reasoning behind his recommendation.

Further, Mr. Meadows realized that the acquisition would probably dilute earnings per share unless the excess capital could be levered up. It was clear that ASB itself could not directly leverage the capital without significantly altering its views on appropriate risk-reward relationships. And while Great Western, because of its strong origination capacity, could leverage ASB's excess capital, Mr. Meadows then wondered if he would be paying a premium to ASB for value that in fact Great Western was creating. Alternatively, Mr. Meadows wondered whether it made more sense to use the excess capital to buy back Great Western stock to reduce earnings-per-share dilution.

Exhibit 1
GREAT WESTERN BANK
Income Statement for the Years Ended December 31, 1986-1988
(millions of dollars except per-share figures)

	1986	1987	1988
Interest income			
Real estate loans	$2,168	$2,086	$2,467
Consumer and other loans	288	323	320
Securities and other interest	173	115	114
Total interest income	$2,629	$2,524	$2,901
Interest expense			
Customer accounts	1,401	1,266	1,514
Borrowings	464	457	542
Total interest expense	$1,865	$1,723	$2,056
Net interest income	$ 764	$ 801	$ 845
Provision for loan losses	56	84	85
Net interest income after provision for loan losses	$ 708	$ 717	$ 760
Other operating income			
Real estate services			
Loan fees	23	22	24
Mortgage banking			
Gain on loan sales	160	102	70
Servicing	23	26	36
Real estate brokerage	18	19	21
Gains and other real estate operations	15	11	15
Total income from real estate services	$ 239	$ 180	$ 166
Retail banking			
Securities brokerage	9	10	6
Fees	35	38	42
Total income from retail banking	$ 44	$ 48	$ 48
Net gain on securities and investments	4	3	14
Net insurance operations	26	55	30
Other	6	51	6
Total other operating income	$ 319	$ 337	$ 264
Other expenses			
Operating and administrative expenses	500	578	617
Write-off of FSLIC secondary reserve	–	49	–
Earnings before taxes on income	$ 527	$ 427	$ 407
Taxes on income	231	215	159
Net earnings	$ 296	$ 212	$ 248
Earnings per share based on average shares outstanding			
Primary	$1.69	$2.68	1.95
Fully diluted	1.66	2.40	1.95

Exhibit 2
GREAT WESTERN BANK
Balance Sheets as of December 31, 1987 and 1988
(millions of dollars)

	1987	1988
Assets		
Cash and securities		
Cash	$ 374	$ 495
Certificates of deposit and federal funds	698	465
Other marketable securities		
(market value $704 and $730)	732	715
Total cash and securities	$ 1,804	$ 1,675
Loans receivable, less accumulated provision		
for estimated losses	25,042	29,144
Real estate held for sale or development, less		
accumulated provision for estimated losses	292	438
Interest receivable and other assets	601	686
Investment in Federal Home Loan Bank System	211	216
Premises and equipment—at cost,		
less accumulated depreciation	365	421
Excess of cost over net assets of companies acquired	200	235
Total assets	$28,515	$32,815
Liabilities		
Customer accounts	$19,974	$22,207
Borrowings	5,882	7,565
Other liabilities and accrued expenses	470	622
Taxes on income, principally deferred	410	438
Total liabilities	$26,736	$30,832
Contingent liabilities		
Stockholders' Equity		
Preferred stock, par value $1.00 a share;		
Authorized 10 million shares and unissued		
Common stock, par value $1.00 a share;		
Authorized 200 million shares;		
Issued 128,223,807 and 128,066,707	128	128
Additional capital	566	567
Retained earnings—substantially restricted	1,139	1,292
Commitment to Employee Stock Ownership Plan	—	(2)
Less treasury stock—at cost, 116,104 and 3,504,050 shares	(54)	(2)
Total shareholders' equity	$ 1,779	$ 1,983
Total liabilities and shareholders' equity	$28,515	$32,815

Exhibit 3

GREAT WESTERN BANK

Atlantic Savings Bank

Summary Income Statements for the Years Ended December 31, 1985-1987
and the 6 months Ended June 30, 1988
(millions)

	Years Ended December 31 1985	1986	1987	6 mos. to 6/30/88*
Interest income on loans	$65.7	$ 94.3	$114.4	$61.3
Interest & div. income on invests.	24.7	31.5	27.5	11.1
Total interest income	$90.4	$125.8	$141.9	$72.4
Interest expenses, customer accounts	66.2	82.0	69.7	36.5
Interest expenses, borrowings	3.0	2.1	12.0	7.1
Total interest expense	$69.2	$ 84.1	$ 81.7	$43.6
Net interest income	$21.2	$ 41.7	$ 60.2	$28.8
Provision for loan losses	.1	.1	.4	.5
Net interest income after provision	$21.1	$ 41.6	$ 59.8	$28.3
Nonrecurring gains	1.6	5.4	—	—
Fee income	1.6	2.1	1.7	.8
Gain or sale of loans	.1	2.7	1.3	.5
Other income	1.0	2.3	1.5	.7
Total income	$25.4	$ 54.1	$ 64.3	$30.3
G&A expenses	11.6	21.5	22.3	11.2
Earnings before tax	$13.8	$ 32.6	$ 42.0	$19.1
Income tax	6.4	8.4	15.9	7.5
Net income extra items	$ 7.4	$ 24.2	$ 26.1	$11.5
Net income	$11.8	$ 30.1	$ 26.1	$11.6

*For the first six months of 1987, total interest income was $69.1 and net income was $13.2.

Exhibit 4

GREAT WESTERN BANK

Atlantic Savings Bank
Summary Average Balance Sheets for the Years Ended
December 31, 1986-1987 and the Six Months Ended June 30, 1988
(millions)

	12/31 1986	12/31 1987	6/30 1988
Assets			
Investments	$ 441	$ 362	$ 313
Loans	894	1,114	1,260
Other, inc. goodwill	104	76	76
Total assets	$1,439	$1,552	$1,649
Liabilities and Equity			
Interest-bearing deposits	$1,235	$1,181	$1,189
Borrowings	24	108	180
Long-term debt	15	15	15
Other	32	30	31
Equity	133	218	234
Total liabilities and equity	$1,439	$1,552	$1,649

Exhibit 5

GREAT WESTERN BANK

Atlantic Savings Bank
Gross Loan Portfolio as of June 30, 1988
(dollars in millions)

	Amount	Percent of Total
Mortgage Loans:		
1–4 family residential	$385.6	43.63%
Commercial real estate	249.3	28.21
Multifamily	176.7	19.99
Total mortgage loans	$811.6	91.83%
Nonmortgage loans:		
Construction and development	52.3	5.92
Other—miscellaneous	12.1	1.37
Consumer	7.8	.88
Total nonmortgage loans	$ 72.2	8.17%
Total gross loans	$883.8	100.00%

Source: FDIC Consolidated Reports of Income and Condition for Savings Banks.

Exhibit 6

GREAT WESTERN BANK

Atlantic Savings Bank
Investment Securities as of June 30, 1988
(dollars in millions)

Security	Book Value	Market Value	Discount
Mortgage-backed	$393.6	$374.7	$18.9
U.S. Treasury/Agency	47.6	46.4	1.2
Tax-exempt	22.2	22.1	.1
Corporate bonds	103.2	97.5	5.7
Preferred stock	19.8	17.0	2.8
Common stock	1.7	1.6	.1
Total	$588.1	$559.3	$28.8

Source: FDIC Consolidated Reports of Income and Condition for Savings Banks.

Exhibit 7

GREAT WESTERN BANK

Purchase Offers from November 1987 to September 1988
for Thrifts with Equity/Asset Ratios Greater Than 10%
(dollars in millions)

Institution	Assets	Equity/ Asset	Offer	Consid- eration	Price/ Book	Price/ Earnings	Price/ Market	Assets
Peoples Savings Bank, FSB, MI	$ 373	10.2%	$44.9	Cash	115%	*×	148%	12.0%
DS Bancor, CT	552	10.7	74.7	Cash/Com.	120	25.4	107	13.6
Brandywine S&LA, PA	180	10.9	27.3	Cash	139	18.0	195	15.2
Central Co-operative Bank, MA	241	11.1	36.5	Cash	131	17.7	126	15.1
Starpointe Savings Bank, NJ	420	10.5	62.5	Cash	133	31.0	157	14.9
Montclair Savings Bank, NJ	424	14.1	80.7	Common	132	20.3	201	19.0
BFS Bancorp, CT	186	11.3	13.6	Common	65	12.7	123	7.3
Marble Financial Corp., VT	368	15.0	67.2	Common	122	17.7	189	18.3
Citizens Financial, RI	2,564	11.8	446.5	Cash	142	17.1	125	17.4
Fidelity First S&LA, TN	925	10.6	121.6	Cash	124	13.7	178	13.1
Richmond Hill Savings Bank, NY	1,113	13.2	160.0	Cash	107	18.0	161	14.1
Beverly Savings Bank, MA	251	12.6	37.4	Cash	119	21.8	186	14.9
Southold Savings Bank, NY	603	17.0	120.0	Cash/Com.	117	13.4	174	19.9
Taunton Savings Bank, MA	205	22.4	55.2	Cash	121	11.5	170	26.9
Average:					121%	18.3×	160%	15.8%

*Not applicable.

Notes

Case 8: INDIANA BANK (A)

Jack Robinson sat in his office overlooking the corner of South Main Street and West Cross, in Logansport, Indiana, contemplating the many alternatives facing Indiana Bank. Indiana Bank was a $250-million community bank located in north-central Indiana. Mr. Robinson, who had joined the bank in 1981, was appointed chief operating officer in 1986 and president and chief executive in 1988. Tomorrow he would lunch with the chairman of the board of directors, who was also the principal shareholder, to celebrate ten years in the bank's employ. It would be an ideal occasion to discuss his recommendations for the future strategic direction of the bank.

The bank had undergone tremendous change during Mr. Robinson's ten-year tenure, achieving a compound annual growth of 25 percent and entering two new geographic markets. New products were developed to serve a more complex and demanding marketplace, and renewed emphasis was placed on community involvement and marketing the bank's quality-service. In addition, young and talented managers had been recruited and developed to add to the strong experience base of longtime executives at the bank. This flurry of activity in the 1980s had positioned the bank to take advantage of opportunities in the financial service markets in the 1990s. It also required that the bank make certain strategic decisions before proceeding too rapidly.

There were several strategies that Indiana Bank could pursue. First, the bank could remain in its current markets and focus on providing high-quality service and a full line of commercial banking products. Growth would be limited by the economic growth of the communities the bank now served and by the bank's ability to differentiate itself and take market share from local competitors. Second, the bank could strive for economies of scale by growing more rapidly through strategic acquisitions. The acquisitions would be of small community banks in the surrounding areas that had quality reputations within their communities and could contribute growth and solid earnings to Indiana Bank. Other acquisition alternatives included buying deposits of failed thrift institutions from the Resolution Trust Corporation or acquiring a bank of equal size, both of which would require additional capital. Finally, an option that had been evaluated in the past was to sell the bank to a large super-regional bank looking for a strong position in Indiana Bank's market.

History

Indiana Bank was founded in the spring of 1887 in Logansport, Indiana, by Peter Huntington, his two sons, and a group of local businessmen. At the time, Logansport was a growing trading center of 10,000 people. There was a great demand for capital to fund the many business endeavors that were available because of the town's strategic position on the Chicago-Indianapolis-New Orleans rail line. There were only two banks serving this growing market in 1887, First National and Farmers Bank, and Huntington and his partners saw an opportunity to capitalize on the community's growing demand for money. Indiana Bank was run by the Huntingtons until 1912, when P.W. Stewart acquired control and became president. Mr. Stewart controlled the bank from 1912 until his death at age 89 in 1952.

With the decline in the railroad industry after World War II, Logansport did not remain the industrial center that it had been during the boom years. After a period of decline, it became a center for light manufacturing for the automobile industry and the trading hub for the surrounding agricultural area.

Considering the economic dislocations, the conservative management of the bank provided by Mr. Stewart was appropriate. In 1912, the bank had capital of $55,000 and assets of $374,000. The speculative boom of the 1920s did not alter the bank's conservative management principles, and it remained solvent through the Great Depression. Forty years later, in 1952, capital was $700,000, and assets reached $10,000,000. These results represented 7 percent and 9 percent compound growth rates in capital and assets, respectively, over the period. By 1990, continuing to follow the same conservative principles, the bank had more than $15 million in capital (8.4 percent compound growth) and assets of $250 million (8.8 percent compound growth) without having raised any new capital.

Over 80 percent of the bank stock was controlled by two families, one of which held about 60 percent of existing shares and was descended from the bank's patriarch, P.W. Stewart. The close control of the bank raised a host of issues such as access to additional capital from existing shareholders, the families' future desire for liquidity and ownership control, and return expectations of the shareholders.

Bank Operations

In 1990 Indiana Bank provided a full line of commercial banking services to three communities in Indiana, as shown in Table 1.

Table 1
Location of Indiana Bank Branches

County	City	Bank Operations
Cass	Logansport	3 Branches (Headquarters)
	Lincoln	1 Branch (merger pending)
Miami	Peru	1 Branch
	North Grove	1 Branch
Marion	Indianapolis	1 Branch
	Lawrence	Business Development Ofc.

Before 1985, the bank had operated solely in the Logansport market. Considering its high capitalization (11 percent equity-to-assets) and the competitive nature of the Logansport market, the directors concluded that a greater return to shareholders could be earned by expanding the bank through acquisition into surrounding markets. In 1985, Indiana Bank bought Peru Community Savings Co., a savings and loan in Miami County, and converted it into a bank. At the same time, Indiana Bank acquired a start-up savings and loan in Indianapolis and operated it as a bank as well. The effect of these two acquisitions was to double Indiana Bank's size without requiring additional capital.

The acquisitions also depressed bank earnings, as shown in Table 2, a financial summary. It took five years for Indiana Bank to return to the 1 percent return-on-asset level that the bank had historically earned and management wished to earn as a minimum in the future. (Exhibits 1a and 1b present the bank's historical financial performance.)

Table 2
Financial Summary
(dollars in millions)

	1984	1985*	1986	1987	1988	1989	1990
Assets	$ 87	$160	$175	$190	$211	$224	$252
Capital	$ 9	$ 10	$ 11	$ 12	$ 14	$ 15	$ 17
Net Income	$.8	($.7)	$1.1	$1.2	$1.4	$1.8	$2.4
ROA (%)	1.00	NA	.65	.65	.70	.85	1.01
ROE (%)	9.30	NA	10.4	10.2	10.9	12.6	14.6

*Earnings include write-off of $828,000 of Indiana Deposit Guaranty Fund after merger with Peru Community Savings Co.

The length of this turn-around illustrated the difficulty of converting a thrift institution into a bank and the costs associated with a start-up operation. The Peru acquisition triggered an $828,000 write-off in 1985 for the Indiana Deposit Guaranty Fund. In addition, it was more difficult than expected to convert the lower interest-rate spreads of a savings and loan to those of a commercial bank. (Exhibit 2 compares the bank's performance to its national peer group and illustrates the effect of the acquisition on return-on-assets, interest-rate spread, and overhead expense.)

In 1990, the board approved a merger agreement with Citizens Community Bank of Lincoln in Cass County, which had a strong history of stable earnings. The merger was now awaiting final state regulatory approval, which was expected in the first quarter of 1991. As shown in Table 3, Citizens added assets of $24 million, capital of $2.5 million, and earnings of $250,000 to Indiana Bank. The acquisition would provide the bank with a strong presence in a market near Logansport. In the last three years, 1987-89, Citizens had earned 1.23 percent,

1.24 percent, and 1.30 percent on average assets. The purchase price was $1.3 million in cash and $1.9 million (3,669 shares) in stock. The total consideration, $3.2 million, translated into a 1.28 multiple to Citizens' book value. Total shares outstanding of Indiana Bank stock after the transaction would be 37,579.

Table 3
Pro Forma Consolidated 1990 Figures
(millions of dollars except per share figures)

	Indiana Bank	Citizens	Consol.
Assets	$252.20	$ 23.70	$275.90
Equity	17.10	2.50	19.60
Earnings	2.35	.25	2.60
Shs Outstand.	33,920		37,579
EPS	$69.30		$69.19

Financial Services Industry

The financial services industry had undergone major change in the 1980s and was facing difficult challenges as it entered the 1990s. The 1980s brought with them deregulation, interstate banking, increased competition, violent fluctuations in interest rates, and rapidly changing technologies and products. Money market funds had emerged as an investment alternative that competed for traditional deposit dollars. Securitization of assets and substitution of credit cards for consumer borrowing removed additional assets from bank portfolios. These developments, along with the downturn in the economy, particularly in the real estate markets in the Northeast and Southwest, had contributed to the current savings and loan crisis and to the poor condition of the country's largest commercial banks.

The Garn–St. Germain Act of 1982 was at the heart of the deregulation of the banking industry. This Act removed deposit rate caps for banks and, for the first time, allowed commercial banks to compete on price for deposits. In addition, the Act expanded the charter of the thrift industry. These developments had the effect of blurring further the lines between financial institutions, intensifying competition, and increasing commercial banks' overall cost of funds.

Interstate banking had a drastic impact on many regions in the country, including Indiana. Before 1985, Indiana banks were restricted to branching within their home county, and they could not be acquired by holding companies outside their county. A law adopted in 1985 allowed statewide acquisition by holding companies and *de novo* branching in contiguous counties. Indiana had been one of the last states to adopt such a law and, as a result, Indiana bank holding companies entered the acquisition arena with a significant size disadvantage compared to institutions in neighboring states. Before the change in law there were 374 Indiana banks, nearly all of which were independent. In 1990, there were 302 banks in total, but only 160 were independent. Ohio and Michigan bank holding companies had been the most active in the acquisition field, including the 1986 acquisition of Indiana's largest bank (American Fletcher) by Banc One, a bank holding company headquartered in Columbus, Ohio.

The role of technology in the financial service industry of the 1990s was very important. Product life cycles had been shortened and had made innovation and maneuverability key success factors. Competitors had either to be of a size to create economies of scale in information technology or had to buy technology from third parties. Banks the size of Indiana Bank were being forced to decide if they could economically develop these capabilities in-house. Indiana Bank had only limited in-house data-processing capabilities. Future demands on this system might lead management to review its information technology strategy.

Recent economic conditions and the fallout of excesses in the 1980s had led to a deterioration in the condition of many of the country's oldest and largest commercial banks. The earnings and stock prices of many money center and regional banks had fallen dramatically over the previous 12 months. As an illustration of this poor condition, on January 6, 1991, the U.S. Government took control of The Bank of New England, the country's 32nd largest bank, which had become insolvent due to economic conditions and poor loan quality.

The savings and loan crisis and fears of other large bank failures offered a bleak prospect for the banking industry in 1991. Mr. Robinson believed, however, that these negative trends created ample opportunity for healthy banks that were financially strong and had a strategy to meet the challenges of the 1990s.

Industry Consolidation and Bank Mergers and Acquisitions

The deregulation of the banking industry and growth of interstate banking triggered industry consolidation in regions throughout the country. In 1988, McKinsey & Company developed a model that illustrated the different stages that occur in the consolidation of the banking industry. (Exhibit 3 provides a summary of the stages described in the model.) This framework suggested what might be in store for the Midwest banking industry over the next few years.

The McKinsey model depicted four stages. In the first stage, "Early Positioning," little acquisition activity occurred as banks concentrated on developing their local franchise. The second stage, "Explosion," occurred after a major change in the industry, such as the change in interstate banking laws. This triggered an explosion of merger activity: banks with strong earnings and market positions rose as stars while others tried to reposition themselves. In the third stage, "Consolidation," the clear leaders emerged with market values that allowed continued acquisition activity without dilution. The followers lost the momentum to keep up in the acquisition field. The number of banks dropped in this stage by as much as 30 to 40 percent, and those banks with low or average market capitalization (that is, not large enough to compete with leaders but too large to be attractive for acquisition) had few opportunities for growth. In the fourth stage, "Differentiation," banks were clearly divided into competitive spheres. The leaders attained super-regional status, and the followers became targets as cross-regional mergers began to take place. "The majority of the pack exist as precarious survivors, although some may be well-positioned for continued viability as community banks."*

Exhibits 4-6 compare the Southeast to the Midwest in stages of bank industry consolidation. In 1986 and 1987, the Southeast banking industry was in the Explosion and Consolidation stages, respectively. The leaders then pulled ahead of the pack and began to fortify their positions, and the Southeast entered the Differentiation stage in 1988. Three groups of players emerged: the clear winners, the followers, and the pack. "Over a very short period, the dynamics of the competitive arena were completely redefined, as a homogeneous, fragmented market was converted into a highly competitive oligopoly with only a few regional survivors."** The Midwest was in the Explosion and Consolidation stages in 1988 and 1991, respectively, and was expected to move into the Differentiation stage within the next year.

Coinciding with the economic downturn in 1990, merger and acquisition activity in the banking industry slowed compared to the 1980s. Three recent phenomena were at the root of this deceleration. First, the slowdown in the economy had created loan portfolio problems, and banks struggling with poor earnings had exited the acquisition field. Second, acquisitive banks had historically used their high priced stock to fund acquisitions. Over the 52 weeks ending December 1990, bank stocks had declined between 20 and 40 percent, as shown in Exhibit 7. At these levels, acquisitions using common stock would be too dilutive to the existing shareholders of the acquiring bank. Finally, the passage of the FIRREA Act, which triggered the wholesale takeover of failing thrifts by the government, created an inexpensive alternative for growth. The Resolution Trust Corporation sold the deposits of failed thrifts for a price of between 3 and 4 percent of core deposits; the buyer did not take the problem loans and troubled investments. Traditionally, healthy thrifts had sold in a range of 6 to 7 percent of core deposits. Unfortunately, there were few failed thrifts in the small communities that Indiana Bank served. Indiana financial institutions had been conservatively run, and the failure rate had been low. Only eight banks failed during the 1980s.

Overall it was a good time to be a buyer in this market. The current conditions had reduced bank valuations and had made acquisition opportunities attractive for those banks with a good performing stock or with sufficient capital to fund acquisitions with cash. The problem thus became identifying attractive target banks and convincing them to sell.

---

*"Mergers and Acquisitions in the Midwest," McKinsey & Company Report to Bank Administration Institute, Detroit, February 22, 1988.

***Ibid.*, p. 25.

Indiana Bank's Options

Mr. Robinson knew there were at least three strategies that the bank could pursue. The stage of consolidation of the Midwest and Indiana banking industry would be a key consideration for the timing of this strategic decision. First, the bank could concentrate on its existing operations and focus on local markets to enhance its market position and earnings. Second, the bank could seek other community banks and make selective acquisitions that would contribute to earnings. Both alternatives offered considerable flexibility. In the immediate future, Indiana Bank would remain independent. Its management would be motivated by the challenge of running an independent institution in close association with the owners. In addition, a proper selection of strategy would allow the sale of the bank at a premium price to a large regional bank sometime in the future should this be in the owners' best interest. Of course, these alternatives also carried the "two-birds-in-the-bush" risk. The third alternative, the bird-in-the-hand option, was to sell the bank now and take advantage of its improved performance since 1985 to enhance the acquisition price.

Maximizing shareholder value was the most important criterion in determining which strategy to follow. Thus, Mr. Robinson's analysis needed to include an assessment of the future and whether the shareholders' investment would achieve higher returns from continued investment in the bank or from cashing out now to pursue other investment alternatives.

Community Bank Strategy

Interstate banking and the reduction of merger restrictions that occurred across the country in the 1980s had led many industry observers to conclude that the small community bank would be swallowed up in an industry consolidation. Others, however, argued that as long as community banks could find a niche within which they could operate profitably, there would be a demand for the personal service that only a local banker could provide. Mr. Robinson and his management team strongly believed there was a viable future for Indiana Bank as a community bank in its existing markets.

The challenges facing Indiana Bank, if it continued operations as a community bank, were to:

- achieve growth in a stable but slowly growing market in which major competitors had a significantly larger market share and greater resources;

- manage the exploding costs of the financial service industry, including modernizing facilities and equipment, controlling processing costs, and developing the sophistication to manage interest rate volatility (Exhibit 8 shows data on scale economies);

- attract and maintain high-caliber staff who could provide the extra service required of a niche player.

Indiana Bank had maintained asset growth of 9.2 percent, loan growth of 14.1 percent, and deposit growth of 9.2 percent over the previous five years. Its stated goal was to achieve overall growth of 10 percent. Loans and deposits were projected to grow between 1 and 2 percent in Cass, 7 and 10 percent in Marion, and 1 and 4 percent in Miami Counties, respectively. These projected growth levels made attaining a 10 percent growth rate impossible without taking market share from local competitors.

In 1990 Indiana Bank earnings reached 1.01 percent return on assets and 14.6 percent return on equity for the first time in over five years. Management expected to continue to enhance earnings through further cost reductions and by concentrating on more profitable lines of business. The bank expected to reach 1.25 percent return on assets in the next several years.

Mr. Robinson was excited about the bank's growth prospects as a community bank, but he wondered what effect this growth might have on the current value of the shareholders' investment. One method of valuation was a discounted cash-flow analysis. This method involved projecting the bank's earnings and cash flows and discounting them at the appropriate cost of capital. This analysis could be done with free cash flows discounted at the weighted average cost of capital or with after-tax "residual" cash flows to equity shareholders discounted at the cost of equity. Mr. Robinson preferred the latter methodology given the amount of leverage in the bank and associated costs of debt ranging from zero percent for demand deposits to traditional bank debt rates.

Exhibit 9 shows conservative five-year financial projections for Indiana Bank. Asset growth reflects management's projection of 10 percent, although Mr. Robinson wondered whether this was a realistic assumption. Loan and deposit levels were maintained near their historic levels, and earnings were projected based on continued improvement of return on assets up to a level of 1.15 percent. A 20 percent dividend payout was assumed. The 30-year Treasury rate on December 13, 1990, was 8.14 percent. The commonly used market premium for the equity market was 5.6 percent. Beta would have to be estimated for Indiana Bank because it was not publicly traded.

Acquisition Strategy

There were many issues to face in pursuing an acquisition strategy: identifying and valuing the target banks, determining the funding method (cash, stock, or both), integrating the new bank into the Indiana Bank system and culture, and raising the required capital for the transaction.

Exhibit 10 provides composite financial information based on several banks within Indiana Bank's region that management believed to be attractive acquisition candidates. In performing an analysis of merger prospects, management assumed a stock transaction as a base analysis. It was important to see how dilutive the transaction would be to existing shareholders at different price levels and the resulting capitalization levels of the combined entity. The dilution created by the acquisition was expected to be made up through increased profitability of the target bank within the first 12 to 24 months of the acquisition. Management thought that Indiana Bank could be a successful bidder at a level of 125 percent of the acquisition bank's book value.

Exhibit 11 shows Indiana Bank's projected performance under an acquisition scenario. The same growth and performance ratios are assumed as in Exhibit 9, together with the acquisition of a "composite bank" (as described above) each year at 125 percent of book value, the premium paid to Citizens. This analysis assumed an all-stock transaction and aggressive return-on-asset figures to provide for recovery of the initial dilution in the first two years.

In its previous acquisitions, Indiana Bank had used a combination of cash and stock to fund its purchases. In the Peru Community Savings Co. and Citizens Community transactions, Indiana Bank shareholders issued stock representing 5 and 10 percent, respectively, of the acquired company. The shareholders of the target companies thus received a portion of the total consideration in cash and a portion in Indiana Bank stock. The amount of Indiana Bank stock issued was determined by its agreed upon value relative to the acquired company. Usually, the target company would receive a premium to its book value, and thus the acquisition would dilute Indiana Bank shareholders' equity. It was important that the acquisition contribute sufficient earnings to make up this initial dilution.

Indiana Bank stock was not publicly traded. Therefore, shareholders had little liquidity. They held the stock for dividend yield, which was minimal compared to other publicly traded bank stocks, for the potential capital appreciation that would occur through continued growth, and for the premium that would be paid to shareholders if the bank were ever sold. Unlike publicly traded banks, Indiana Bank had to negotiate the value to place on Indiana Bank stock when it was used in a transaction. Also, new shareholders would have no liquidity in their stock. Thus, Indiana Bank was at a disadvantage in competing against larger banks whose stocks were publicly traded and had historically traded at a premium to book value. These banks had made nondilutive acquisitions because of the high values of their own shares.

The current market conditions, however, had somewhat diminished this handicap. Indiana Bank was now able to compete head-to-head with larger banks whose stock price was down and whose offer of cash would lack the tax advantage of a stock transaction.

Sale of the Bank

The potential sale of Indiana Bank had been reviewed many times in the past. The shareholders had always concluded that the opportunities for growth and appreciation of the bank's value as an independent entity outweighed the prospects of a sale. However, many banks of a similar size had been acquired at healthy premiums over the previous five years, and management wished to remain open to this possibility. The McKinsey model suggested that an independent bank's value as an acquisition might vary dramatically depending on the industry phase in which the bank was operating.

Mr. Robinson thought that a buyer would value the bank using one or more valuation methods, including discounting the bank's projected cash flows and valuing core deposits in the bank based on each type of deposit and its projected duration with the bank. A more common and quicker method was to apply market multiples to earnings and book value. In the last few years, outright sales of Indiana banks had been priced, on average, at 180 percent of book value. (Nationally, this figure was 170 percent.) Premiums, however, had fallen from levels over 200 percent of book value in 1986 to under 150 percent in 1990. (Exhibits 12 and 13 provide information about recent bank merger transactions.)

Mr. Robinson thought that it was important to continue to entertain the option of a sale; however, with the current low valuations of banks and the reduced volume of merger activity, shareholders might be better served if the bank focused on its existing markets and on developing new markets to enhance asset and earnings growth and shareholder value. The tax liability to the majority shareholders associated with a sale also detracted from this option if sufficient return on investment could be earned within the bank.

Financing Alternatives

Mr. Robinson knew that even if management opted not to sell the bank now, at some point Indiana Bank shareholders would require liquidity in their holdings of Indiana Bank stock. In addition, if the bank went ahead with an acquisition strategy, it would probably require additional capital. Therefore, financing alternatives needed to be investigated. Indiana Bank's capital ratios were well within regulatory limits. Bank examiners, however, suggested that the bank was undercapitalized relative to its peer group, which had a capital-to-asset ratio of 8.5 percent. Management considered issuing shares of common stock or floating convertible debentures as ways to raise additional capital.

Should the bank issue common shares, pricing would be a major question for existing shareholders as well as for prospective investors. Making the security attractive to new investors would require revising the dividend policy and creating a strong story behind Indiana Bank. Local investment bankers believed there was solid demand for Indiana Bank stock within the Logansport community. The stock would require a large enough dividend to yield 3 percent if it were to achieve a price of 125 percent of book value in normal markets, although possible multiples could range from one to one-and-a-half times book value. Mr. Robinson wanted to evaluate stock offerings of between 1,500 and 7,500 shares to determine the effect on earnings per share and financial ratios. It would possibly be necessary to split the stock between ten- and twenty-to-one to bring its share price to a reasonable range, but Mr. Robinson thought he could complete his analysis without this small complication.

Mr. Robinson recognized that the present was not a particularly attractive time to raise funds in the market, due to the depressed prices of bank stocks. He was also concerned about ownership dilution and considered the possibility of issuing a class of nonvoting stock.

Another option was to offer $4 million to $5 million of a convertible debenture with an 8.5 percent coupon and 20 percent conversion premium. This option, which Mr. Robinson believed was saleable in the local market, would allow the bank to raise more capital with less dilution and receive a premium price in the market. If the bank performed well, this security would never be repaid but rather converted to equity. For regulatory capital purposes, however, it would not count as equity capital until the conversion had taken place.

Conclusion

As the light dimmed on Main Street, Jack Robinson packed up his briefcase to head home. There were plenty of issues to think about before his lunch meeting. Though he had revisited these issues many times in the last nine years and felt comfortable with them, the answer was no clearer now than it was when he had joined the bank in 1981. Indiana Bank was a much different organization than the one he had joined, and the financial service industry had changed dramatically. Mr. Robinson wanted to take the evening to re-evaluate where Indiana Bank had been in the last five years and assess its options for the future before talking with the chairman.

Exhibit 1a

INDIANA BANK (A)

Statements of Financial Condition
(dollar figures in thousands)

	1983	1984	1985	1986	1987	1988	1989	1990	Proj. 1991 *	5-year Average as a Percent of Assets
Assets										
Cash	$ 5,807	$ 5,809	$ 8,125	$ 7,247	$ 9,835	$ 14,721	$ 9,549	$ 10,406	$ 8,359	4.9%
Investments	25,198	25,557	45,929	47,204	44,618	36,539	48,869	52,638	58,723	22.1
Temporary investments	2,250	2,475	6,720	1,530	4,170	3,200	5,500	5,930	9,166	1.9
Net loans	40,914	48,236	91,358	111,452	122,982	148,828	151,455	172,053	214,049	67.0
Bank premises & equipment	2,031	2,700	4,217	4,178	5,203	5,062	5,264	5,244	6,464	2.4
Other assets	1,836	2,014	3,289	3,073	2,899	2,936	3,325	5,946	3,829	1.7
Total Assets	$ 78,036	$ 86,791	$159,638	$174,684	$189,707	$211,286	$223,962	$252,217	$300,590	100.0%
Liabilities										
Deposits										
Noninterest bearing	$ 11,560	$ 12,634	$ 11,612	$ 17,320	$ 16,273	$ 20,021	$ 18,637	$ 19,945	$ 20,235	8.8%
Interest bearing	55,396	61,549	133,858	142,788	156,128	172,466	186,137	208,878	252,439	82.3
Total deposits	$ 66,956	$ 74,183	$145,470	$160,108	$172,401	$192,487	$204,774	$228,823	$272,674	91.2%
Temporary borrowings	1,600	2,244	2,755	1,660	3,205	2,987	1,875	3,656	2,031	1.3%
Other liabilities	892	1,016	1,335	1,778	1,863	2,255	2,203	2,615	3,785	1.0
Total liabilities	$ 69,448	$ 77,443	$149,560	$163,546	$177,469	$197,729	$208,852	$235,094	$278,490	93.4%
Capital	8,588	9,348	10,078	11,138	12,238	13,557	15,110	17,123	22,100	6.6%
Total Liabilities and Capital	$ 78,036	$ 86,791	$159,638	$174,684	$189,707	$211,286	$223,962	$252,217	$300,590	100.0%

* 1991 projected figures include Citizens Community Bank.

Exhibit 1b

INDIANA BANK (A)

Statements of Income and Expenses
(dollar figures in thousands)

	1983	1984	1985	1986	1987	1988	1989	1990	Proj. 1991 *
Income									
Interest income									
Investments	$ 2,947	$ 2,616	$ 3,976	$ 4,633	$ 3,780	$ 3,691	$ 3,528	$ 4,171	$ 4,825
Temporary investments	214	226	397	225	135	212	632	373	708
Loans	5,054	6,239	11,266	11,813	12,866	15,159	17,858	20,179	24,377
Total interest income	$ 8,215	$ 9,081	$15,639	$16,671	$16,781	$19,062	$22,018	$24,723	$29,910
Noninterest income	405	424	419	886	566	1,013	1,001	1,352	1,589
Total operating income	$ 8,620	$ 9,505	$16,058	$17,557	$17,347	$20,075	$23,019	$26,075	$31,499
Expenses									
Interest expense	$ 4,728	$ 5,424	$10,751	$10,340	$ 9,521	$11,042	$12,787	$13,743	$16,975
Noninterest expense									
Salaries & benefits	1,433	1,518	2,276	2,832	3,242	3,560	3,837	4,372	5,195
Occupancy	443	511	799	1,018	1,155	1,245	1,262	1,330	1,546
Other	1,025	1,040	1,674	1,814	2,027	2,047	2,424	2,772	2,891
Total noninterest expense	$ 2,901	$ 3,069	$ 4,749	$ 5,664	$ 6,424	$ 6,852	$ 7,523	$ 8,474	$ 9,632
Provision for loan loss	108	250	629	280	248	502	415	530	558
Total operating expense	$ 7,737	$ 8,743	$16,129	$16,284	$16,193	$18,396	$20,725	$22,747	$27,165
Income (loss) before taxes and securities transactions	$ 883	$ 762	$ (71)	$ 1,273	$ 1,154	$ 1,679	$ 2,294	$ 3,328	$ 4,334
Securities gains (losses)	5	62	32	277	271	237	233	0	0
Income tax (credit)	(139)	0	111	(448)	(340)	(513)	(719)	(976)	(1,327)
Extraordinary items (net of taxes)	0	0	(829)	0	100	0	0	0	0
Net Income	$ 749	$ 824	$ (757)	$ 1,102	$ 1,185	$ 1,403	$ 1,808	$ 2,352	$ 3,007

* 1991 projected figures include Citizens Community Bank.

Exhibit 2

INDIANA BANK (A)

Indiana Bank Asset Utilization Ratios
Compared to Peer Group

	1987	1988	1989	3 Year Averages
Net income/Average assets (ROA)				
Indiana Bank	0.65%	0.70%	0.83%	0.73%
Peer Group	0.98%	1.06%	1.09%	1.04%
Interest income/Average assets				
Indiana Bank	9.17%	9.40%	10.10%	9.56%
Peer Group	9.13%	9.23%	9.82%	9.39%
Interest expense/Average assets				
Indiana Bank	5.22%	5.47%	5.89%	5.53%
Peer Group	4.87%	5.06%	5.68%	5.20%
Net interest margin/Average assets				
Indiana Bank	3.95%	3.93%	4.21%	4.03%
Peer Group	4.28%	4.14%	4.16%	4.19%
Noninterest expense/Average assets				
Indiana Bank	3.09%	3.01%	2.89%	3.00%
Peer Group	2.17%	2.16%	2.12%	2.15%
Noninterest income/Average assets				
Indiana Bank	0.44%	0.40%	0.59%	0.48%
Peer Group	0.57%	0.59%	0.61%	0.59%
Overhead expense/Average assets				
Indiana Bank	3.53%	3.41%	3.48%	3.47%
Peer Group	2.74%	2.79%	2.76%	2.76%

Exhibit 3
INDIANA BANK (A)

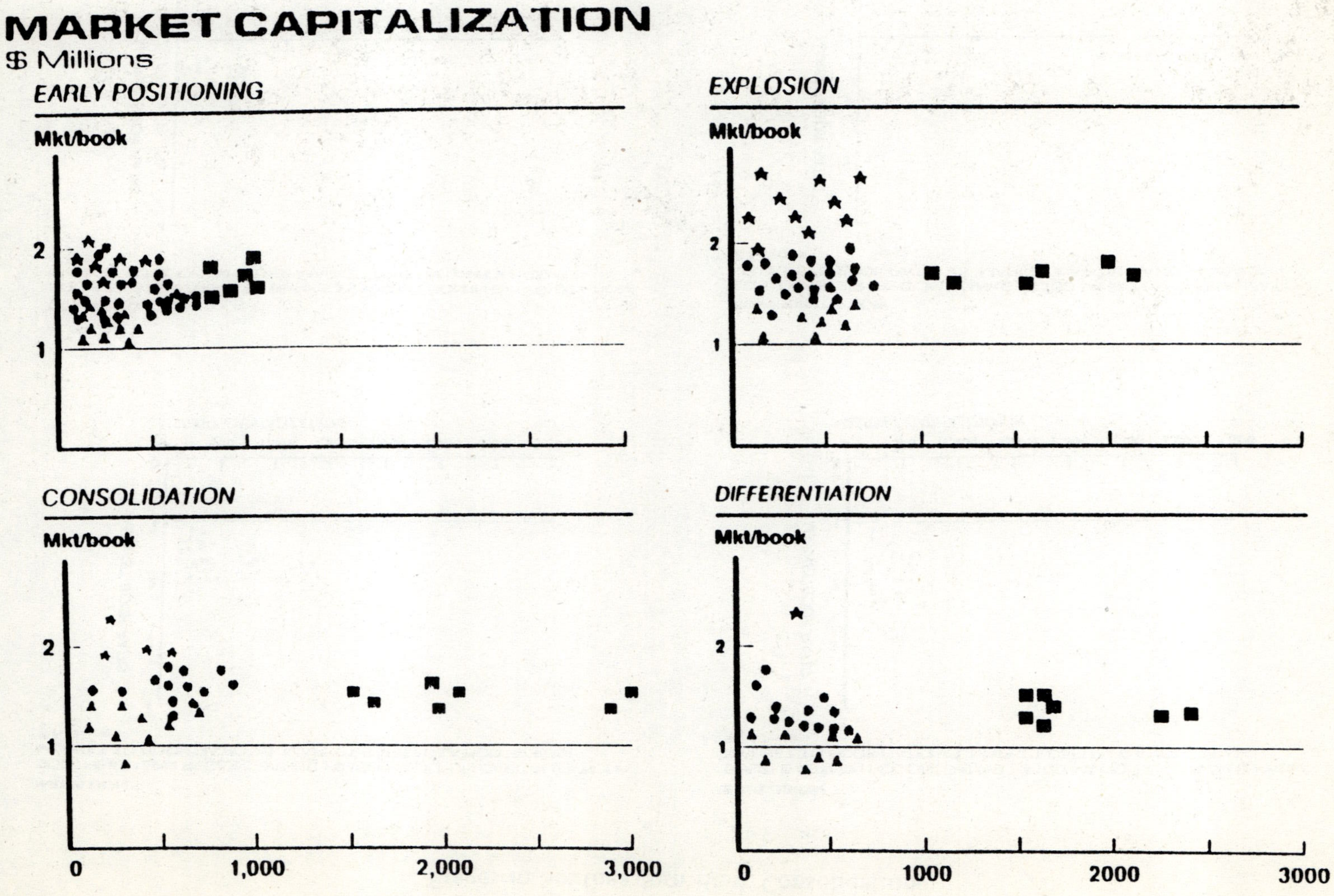

Source: McKinsey & Company, Inc.

Exhibit 4
INDIANA BANK (A)
Stages in Southeastern Bank Consolidation

INITIATION
SOUTHEASTERN REGION, BANKS >$ 100 MILLION IN CAPITALIZATION
MARKET TO BOOK RATIO VS. MARKET CAPITALIZATION (6/3/85)
$ Millions

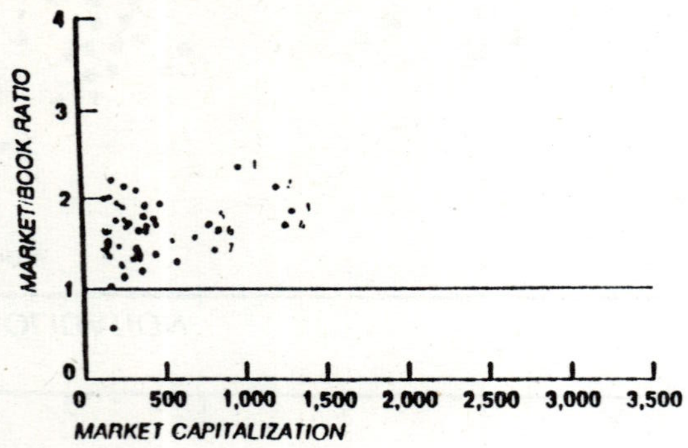

EXPLOSION
SOUTHEASTERN REGION, BANKS >$ 100 MILLION IN CAPITALIZATION
MARKET TO BOOK RATIO VS. MARKET CAPITALIZATION (1/6/86)
$ Millions

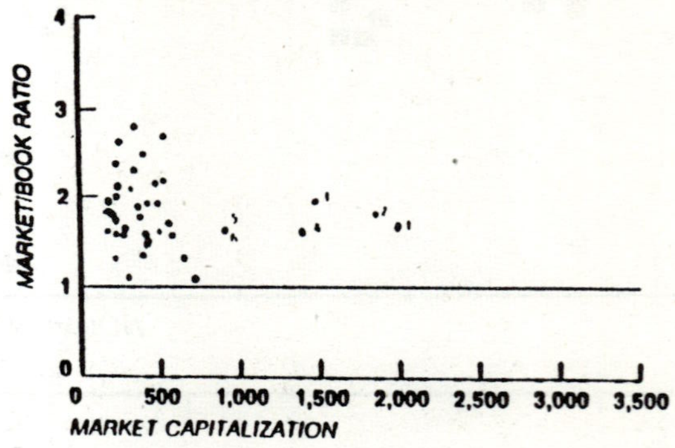

CONSOLIDATION
SOUTHEASTERN REGION, BANKS >$ 100 MILLION IN CAPITALIZATION
MARKET TO BOOK RATIO VS. MARKET CAPITALIZATION (9/3/87)
$ Millions

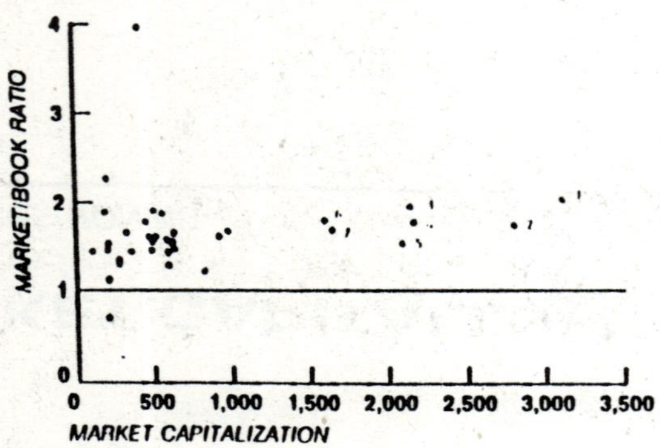

DIFFERENTIATION
SOUTHEASTERN REGION, BANKS >$ 100 MILLION IN CAPITALIZATION
MARKET TO BOOK RATIO VS. MARKET CAPITALIZATION (1/5/88)
$ Millions

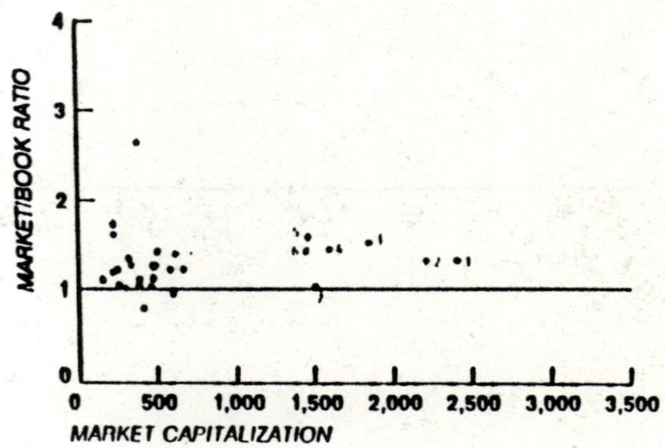

Source: McKinsey & Company, Inc.

Exhibit 5
INDIANA BANK (A)
Phase II of Bank Consolidation: Midwest versus Southeast

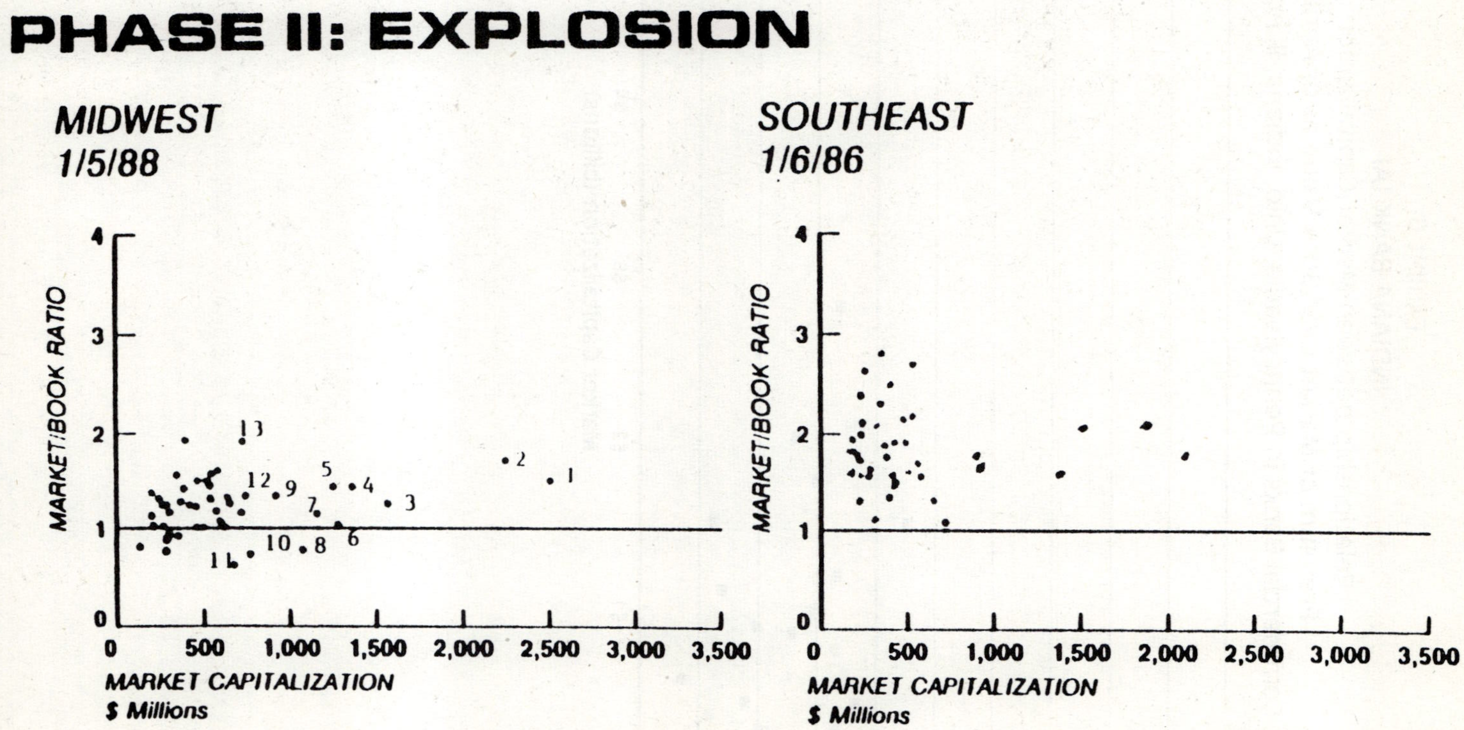

Source: McKinsey & Company, Inc.

Exhibit 6
INDIANA BANK (A)
Relationship between Market Capitalization and
Premium of Market over Book Value as of April 1991
for Commercial Banks in Pennsylvania, Ohio, Indiana, Illinois, and Michigan

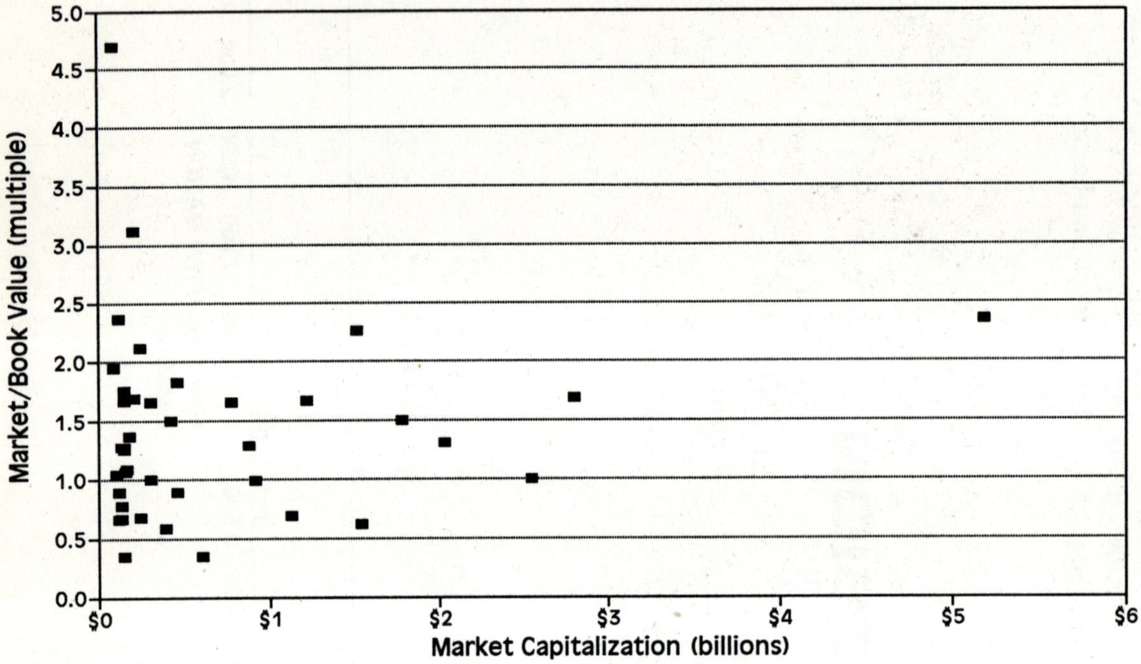

Exhibit 7
INDIANA BANK (A)
Recent Performance of Selected Bank Stocks
as of December 1990
(dollar figures, except per-share information, in millions)

	City	Total Assets	Total Equity	Equity/ Assets	Price 12/13/90	FYE EPS	52-Week Percent Change	Price/ Earnings Ratio ①	Market/ Book	ROA	ROE	7/90 Beta
Indiana Bank Stocks												
INB Financial Corp	Indianapolis	$6,015	$435	7.2%	$18.75	$3.37	–29.0%	7.10	0.78	1.0%	13.6%	0.85
Merchants National Corp	Indianapolis	5,577	369	6.6	15.25	2.82	–47.0	26.75	0.61	0.7	11.2	0.90
Old National Bancorp	Evansville	2,184	174	8.0	24.50	1.97	– 9.0	12.83	1.64	1.0	12.7	N.A.
Fort Wayne National Corp	Fort Wayne	1,755	142	8.1	18.63	2.41	–22.0	8.39	1.01	1.1	13.1	N.A.
Averages							–26.8%	9.44②	1.01	1.0%	12.7%	0.88
Ohio Bank Stocks												
BancOne Corp	Columbus	$26,552	$2,279	8.6%	$26.63	$2.52	– 5.0%	10.16	1.85	1.4%	16.1%	0.95
National City Corp	Cleveland	22,972	1,507	6.6	29.00	4.34	–22.0	6.61	1.16	1.1	17.5	0.90
Huntington Bancshares	Columbus	11,680	721	6.2	12.50	2.11	–29.0	8.56	1.02	0.9	15.0	0.75
Ameritrust	Cleveland	11,233	718	6.4	9.75	3.10	–60.0	69.64	0.51	1.0	16.2	0.80
Society Corp	Cleveland	10,903	746	6.8	31.50	5.06	– 6.0	9.52	1.39	1.0	15.3	0.90
Fifth Third Bancorp	Cincinnati	7,143	699	9.8	31.75	2.77	–11.0	10.69	1.79	1.5	15.5	0.75
Averages							–22.2%	7.59③	1.29	1.2%	15.9%	0.84
Other Regional Bank Stocks												
Security Pacific Corp	Los Angeles	$83,943	$4,637	5.5%	$22.00	$6.39	–48.0%	3.81	0.58	0.9%	18.0%	1.00
First Chicago Corp	Chicago	47,907	2,692	5.6	19.00	5.49	–51.0	4.35	0.47	0.7	15.8	1.15
PNC Financial Corp	Pittsburgh	45,661	2,830	6.2	23.38	4.03	–44.0	9.28	0.79	0.8	13.3	0.85
Continental Bank Corp	Chicago	29,549	1,680	5.7	9.13	2.96	–58.0	(9.31)	0.27	0.5	12.1	1.10
Comerica	Detroit	12,149	705	5.8	42.75	4.72	–10.0	5.71	1.00	0.6	11.6	0.85
Northern Trust Corp	Chicago	10,938	591	5.4	28.75	6.52	–12.0	8.87	1.65	1.0	21.3	0.95
Averages							–37.2%	6.40④	0.79	0.8%	15.4%	0.98
Money Center Bank Stocks												
Citicorp	New York	$230,643	$10,116	4.4%	$14.00	$1.53	–51.0%	(21.54)	0.46	0.2%	6.0%	1.20
Chase Manhattan Corp	New York	107,369	4,998	4.7	11.38	(5.90)	–67.0	(4.26)	0.29	-0.6	-16.2	1.10
Bankamerica Corp	San Francisco	98,764	5,534	5.6	24.38	5.24	– 8.0	7.13	0.94	1.1	22.5	0.95
Averages							–42.0%		0.56	0.7%⑤	14.3%	1.08

①Based on latest 12-months earnings
②Average excludes Merchants National
③Average excludes Ameritrust
④Average excludes Continental Bank
⑤Average excludes Chase Manhattan

Exhibit 8

INDIANA BANK (A)

Bank Operating Cost Economies as a Function of Size

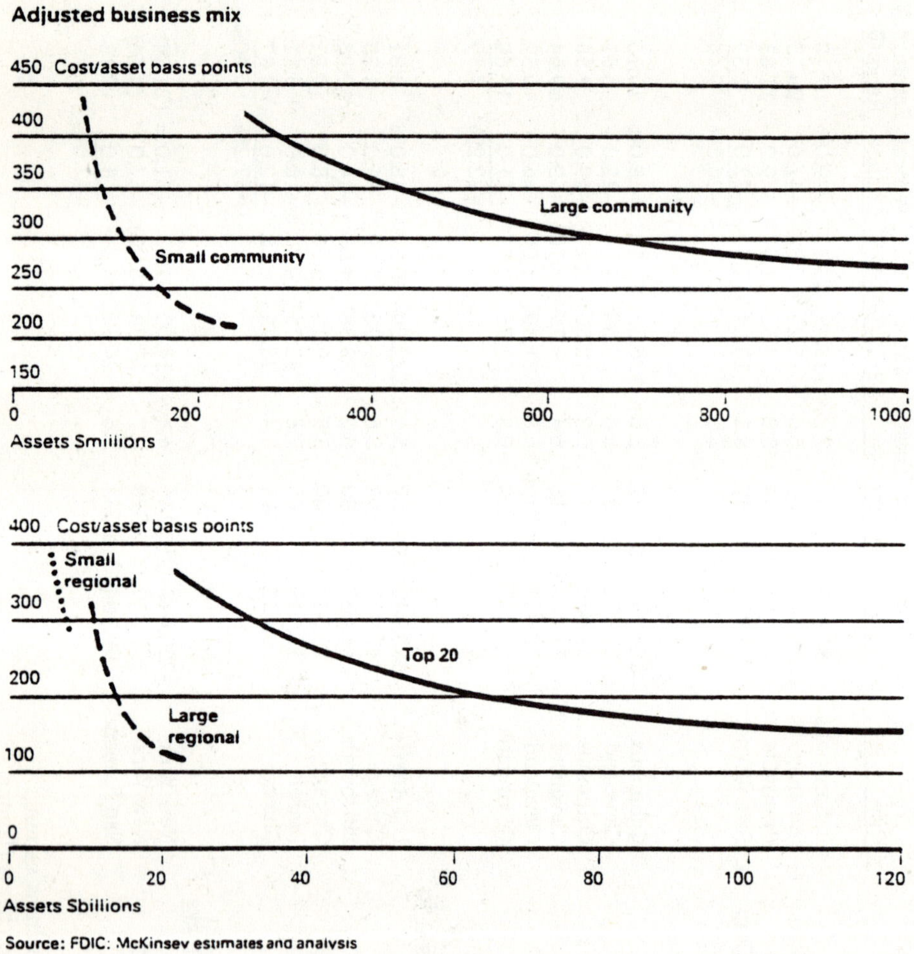

Source: FDIC: McKinsey estimates and analysis

Exhibit 9

INDIANA BANK (A)

Five-Year Projections, 1991-1995
(dollar figures, except per-share figures, in thousands)

	Actual 1989	Adj* 1990	1991	1992	1993	1994	1995
Total assets	$223,962	$275,897	$303,487	$333,835	$367,219	$403,941	$444,335
Loans	$151,455	$188,962	$212,441	$233,685	$257,053	$282,759	$311,034
percent of assets	67.6%	68.5%	70.0%	70.0%	70.0%	70.0%	70.0%
Deposits	$204,774	$249,924	$273,138	$300,452	$330,497	$363,547	$399,901
percent of assets	91.4%	90.6%	90.0%	90.0%	90.0%	90.0%	90.0%
Capital	$ 17,123	$ 19,636	$ 22,011	$ 24,688	$ 27,703	$ 31,096	$ 34,913
percent of assets	7.6%	7.1%	7.3%	7.4%	7.5%	7.7%	7.9%
Net income	$ 2,352	$ 2,600	$ 2,969	$ 3,346	$ 3,768	$ 4,241	$ 4,772
Return on average assets	0.85%	1.04%	1.03%	1.05%	1.08%	1.10%	1.13%
Return on average equity	12.6%	14.1%	14.3%	14.3%	14.4%	14.4%	14.5%
Dividends	$ 254	$ 339	$ 594	$ 669	$ 754	$ 848	$ 954
Per Share:							
Net income	$62.58	$69.19	$79.02	$89.04	$100.27	$112.87	$126.97
Book value	$455.65	$522.53	$585.74	$656.97	$737.19	$827.48	$929.06

ASSUMPTIONS

Asset growth	10.0%
Loans/Assets	70.0%
Deposits/Assets	90.0%
Begin ROA	1.0%
Increment improvement ROA	0.025%
Maximum ROA	1.25%
Dividend payout/Income	20.0%
Shares outstanding*	37,579

*These figures have been adjusted to give effect for the acquisition of Citizens Community Bank.

Exhibit 10

INDIANA BANK (A)

Composite Bank
Five-Year Projections, 1991-1995
(dollar figures in thousands)

	Preacquisition 1989	1990*	1991	1992	1993	1994	1995
Total assets	$ 75,469	$ 83,016	$ 91,318	$100,450	$110,495	$121,544	$133,699
Capital	$ 6,215	$ 7,045	$ 8,056	$ 9,226	$ 10,576	$ 12,130	$ 13,917
percent of assets	8.2%	8.5%	8.8%	9.2%	9.6%	10.0%	10.4%
Net income	$ 755	$ 830	$ 1,264	$ 1,462	$ 1,688	$ 1,943	$ 2,233
Return on average assets	1.00%	1.05%	1.45%	1.53%	1.60%	1.68%	1.75%
Return on average equity	12.1%	12.5%	16.7%	16.9%	17.0%	17.1%	17.1%
Dividends	NM	$ 0	$ 253	$ 292	$ 338	$ 389	$ 447

ASSUMPTIONS	
Asset growth	10.0%
Begin ROA	1.45%
Increment improvement ROA	0.075%
Dividend payout/Income	20.0%

*Projected 1990 based on above assumptions.

Exhibit 11

INDIANA BANK (A)

Proforma Consolidated Acquisition Scenario
Five-Year Projections, 1991-1995
(dollar figures, except per-share information, in thousands)

	Actual 1989	Preacq. 1990*	1991	1992	1993	1994	1995
Total assets	$223,962	$275,897	$386,528	$507,642	$640,248	$785,451	$944,465
Loans	$151,455	$188,962	$270,569	$355,350	$448,174	$549,816	$661,126
percent of assets	67.6%	68.5%	70.0%	70.0%	70.0%	70.0%	70.0%
Deposits	$204,774	$249,924	$347,875	$456,878	$576,223	$706,906	$850,019
percent of assets	91.4%	90.6%	90.0%	90.0%	90.0%	90.0%	90.0%
Capital	$ 17,123	$ 19,636	$ 30,034	$ 41,878	$ 55,428	$ 70,972	$ 88,836
percent of assets	7.6%	7.1%	7.8%	8.2%	8.7%	9.0%	9.4%
Net income	$ 2,352	$ 2,600	$ 4,191	$ 6,000	$ 8,131	$ 10,624	$ 13,524
Return on average assets	0.85%	1.04%	1.27%	1.34%	1.42%	1.49%	1.56%
Return on average equity	12.6%	14.1%	16.9%	16.7%	16.7%	16.8%	16.9%
Dividends	$ 254	$ 339	$ 838	$ 1,200	$ 1,626	$ 2,125	$ 2,705
Shares outstanding:							
Preacquisition	37,579	37,579	37,579	54,432	70,392	85,194	98,729
Postacquisition			54,432	70,392	85,194	98,729	110,979
Per-share fully diluted							
Net income	$62.58	$69.19	$76.99	$85.23	$95.44	$107.61	$121.86
Book value	$455.65	$522.53	$551.76	$594.93	$650.61	$718.86	$800.47

ASSUMPTIONS

Loans/Assets	70.0%
Deposits/Assets	90.0%
Dividend payout/Income	20.0%
Shares outstanding	110,979

*These figures have been adjusted to give effect for the acquisition of Citizens Community Bank.

NOTE: These projections assume all stock transactions and consolidation on a pooling basis.

Exhibit 12

INDIANA BANK (A)

Recent Merger Transactions
1986-1990

Qtr	Year	Price/ Book	Annual Averages
3	86	2.22×	
4	86	1.68	1.95×
1	87	2.25	
2	87	1.72	
3	87	1.94	
4	87	1.62	1.88×
1	88	1.54	
2	88	1.72	
3	88	1.82	
4	88	1.55	1.66×
1	89	1.49	
2	89	1.40	
3	89	1.93	
4	89	1.49	1.58×
1	90	1.35	
2	90	1.53	
3	90	1.52	1.47×
	Four-year average		1.69×

Exhibit 13

INDIANA BANK (A)

Recent Indiana Bank Merger Statistics
July 1987 through August 1989

	1	2	3	4	5	6	7	8	9	10	11
Type of consideration	Stock	Stock	Cash/Stk	Stock	Stock	Stock	Stock	Cash/Stk	Stock	Stock	Stock
Date of announcement	7/87	10/87	12/87	12/87	1/88	3/88	8/88	1/89	2/89	5/89	8/89
Approx. value at date of announcement (000)	$ 17,000	$ 36,667	$ 24,500	$ 26,447	$ 14,000	$ 8,046	$ 36,209	$ 8,301	$ 58,609	$ 25,459	$186,732
Financial highlights:											
Period ending	9/87	12/87	12/87	9/87	12/87	12/87	9/88	12/88	12/88	3/89	6/89
Total assets (millions)	$134.3	$257.0	$188.4	$173.8	$98.7	$68.0	$191.1	$43.0	$255.2	$135.5	$1,007.5
Total equity (000)	9,341	20,923	17,942	15,440	8,556	4,680	16,411	4,634	23,213	13,427	90,805
Net income (last 12 months) (000)	1,063	2,067	1,198	1,514	960	607	2,660	578	5,091	2,003	7,798
Condition comparisons:											
Equity/Assets	7.0%	8.1%	9.5%	8.9%	8.7%	6.9%	8.6%	10.8%	9.1%	9.9%	9.0%
Performance comparisons:											
Return on equity	11.4%	9.9%	6.7%	9.8%	11.2%	13.0%	16.2%	12.5%	21.9%	14.9%	8.6%
Return on assets	0.79%	0.80%	0.64%	0.87%	0.97%	0.89%	1.39%	1.34%	2.00%	1.48%	0.77%
Valuation comparisons:											
Price times earnings	16.0×	17.7×	20.5×	17.5×	14.6×	13.3×	13.6×	14.4×	11.5×	12.7×	23.9×
Price/Book	182%	175%	137%	171%	164%	172%	221%	179%	252%	190%	206%

Source: McDonald & Company Securities, Inc.

Notes

Case 9: NAVY FEDERAL CREDIT UNION

C.M. "Toby" Baker, director of planning at Navy Federal Credit Union (NFCU), was debating in early 1991 whether the time had come to recommend to the board of directors a change in the institution's capital reserve policy. NFCU was the largest credit union in the country, with assets in 1990 of over $4.5 billion. Incorporated in 1933, NFCU had been founded to provide a way for Department of the Navy employees to pool their funds to meet money emergencies during the depression. During its first year of operation, NFCU had 49 members and assets of $450. Over the next 60 years, both the membership base and the institution's size had grown dramatically, but membership continued to be restricted primarily to Navy and Marine Corps personnel and their families.

At its annual planning meeting in 1982, the board had approved a reserve policy that had carried NFCU through the mid-1980s. Recent events, however, had changed the fundamental nature of the financial services industry as well as the outlook for NFCU. Increased competition arising from deregulation suggested the need to lower reserve requirements so credit unions could pay out higher dividends or charge lower loan rates to attract and retain members. The recent savings and loan crisis, however, made depositors and regulators wary and suggested the need for increased reserves for all financial service organizations. In addition, the planned cutbacks in armed forces personnel threatened the membership base for all military-related credit unions.

Credit union regulators had imposed certain capital requirement levels on credit unions, and NFCU exceeded those levels in 1990. The issue facing Mr. Baker was how to determine the proper reserve level for NFCU above and beyond the federally mandated levels, given NFCU's asset structure and membership base.

Mr. Baker considered an adequate reserve level important for two reasons. First, reserves provided a way to cover unexpected losses and maintain an ability to pay consistent dividends even in difficult financial times. Second, because these reserves represented free capital, their earnings were used to offset expenses, thus allowing the credit union to offer lower loan rates, pay higher dividends, and provide to members additional services that might not be profitable at all locations.

There were, however, two schools of thought on the issue of capital accumulation. The first held that all available earnings, above those required to be added to the reserve base, should be distributed during the period in which they were earned, to benefit current members. In this view, any excess retention of capital benefited future members at the expense of current members. The second theory held that building a strong capital base benefited current members by allowing credit unions to reduce interest rate spreads and provide services to members. A strong capital base also protected the interests of all members, existing and future.

Credit Unions

Credit unions were member-owned, not-for-profit cooperative financial institutions formed to permit members to pool their savings, lend them to one another, and own the organization where they saved, borrowed, and obtained related financial services. Members were united by a common bond and democratically operated the credit union under state or federal regulation. Membership was restricted to a defined group, such as employees of a given company or plant, or individuals living or working in a specified geographic area, or a combination of the two. About 80 percent of the nation's credit unions had an occupational membership base, 14 percent had an associational base (such as a church group), and 6 percent had a community base.

The credit union industry was structured as a pyramid. (Exhibit 1 outlines the organizational structure of the credit union system in 1990.) The National Credit Union Administration (NCUA) and the National Credit Union Share Insurance Fund (NCUSIF) supervised and insured, respectively, about 8,600 federal credit unions and 4,400 state-chartered credit unions as of June 30, 1990. Most credit unions were themselves members of, and depositors in, "corporate credit unions," which provided investment and liquidity services to their members. The corporate credit unions were, in turn, members of the U.S. Central Credit Union, a credit union affiliated with the Credit Union National Association (CUNA was the principal national trade association for credit unions). U.S. Central, with assets of over $25 billion, provided investment opportunities, as well as other wholesale financial and payment services, to corporate credit unions and their member credit unions.

The Central Liquidity Facility (CLF) was a mixed-ownership government corporation managed by the NCUA. The NCUA could, under certain conditions, authorize the CLF to advance funds to the NCUSIF. Also under certain conditions, the Secretary of the Treasury was authorized to lend up to $500 million to the CLF. U.S. Central, acting as agent for its corporate credit union members, owned a large percentage of the stock of the CLF. Thus, most credit unions, either directly or through their ties with corporate credit unions, were members of the CLF.

Credit unions were evaluated annually by the NCUA using the CAMEL rating system. Both quantitative and qualitative aspects of each credit union were checked in five areas: capital adequacy, asset quality, management, earnings, and liquidity. (Exhibit 2 outlines key and secondary ratios included in the CAMEL rating system.) In addition, the NCUA evaluated credit unions on management of cash flows, balancing or matching of assets and liabilities, and management of interest rate risk.

Upon completion of its evaluation, NCUA derived a composite rating for each credit union on a scale of 1 to 5. Composite ratings were as follows:

(1) Institutions that are sound in almost every respect, highly resistant to external economic and financial disturbances, and capable of withstanding most business fluctuations.

(2) Institutions that are fundamentally sound, but with modest weaknesses correctable in the normal course of business. These institutions are also well able to withstand most business fluctuations.

(3) Institutions that exhibit a combination of weaknesses ranging from fair to unsatisfactory, are only nominally resistant to the onset of adverse business conditions, and consequently require more than normal supervisory attention.

(4) Institutions with a more than moderate volume of asset weaknesses or a combination of other conditions that are unsatisfactory. These institutions require prompt action to correct these conditions and close supervisory attention.

(5) Institutions whose overall condition is worse than that defined under composite rating number 4. These institutions are clearly insolvent, will not survive more than 12 months, and are immediately targeted for merger or liquidation.

At the end of 1989, assets of federally insured credit unions totaled $189 billion, accounting for 3.7 percent of the assets held by the nation's depository institutions. This represented substantial growth since 1970, when credit unions held $10.6 billion in assets (1.3 percent of total assets in depository institutions), and 1980, when assets totaled $60.9 billion (2.3 percent of total assets in depositories).

Since 1980 the major change for credit unions had been the rapid growth in loans secured by one- to four-family dwellings, which had risen from less than 5 percent of assets in 1980 to 21.8 percent in 1990. This rate of growth had recently begun to slow. Exhibit 3 outlines the aggregate asset distribution of credit unions and commercial banks as of December 31, 1990.

Credit Union Capital and Reserve Policies

Credit unions were chartered without capital, which they had to accumulate by retaining earnings. No stock or debt instruments to provide initial capital were permitted. By statute, credit union reserve requirements were based on the amount of risk assets that a credit union had on its balance sheet. Risk assets were defined as all assets except cash and government-guaranteed loans or investments with maturities of less than three years.

Credit unions had to transfer a certain percentage of gross income to a regular reserve at the end of each accounting period. A credit union in operation more than four years and having assets of $500,000 or more had to set aside 10 percent of gross income until the regular reserve equaled 4 percent of outstanding loans and risk assets. The allocation then dropped to 5 percent of gross income until the regular reserve equaled 6 percent of loans and risk assets. Credit unions in operation less than four years or having less than $500,000 in assets had the same transfer rates but higher reserve level requirements, 7.5 and 10 percent, respectively. Exhibits 4a and 4b outline the aggregate capital structures of credit unions and commercial banks as of December 31, 1989.

Legislation passed by Congress in 1984 also required federally insured credit unions to deposit and maintain in the NCUSIF fund an amount equal to 1 percent of insured shares. Although credit unions did not expense this deposit but instead carried it on their books as an asset, credit unions did not receive the income earned by the deposit. The income inured to the benefit of the insurance fund. In normal years, the income from investment of the aggregate deposit was sufficient to enable the NCUSIF to waive any insurance premium. The NCUSIF, however, was also allowed to assess a premium of one-twelfth of 1 percent of insured shares if its investment income was not enough to pay for losses. On the other hand, if the fund's equity ratio (calculated by dividing insurance fund reserves by total insured shares) exceeded 1.3 percent of insured shares, the balance above that level had to be distributed on a *pro rata* basis to the insured credit unions. No premium had been assessed since 1984; distributions were made only in 1985. As of June 30, 1990, the NCUSIF had over $2 billion in assets and an equity ratio of 1.28 percent.

Credit union officials believed that the existing mandated reserve requirements, combined with the NCUSIF fund, were sufficient to protect their members' interests. Further additions to capital were discretionary, to be made according to the specific characteristics of each credit union. Unlike commercial bank owners, who acquire assets with a small up-front investment and by attracting federally insured deposits, credit unions might be less likely to take risks with the institution's capital because the credit union was owned equally by all of its members. Credit unions had true mutuality — they accepted savings from, lent to, or otherwise served only credit union members. The prevailing practice was one member, one vote — not one dollar, one vote. Because the ownership of credit unions was so widely distributed over the membership, there was supposed to be little incentive for owners or management to engage in excessive risk-taking. There was little chance of personal gain from such actions.

The credit union practice of lending to and borrowing from a fixed group of members "closed" the field of operations on both ends. This practice had a positive impact because it discouraged excessive risk-taking on the part of management, and members had more direct information about the uses management made of their deposits. The structure also could pose problems, however, for smaller, single-employer-based credit unions faced with plant closings or other unforeseen reductions in membership and subsequent "runs" on the credit union. Members would need to consume their savings but at the same time would have difficulty servicing their debt.

Historically, credit unions had experienced lower failure rates than either commercial banks or savings and loans. Credit union failures and assisted mergers were at record low levels in 1988 (35 failures and 50 mergers) and 1989 (54 failures and 60 mergers). The industry average capital ratio for credit unions was 7.4 percent in 1989, compared to 6.2 percent for commercial banks and 2.6 percent for savings and loans. Credit unions had avoided some pitfalls experienced by savings and loans by maintaining conservative investment practices and short-term consumer loan portfolios. Credit unions were not even granted mortgage lending power until 1978.

Navy Federal Credit Union

Since its inception, NFCU's membership base had expanded to include the following:

- active-duty commissioned officers in the Navy and Marine Corps, regardless of location;
- active-duty enlisted personnel, inactive personnel undergoing training, and Navy Department civilian employees in the Washington D.C. area and 22 other states in the continental U.S., except those eligible for membership in other occupational-type credit unions;
- Navy civilians and active-duty enlisted personnel in a foreign country or on a ship home ported in a foreign country;
- certain active-duty Coast Guard personnel;
- certain persons retired by the U.S. Government; and
- immediate family of primary members.

As a result of its willingness to serve those eligible, NFCU experienced substantial growth in members and assets. Exhibit 5 provides a summary of NFCU's financial performance over the period 1980-1990.

From the outset, NFCU recognized the transient nature of its membership base and developed a growth strategy to accommodate the unique needs of its members. Navy and Marine Corps personnel were rarely stationed in one place for long, and NFCU provided ways for its members to maintain a primary financial relationship with the same institution as they moved around the globe, sometimes on very short notice. During 1990, NFCU operated over 80 branch offices, including 30 overseas, thus living up to its motto: "NFCU serves where you serve."

Historically, NFCU's competition included individual credit unions on military bases and other financial institutions such as commercial banks and savings and loans. Within recent years, organizations such as the United Services Automobile Association (USAA) had encroached on the membership base of NFCU by offering investment and banking services, as well as traditional insurance services, to commissioned and former officers in the armed forces and their dependents. NFCU maintained its competitive advantage through its size, which afforded economies of scale and extensive automation of services, and through its geographic distribution, which provided convenience for members. In 1990, 50 to 55 percent of all existing members considered NFCU their primary financial institution.

To maintain the loyalty of its members, NFCU strove to provide the utmost in convenience for them. Continually enhancing automation capabilities was one way in which NFCU provided superior service. NFCU accepted member loan applications over the phone and provided touch-tone teller service for fund transfers and automated loan payments. In 1990, NFCU also operated over 100 proprietary ATMs worldwide, and members had access to funds through over 3,000 ATMs worldwide through the Armed Forces Financial Network and over 50,000 ATMs worldwide through the PLUS network. During 1990, over 60 percent of teller transactions were done through ATMs.

NFCU's stated primary goal was to "protect, preserve and safeguard the assets of the credit union." To achieve this goal, NFCU engaged in conservative lending practices and maintained stringent capital accumulation policies. NFCU's capital-to-assets ratio increased from 4 percent in 1980 to 7.9 percent in 1990, and yet the board still transferred at least 10 percent of gross income to reserves, more than required by federal mandate. Management's goal, as established at the 1982 planning meeting, was to have sufficient earnings from reserves to cover 30 percent of operating expenses. Management believed that increased levels of capital would enable NFCU to reduce the spread between borrowing and lending rates, as well as provide additional, low-cost services to members.

Asset/Liability Structure

Consistent with the cooperative nature of credit unions, over 70 percent of NFCU's assets in 1990 were loans to members. The remainder was in cash, investments, and other assets. (Exhibits 6 through 9 provide financial information for NFCU for the period 1988-1990.) As of December 31, 1990, about 60 percent of all loans outstanding were consumer loans, and 60 percent of those were auto loans. The average maturity on a consumer loan was four to five years, with an average portfolio repricing of 24 months.

Eighteen percent of loans were one- to four-family mortgages, either held for sale on the secondary market through U.S. Government-sponsored enterprises, or held in portfolio. Loans held in NFCU's portfolio consisted of 15-year mortgages with average portfolio repricing of seven years. Existing policy stated that no more than 15 percent of NFCU's assets were to be mortgages held in the portfolio. The policy also stated that not more than 10 percent of assets were to be mortgages held for sale in the secondary market. Loans held for sale were typically sold within three months, although the portfolio manager had some latitude about the timing of these sales, depending upon an assessment of the trends in prevailing interest rates. The portfolio manager was not restricted by the amount of time a loan stayed on the books but rather by the cumulative dollar amount of mortgages held for sale. Rapid sale of the mortgages minimized NFCU's exposure to principal loss and adverse movements in interest rates.

Consistent with management's desire to provide excellent service to members, NFCU kept the servicing function for all loans sold in the secondary market. By keeping the servicing function, the change in ownership was transparent to members, and the servicing of these loans provided substantial income for NFCU. At year-end 1990, NFCU was servicing over $2 billion in mortgage loans and received servicing fees of over $500,000 a month.

Other loans to members included home equity loans (the most rapidly growing asset class), lines of credit, student loans, and credit card loans. NFCU did not make any commercial loans; however, it would make loans of up to $25,000 to individual members for business purposes.

NFCU's loan loss exposure was low: the monthly consumer loan delinquency ratio was 0.31 percent in 1990. The net charge-off as a percentage of average loans outstanding was 0.35 percent in 1989 and 0.37 percent in 1990. Not surprisingly, credit card loans had the highest potential for loss. NFCU provided loan-protection-life-insurance policies up to $10,000 per borrower at no cost to members.

Other assets included cash and investments. Cash assets included vault and ATM cash, required Federal Reserve deposits, and deposits in banks supporting branch office operations. Investments consisted of certificates of deposit or Federal Funds accounts at any of the 100 largest national banks in the country (according to asset size) as well as U.S. Government and agency securities. Management's policy was to look for investments that provided safety, liquidity, and yield, in that order. Investments could not have maturities of more than seven years and could not include corporate shares or bonds.

Sources of funds primarily consisted of members' accounts plus reserves and undivided earnings. To become a member, an eligible individual had to purchase at least one five-dollar share in Share Savings. NFCU offered Share Savings and Sharechek accounts, similar to commercial bank savings and checking accounts. NFCU also offered one- to five-year Share Certificate accounts (similar to commercial bank CDs), 26-week money market certificates, and individual retirement accounts. Members could deposit or withdraw funds from any of these accounts according to minimum dollar and maturity guidelines established by NFCU's board.

Dividends were paid to shareholders according to the type and size of account they held. The dividends were similar to interest payments on commercial banking accounts; however, because the payments were considered returns to equity shareholders, they were not guaranteed. In practice, however, the dividend payments were always disbursed and, in fact, were treated like interest payments for members' tax purposes. NFCU's capital reserves allowed it to offer competitive dividend rates even in uncertain economic times; during the downturn of 1990, dividend rates fell more slowly than comparable commercial bank savings rates while loan rates remained competitive. (Exhibit 10 provides year-end 1990 typical savings and consumer loan rates for NFCU and U.S. commercial banks.) Principal amounts held in share accounts were insured up to $100,000 per member by the NCUSIF.

In the late 1980s the federal government mandated that all armed services personnel receive their pay via direct deposit in a financial institution. During 1990, NFCU estimated that it received direct deposit payments during each pay period of over $100 million for its Navy members and $30 million for its Marine Corps members. This development helped to secure NFCU's membership base. Funds that were directly deposited into NFCU accounts in Washington were automatically available to members either at branch offices worldwide or through NFCU's extensive ATM network. About 50 to 55 percent of all members had transaction accounts (Sharechek) with NFCU.

NFCU's reserve accounts included undivided earnings, regular reserve, and capital reserve accounts. The regular reserve account was required by and maintained in accordance with the Federal Credit Union Act. A percentage of earnings, net of additions to loan loss reserves, was transferred to this account each period. Funds in the regular reserve account were not available for the payment of dividends. The capital reserve account was established at the discretion of the board to protect the interests of members, including an assurance of dividend payments in the event of unforeseen economic hardship. The board made discretionary contributions to this fund as earnings permitted in a given period. Earnings on both the regular and capital reserves were available to cover operating expenses.

Conclusion

Mr. Baker recognized the need for a capital accumulation policy, but he was not sure how to determine the "proper" reserve levels for NFCU. There was a necessary trade-off between dividend payments to members and capital accumulation. If NFCU was too aggressive in building reserves, returns to members might suffer, and NFCU might lose some of its competitive edge. If dividend payments were too high, however, reserves might suffer, decreasing the amount of protection afforded to members as well as the ability of NFCU to provide services to members, both immediately and in the future.

Mr. Baker had identified six key factors which he wanted to consider in making his recommendation to the board:

(1) In a questionable economic environment, it was important to maintain adequate reserves to cover unexpected losses and maintain dividend payments to members.

(2) Earnings on reserves enabled NFCU to reduce the required interest rate spread, minimize service charges for current members, and develop new services for the convenience of all members.

(3) NFCU's mortgage holdings required the availability of long-term capital, especially in situations when the portfolio manager delayed the sale of mortgages in the secondary market during unattractive interest rate periods.

(4) Credit unions were not subject to state or federal income taxes in 1990; however, there was growing pressure within the financial service industry to make credit unions taxable entities. Would it be prudent to build a large capital base immediately? If credit unions were eventually taxed, would it be more difficult to build reserves with after-tax earnings?

(5) In an era of savings and loan and bank failures, NFCU had to maintain adequate reserves in the event other credit unions failed and the NCUSIF imposed an additional insurance premium.

(6) Proposed government cutbacks of up to 20 percent of armed forces personnel might lead to distress at other military-based credit unions, and NFCU management wanted to maintain adequate reserves to enable NFCU to merge with or purchase the assets of troubled credit unions, should it choose to do so.

As Mr. Baker packed up his briefcase for the night, he reflected on the unique characteristics of NFCU's membership base and the resulting operating guidelines established by the board. He wanted to recommend a capital reserve policy that would protect the interests of existing members as well as anticipate future needs of the institution.

Exhibit 1

NAVY FEDERAL CREDIT UNION

Credit Union System Structure
as of June 30, 1990

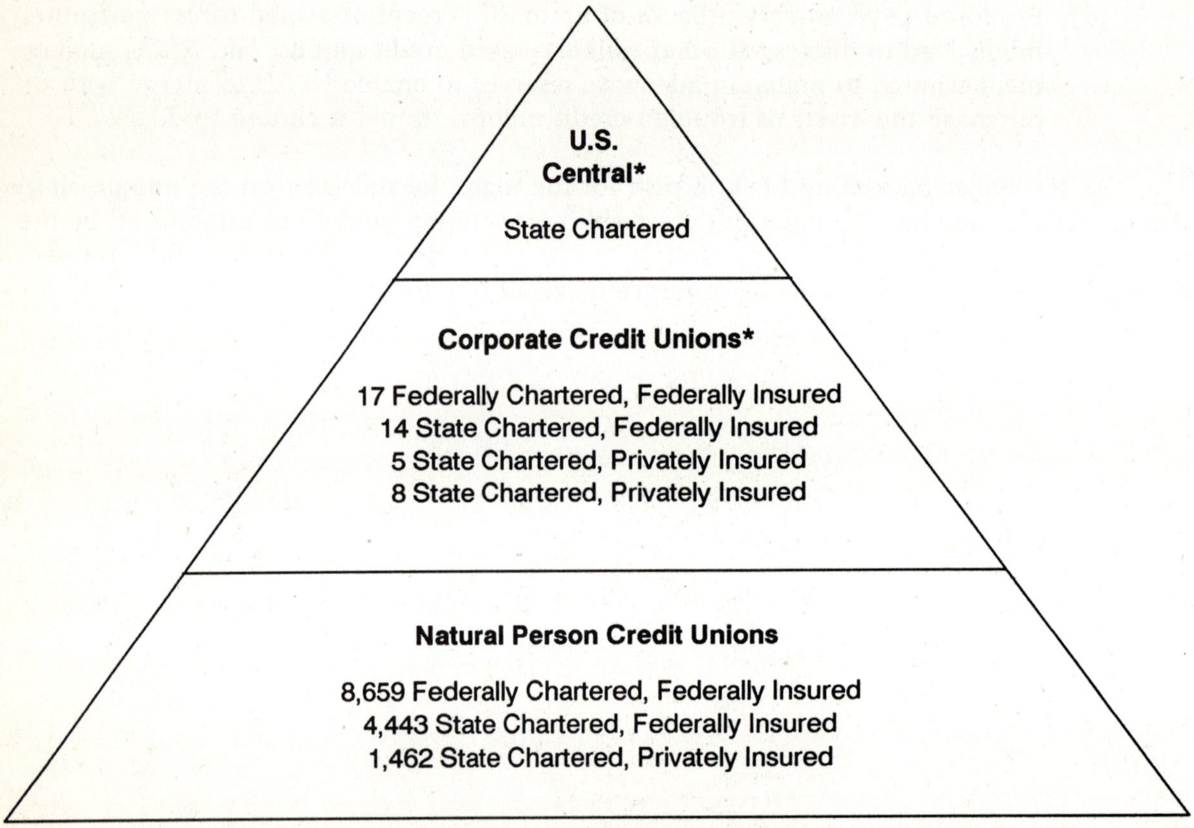

*U.S. Central and the Corporate Credit Unions comprise the Corporate Credit Union System, which includes a total of 45 institutions.

Exhibit 2

NAVY FEDERAL CREDIT UNION

CAMEL Ratios

CAPITAL ADEQUACY

Key ratios:

Capital/Assets	(Allowance for loan loss reserves + Allowance for investment losses + Regular reserve + Investment valuation reserve + Other reserves + Undivided earnings) ÷ (Total assets)
Net Capital/Assets	(Capital − (Loan losses + Investment losses + Other identified losses)) ÷ (Total assets)

Supporting ratios:

(Total Capital plus Shares and Deposits)/ Shares and Deposits	(Capital + Total shares) ÷ (Total shares)
Total Delinquent Loans/ Capital	(Total delinquent loans) ÷ (Capital)
Solvency Equation	(Total assets + Allowance for loan losses − Liabilities − Collection problem loans − Other potential losses) ÷ (Total shares)
Classified Assets/ Capital	(Collection problem loans + Other potential losses) ÷ (Capital)

ASSET QUALITY

Key ratios:

Delinquent Loans/Loans	(Total of delinquent loans more than 2 months) ÷ (Total loans)
Net Charge Offs/ Average Loans	(Total of loans charged off in previous 12-month period − Total recoveries in same period) ÷ (Average loans)

Supporting ratio:

Total Classified Assets/ Total Assets	(Collection problem loans + Other potential losses) ÷ (Total assets)

EARNINGS

Key ratios:

Net Income/Avg Assets (before reserve transfer)	(Net income (loss) after all operating expenses and all cost of funds) ÷ (Current period assets plus prior period assets ÷ 2)
Net Income/Avg Assets (after reserve transfer)	(Net income (loss) after all operating expenses and all cost of funds and net required reserve transfer) ÷ (Current period assets plus prior period assets ÷ 2)

Exhibit 2 (continued)

NAVY FEDERAL CREDIT UNION

Operating Expenses/ Average Assets	(Total operating expenses − provision for loan losses) ÷ (Current period assets plus prior period assets ÷ 2)

Supporting ratios:

Gross Income/ Average Assets	(Gross income) ÷ (Current period assets plus prior period assets ÷ 2)
Cost of Funds/ Average Assets	(Cost of funds) ÷ (Average assets)

LIQUIDITY

Key ratios:

Long-term Assets/Assets	(Long-term investments (> 3 years) + Real estate loans + Commercial loans + Agricultural loans + Fixed assets) ÷ (Total assets)
Net Long-term Assets/ Assets	(Long-term investments (> 3 years) + Fixed rate real estate loans (> 3 years) + Commercial loans + Agricultural loans + Fixed assets) ÷ (Total assets)
Estimated Short-term Cash Availability	(Cash + Investments with maturities or repricing in less than 1 year + Estimated loan repayments − Share certificates maturing in less than 1 year − IRA, Keogh, and retirement accounts maturing in less than 1 year − Note payable − 25% of all other shares) ÷ (Total assets − Total reverse repurchase agreements)

Supporting ratios:

Total Borrowings/ Total Shares & Capital	(Note and interest payable) ÷ (Total shares + Capital)
Regular Shares/Total Shares & Borrowings	(Regular shares) ÷ (Total shares + Notes and interest payable)
Total Loans/Total Shares	(Total loans) ÷ (Total shares)
Liquid Assets/Short-term Liabilities & Shares	(Short-term investments + Marketable long-term investments (at market value) + Cash − Liabilities secured by short-term or marketable investments) ÷ (Total shares + Total short-term liabilities − Liabilities secured by short-term or marketable investments − Nonpublic unit long-term share certificates over $100,000 − Public unit funds)

Exhibit 3

NAVY FEDERAL CREDIT UNION

Asset Distribution of Credit Unions and Commercial Banks
as of December 31, 1990
(dollar figures in billions)

	Credit Unions		Commercial Banks	
	Dollar Amount	Percent of Total	Dollar Amount	Percent of Total
Total assets	$198.2	100.0%	$3,420.2	100.0%
Total loans	127.1	64.1	2,122.7	62.4
Consumer	82.1	41.4	403.4	11.9
Commercial/industrial	1.4	0.7	615.2	18.1
1- to 4-family real estate	43.3	21.8	400.3	11.8
Commercial and other real estate	0.0	0.0	428.7	12.6
Other loans	0.3	0.2	275.2	8.1
Total investments	61.9	31.2	947.4	27.8
Cash	4.4	2.2	215.4	6.3
Other assets	4.7	2.4	116.7	3.4

Source: Credit Union National Association

Exhibit 4a
NAVY FEDERAL CREDIT UNION
Distribution of Number, Capital, and Assets of Credit Unions by Capital Ratios
as of December 31, 1989
(dollar figures in millions)

Capital Ratio	Number	Percent of Total	Total Capital	Percent of Total	Total Assets	Percent of Total
Less than 0	78	0.6%	($ 149)	–1.0%	$ 1,970	1.0%
0% to 3%	367	2.9	$ 111	0.7	5,921	3.0
3% to 3.99%	397	3.1	244	1.6	6,820	3.5
4% to 4.99%	642	5.0	652	4.3	14,016	7.2
5% to 5.99%	993	7.8	1,598	10.6	28,635	14.7
6% or more	10,356	81.2	12,584	83.9	137,522	70.6
Total	12,755	100.0%	$15,040	100.0%	$194,884	100.0%

Exhibit 4b
NAVY FEDERAL CREDIT UNION
Capital Ratios of Credit Unions and Banks by Size
as of December 31, 1989
(dollar figures in millions)

Commercial Banks:

Asset Size (millions of dollars)	Number of Banks	Percent of Total	Assets	Capital	Capital/ Assets
0 to 2	18	0.1%	$ 23	$ 16	68.3%
2 to 10	609	4.9	4,393	627	14.3
10 to 50	5,867	47.5	163,029	14,999	9.2
50 to 100	2,759	22.4	193,978	16,720	8.6
Over 100	3,088	25.0	3,040,748	186,537	6.1
Total	12,341	100.0%	$3,402,172	$218,899	6.4%

Credit Unions:

Asset Size (millions of dollars)	Number of Credit Unions	Percent of Total	Assets	Capital	Capital/ Assets
0 to 2	5,500	42.9%	$ 4,198	$ 476	11.3%
2 to 10	4,160	32.4	20,032	1,811	9.0
10 to 50	2,376	18.5	53,214	4,179	7.9
50 to 100	415	3.2	29,079	2,031	7.0
Over 100	382	3.0	91,685	6,542	7.1
Total	12,833	100.0%	$198,208	$15,039	7.6%

Source: Credit Union National Association

Exhibit 5

NAVY FEDERAL CREDIT UNION

Financial Summary, 1980-1990
(dollar figures in millions)

	1980	1990	10-year CAGR*
Assets	$ 866.2	$4,574.6	18.11%
Loans outstanding	$ 695.7	$3,220.7	16.56
Mortgage loans serviced	43.0	2,073.1	47.34
Shares (other than Share certificates)	$ 599.5	$2,827.7	16.78
Share certificates	137.2	921.2	20.98
Reserves	$ 34.8	$ 346.3	25.83
Gross income	$ 87.4	$ 432.7	17.35
Operating expenses	44.7	154.0	13.17
Dividends	42.3	224.3	18.15
Members	551,313	1,098,542	7.14
Sharecheks processed	6,334,880	88,729,789	30.21
Share purchases	3,779,662	19,586,931	17.88
Share withdrawals	1,741,882	7,674,173	15.98
Mortgage loans made	471	6,757	30.52
Consumer loans made	154,796	211,189	3.16

*CAGR = compound annual growth rate

Exhibit 6
NAVY FEDERAL CREDIT UNION
Statements of Financial Condition as of December 31, 1988-1990
(dollar figures in thousands)

	1988	1989	1990
Assets			
Auto loans	$ 911,459	$1,132,450	$1,182,230
Other consumer loans	670,764	699,566	736,901
Mortgages	549,934	583,521	575,574
Home equity loans	91,889	196,107	311,368
Credit card loans	193,303	267,724	333,997
Lines of credit	79,120	79,619	80,620
Total loans to members	$2,496,469	$2,958,987	$3,220,690
Loan loss reserve*	(12,833)	(14,711)	(16,326)
Net loans to members	$2,483,636	$2,944,276	$3,204,364
Cash	55,810	61,484	74,730
Investments	812,221	707,279	1,080,559
Accrued interest receivable	16,636	20,976	26,966
Fixed assets (net)	52,598	69,927	69,782
Prepaid and other assets	48,660	57,233	70,510
Mortgage loans in process	14,615	24,022	16,664
Deposit—NCUSIF	25,439	28,485	31,000
Total assets	$3,509,615	$3,913,682	$4,574,575
Liabilities and Members' Equity			
Securities sold under repurchase agreements	$ 191,451	$ 219,093	$ 359,136
Drafts payable	41,935	46,854	44,122
Dividends payable	33,770	38,280	41,380
Accrued expenses and accounts payable	19,488	25,652	34,742
Total liabilities	$ 286,644	$ 329,879	$ 479,380
Members' accounts:			
Share savings accounts	$1,408,595	$1,407,160	$1,521,380
Sharechek accounts	418,561	504,107	572,158
Share certificate accounts	569,919	754,738	921,248
Individual retirement accounts	575,509	625,959	734,110
Total members' accounts	$2,972,584	$3,291,964	$3,748,896
Reserves and undivided earnings:			
Regular reserve	$ 83,577	$ 102,570	$ 116,998
Capital reserve	166,310	188,769	228,801
Undivided earnings	500	500	500
Total reserves and undivided earnings	$ 250,387	$ 291,839	$ 346,299
Total members' equity	$3,222,971	$3,583,803	$4,095,195
Total liabilities and members' equity	$3,509,615	$3,913,682	$4,574,575

*Breakdown of Loan Loss Reserve:	1988	1989	1990
Balance, beginning of year	$10,520	$12,833	$14,711
Provision charged to operations	11,400	11,400	12,984
Loans and accrued interest charged off	(9,901)	(11,206)	(12,577)
Recoveries	814	1,684	1,208
Balance, end of year	$12,833	$14,711	$16,326

Exhibit 7

NAVY FEDERAL CREDIT UNION

Statements of Operations
(dollar figures in thousands)

	1988	1989	1990
Interest on loans to members	$248,631	$294,569	$338,873
Investment income	45,303	62,705	67,534
Other income	13,391	19,141	26,340
Total income	$307,325	$376,415	$432,747
Dividend and interest expense:			
Dividends	$165,168	$196,208	$224,282
Interest on securities sold under repurchase agreements	2,883	22,575	21,644
Total dividend and interest expense	$168,051	$218,783	$245,926
Net interest and other income	$139,274	$157,632	$186,821
Provision for loan losses	11,400	11,400	12,984
Net interest and other income after provision for loan losses	$127,874	$146,232	$173,837
Operating expenses:			
Salaries and employee benefits	$ 51,189	$ 58,981	$ 65,477
Office operating expenses	33,320	40,323	47,780
Loan protection life insurance	3,375	3,474	3,891
Life savings insurance	899	846	963
Education and publicity	768	1,005	990
Federal supervision and examinations	188	219	271
Total operating expenses	$ 89,739	$104,848	$119,372
Net operating income	$ 38,135	$ 41,384	$ 54,465
Nonoperating (loss) income	6	68	(5)
Net income	$ 38,141	$ 41,452	$ 54,460

Exhibit 8

NAVY FEDERAL CREDIT UNION

Statements of Reserves and Undivided Earnings
as of December 31, 1987-1990
(dollar figures in thousands)

	Regular Reserve	Capital Reserve	Undivided Earnings	Total
Balance at December 31, 1987	$ 73,143	$138,603	$ 500	$212,246
Net income	0	0	38,141	38,141
Transfers:				
Statutory	21,834	0	(21,834)	0
Discretionary	0	27,707	(27,707)	0
Provision for loan losses	(11,400)	0	11,400	0
Balance at December 31, 1988	$ 83,577	$166,310	$ 500	$250,387
Net income	0	0	41,452	41,452
Transfers:				
Statutory	30,393	0	(30,393)	0
Discretionary	0	22,459	(22,459)	0
Provision for loan losses	(11,400)	0	11,400	0
Balance at December 31, 1989	$102,570	$188,769	$ 500	$291,839
Net income	0	0	54,460	54,460
Transfers:				
Statutory	27,412	0	(27,412)	0
Discretionary	0	40,032	(40,032)	0
Provision for loan losses	(12,984)	0	12,984	0
Balance at December 31, 1990	$116,998	$228,801	$ 500	$346,299

Exhibit 9
NAVY FEDERAL CREDIT UNION
Statements of Cash flows
(dollar figures in thousands)

	1988	1989	1990
Cash flow from operating activities			
Net income	$ 38,141	$ 41,452	$ 54,460
Adjustments:			
Provision for loan losses	11,400	11,400	12,984
Depreciation and amortization	5,797	8,156	9,013
Loss (gain) on disposition of fixed assets	(6)	(68)	5
Mortgage loans originated for sale	*	(297,448)	(496,594)
Mortgage loan sales	*	305,400	433,854
Increase in interest receivable	(4,585)	(4,340)	(5,990)
Increase in dividends payable	3,258	4,510	3,100
Other, net	(6,886)	2,510	(6,919)
Net cash provided by operations	**$ 47,119**	**$ 71,572**	**$ 3,913**
Cash flows from investing activities			
Net (increase) decrease in Federal Funds and other short-term investments	($ 91,439)	$187,848	($134,459)
Purchase of investment securities	(323,582)	(650,278)	(383,890)
Proceeds from maturity or sale of investment securities	138,609	567,372	145,069
Net increase in loans disbursed to members	(261,666)	(479,992)	(210,332)
Net decrease (increase) in loans in process	(10,481)	(9,407)	7,358
Net additions to fixed assets	(10,415)	(25,417)	(8,873)
Increase in deposit to NCUSIF	(4,045)	(3,046)	(2,515)
Net cash used by investing activities	**($563,019)**	**($412,920)**	**($587,642)**
Cash flows from financing activities			
Net increase in members' equity accounts excluding reserves and undivided earnings	$ 323,418	$ 319,380	$ 456,932
Net increase in securities sold under repurchase agreements	191,451	27,642	140,043
Net cash provided by financing activities	**$ 514,869**	**$ 347,022**	**$ 596,975**
Net increase (decrease) in cash	($ 1,031)	$ 5,674	$ 13,246
Cash at beginning of year	56,841	55,810	61,484
Cash at end of year	$ 55,810	$ 61,484	$ 74,730

*Net effect included in "Net increase in loans disbursed to members."

Exhibit 10

NAVY FEDERAL CREDIT UNION

Comparison of Saving and Lending Rates
as of December 31, 1990

	NFCU	Commercial Banks
1-year CD (> $1,000)	8.00%	6.85% – 7.50%
5-yr CD (> $1,000)	8.25%	6.70% – 7.72%
Savings (> $5)	6.00%	4.25% – 5.00%
IRA (< $10,000)	7.50%	6.20% – 7.40%
Credit card	14.00%	16.00% – 19.00%
Personal line of credit (< $5,000)	14.50%	14.00% – 15.00%
Home improvement loan (< 15 years)	13.50%	11.50% – 12.75%
Auto loan (new autos)	9.90% – 11.90%	10.80% – 12.25%

Note: This information represents a sampling of publicly listed rates. Specific loan and savings account covenants and fees may differ between instruments.

Case 10: ROCKHARD INSURANCE

In July 1989, Janet James, senior vice president for strategic planning for Rockhard Insurance Company, an $11-billion-asset mutual life insurance company, had finished reading an article about the diversification activities of the Prudential Insurance Company, the largest life insurance company in the United States. As Ms. James thought about the article and Prudential's new activities, she wondered what the implications were for her company, Rockhard Insurance, in the coming decade. In particular, she wondered whether her company should adopt a similar strategy to Prudential's.

Rockhard Insurance

Rockhard Insurance was founded in 1902 in Hartford, Connecticut, as a mutual insurance company providing industrial life insurance for the common worker. Its sales force initially called on workers as they left their work sites to sell its policies. Premiums were usually paid weekly, and the same sales representatives who sold the initial policies collected the premiums.

Over the years, Rockhard had diversified from its initial industrial life insurance products into a full line of life insurance products, and its customer base had expanded from the common worker to a representative cross section of the life-insurance–buying public. Growth for Rockhard had been slow but steady; its profitability had been similar to other mutual life insurance companies of similar size. By 1989, Rockhard was a well-established, middle-tier life insurance company with policyholders in all 50 states and a distribution network of independent agents throughout the United States. (Exhibits 1 and 2 show Rockhard's financial statements for 1987 and 1988.)

Rockhard was a conservatively managed company. This approach had filled its portfolio with high-quality assets (the company was rated AAA by Standard and Poor and Aaa by Moody) but had put Rockhard in the position of being a follower rather than an industry innovator in products and diversification. Rockhard's management considered its conservatism a strength, believing it allowed the company to provide superior service to its policyholders through concentration of resources and to avoid disastrous losses by poorly planned or implemented diversification.

The company therefore provided the standard life insurance, disability insurance, health insurance, and annuity products that were available from most mutual insurance companies. It also offered institutional investment management services for pension funds. It had not diversified into activities such as securities brokerage, investment banking, and mutual fund management and distribution, as had many of its life-insurance competitors. It had not expanded into other insurance areas, such as property casualty and liability insurance, though most other large and middle-tier insurance companies were in both major categories of business.

Furthermore, Rockhard's status as a mutual company, owned by its policyholders, presented a problem in raising new capital. Its "Contingency Reserves," equivalent to owners' equity, could be increased only by the retention of net income. It was not possible to issue new equity without converting to a stock-company structure, although the mutual structure also protected Rockhard from any takeover threats.

It could invest in noninsurance businesses, through a cash purchase or through a separate subsidiary, provided the proper procedures and regulatory rules were followed. There was always the chance, however, that the regulatory authorities would decide a venture was too risky. In that case, they would require that the investment be written down in part or completely. The result would be a decrease in contingency reserves and a possible constraint on growth because the volume of insurance was restricted to a multiple of the reserves.

The use of partly owned subsidiaries was one method a mutual company could use to raise equity capital for a new venture. The mutual company could sell stock in the subsidiary or use it as a joint venture.

The Insurance Industry

The insurance industry began in the marine merchant business, when individuals, for a fee, would guarantee the delivery of goods regardless of storms or piracy on the high seas. From these practical beginnings, the industry grew to write over 14 million policies annually in the United States alone. The industry provided a million jobs to upper-level managers, data processors, actuaries, salesmen, and clerical staff. It was a major financial intermediary, investing its assets in senior corporate debt and in real estate mortgages in order safely to generate earnings and cash necessary to meet its obligations.

Insurance was the exchange of a small certain payment, called a premium, for a large but uncertain loss. The uncertainty might be a point in time, as with life insurance, or a dollar sum, as with property-casualty insurance. The insurance companies made their money by spreading the losses of a few policyholders over the premiums of many. In fact, providing insurance coverage was simply playing a game of calculated risks. Actuaries looked at historical trends and ran thousands of regressions: with enough data, they could predict the number and size of the losses for any given coverage—life, property, or liability—and thus they could estimate the price each policyholder should pay for the risks the insurance covered.

To calculate the size and number of losses, actuaries looked at environmental changes, such as alterations in weather patterns, the change in the price of oil, or the increase in terrorism. They also looked at behavior trends of policyholders: changing driving records, mortality rates, and length and number of hospital stays. In short, actuaries were masters at quantitative analysis; they drew decision trees, ran computer simulations, and performed detailed regression analyses.

Insurance coverage could be classified as life products and all others (such as property, casualty, and suretyship). Life insurance covered the risk of early death. With property insurance, the risk covered was damage to an insured's possessions, whether it be from fire, theft, or natural causes such as wind. Casualty (often referred to as liability) insurance covered the damages suffered by a third party due to the insured's negligence or accident. Policies could be written to cover specific lines, such as home, auto, fire, boat, or personal article, or could be written as multiline coverage. Most home policies written included fire coverage and often had provisions for limited personal article coverage. The number of products made available was directly related to the type of customers—lower- and middle-income individuals (auto, home), wealthy individuals (personal articles, boat and yacht), small businesses (limited liability), and large corporations (worker's compensation, group health, commercial liability).

Life Insurance

Life-insurance companies held a long and often distinguished position in American history, offering risk-protection services in the United States for over 225 years. The Presbyterian Ministers Fund, incorporated in Philadelphia in 1759 as the Corporation for Relief of Poor and Distressed Presbyterians and of the Poor and Distressed Widows and Children of the Presbyterian Church, held the distinction of being the oldest-life insurance company in the world. It also predated by more than two decades the establishment of the first commercial bank in the United States, which was formed in 1781.

The concept of life insurance took general hold at the time of the Civil War. One innovation that fueled this growth was the introduction of small policies peddled door-to-door with weekly payments collected in person by the agent. Another innovation was the incorporation of systematic saving through tontine plans. Subscribers formed a pool of money that, together with interest, went to the final surviving member. Insurance companies grew steadily through the 20th Century, until at the end of 1986 there were over 2,300 life-insurance companies in the United States with combined assets of about $937 billion. These companies had about 400 million life-insurance policies in force, which generated annual premiums of $194 billion.

In 1986, 785,000 people were directly employed by life and health companies, and several hundred thousands more were employed by agencies selling life and health insurance.

Life insurance companies were the fourth largest financial intermediary, offering public products involving both insurance protection in the case of death and a way of saving for over 80 percent of all families in the United States. Life insurance was designed to provide, on the death of the insured, cash benefits to third parties called beneficiaries, although the beneficiaries were not necessarily parties to the contract. The basic contracts were term, whole life (cash value available), and endowment. These could be sold on an individual or group basis, with group term insurance a common employee benefit. Unfortunately for the life-insurance companies, this product was one of their least profitable.

To enhance profitability, life-insurance companies had grown increasingly ingenious in developing tax-related products that allowed the policyholder's investment to compound on a before-tax basis or offered some other tax-deferring or tax-escaping opportunity. The Internal Revenue Service was equally ingenious in ending these opportunities, either by regulation or by Congressional action.

The life-insurance sector was a maturing one. Its customers were becoming more sophisticated (such as companies buying benefit plans rather than individuals buying endowment policies) in selecting low-cost products. Competition was increasing for its more profitable products. These developments were reflected in the industry's rate of asset growth, which was one of the lowest of the major types of financial intermediaries. Its profitability was the lowest of all major types of financial intermediaries, as shown in Exhibits 3, 4, and 5. Return on equity had been comparatively respectable for stockholder-owned companies but poor for mutual companies, as Exhibit 6 shows. It was also a concentrated industry, dominated by the largest companies, as indicated by Exhibits 7 and 8. The fastest-growing product of the life insurance industry was annuities, a tax-related investment product, as Exhibit 9 shows, presaging a fundamental change in market demand for life-insurance products.

The Casualty Insurance Business

Casualty insurance companies were in the unique position of not knowing the costs of their products until months, perhaps years, after their product's sale had been completed; actuaries could only guess at ball-park figures, and unforeseen catastrophes could sharply change expected profits to real and costly losses. To soften the blow of later losses, insurance casualty companies were required by law to keep a certain cash balance in reserve. The size of the reserves varied with the size of the claims expected during any given period.

Casualty companies made their money two ways: through direct profit on their products and through investments made with cash generated through premium payments. Especially during times of high interest rates, companies could actually lose money on their insurance business (recording an "underwriting loss") but make more than enough to offset that loss with their investment portfolios. In recent years, the pressure for the underwriting business to be profitable in its own right had mounted as a result of low interest rates and increased competition attracted to the business by previously higher rates.

Casualty companies often reinsured a portion of the risks they underwrote with other casualty companies, much as a bank might sell a participation in a loan to another bank and buy a participation in a loan the other bank had made. At a wholesale level, several specialized reinsurance companies dealt only with other insurance companies, having no retail business of their own. The pinnacle of the reinsurance industry was Lloyd's of London. This was a unique reinsurance organization of professionals who made commitments on behalf of syndicates of "names," individuals who had invested in the syndicate but who were liable to the full extent of their net worth for the obligations of the syndicate.

Because even a simple revision to a customer's insurance policy required an immediate change, and such a change often resulted in price changes, it was very important that all records were kept up to date. Casualty insurance products especially involved massive record keeping, information flow, and rate processing: policy description; reports of changes and accidents; endorsements; claim verification; quantification of demographic and environmental changes that directly affected premium rates. In the 1980s, paperless computer systems had absorbed many of the functions previously done by hand, and well-designed and well-operated computer systems had become one of the most crucial factors in determining a company's success.

Administration and Marketing Requirements

Another crucial success factor for all insurance companies was adequate service. Servicing an account—be it a corporate account for a major company or a nonprofit organization, or a private, personal account—involved not just handling the premium payments, but other functions as well, including but not limited to:

- understanding the needs of the customer and recommending suitable products
- assessing the value of the insured's property to ensure proper coverage
- pricing the individual policies
- handling the cash transaction
- reporting the claim
- investigating the claim
- reimbursing the claim

Because many companies' products were similar (having been based on similar actuarial studies), timeliness and accuracy were important factors that distinguished good service from bad and good companies from poor ones.

Traditionally, insurance companies had shared the burden of providing good service with middlemen—insurance agents and brokers. Agents were salesmen usually licensed to sell one company's product only and who assumed responsibility for their customers' payment of premiums. Brokers were agents who were licensed to do business with more than one company and who took no credit risk. Brokers also sold other types of financial instruments, such as mutual funds; agents concentrated on insurance products only. The brokers varied in size and sophistication and thus in the amount of service they provided. Large, national brokers, referred to in the industry as "the alphabet houses"—Alexander & Alexander ("A&A"), Marsh and McLennon ("M&M"), Johnson and Higgins ("J&H"), and others—usually had computer linkups with the companies they served. These brokers wielded considerable power over the companies because the companies depended on them for sales and claims management, especially for large and lucrative corporate accounts. Smaller agents, who ran "Mom-and-Pop" shops, were valuable to the large insurance companies because they could build better relations with the individual customers in the communities in which they lived.

A few insurance companies had almost circumvented the middleman by doing all sales and service themselves or through captive agents. For example, Sears' Allstate marketed auto insurance directly through its retail customer base. Often considered budget insurance, these companies were known for their simple product lines and low prices (since less selling costs were necessary), and, not surprisingly, they could have a reputation for poor service.

The property and casualty underwriting business ran on very tight margins. The servicing costs were extremely high. The distributors were usually paid commissions. Sophisticated data-processing equipment created costly overhead. The business was subject to unpredictable losses and costly catastrophes. And, despite these drawbacks, competition was fierce. Underwriting losses in property and casualty insurance were not unusual. Analysts referred to underwriting profitability by using a combined ratio: the fraction of costs assumed over premium generated. A typical combined ratio was 1.1 or 1.2; an excellent ratio was .98 or .99.

Because of the tight margins, the cyclicality of the business, and the synergies between insurance products and other finance-related products (for example, real estate mortgages and IRAs), many insurance companies had diversified into other financial services.

The Prudential Insurance Company

The Prudential Insurance Company at the end of 1988 was the largest insurance company and the second largest financial institution in the United States. Though its most important business was life insurance, it was also active in a range of other financial service businesses including mortgage origination, home and auto insurance, reinsurance, commercial lending, mutual fund distribution, securities underwriting, and investment management. During the 1980s the story of Prudential Insurance was the history of its evolution from a mutual life-insurance company into an innovative diversified financial services giant.

In the early 1980s, Prudential entered the securities business with its acquisition of Bache and Company, a major retail brokerage firm. In June 1989, it expanded its reach in the securities business by acquiring Thomson McKinnon, the ninth-largest retail brokerage firm, with 4,700 employees and 154 branch offices. Though the acquisition made Prudential-Bache one of the nation's five largest retail brokerage firms, with over 8,000 retail brokers, Prudential did not ignore the investment banking and related businesses. In addition to the investment banking activities housed in its Prudential-Bache unit, Prudential had significant investment banking functions in other parts of the company. Under its Investment Division, headed by a vice chairman, Prudential provided a range of merchant banking activities through subsidiaries in Europe and Asia and through Prudential Capital, which was also the largest medium-term lender in the United States.

In 1987, Prudential entered the commercial banking business by setting up its "non-bank" bank, Prudential Bank and Trust Company. By the end of 1988, Prudential Bank and Trust Company had reached $1.1 billion in assets and had developed a broad product line including certificates of deposit, money market deposit accounts, home equity and second mortgage loans, small business loans, and a collective-trust product for 401K-type retirement plans.

Trends in the Financial-Services Industry

The financial-services industry had experienced dramatic change in the 1980s. Rocked by rapidly changing interests rates, inflation turning to deflation, new technology, and deregulation, the 1980s had been a period of turmoil for a traditionally conservative industry. The barriers blurred between various segments of the industry, such as banking, securities, and insurance. Major insurance firms bought securities firms, commercial banks moved into a wide range of investment banking activities, and securities firms began to sell insurance products and a range of bank products such as mortgages and depository services.

The merger of different industry segments, however, was not without its casualties. Sears and its insurance subsidiary, Allstate Insurance, in 1988 closed down their California thrift, which they had operated for many years, after using it to make a much publicized but apparently unsuccessful thrust into nationwide consumer banking. Equitable, the third largest life-insurance company in the United States, experienced mass resignations of senior executives and the designation of a new CEO in 1988, the result of a disastrous fall in profits in 1987 caused by losses on guaranteed investment contracts.* And the problems in Southwestern real estate created difficulties for some companies in their more traditional mortgage investments.

Overall, the insurance industry had experienced squeezed profits and increasing numbers of insolvencies as its members diversified and moved into riskier, interest-sensitive products. The most notable casualties had been Baldwin-United and Charter Company, which

---

*Guaranteed investment contracts (GIC) were one of the hot insurance products of the early 1980s. Under these contracts, insurance companies promised an investor that the investor would be able to invest funds under the conditions and rates specified in the contract. If the rates promised were higher than the insurance company could earn on its investments, the insurance company would lose money. GICs were popular with individuals, with corporate pension trustees, and with designers of securitized instruments who needed a fixed rate at which prepayments could be reinvested.

collapsed in the early 1980s after heavy losses on a single-premium deferred annuities scheme.*

The decade of the 1990s promised to be even more difficult for the financial-services industry. Continued consolidation of depository institutions was widely anticipated, and securities and insurance activities were expected to become more competitive as the result of new players entering from the banking sector.

Developing Rockhard's Strategy

As Ms. James analyzed Prudential's strategy of diversification and noted the various trends in financial services toward the blurring of distinctions between different types of financial institutions, she wondered where the logical areas of extension for Rockhard were. Financial supermarket strategies had met with mixed success, but it was also clear that it would be hard to expand revenues and profits in Rockhard's basic business of life insurance and related services.

Unfortunately, no specific area of financial services stood out as a clear growth area for the 1990s. Investment banking had enjoyed spectacular profits in the 1980s, but Wall Street had begun to experience reduced profits and consolidation as the decade had come to a close. Depository institutions (commercial banks and thrifts) suffered from overcapacity, and in the thrift area the problems were so severe that Congress was currently debating a $150 billion bailout bill. Pension funds and mutual funds were expected to show strong growth in the 1990s, but competition in these businesses was strong. Success required strong investment management skills.

Ms. James knew that she had to build on Rockhard's strengths in developing a growth strategy, but she also knew that those strengths could make it difficult to expand successfully into non–life-insurance areas.

---

*Like GICs, these policies guaranteed investors a compounded rate of return on a single-payment insurance policy. If the guaranteed rate was greater than the insurance company could earn, the insurance company would lose money on the policy. Because of the tax advantages that existed at the time, these policies were attractive ways of compounding interest before taxes.

Exhibit 1

ROCKHARD INSURANCE

Consolidated Statement of Income
Years Ended December 31, 1987-1988
(millions)

	1987	1988
Revenue		
Premium income	$1,375.5	$1,428.3
Net investment and other income	784.3	887.6
Total	$2,159.8	$2,315.9
Disposition of Revenue		
Policy benefits & payments	761.2	707.1
Increase in policyholders' reserves & funds	894.1	1,051.8
Operating expenses	144.5	169.1
Commissions	90.9	94.8
Taxes	18.8	19.3
Total	$1,909.5	$2,042.1
Net gain before dividends	$ 250.3	$ 273.8
Dividends to policyholders	237.6	246.2
Net gain from operations	$ 12.7	$ 27.6
Net realized capital (loss) gain	13.0	(2.4)
Net income	$ 25.7	$ 25.2

Exhibit 2

ROCKHARD INSURANCE

Consolidated Statement of Financial Position
as of December 31, 1987 and 1988
(millions)

	1987	1988
Assets		
Bonds	$ 4,875.9	$ 5,556.9
Common stocks	59.0	65.8
Mortgage loans	1,975.7	2,493.5
Real estate:		
Investment	128.5	190.2
Other	32.4	34.0
Other investments	199.4	262.5
Policy loans	1,053.5	1,034.1
Cash and short-term investments	448.2	271.1
Investment & insurance amounts receivable	328.1	369.4
Separate account assets	904.8	997.5
Other	15.5	19.4
Total Assets	$10,021.0	$11,294.4
Reserves and Liabilities		
Policyholders' reserves & funds	$ 7,899.3	$ 8,938.0
Policyholders' dividends	253.9	259.0
Policy claims & other benefits payable	189.3	214.0
Federal income taxes	14.6	18.0
Long-term debt	50.0	50.0
Mandatory securities valuation reserve	72.6	90.7
Separate account reserves & liabilities	904.2	996.7
Other	133.2	219.4
Total reserves & liabilities	$ 9,517.1	$10,785.8
Contingency Reserves		
Designated	19.7	20.4
General	484.2	488.2
Total contingency reserves	$ 503.9	$ 508.6
Total Reserves, Liabilities, & Contingency Reserves	$10,021.0	$11,294.4

Exhibit 3

ROCKHARD INSURANCE

Total Assets of Financial Intermediaries at Year-End
Selected Years Between 1960 and 1987
(billions of dollars)

Financial Intermediary	1960	1970	1975	1980	1985	1987*
Commercial banks	$257.6	$ 576.2	$ 964.9	$1,703.7	$2,483.8	$2,847.1
Savings institutions						
Savings associations	71.5	176.2	338.2	629.8	1,080.6	1,262.0
Savings banks	40.6	79.0	121.1	171.6	216.8	260.2
Total	$112.1	$ 255.2	$ 459.3	$ 801.4	$1,297.4	$1,522.2
Life-insurance companies	119.6	207.3	289.3	479.2	825.9	1,052.2
Private pension funds	38.1	112.0	194.5	383.6	606.3	700.8
State and local pension funds	19.7	60.3	104.8	198.1	404.7	529.3
Finance companies	27.6	64.1	99.1	202.4	354.4	447.8
Money market funds	—	—	3.7	76.4	243.8	316.1
Investment companies	17.0	47.6	42.2	58.4	251.7	453.8
Credit unions	6.3	18.0	36.9	69.0	137.2	183.7
Total	$598.0	$1,340.7	$2,194.7	$3,972.2	$6,605.2	$8,053.0

*Preliminary

Exhibit 4
ROCKHARD INSURANCE COMPANY
Assets of Financial Intermediaries

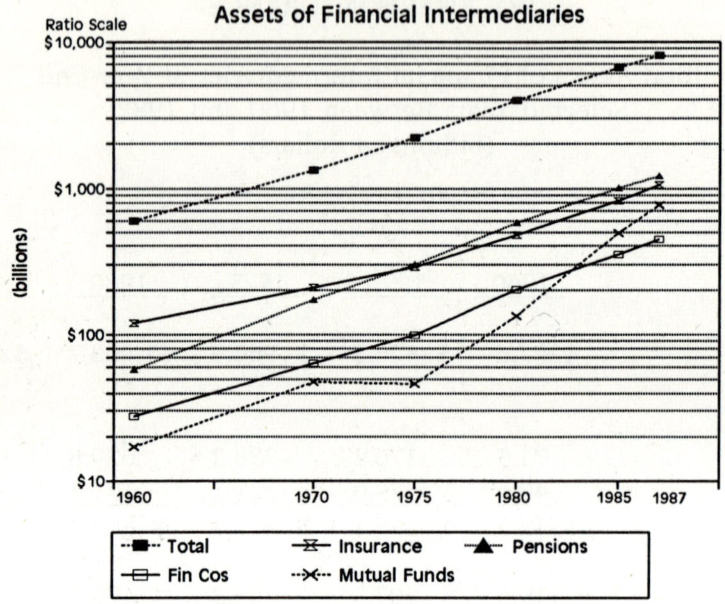

Exhibit 5
ROCKHARD INSURANCE COMPANY
Assets of Large Financial Institutions

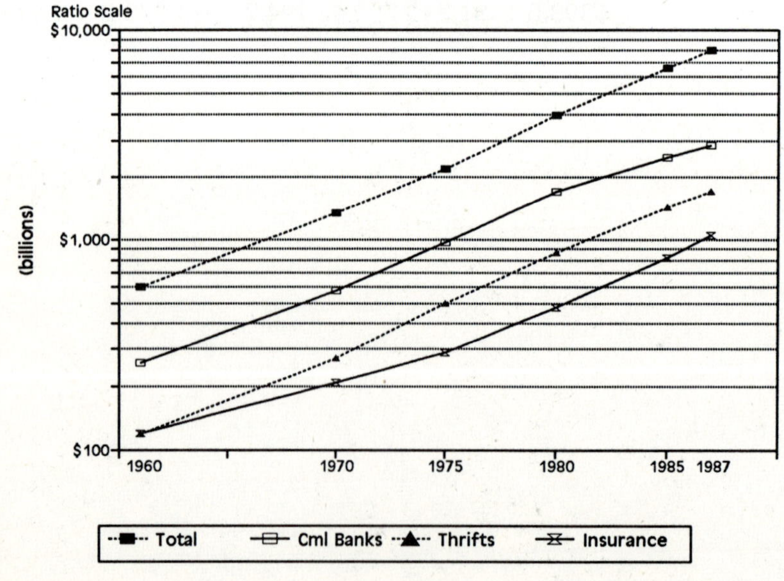

Exhibit 6

ROCKHARD INSURANCE

Return on Equity at Selected Types of Financial Institutions, 1975-1984[1]

Industry	1975-1984	1980-1984
Commercial banking	12.3%	12.2%
Multinational bank holding companies	13.1[2,3]	13.0[3]
Finance companies[4]	11.4	12.6
Mortgage companies[4]	13.7[5]	13.1
Securities firms	16.4	18.7
Investment banks	21.5	26.0
Other securities firms	14.5	15.8
Life insurance	13.7	13.4
Stockholder-owned companies	15.6	15.2
Mutual companies	10.6	10.5
Property and casualty insurance	10.9[6]	7.4
Stockholder-owned companies	11.2[6]	7.7
Mutual companies	9.8[6]	7.4
Insurance brokerage firms		
Large firms	22.5[6]	18.3
Small firms	12.5[6]	9.2
Diversified financial firms[7]	14.0	13.1

[1]Returns for commercial banks, securities firms, life insurers, and property and casualty insurers are based on average equity. Because of limited availability of data, returns for finance companies, mortgage companies, and insurance brokers are based on year-end equity. By way of comparison, nonfinancial firms (represented by those included in Standard & Poor's 400 stock index) reported average returns of 13.7 percent over 1980-84 and 14.0 percent over 1975-84.

[2]Excludes Crocker and Continental Illinois in 1984.

[3]1976-1984.

[4]Excluding subsidiaries of bank holding companies.

[5]1978-1984.

[6]1976-1984, one complete underwriting cycle.

[7]Aetna Life & Casualty, American Express, Beneficial Corporation, Household International, E.F. Hutton, Merrill Lynch, Transamerica, and Sears Roebuck.

Source: Federal Reserve Bank of New York, Recent Trends in Commercial Bank Profitability, A Staff Study. New York: Federal Reserve Bank of New York, 1986.

Exhibit 7

ROCKHARD INSURANCE

Share of Total Industry Base of the Ten Largest Firms,
By Rank of Concentration, 1984

Industry	Number of Firms	Top Ten Share of Total (percent)	Base	Total Base (billions)
Securities	339	54.4%	Capital	$ 11.6
Life insurance	2,134	48.7	Assets	723.9
Property & casualty insurance	3,468	43.5	Assets	264.7
Commercial banks	15,000	22.9	Assets	1,956.9
		16.6	Deposits	1,727.1
Thrift institutions	3,521	13.4	Assets	1,181.3
		12.5	Deposits	965.1

Exhibit 8

ROCKHARD INSURANCE

Share of Total Industry Assets of The Ten Largest Life Insurance Companies, 1984

	Assets (billions of dollars)	Share of Total (percent)
All companies	$ 723.9	100.0%
Ten largest companies	352.7	48.7
Prudential	78.9	10.9
Metropolitan	67.4	9.3
Equitable	44.5	6.1
Aetna	34.0	4.7
New York Life	25.6	3.5
John Hancock	24.7	3.4
Travelers	23.3	3.2
Connecticut General	19.2	2.7
Teachers	19.2	2.7
Northwestern Mutual	15.9	2.2

Exhibit 9

ROCKHARD INSURANCE

Ordinary Life-Insurance Premium Receipts
U.S. Life-Insurance Companies
(millions)

	1982	1983	1984	1985	1986
Life-Insurance Premiums					
Ordinary	$ 38,371	$ 37,978	$ 38,625	$ 46,096	$ 51,618
Group	9,433	9,560	9,702	11,041	11,826
Industrial	1,484	1,066	1,108	905	787
Credit	1,512	1,661	1,839	2,085	1,982
Total Life-Insurance Premiums	$ 50,800	$ 50,265	$ 51,274	$ 60,127	$ 66,213
Annuity Considerations					
Individual	$ 15,196	$ 14,003	$ 15,706	$ 20,891	$ 26,117
Group	19,448	16,541	27,153	33,008	57,595*
Total Annuity Considerations	$ 34,644	$ 30,544	$ 42,859	$ 53,899	$ 83,712
Health-Insurance Premiums					
Individual	$ 7,168	$ 7,926	$ 8,626	$ 9,143	10,379
Group	26,930	29,131	30,704	31,023	32,130
Credit	862	1,144	1,341	1,671	1,644
Total Health-Insurance Premiums	$ 34,960	$ 38,201	$ 40,671	$ 41,837	$ 44,153
Total Premium Receipts	$120,404	$119,010	$134,804	$155,863	$194,078

Note: Credit Life Insurance is limited to insurance on loans of 10 years or less duration.
*Unusually large increase in group annuity considerations due to an NAIC-mandated change in statutory reporting methods.
Source: American Council of Life Insurance, *1987 Life Insurance Fact Book*, Update, p. 28.

Notes

Case 11: FIRST BOSTON, INC.

Earl Fisher, senior investment officer at a major mutual fund group, put down the February 4, 1988, issue of the *Wall Street Journal*. He had read that Campeau Corp. and Henley Group, Inc. were retaining the firm of Wasserstein, Perella & Co. as advisors to their separate takeover fights. Both firms had been using First Boston as adviser. As officer in charge of his firm's equity investments, Mr. Fisher was concerned about the stock of First Boston, which he had purchased over 18 months ago. This investment did not represent a large percentage of his portfolios, but it was more than 5 percent of First Boston's common stock.

His uneasiness began in late 1987 when rumors surfaced of internal management problems at First Boston. The magnitude of the problems became quite clear on February 2, 1988, when Bruce Wasserstein and Joseph R. Perella, coheads of First Boston's Investment Banking Department, resigned to start their own firm. This marked the end of a more than ten-year relationship, which was credited with bringing First Boston back from the verge of obsolescence to a position as one of the prominent firms in the industry. By the end of trading on February 3, First Boston's stock price had tumbled from 26¼, on the day of the announcement, to close at 22⅞, a 13 percent drop. By comparison, the Dow Jones Industrial Average declined only 1 percent over the same period.

Mr. Fisher had quite a bit to consider. Wasserstein and Perella had taken with them a core of top bankers from First Boston. It was unclear how many clients would leave due to the loss of the two stars and how many more bankers would leave to join the pair or other competing firms. Mr. Fisher also knew that many of the mergers and acquisitions (M&A) clients used other services offered by First Boston, so those departments could potentially lose business, too.

Should he sell his First Boston stock, or buy more? Considering the current state of investment banking, maybe he should get out of the industry altogether until the dust settled.

First Boston, Inc.

In 1978, blunt-spoken, long-time trader for First Boston, Peter Buchanan, became president of the firm. He had his work cut out for him. At the end of 1978, First Boston showed net income of $1.8 million on $94.2 million in revenue, the lowest income level since the Depression. Those results were not aberrations: both revenues and profits had been

---

This case was prepared from publicly available information.

slipping steadily during the 1970s. Teaming up with then chairman and CEO, George Shinn, Mr. Buchanan engineered a recovery that established First Boston as one of the strongest of the Big Five investment banks. In 1983, First Boston had $515.4 million in total revenues and net income of $80.2 million.

Much of the credit for the firm's turnaround had been attributed to the M&A department, headed by Joe Perella and Bruce Wasserstein. Mr. Perella had joined First Boston in 1973 and ran the one-man department in relative obscurity until Mr. Shinn became CEO in 1975. Mr. Shinn's strategy emphasized M&A, and therefore Mr. Perella was allocated the resources necessary to hire talent and expand business. This included hiring Bruce Wasserstein in 1977.

The M&A department generated just over $3 million in fees in 1977 with nine staff members. By 1985, the group had grown to 100 bankers and analysts, generating close to $200 million in fees at more than the firm's average margin. This represented almost one-quarter of First Boston's total revenue of $888 million. (Financial statements are provided in Exhibits 1 and 2.) In 1986, First Boston was ranked first in both the number and dollar value of those M&A transactions in which it served as adviser. The final numbers had not yet been tabulated, but Mr. Fisher expected First Boston to maintain that number-one position for 1987.

Perella and Wasserstein pioneered the evolution of specialists instead of generalists. They wanted to be perceived as the most professional M&A department on Wall Street. First Boston's bankers had to become the most knowledgeable about the conceptualization, analysis, and implementation of transactions.

By mid-1987, however, tension was mounting. First Boston's M&A department generated $350 million in fees, but the firm only netted $108 million on $1.3 billion in total revenue. This profit included a one-time $80 million pretax gain from selling the headquarters building. Mr. Wasserstein was reportedly very critical of the firm's direction. He blamed the trading side for the problems and wanted that business eliminated as a profit center. He thought it should function strictly as support for his department's activities. According to press reports, he and Mr. Perella had come close to leaving in early 1987, but Mr. Buchanan soothed their emotions by commissioning a detailed analysis of the firm's direction. In January 1988, Mr. Buchanan reviewed the analysis and, realizing Mr. Wasserstein's recommendations would result in huge layoffs, announced there would be no change in the firm's strategy.

Mr. Fisher's acquaintances in the firm were not much help in interpreting events. They seemed evenly divided between those who were sure Wasserstein and Perella were the backbone of First Boston and those who felt First Boston had competent, albeit not as creative, replacements. Mr. Fisher's acquaintances did indicate that both Perella and Wasserstein had wanted to be invited onto First Boston's executive committee and that Mr. Wasserstein had also pushed for a commitment from top management that he would become president of the firm. Nothing had materialized, however, with respect to their requests. Both were understood to be well compensated, with published rumors suggesting each was being paid about $6 million annually.

Current Industry Environment

First Boston was one of the first major investment banking firms to become a publicly held firm. It took many years, but by 1987 most other major firms in the industry had either become a public entity or had been acquired by a public entity, with one notable exception—Goldman, Sachs. The need for capital prompted these changes. As deals became larger, many firms realized that they could not or would not be able to participate due to the size of their capital bases.

The one element that frequently did not make the transition to a publicly held firm was management. Most of the firms were partnerships steeped in tradition. The partners, however, were not professional managers. With a rapidly changing environment, Mr. Fisher was concerned with the risky decisions these managers faced and with their ability to implement the selected plans.

1987 was a year no one in the industry would forget. First, the M&A experts were nervous about the new tax laws that became effective January 1, 1987. These laws increased the tax liability of sellers and consequently reduced the attractiveness of making acquisitions. Prices had to be higher for the same net proceeds; generating gains over a short holding period was more difficult. Industry analysts anticipated a huge decrease in the number of transactions. As it turned out, if it were not for Black Monday, the volume of transactions as well as the total dollar value of those transactions would have probably matched 1986's record of 4,323 transactions totalling $204 billion. For 1987, the number of transactions decreased to 3,701, and the total dollar value decreased to $168 billion.

Overall profitability, however, was a continuing problem in 1987. In the second quarter, total investment industry pretax earnings had decreased 73 percent from the previous quarter, to $532 million. The second quarter of 1986 had generated pretax earnings of $1.3 billion. Revenues had dipped only 14 percent from the prior quarter to $12.6 billion. Admittedly, these dismal second quarter results were accentuated by a $377 million pretax bond trading loss at Merrill Lynch & Co. and a loss of $100 million reported by First Boston. (The Merrill Lynch loss was due to a mispricing on a mortgage securitization; the First Boston loss was due to trading losses on fixed income securities.) Overall, the third quarter was only slightly better than the second; however, results were mixed. Business had increased in marginally profitable areas, such as trading, but other areas recorded flat or declining sales. Nevertheless, expenses in most firms continued to outpace revenues in the third quarter.

In response to the reduced industry-wide operating profits, many firms had revealed action plans before the October 19, 1987, stock market crash. Staff reductions and cost controls were the items targeted by the industry. Mr. Fisher was increasingly uncomfortable with the rate at which the industry had been hiring. Between the eagerness to expand overseas and the increased activity in the United States, the number of employees and level of compensation had grown astronomically over the years immediately before 1987. By Black Monday, Wall Street had already laid off 1,100 employees, including a total of 900 at Salomon and Kidder, Peabody, and more layoffs were expected. Black Monday served to speed up the pruning process the industry was undertaking. By the end of January 1988, more than 10,000 layoffs either had occurred or had been announced, including 5,000 to 6,000 people targeted by Shearson Lehman after its acquisition of E.F. Hutton.

The departments most under scrutiny were the municipal, corporate, and government bond businesses, money market and commodities operations, and mortgage and real estate brokerage units. The plunging bond market and huge trading losses revealed many unprofitable departments, poor management controls, and the high overhead built up during the rapid expansion in the industry.

The industry's response to diminishing returns was not only evident in its staff and other cost reductions but in increased risk-taking. Merchant banking became the name of the game. In the United States, merchant bankers invested their firms' capital in takeovers and leveraged buy-outs resulting in higher risks but also potentially in higher profits. As competition heated up in this arena, the deals simply got bigger.

The market's crash uncovered one of the risks involved with merchant banking bridge financing. Bridge loans were increasingly provided by the investment banking firms as temporary financing for acquisitions they were working on. These loans were typically refinanced with high-yield bonds, also known as "junk bonds." When the stock prices dropped so dramatically, the loss of equity values behind these loans exposed the firms' capital to potential loss as the loans were refinanced. It was estimated that Salomon Brothers had $600 million in bridge loans outstanding, Kidder, Peabody & Co. had advanced $200 million, and Shearson Lehman was on the hook for $280 million. It was too soon to tell how much money would eventually be lost.

Fortunately, the major firms were not significantly hurt by losses incurred in accounts failing to meet margin calls after the crash, although a subsidiary of Continental Bank in Chicago engaged in clearing option trades lost $90 million, including a loss of $50 million from one customer involved in exceptionally risky investments.

Due to the high number of deals in the pipeline, however, risk arbitrage losses were heavy. (Risk arbitrage was the name given to the process of investing in stocks of companies on both sides of an acquisition.) First Boston lost $60 million in these risky investments. Underwriting losses were widespread. Many firms lost as much as $50 million. Four firms stood to lose $100 million each just from the $12.33 billion underwriting of British Petroleum Co. even after the British government had modified the terms to ameliorate the problems the underwriters faced.

By the time Perella and Wasserstein resigned, the street was full of rumors that other major firms were having similar internal conflicts. Salomon Inc.'s investment bankers were publicly complaining that they did not have enough representation on the firm's board. Investment bankers throughout the industry resented subsidizing the traders. To throw more wood on the fire, the trading losses resulted in smaller year-end bonuses than in the past. With the investment banking side of the business so profitable, especially mergers and acquisitions, top management at the firms had some serious issues to contend with and issues that needed to be resolved quickly before others followed Perella and Wasserstein.

Conclusion

Mr. Fisher took pride in his reputation. He was known to be an industry expert, but the current environment appeared very unstable. He did not know if more M&A experts would leave to form their own firms and, if so, whether the development would significantly depress the future earnings of the full-service companies. After all, Mr. Fisher knew that distribution was very important to the M&A field, and only the larger firms, such as First Boston, had that kind of capability. It would be too expensive for the new M&A "boutiques" to develop their own distribution system. He looked at financial comparatives he had prepared (Exhibits 3, 4, and 5) and wondered if he could find some answers in that information.

There were some strong positive points that made Mr. Fisher feel a bit more comfortable about the industry's prospects. The year 1988 was off to a good start, according to Mr. Fisher's sources at the various firms. Several large M&A deals were apparently in the works. Mr. Fisher was also relieved that the firms were finally being forced to deal with their problems. He knew that if the problems were handled professionally, 1988 would be a better year.

Mr. Fisher expected his company's president to call him within the next couple of days, and Mr. Fisher wanted to tell him confidently whether or not the firm was going to sell its position in First Boston.

Exhibit 1

FIRST BOSTON, INC.

Income Statement for the Years Ended December 31, 1983-1987
(millions except for per share figures)

	1983	1984	1985	1986	1987
Revenues:					
Principal transactions	$ 176.7	$ 196.4	$ 311.9	$ 397.2	$ 211.6
Investment banking	198.0	220.1	383.3	670.4	849.6
Interest and other	140.7	149.3	193.1	242.2	261.1
	$ 515.4	$ 565.8	$ 888.3	$1,309.8	$1,322.3
Expenses:					
Employee compensation	283.3	297.6	472.4	705.6	730.9
Other	123.9	150.8	233.9	359.1	471.8
	$ 407.2	$ 448.4	$ 706.3	$1,064.7	$1,202.7
Income before taxes and Equity in earnings of affiliate*	108.2	117.4	182.0	245.1	119.6
Income taxes	42.4	53.2	73.2	96.9	44.1
Equity in earnings of affiliate	14.4	15.4	21.5	32.4	33.4
Net income	$ 80.2	$ 79.6	$ 130.3	$ 180.6	$ 108.9
Dividends declared	$22.3	$24.7	$27.0	$30.9	$31.9
Shares outstanding (millions)	22.5	24.9	28.6	33.1	33.2
Earnings per share:					
Primary	$3.32	$3.11	$4.29	$5.14	$3.12
Fully diluted	3.06	2.94	4.07	5.01	3.12

* In 1978, First Boston acquired approximately 28 percent of the capital stock of Financiere Credit Suisse-First Boston (FCSFB). Concurrently, FCSFB purchased 1.1 million shares of First Boston, Inc. As of December 31, 1987, First Boston had increased its percentage ownership in FCSFB to 34 percent and FCSFB had increased its ownership in First Boston, Inc. to 40 percent.

Exhibit 2

FIRST BOSTON, INC.

Balance Sheets as of December 31, 1983-1987
(millions of dollars)

	1983	1984	1985	1986	1987
Assets					
Cash and deposits	$ 259.3	$ 419.4	$ 724.0	$ 1,548.2	$ 1,360.0
Trading and investment securities	5,983.5	11,697.2	17,744.0	19,616.1	12,188.9
Resale agreements	8,856.3	10,897.5	18,265.4	20,017.5	19,300.5
Receivables	6,495.9	1,750.8	6,774.0	3,293.3	2,314.9
Other	408.3	531.6	2,023.7	1,085.6	983.3
Total assets	$22,003.3	$25,296.5	$45,531.1	$45,560.7	$36,147.6
Liabilities and Stockholders' Equity					
Loans/Notes payable	$ 1,506.9	$ 2,126.2	$ 3,384.8	$ 3,839.8	$ 2,012.1
Repurchase agreements	9,366.7	15,872.9	22,071.3	24,064.8	25,005.5
Securities sold not yet purchased	5,667.5	4,523.4	10,484.7	10,771.3	2,990.2
Payables	4,822.3	1,725.9	6,051.1	3,761.2	3,284.0
Other	254.1	585.0	2,835.4	2,164.8	1,793.7
Total liabilities	$21,617.5	$24,833.4	$44,827.3	$44,601.9	$35,085.5
Capital stock & surplus	152.7	179.5	312.9	414.9	434.2
Foreign currency translation adj.	(1.1)	(3.0)	(2.9)	(2.1)	2.5
Retained earnings	250.6	305.6	408.8	558.4	635.5
Less: Treasury stock	16.4	19.0	15.0	12.4	10.1
Total equity	$ 385.8	$ 463.1	$ 703.8	$ 958.8	$ 1,062.1
Total liabilities and stockholders' equity	$22,003.3	$25,296.5	$45,531.1	$45,560.7	$36,147.6

Exhibit 3

FIRST BOSTON, INC.

Industry Comparisons
(dollar figures in millions)

First Boston	1983	1984	1985	1986	1987
Total revenue	$1,482	$2,015	$2,452	$3,258	$3,405
Investment banking	$198	$220	$383	$671	$850
(as % of tot. rev.)	15.3%	12.2%	15.6%	20.6%	25.0%
Commission revenue	$72	$75	$85	$123	$183
(as % of tot. rev.)	5.6%	4.2%	3.5%	3.8%	6.0%
Gross divs. & interest	$1,025	$1,508	$1,661	$2,055	$2,146
(as % of tot. rev.)	79.1%	83.6%	67.7%	63.1%	63.0%
Interest expense	$967	$1,449	$1,564	$1,948	$2,083
Net worth	386	463	704	957	1,062
Net income	80	80	130	181	109*
P/E ratio	12.6×	17.6×	10.2×	8.2×	8.0×

12/31/87 Beta: 1.4

*Includes a pretax profit of $80 million from the sale of corporate headquarters.

Merrill Lynch	1983	1984	1985	1986	1987
Total revenue	$5,687	$6,038	$7,117	$9,606	$10,659
Investment banking	$745	$580	$719	$980	$991
(as % of tot. rev.)	13.1%	9.6%	10.1%	10.2%	9.3%
Commission revenue	$1,523	$1,217	$1,582	$2,200	$2,400
(as % of tot. rev.)	26.8%	20.2%	22.2%	22.9%	22.5%
Gross divs. & interest	$1,792	$2,433	$2,565	$3,047	$3,475
(as % of tot. rev.)	31.5%	40.3%	36.0%	31.7%	32.6%
Interest expense	$1,433	$2,109	$2,218	$2,698	$3,031
Net worth	1,888	2,079	2,341	2,876	3,331
Net income	230	95	224	454*	391*
P/E ratio	11.9×	26.2×	15.2×	8.5×	6.3×

12/31/87 Beta: 1.4

*1986 and 1987 include one-time gains of $131.2 million and $192.7 million, respectively.

Exhibit 3 (continued)

FIRST BOSTON, INC.

Morgan Stanley	1983	1984	1985	1986	1987
Total revenue	$860	$1,341	$1,795	$2,464	$3,148
Investment banking	$212	$267	$424	$655	$711
(as % of tot. rev.)	24.7%	19.9%	23.6%	26.6%	22.6%
Commission revenue	$131	$130	$154	$216	$297
(as % of tot. rev.)	15.2%	9.7%	8.6%	8.8%	9.4%
Gross divs. & interest	$415	$795	$938	$1,063	$1,421
(as % of tot. rev.)	48.3%	59.3%	52.3%	43.1%	45.1%
Interest expense	$391	$748	$900	$1,035	$1,380
Net worth	207	238	314	798	1,137
Net income	51	61	106	201	231
P/E ratio		(not traded until 3/86)		8.4×	9.0×

12/31/87 Beta: Not meaningful

PaineWebber	1983	1984	1985	1986	1987
Total revenue	$1,541	$1,553	$1,885	$2,385	$2,437
Investment banking	$237	$166	$207	$293	$273
(as % of tot. rev.)	15.4%	10.7%	11.0%	12.3%	11.2%
Commission revenue	$559	$461	$537	$762	$787
(as % of tot. rev.)	36.3%	29.7%	28.5%	31.9%	32.2%
Gross divs. & interest	$422	$631	$761	$800	$837
(as % of tot. rev.)	27.4%	40.6%	40.3%	33.5%	34.3%
Interest expense	$331	$565	$692	$720	$676
Net worth	322	326	431	633	1,093
Net income	91	13	34	72	75
P/E ratio	1.5×	8.8×	4.0×	2.5×	2.5×

12/31/87 Beta: 1.7

Exhibit 3 (continued)

FIRST BOSTON, INC.

Shearson Lehman	1983	1984	1985	1986	1987
Total revenue	$1,811	$2,262	$4,259	$6,442	$6,228
Investment banking	$386	$423	$613	$865	$684
(as % of tot. rev.)	21.3%	18.7%	14.3%	13.4%	11.0%
Commission revenue	$598	$536	$712	$914	$1,118
(as % of tot. rev.)	33.0%	23.7%	16.7%	14.2%	18.0%
Gross divs. & interest	$351	$584	$1,886	$3,206	$3,129
(as % of tot. rev.)	19.4%	25.8%	44.3%	49.8%	50.2%
Interest expense	$206	$467	$1,729	$3,024	$2,892
Net worth	710	949	1,177	1,358	1,742
Net income	174	105	151	338	169
P/E ratio		(not traded until 5/87)			17.0×

12/31/87 Beta: Not meaningful

Salomon Inc.	1983	1984	1985	1986	1987
Total revenue	$3,123	$4,039	$5,701	$6,789	$6,003
Investment banking	N/A	N/A	N/A	N/A	N/A
(as % of tot. rev.)	—	—	—	—	—
Commission revenue	N/A	N/A	N/A	N/A	N/A
(as % of tot. rev.)	—	—	—	—	—
Gross divs. & interest	N/A	N/A	N/A	N/A	N/A
(as % of tot. rev.)	—	—	—	—	—
Interest expense	$N/A	$2,504	$3,622	$4,484	$3,965
Net worth	2,240	2,406	2,954	3,454	3,481
Net income	470	212	557	516	142
P/E ratio	9.5×	21.6×	11.5×	11.1×	22.8×

12/31/87 Beta: 1.7

Exhibit 4

FIRST BOSTON, INC.

Industry Five-Year Merger Completion Record
1983-1987

	Number of Transactions	% Change	$ Value (in millions)	% Change	$ Value/Number (in millions)
1983	2,387	–	$ 52,579.7	–	$ 22.0
1984	3,158	+ 32.3%	125,986.3	+ 139.6%	39.9
1985	3,428	+ 8.6	145,397.8	+ 15.4	42.4
1986	4,323	+ 26.1	204,438.9	+ 40.6	47.3
1987	3,701	- 14.4	167,519.2	- 18.1	45.3

	Number of $2+ Bill. Transactions	Largest transaction (in millions)
1983	1	$ 2,300
1984	7	13,300
1985	10	5,670
1986	10	6,250
1987	9	7,995

Exhibit 5
FIRST BOSTON, INC.
Industry Four-Year U.S. Underwriting Record
(Full Credit to Lead Manager)
1984-1987

	1984		1985	
	$ Value (in billions)	No. of Issues	$ Value (in billions)	No. of Issues
Salomon	$ 23	185	$ 30	279
First Boston	10	122	21	265
Goldman, Sachs	8	77	15	134
Merrill Lynch	9	102	14	174
Morgan Stanley	5	59	9	94
Drexel Burnham	11	107	12	172
Shearson Lehman*	7	93	9	157
Kidder, Peabody	2	44	4	79
Bear Stearns	1	24	1	35
Prudential-Bache	2	34	1	42
Total other	20	N/A	22	733
Total	$ 96**	N/A	$138	2,164

	1986		1987	
	$ Value (in billions)	No. of Issues	$ Value (in billions)	No. of Issues
Salomon	$ 49	429	$ 40	328
First Boston	44	398	37	254
Goldman, Sachs	29	252	34	298
Merrill Lynch	29	293	32	291
Morgan Stanley	28	249	30	303
Drexel Burnham	30	260	20	213
Shearson Lehman	16	259	20	251
Kidder, Peabody	10	189	10	139
Bear Stearns	4	85	5	76
Prudential-Bache	4	77	5	81
Total other	43	1,274	38	977
Total	$286	3,765	$271	3,211

*In May 1984, Shearson merged with Lehman Brothers. For the purposes of this presentation, the transactions prior to the merger have been added to the postmerger activities for that year.

**Estimated. Sources of 1985-1987 data, *Institutional Investor* (various issues).

Exhibit 5 (continued)

FIRST BOSTON, INC.

Industry Four-Year International Underwriting Record
(Full Credit to Lead Manager)
1984-1987

	1984*		1985*	
	$ Value (in billions)	No. of Issues	$ Value (in billions)	No. of Issues
Nomura Securities	$ 5	49	$ 8	86
CSFB/First Boston	14	84	21	119
Daiwa Securities	2	36	4	47
Nikko Securities	2	25	3	43
Deutsche Bank	6	60	10	79
Yamaichi Securities	2	27	3	39
Goldman, Sachs	2	26	7	52
Union Bank of Switzerland	2	31	6	60
Morgan Stanley	5	44	8	76
Salomon	7	36	11	83
Total Other	49	N/A	85	1,018
Total	$ 96	N/A	$166	1,702

	1986		1987	
	$ Value (in billions)	No. of Issues	$ Value (in billions)	No. of Issues
Nomura Securities	$ 17	146	$ 20	131
CSFB/First Boston	21	127	15	146
Daiwa Securities	10	94	9	83
Nikko Securities	6	60	9	64
Deutsche Bank	15	91	8	75
Yamaichi Securities	5	62	8	75
Goldman, Sachs	5	34	8	42
Union Bank of Switzerland	8	82	7	58
Morgan Stanley	11	96	6	59
Salomon	10	65	6	56
Total Other	112	N/A	85	N/A
Total	$220	N/A	$181	N/A

*1984 and 1985 include only bond underwritings.

Notes

Case 12: PRIMERICA CORPORATION

As chairman of the board of Primerica Corporation, Gerald Tsai, Jr., had overseen one of the most radical corporate transformations in modern business history. He had changed American Can Company from a container manufacturer and retail-store operator into a service conglomerate in the insurance, brokerage, and retailing businesses, as shown in Exhibit 1. In July 1987, the newly named Primerica Corporation had purchased Smith Barney, Harris Upham & Company, Inc., a major retail investment banking firm, further deepening Primerica's commitment to the financial service industry. By February 1988, however the situation had changed.

Primerica's future was devastated by the stock market crash of October 19, 1987. Its stock had been trading at a price of $48 per share the week of October 16, 1987, but the price had fallen to $21.75 by early December. The crash came immediately after Primerica had finished implementing its acquisition strategy, and debt was a comparatively high percentage of the company's capital structure. Primerica's share price had rebounded modestly to $28.25 by the third week in February 1988, but Mr. Tsai could hardly be satisfied with the market's perception of the worth of his company. The 1987 annual report stated, "Primerica is dedicated to a primary purpose—to maximize shareholder value," yet the value of the company's shares had declined by over 40 percent since October.

Mr. Tsai's ability to react to the changes in the financial markets was limited by Primerica's relative financial inflexibility. Much of the company's debt had been taken on to finance acquisitions, yet the value of the acquisitions had plummeted on October 19. The company's announced long-term plan was to continue to expand its financial service businesses, purchase new businesses, and divest itself of its retail operations. Thus, the company was in a "catch 22": it had to raise cash by selling nonstrategic businesses to reduce its leverage and to fund internal growth; but its method of raising cash, by selling off business units, had been devalued by the market's crash.

Would selling a nonstrategic subsidiary increase the stock price of the parent if the price received for the subsidiary was what the market had expected? If the answer to this question was "no," then Primerica's selling of a subsidiary would not affect the share price. However, if the market was undervaluing Primerica's assets, then the selling of assets would result in a per-share value greater than the present market value of the shares.

This case was prepared from public information.

There were rumors on Wall Street that Mr. Tsai was considering either taking the company private with a leveraged buy-out (LBO) or selling the company to a third party. An additional alternative was to sell off the company in pieces, if that would bring larger total proceeds. These options all implied that management thought the assets were undervalued.

Thus, the issues were:

1. Was Primerica's value being properly represented in its share price, or was the company worth more than the markets perceived?

2. What was the debt/equity ratio needed to maximize shareholder value?

3. How could Primerica raise cash most efficiently to fund its growing business, pay back debt (if so desired), and, most importantly, maximize shareholder value?

Many issues complicated each of the alternatives, not the least probably being the natural desire of Mr. Tsai to keep his reputation intact as one of the most astute financial strategists of the generation.

Financial Highlights of 1987

Primerica's financial strategy evolved in calendar year 1987 with the changes in the financial markets. In the early (precrash) part of the year, Primerica sold a minority interest in one of its subsidiaries to the public to take advantage of the relatively high multiples in the stock market. The company also assumed a significant amount of debt in July 1987 to purchase Smith Barney. After October 19, however, Primerica was primarily interested in reducing its debt load. (Exhibits 2 through 5 present recent financial information for Primerica.)

Before the stock market crash, Primerica also offered for sale the partial ownership of two of its subsidiaries: a minority share of its equity in American Capital Management & Research, Inc. (ACM&R), in March 1986, and approximately 19 percent of its 100 percent ownership in The Musicland Group, in February 1987. ACM&R was currently trading on the New York Stock Exchange (NYSE) at $13 a share; Primerica owned 20.2 million shares, about 83 percent of ACM&R's outstanding shares. Primerica kept 82.1 percent of Musicland's shares, 9.147 million shares, which were currently trading at $33 a share on the NYSE.

In early 1987, Primerica authorized a two-for-one stock split in the form of a 100 percent stock dividend. This move caused the price of the firm's shares to drop by one-half while doubling the number of shares outstanding. In addition, the company completed the repurchase of six million shares that had been authorized by the board of directors in the third quarter of 1986. In November 1987, the board authorized the repurchase of an additional five million shares.

Following the stock market crash and after publishing its year-end financial statements, Primerica announced in January 1988 its intention to form a new company with the A.L. Williams Corporation. A.L. Williams had one of the largest insurance sales forces in the country, with over 180,000 agents. It specialized in selling term life insurance. Primerica would acquire 69.8 percent of the new firm in exchange for its wholly owned subsidiary, Massachusetts Indemnity and Life Insurance Company (MILICO). A.L. Williams would receive the balance of the stock in exchange for its outstanding shares. In effect, Primerica would be giving up 30.2 percent of MILICO to acquire 69.8 percent of the A.L. Williams Corporation.

To reduce its $2 billion debt, in 1987 Primerica sold its subsidiary, Looart Press, Inc., for $180 million. The company also sold substantially all of its remaining timberlands for about $85 million.

According to the 1987 annual report, it was Primerica's "intention to divest additional nonstrategic assets in order to enhance our future position, and to allow us to focus on future growth." Thus, in February 1988, Primerica sold its common stock investment in Triangle Industries, Inc., for $124 million in cash. (Triangle Industries had purchased the old core business, the can operations.) Also in February (after the financial statements had been prepared), "Primerica signed an agreement in principle which would result in the sale of its remaining interest in The Musicland Group to a group of investors for approximately $330 million." The Musicland Group represented substantially all of Primerica's specialty retailing revenues and operating income. The sale would cause an after-tax gain of about $130 million, or $2.50 per common share, in the second quarter of 1988. Primerica stated in its annual report, "We plan to use the net proceeds to reduce debt." Many analysts wanted to examine the transaction to see whether Primerica had received a fair price for the subsidiary or had sold the subsidiary under "fire sale" pressures.

Smith Barney Acquisition

Primerica purchased Smith Barney for $750 million in July 1987. In retrospect, the timing could not have been less fortunate. Smith Barney's risk arbitrage group suffered heavy losses on October 19, resulting in an operating loss of $93 million for the year and effectively raising the purchase price of the firm to Primerica. The October market disruption also damaged Smith Barney's future profit potential. The firm was heavily dependent on its retail accounts to generate revenue. After the crash, retail volume fell off dramatically.

Market rumors hinted at a general dissatisfaction with Mr. Tsai at Smith Barney. The dismissal of the entire risk arbitrage department insured there would be no other trading losses, but the decision was resented by the Smith Barney employees as an inappropriate response. Mr. Tsai's unwillingness to commit the capital of the organization to support merger and acquisition transactions was taken as symbolic of a lack of commitment to the firm. The profitability of Smith Barney was unaffected, but morale was reportedly depressed because the employees believed that Mr. Tsai did not plan to support the organization's growth.

Methods to Raise Cash

Primerica needed to raise cash to fund its growing businesses. This task had been done historically, at least partially, by selling assets and unwanted subsidiaries. At this point, additional options had to be considered.

Raise Equity

The equity markets had not recovered significantly since the stock market crash. More importantly, the share price of Primerica was significantly lower than its precrash value. If Primerica issued new shares, it would be offering equity at the worst possible time, the low point of the market. Raising equity remained a possibility, however, if the company wanted to maintain its debt-equity ratio and pursue other financial-service acquisitions.

Another factor weighing against raising equity was that it would further dilute the earnings of the company. Dilution could have the effect of lowering, not raising, the stock price unless, of course, the money raised through an offering could be used to acquire an "undervalued" asset.

Sell Smith Barney

After the October crash a rumor started that Mr. Tsai was considering selling the firm. Later rumors suggested that he had been unable to interest prospective buyers in paying anywhere near the $750 million purchase price Primerica had paid. (Exhibit 6 contains information on firms in the investment banking industry.) Smith Barney was apparently going to post a $15 million profit before tax in the first quarter of 1988.

The first of many issues that complicated the potential sale of Smith Barney was the general debate on whether it would be possible to sell such a people-intensive business twice in one year. First, the purchaser would have to deal with the unrest at the firm. To stabilize the situation, a potential purchaser would at least have to convince the employees that it would support the firm with needed capital, would pay competitive wages and bonuses, and would allow the managing directors the needed autonomy. Second, a sale of Smith Barney for less than $750 million would cause Primerica to post a loss before taxes. If this was classified as a capital loss, it would not be allowed as a write-off for tax purposes against ordinary income. Finally, a sale at a loss might indicate that Mr. Tsai had made a poor business decision, which he might be reluctant to make evident so clearly.

Sell Other Subsidiaries

Primerica's rapid diversification and subsequent acquisition spree left it with a group of companies run independently by their respective CEOs. Primerica had announced in late 1987 that it was considering selling its catalog companies, and it had already disposed of one subsidiary. The remaining companies, Fingerhut, Figi's, and Michigan Bulb, generated over $1 billion in revenues for Primerica. (Exhibits 7 and 8 contain information on retailing and mail-order firms.)

Primerica had two ways to sell its subsidiaries: it could either "spin off" the subsidiary through an initial public offering (IPO) or it could sell the division in its entirety to another company or to management through an LBO. "Spinning off" subsidiaries through a stock offering was questionable for the same reasons that Primerica's own equity offering would not be attractive: the market was viewed to be at a low point. However, because Primerica now owned an investment bank, the cost of an IPO would be reduced.

The outright sale of a division or of multiple divisions could be attractive to Primerica. Many of the divisions could be sold for prices that would far exceed what Primerica had paid for them and at multiples of earnings well above Primerica's own price-earnings ratio. However, if Primerica was forced to sell off an insurance division to reach a targeted debt structure, the action might be perceived by the financial markets as retrenching. (Data on the insurance industry are provided in Exhibit 9.) The difficulty in this evaluation was trying to calculate the market's appetite for each division. Who would be willing to pay, and what kind of premium would they pay, for a mail-order catalog business? for insurance companies? Most important, would the sales bring in enough cash to allow Primerica to reach its target debt structure and expand its remaining businesses? Maybe it would be easier, and more cost effective, given the potential disruptions in the subsidiaries, to sell the company as one entity.

Issue Debentures or Take the Company Private (LBO)

In March 1988, a rumor circulated that Mr. Tsai was considering taking Primerica private. As with all LBOs, this would entail levering up the company substantially and using the proceeds to buy out the existing shareholders. The questions in the minds of investors were whether Mr. Tsai was serious and whether an LBO was possible. Many doubted that Primerica's underlying assets could support the debt needed for an LBO. The company was already substantially levered.

Sell the Entire Company

Mr. Tsai had also had highly confidential discussions with Mr. Sandy Weill, chairman of the board of Commercial Credit Corporation (CCC) and former head of Shearson Lehman Brothers (owned by American Express), about selling Smith Barney to CCC. Recently, however, Mr. Weill had proposed a merger of both organizations. As proposed, the merger would be a sale of Primerica to CCC through a stock swap. There appeared to be a good match between CCC's cash-generating businesses and Primerica's growth businesses.

CCC had gone public late in 1986. Its strategy was to provide broad financial services to consumers and select insurance products to the commercial market. Consequently, the company had divested or closed several companies and product lines such as vehicle leasing, group health, and certain life-insurance products. CCC's stock was trading at about $27, having risen from $23 early in 1988. Summary financial information is provided in Exhibit 10.

The amount of stock to be exchanged had yet to be established, so the value of Primerica had to be determined. If Primerica's value was, for example, $60 per share, it might not be financially feasible for CCC to effect a merger.

Other Considerations

Mr. Tsai was also said to be going through a personal metamorphosis. He had recently married and was said not to be spending as much time at the office as he once had. Instead, he was spending time with his wife and enjoying activities for which he had not had time when he was putting in 80-hour weeks in the 1960s and 1970s. Primerica was probably the last stage of a long and successful career that Mr. Tsai undoubtedly wanted to end on a high note.

The senior management at Primerica was rumored to have lucrative "golden parachutes" in place. If the rumors were true, a sale of the entire entity would be the most financially attractive alternative for the personal financial positions of the senior officers. The question was whether this alternative would be in the best interests of the shareholders.

Although interest rates dropped temporarily following the October 1987 market break, they quickly recovered. Ninety-day Treasury bills had been averaging 5.7 percent and long-term Treasury bonds were yielding 8.4 percent to 8.5 percent during the December 1987-February 1988 period.

Exhibit 1
PRIMERICA CORPORATION
Business Segments

	Acquired	Price (millions)
A. Financial Services Businesses		
I. Insurance		
Pennsylvania Life Insurance Company and affiliates; Massachusetts Indemnity and Life Insurance Company (wholly owned as of 12/31/87 but involved in the A. L. Williams transaction. Major subsidiaries include Trans Pacific Life Insurance Company and Executive Fund Life Insurance Company, originally part of Penn. Life Co.)	1/83	$295
Transport Life Insurance Company	9/82	$152
National Benefit Life Insurance and Triad Life Insurance Corporation	4/82	$127
Voyager Group, Inc.	9/83	$ 45
A. L. Williams (majority ownership acquired 2/88)	9/83	$ 38*
II. Mutual Fund and Asset Management		
American Capital Management & Research (83% owned by Primerica)		
RCM Capital Management	6/86	Joint Venture
III. Mortgage Banking	5/85	$125
Berg Enterprises, Inc.		
Margaretten & Company, Inc. (sub. of Berg)	7/87	$750
IV. Investment Banking & Securities Brokerage		
Smith Barney, Harris Upham & Company, Inc.		
B. Specialty Retailing Businesses	1978	$137
I. Direct-Mail Marketing		
Fingerhut Corporation		
Figi's, Inc.	1981	$ 23.5
Michigan Bulb Company	1984	$ 22
II. Specialty Stores	1977-	$103**
The Musicland Group, Inc. (Pickwick & Sam Goody) (81.8% owned by Primerica as of 12/31/87)	1978	
Dunham's Athleisure Corporation	2/85	$ 11

*In 1986, sold 17% of ACM&R to public for $79.2 million. The cost basis was $9.9 million.

**In 1987, Musicland sold shares of common stock for $36 million. Primerica's ownership was thereby reduced by 82%, and Primerica recorded a pretax gain of $15.2 million.

Exhibit 2
PRIMERICA CORPORATION
Income Statement for the Years Ended December 31, 1984-1987
(millions of dollars except per-share amounts)

	1984	1985	1986	1987
Revenues				
Insurance, mutual funds, asset management, and mortgage banking	$1,045	$1,280	$1,464	$1,589
Investment banking and securities brokerage	—	—	—	399
Specialty retailing	995	1,156	1,380	1,696
Other businesses	313	40	43	78
Total revenues	$2,353	$2,476	$2,887	$3,762
Operating Costs and Expenses				
Insurance, mutual funds, asset management, and mortgage banking	888	1,100	1,178	1,324
Investment banking and securities brokerage	—	—	—	492
Specialty retailing	923	1,054	1,270	1,529
Other businesses	312	30	30	23
Total operating costs and expenses	$2,123	$2,184	$2,478	$3,368
Business operating income	$ 230	$ 292	$ 409	$ 394
Corporate Expenses	70	68	91	54
Interest expense and other, net	82	83	99	114
Net operating income	$ 78	$ 141	$ 219	$ 226
Gain (loss) on sale or issuance of stock of subsidiaries and equity investments	(1)	33	70	69
Income from continuing operations before income taxes and minority interests	$ 77	$ 174	$ 289	$ 295
Provision (benefit) for income taxes	(9)	72	64	87
Income from cont. operations before minority interests	$ 86	$ 102	$ 225	$ 208
Discontinued operations, net of taxes	46	47	33	—
Minority interests, net of income taxes	—	—	(5)	(9)
Income from cont. operations before extraordinary items	$ 132	$ 149	$ 253	$ 199
Extraordinary items	4	—	(23)	—
Cumulative effect of change in accounting for taxes	—	(60)	—	—
Net Income	$ 136	$ 89	$ 230	$ 199
Dividends on preferred stock	26	26	21	20
Net income applicable to common stock	$ 110	$ 63	$ 209	$ 179
Earnings per share (diluted) from continuing operations	$ 1.35	$ 1.51	$ 3.44	$ 3.16
EPS from net income	$ 2.32	$ 1.26	$ 3.60	$ 3.16

Exhibit 3

PRIMERICA CORPORATION

Statements of Financial Position as of December 31, 1986 and 1987
(millions)

	1986	1987
Assets		
Cash and short-term investments	$ 209	$ 236
Insurance, mutual funds, asset management, and mortgage banking:		
Investments	1,671	1,882
Receivables, net	272	243
First mortgage loans held for sale	591	420
Value of insurance in force	219	222
Deferred policy acquisition costs	592	779
Other assets	342	362
	$3,687	$ 3,908
Investment banking and securities brokerage:		
Cash and securities segregated under federal and other brokerage regulations	—	50
Securities purchased under agreements to resell	—	2,701
Receivables from customers	—	922
Receivables from brokers and dealers	—	818
Trading securities owned, at market value	—	2,501
Other assets	—	290
		$ 7,282
Specialty retailing:		
Receivables, net	352	275
Inventories	217	236
Other assets	227	163
	$ 796	$ 674
Cost of acquired businesses in excess of net assets	387	748
Other assets	271	371
Total Assets	$5,350	$13,219

Exhibit 3 (continued)

	1986	1987
Liabilities		
Policy liabilities and accruals	$1,124	$1,297
Notes payable, principally collateralized by first mortgage loans	574	429
Short-term brokerage borrowings	—	1,009
Securities sold under agreements to repurchase	—	2,956
Payables to brokerage customers	—	504
Payables to brokers and dealers	—	811
Trading securities sold not yet purchased, at market	—	1,081
Accounts payable and other liabilities	1,271	1,525
Debt obligations	665	1,998*
Deferred income taxes	227	155
Total Liabilities	$3,861	$11,765
Redeemable preferred stock	163	150
Common Shareholders' Equity		
Common stock (issued: 1987—59,770,848 shares; 1986—58,087,278 shares)	58	60
Capital in excess of par value	622	658
Net unrealized depreciation of equity securities	(9)	(40)
Cumulative translation adjustments	(2)	3
Earnings reinvested	797	891
Treasury stock, at cost (1987—8,662,270; 1986—4,624,446 shares)	(140)	(268)
Total Stockholders' Equity	$1,326	$ 1,304
Total Liabilities and Equity	$5,350	$13,219

*Primerica's cost of debt was 9.7% in 1987.

Exhibit 4
PRIMERICA CORPORATION
Statements of Changes in Financial Position, Years Ended December 31, 1985-1987
(millions of dollars)

	1985	1986	1987
Operations			
Income from continuing operations before extraordinary items and cumulative effect of a change in accounting for income taxes	$101	$221	$199
Charges and credits to income not affecting funds:			
Increase in policy liabilities and accruals and other policyholder funds	156	137	172
Amortization of value of insurance in force and deferred policy acquisition costs	169	183	228
Deferred income taxes	87	29	78
Depreciation	30	35	45
Other, primarily nonrecurring items and realized gains on investments	(14)	(122)	(93)
	$530	$483	$629
Increase in securities purchased under agreements to resell, net of securities sold under agreements to repurchase	—	—	102
Trading securities, net	—	—	(338)
Additions to deferred policy acquisition costs	(295)	(313)	(397)
Changes in:			
Receivables	(85)	(81)	75
Inventories	(10)	(43)	(35)
Accounts payable and other liabilities	94	38	(105)
Payables to broker and dealers, net of receivables	—	—	(31)
Payables to brokerage customers, net of receivables	—	—	286
Other	(63)	57	(82)
Funds provided by continuing operations	**$171**	**$141**	**$104**
Investment Activities			
Business acquisitions	(135)	(154)	(760)
Business divestments	19	491	242
Sale or maturity of investments	538	461	784
Purchases and increases in investments	(785)	(795)	(1,100)
Sale of corporate headquarters	—	151	—
Sale of subsidiary headquarters building	—	—	23
Sale or issuance of subsidiary common stock	—	79	36
Sale of remaining interest in James River Corporation	161	—	—
Additions to property, equipment, and leasehold improvements	(44)	(49)	(68)
Funds (used) provided by investment activities	**($246)**	**$184**	**($845)**
Financing Activities			
Dividends paid	(96)	(102)	(105)
Issuances of common stock	160	23	13
Redemption of redeemable preferred stock	—	(31)	—
Purchases of treasury stock	(2)	(77)	(148)
Debt transactions:			
Proceeds from debt obligations	231	239	1,241
Reductions of debt obligations	(77)	(408)	(99)
Net change in short-term brokerage borrowings	—	—	(162)
Other	4	(22)	27
Funds (used) provided by financing activities	**$221**	**($378)**	**$767**
Net funds (used) provided by discontinued operation	31	(10)	—
Change in cash and short-term investments	**$177**	**($ 63)**	**$ 26**

Exhibit 5
PRIMERICA CORPORATION
Business Segment Analysis
(in millions of dollars except per-share amounts)

	1986	1987
Revenues by Source		
Insurance premiums	$1,052	$ 1,148
Net investment income	156	196
Mutual fund management fees and sales commissions	129	121
Mortgage banking and other	127	124
	$1,464	$ 1,589
Investment banking and securities brokerage	—	399
Direct-mail marketing	904	1,111
Specialty retailing stores	476	585
Other businesses	43	78
	$1,423	$ 2,173
Total revenue	$2,877	$ 3,762
Business Operating Income		
Life insurance	159	183
Insurance, mutual funds, asset management, and mortgage banking	129	82
Investment banking and securities brokerage	—	(93)
Specialty retailing	111	167
Other businesses	12	55
Total business operating income	$ 409	$ 394
Asset Composition		
Insurance, mutual funds, asset management, and mortgage banking	3,940	4,159
Investment banking and securities brokerage	—	7,717
Specialty retailing	929	735
Other businesses	41	11
Corporate	441	597
Total assets	$5,351	$13,219
Depreciation		
Insurance, mutual funds, asset management, and mortgage banking	13	13
Investment banking and securities	—	10
Specialty retailing	13	17
Other businesses	4	1
Corporate	6	4
Total depreciation	$ 35	$ 45

Exhibit 6
PRIMERICA CORPORATION
Comparable Investment Banks, Fiscal Year Ended Closest to December 1987
(dollars in millions except per-share figures)

Firm	Rev. (1)	Net Inc. (2)	EPS (3)	Beta (4)	P/E Ratio (5)	Annual % Chng Mkt. Pr. (6)	Mkt. ÷ Bk. (7)	Int. Exp. (8)	Depn. (9)	Income Before Tax (10)	Shrs. Outs. (11)	MP/ Share (12)	D/E (13)
Merrill Lynch	$10,868	$391	$3.50	1.05	9.15×	(25)%	.84×	$3,031	$250	$429.0	104.6	$27.88	1.58×
Shearson Lehman	6,228	151	1.18	.81	*n.a.	(19)	*n.a.	3,159	151	153.0	85.6	*n.a.	2.15
Salomon, Inc.	6,003	142	1.08	1.45	20.19	(23)	.99	3,965	40	225.0	131.5	26.38	.37
Morgan Stanley	3,148	231	9.33	1.25	5.95	(3)	1.63	1,380	39	364.2	23.8	81.00	.52
Paine Webber	2,437	72	2.48	1.08	20.49	(45)	.47	676	22	110.3	29.0	17.25	.32
Bear Stearns	1,888	143	1.75	.99	7.61	(35)	.94	550	17	329.0	81.5	10.39	.38
First Boston	1,322	109	3.41	.77	12.97	12	1.46	2,083	35	119.6	32.3	48.75	.40
A. G. Edwards	505	36	1.76	1.15	14.96	(28)	1.46	3	10	56.5	20.4	15.50	-0-
Alex Brown	298	21	1.29	1.77	17.89	(41)	1.00	26	3	38.1	15.8	10.50	.15
Industry averages (includes other companies)				.91	12.1		1.58						.12
5-year high					13.2								
5-year low					7.5								

*in the process of a merger.

Other valuation multiple: Industry average, Price per share ÷ Revenue per share = .32

Column Content, Exhibits 6-9 (except as noted):

(1) Revenues
(2) Net income
(3) Earnings per share on a fully diluted basis
(4) Beta
(5) Price per share ÷ earnings per share
(6) Percent change in market price over the company's fiscal year
(7) Total market price of the company ÷ total book value of the company
(8) Interest expense
(9) Depreciation
(10) Income before tax
(11) Number of shares outstanding
(12) Price per share
(13) Debt to equity. Debt is defined as total liabilities less accruals, payables, repos, and short-term payables.

Exhibit 7

PRIMERICA CORPORATION

Comparable Retail Companies
(dollars in millions except per-share figures)

Firm	Rev. (1)	Net Inc. (2)	EPS (3)	Beta (4)	P/E Ratio (5)	Annual % Chng Mkt. Pr. (6)	Mkt.÷Bk. (7)	Int. Exp. (8)	Depn. (9)	Income Before Tax (10)	Shrs. Outs. (11)	MP/ Share (12)	D/E (13)
Sears	$48,440	$1,649	$4.35	1.27	9.48x	n/a%	1.06×	$2,716	560	$1,931	379	$43.25	.70×
Kmart	25,627	692	3.40	1.44	10.76	n/a	1.75	308	401	1,171	199	38.00	.27
Wal-Mart	15,959	628	1.11	1.30	22.10	(6)	8.08	114	166	1,069	565	31.13	.08
J.C. Penney	15,332	608	4.41	1.32	10.86	(5)	1.60	300	241	925	132	53.63	.62
Dayton Hudson	10,677	228	2.68	1.43	16.58	(28)	1.77	152	231	743	150	42.13	.85
May	10,581	444	2.98	1.57	12.87	(6)	2.07	113	0	530	89	36.25	.45
Woolworth	7,134	251	3.90	1.49	13.89	18	2.08	51	147	406	66	52.87	.29
Best	2,067	30	1.23	.93	34.20	102	1.22	46	64	48	25	26.25	.63
Family Dollar	565	25	.86	1.40	16.49	25	2.69	0	9	47	3	16.25	.05
Industry averages (includes other companies)				1.38	17.70		2.97						.55
5-year high					21.40								
5-year low					11.50								

Other valuation multiple: Industry average, Price per share÷Revenue per share = .56

Exhibit 8

PRIMERICA CORPORATION

Comparable Mail-Order Companies
(dollars in millions except per-share figures)

Firm	Rev. (1)	Net Inc. (2)	EPS (3)	Beta (4)	P/E Ratio (5)	Annual % Chng Mkt. Pr. (6)	Mkt.÷Bk. (7)	Increase in Sales (8)	Int. Exp. (9)	Income Before Tax (10)	Shrs. Outs. (11)	MP/ Share (12)	D/E (13)
Spiegel	$927	$49*	$1.28	.94	9.90×	(36)%	2.08×	6.3%	$40.0	$72	38.5	$9.88	1.79×
New Process	363	23	2.42	.54	11.70	30	3.70	.8	0	40	9.4	38.88	n.a.
Lands' End	336	22	1.10	1.44	22.71	26	10.50	26.9	1.4	38	20.0	25.13	.08
Medco Cont.	283	12	.69	1.53	30.87	(2)	3.59	108.2	3.9	34	42.3	12.88	.08
Inmac Corp.	165	8	.86	1.83	13.73	(44)	3.81	33.0	.7	15	9.0	13.75	-0-
Sharper Image	151	6	.68	1.77	14.24	(33)	2.07	32.9	0	10	8.3	6.38	-0-
Williams Sonoma	137	3	.87	.30	26.20	8	3.90	36.3	1.6	5.8	4.0	21.00	.32
Lillian Vernon	126	3	.53	1.20	8.02	(22)	1.81	8.9	0	11.3	8.3	6.38	-0-
Industry averages				.55	18.9		2.58						.44
5-year high					18.9								
5-year low					10.4								

Other valuation multiple: Industry average, Price per share÷Revenue per share = .58

* Net income before extraordinary items and after tax was $41 million.

Note: Column 8 lists revenue growth over the previous fiscal year and Column 9 lists interest expense.

Exhibit 9

PRIMERICA CORPORATION

Comparable Insurance Companies
(dollars in millions except per-share figures)

Firm	Rev. (1)	Net Inc. (2)	EPS (3)	Beta (4)	P/E Ratio (5)	Annual % Chng Mkt. Pr. (6)	Mkt. ÷ Bk. (7)	Int. Exp. (8)	Depn. (9)	Income Before Tax (10)	Shrs. Outs. (11)	MP/ Share (12)	D/E (13)
Aetna Life	$22,114	$921	$7.95	.81	7.89×	(14)%	.92x	$77.9	n.a.	984.8	113.63	$50.38	.12×
Transamerica	7,175	427	5.67	1.02	7.36	(14)	1.01	325.4	132.0	429.0	75.37	34.25	2.62
American General	7,157	563	4.34	.86	9.14	(7)	.97	334.0	n.a.	661.0	146.92	39.75	1.57
Kemper	3,669	251	4.32	.87	8.13	(13)	.93	61.0	n.a.	242.8	58.24	25.00	.09
Capital Holding	3,351	172	1.59	1.03	9.24	0	.71	43.7	17.23	229.1	47.19	32.25	.23
Jefferson Pilot	1,052	148	3.75	1.01	15.04	(2)	1.12	0	32.8	129.9	39.35	34.00	.20
Northwestern Ntl.	2,052	38	1.64	.44	7.37	13	.87	0	37.6	53.9	11.20	33.75	.40
USLife Corp.	1,189	80	n.a.	1.06	9.78	1	.72	35.4	9.1	112.0	24.97	26.75	.28
Independent Ins.	456	29	4.36	.46	8.87	(12)	.71						
Industry averages (includes other companies)				.74	11.30		.95						.12
5-year high					11.90								
5-year low					7.60								

Other valuation multiple: Industry average, Price per share ÷ revenue per share = .32

Exhibit 10

PRIMERICA CORPORATION

Summary Financial Information of Commercial Credit Corporation

	December 31		
	1985	1986	1987
(in millions)			
Revenues	$ 963.0	$1,020.9	$ 912.3
Net earnings	(4.8)	45.9	23.7
Assets	6,370.0	4,827.8	4,306.4
Total liabilities	5,529.4	3,877.8	3,660.0
Equity	840.6	950.0	646.4
(per share)			
Earnings from continuing opns.	$ –	$ 0.95	$ 2.00
Earnings from discontinued opns.	(0.13)	0.22	(1.52)
Net earnings	(0.13)	1.17	0.48

Notes

Case 13: FIRST WACHOVIA CORPORATE FINANCE GROUP

Samuel Tallman, senior vice president and group executive in charge of the Corporate Finance Group (CFG) of First Wachovia Corporation, was reviewing results of a new loan-participation program. By February 1989, the program, a corporate-finance product introduced in the summer of 1988, had been in operation for six months. Because this product was the first one developed and introduced by the newly organized CFG, Mr. Tallman was interested in both the product's relative success and the lessons to be learned from its first six months.

First Wachovia Corporation

First Wachovia Corporation was one of the largest regional bank holding companies in the United States and one of the dominant banks in its primary market, the Southeast. Formed in 1985 by the merger of First Atlanta Corporation of Atlanta, Georgia, and Wachovia Corporation of Winston-Salem, North Carolina, First Wachovia was the 29th largest bank holding company in the nation. At the end of 1987, its assets totaled $19.3 billion.

Known for its conservative lending practices and high-quality middle-market customer base, First Wachovia was well regarded by Wall Street analysts. The bank enjoyed an average price-earnings ratio of 12.1 times in 1987 and 8.8 times in 1988 (compared with an industry average of 6.4 times for that year). Its market price averaged 1.38 times its book value. The holding company's return on assets had increased to 1.12 percent in 1988 from .91 percent in 1987. Return on equity was 15.7 percent, up from 13.6 percent.

As a result of the market's favorable view, First Wachovia enjoyed one of the highest market-price capitalizations of any major bank holding company. First Wachovia's management viewed its reputation and high market capitalization as important assets to be safeguarded. Among the bank's specific strengths that were significant for its corporate-finance work were its correspondent-bank network (the largest in the Southeast), its position as the largest bond and money-market dealer in the Southeast, and its strong cash-management business.

First Wachovia had a strong position with the upper end of the corporate middle market in the Southeast, a highly competitive area because of the other large, aggressive super-regional banks in the region. First Wachovia's customers were typically conservatively managed companies with strong financial positions, which made them attractive potential customers for competing banks.

First Wachovia's Corporate Finance Group

The CFG was formed in the spring of 1987. Its mission was to develop products for the bank's traditional corporate market segment to tie these customers more tightly to First Wachovia. An early project was to develop a way of matching corporate customers' borrowing needs that could not economically be satisfied directly by the bank with the investment interests of individuals, other institutions, and other corporate customers with surplus funds.

Developing the ability to sell existing and new loans was an important goal for several reasons. The sale of a loan would reduce the assets on the bank's books. This change, together with the fee for managing the transaction, could enhance the bank's return on assets. Because of the very competitive pricing in the marketplace, the return on assets could not easily be increased by raising interest rates. Management also wished to maintain and improve service to Wachovia's customer base to prevent its erosion by competitors, especially by money-center banks with national and international scope. Experience with loan sales would build the distribution skills, capacity, and market reputation that were essential to establishing future corporate-finance products.

The CFG provided a range of services from making private placements of $10 million and higher for borrowers to arranging short-term loan participations of $500,000 or more for investors. Tax-exempt financing of $1 to $10 million, financing of Employee Stock-Ownership Plans, and interest-rate protection were among the other services provided by the CFG. A long-term goal of the group was to build a securitization system. The new loan-participation product, which provided an alternative to commercial paper, could be the first element of the system.

The eight-person CFG served as a support department for the corporate bankers who managed First Wachovia's relationships with individual companies. These account-relationship managers identified company needs and, when necessary, called in specialists (such as those in the CFG) to structure complex transactions. The CFG members were responsible for using their credit expertise to design new products. They were also responsible for arranging the implementation of these products. Legal and structural aspects had to be developed and coordinated with appropriate bank departments. Line management and account managers had to be educated about a product's features because they would be responsible for marketing it. CFG received reimbursement for its expenses, but profits were allocated to line departments. Mr. Tallman estimated that one member of his department would ultimately be spending full time on the loan-participation product, at an annual cost of $45,000.

First Wachovia's Loan-Sale Program

First Wachovia's loan-sale program was established in the summer of 1988. The purpose of the program was to lower the borrowing costs for First Wachovia's most valued corporate customers and to provide them with an attractive alternative both to capital-market borrowing options, such as commercial paper, and to loan-sale programs offered by other commercial (primarily, money-center) banks. Some benefits First Wachovia foresaw for its customers were: lower borrowing costs, ease of execution, and a dependable source of financing. First Wachovia's relationship with the customer would be maintained because First Wachovia would always keep a piece of the transaction.

The loan-sale program was structured to meet the financial needs of companies with at least $250 million in sales whose common stock was publicly traded because their filings with the Securities and Exchange Commission were available without additional expense to the borrower. On the investment side, the program was aimed at a range of investors with needs for high-quality, short-term instruments in variable amounts who were willing to take a slightly higher risk to gain a higher return than U.S. government debt provided. These investors included other financial institutions (particularly First Wachovia's correspondent banks), nonfinancial corporations with more than $5 million in assets, and individuals with net worths of $1 million or annual incomes more than $200,000.

The loan-participation program was structured as follows: One of First Wachovia's operating banks (First National Bank of Atlanta or Wachovia Bank and Trust Company, N.A.) would make a loan commitment to a customer for a series of short-term (90 days or less) floating-rate rollover loans. Investors previously identified as having an interest in the program would be offered a participation in the initial short-term loan on a nonrecourse basis with the right of first refusal at market rates on participations in subsequent renewals. Any subsequent participations that were not taken up would be offered to other investors. First Wachovia would ultimately keep any balance not sold in addition to the 5 to 10 percent it expected to hold as a matter of policy, but the retained balance and subsequent rollovers would be available for sale at any time.

Investors offered the participation would have already executed a master participation agreement with one of First Wachovia's operating banks. They would then be contacted about available participations by First Wachovia's Bond and Money Market Group, just as they would be about other types of money-market instruments. Participations were normally sold in minimum sizes of $500,000 but might range up to $20 million. Mr. Tallman did not think the Bond and Money Market Group sales staff would require additional personnel to sell this product, although three of that group's traders would work part-time on it. Mr. Tallman estimated the cost of this effort to be $25,000.

The Review

The data in front of Mr. Tallman (presented in Exhibits 1, 2, and 3) showed that the CFG had made good progress toward the goal for the loan-sale program. By the end of 1988, an average of over $90 million in loans sold was outstanding. For 1989, Mr. Tallman expected the program to average over $200 million in loans sold outstanding and to grow steadily to the CFG's goal of $1 billion outstanding. Despite the progress in developing the volume of the loan-sale program, however, Mr. Tallman noted that it did not appear to be highly profitable. Gross income from the program in 1988 was just over $69,000 before CFG expenses. On the other hand, most of the customers of the participation program were existing customers of the bank who would not be using the bank's line of credit at profitable levels. Thus, the loan-sale program represented a way to generate additional revenue to cover the internal cost of qualifying and carrying the customer from a credit standpoint.

Did the profits generated by the loan-sale program and the strengthening of Wachovia's customer relationships that resulted from the program compensate adequately for the risks of the program? Mr. Tallman knew that a variety of factors needed to be considered in evaluating the program. Factors that were positive for the program included the fact that it was helping to develop distribution capability and new customers for other Wachovia money-market products, that it was helping to build experience and capability in the CFG, and that its development was helping to resolve systems problems between the Corporate Banking Group and the Bond and Money Market Group. In addition, a U.S. Supreme Court decision in December 1988 allowing major commercial banks to underwrite commercial paper through a securities affiliate could open new doors for the CFG.

The major negative factor for the program was the thin spread Wachovia earned on the loan sales; any significant losses on bad loans might far exceed any revenues generated by the program. The loan-loss provision in 1988 had been less than 0.5 percent of loans, however.

Loan losses could fall into two categories. The first would be losses on the portion of a bad loan that Wachovia had retained on the initial sale of a loan. This loss would not generate an incremental loss to Wachovia's income statement at the time the loan went bad because the deduction would be charged to the bank's loan-loss reserve (which was created by periodic charges against the income statement). The second category would be losses on the portion of a bad loan that Wachovia had sold but might feel compelled to repurchase to protect its reputation. Any repurchase of bad loans would be an incremental loss recorded on Wachovia's income statement at the time of repurchase. In either case, a tax deduction would be allowed only when the loss was actually recognized.

Mr. Tallman further wondered how the loan-sale program might be structured differently to make it more attractive to customers and more beneficial to Wachovia.

Exhibit 1

FIRST WACHOVIA CORPORATE FINANCE GROUP

Loan-Participation Profitability Report

Period	$ Participation Amount*	Bond Dept. Spread Income** +	Net Carry Income† =	Gross Income −	Income to Corporate Banking†† =	Bond Dept. Net Income
Inception Through June 1988						
Subtotal	$192,500,000.00	$ 9,317.19	$ 3,720.91	$13,038.10	$ 5,132.87	$ 7,905.23
June 1988 to September 1988						
Subtotal	$333,342,000.00	$23,864.90	$ 5,143.24	$29,008.14	$12,738.85	$16,269.29
Fourth Quarter — 1988						
Subtotal	$285,037,000.00	$18,133.06	$ 9,303.51	$27,436.57	$ 7,442.34	$19,994.23
1988 Grand Total	$810,879,000.00	$51,315.15	$18,167.66	$69,482.81	$25,314.06	$44,168.75

*Volume of loans transferred to Bond Department for sale. Average balance *outstanding* in 1988 was $90 million.

**Spread earned on participations sold.

†Earnings on unsold amounts held in inventory.

††Earnings allocated back to the lending groups for amounts sold. Does not include the spread earned by the lending groups on the residual loans retained by the unit of origin. The spread on the retained loans would be the figures shown in the fifth column of Exhibit 3.

Exhibit 2

FIRST WACHOVIA CORPORATE FINANCE GROUP

Management Information Update:
Sales of Loans Less Than One Year in Maturity Outstanding as of 1/13/89

(dollars in millions)

Name	Sold	Inventory	Residual Loan*	Total
(names omitted)	$ 38.7	$ 0.3	$ 1.0	$ 40.0
	15.0	0.0	0.0	15.0
	17.0	0.0	3.0	20.0
	10.0	0.0	3.0	13.0
	19.5	0.5	5.0	25.0
	19.8	0.2	2.0	22.0
	9.8	0.0	1.0	10.0
	7.0	0.0	3.0	10.0
	0.1	3.9	1.0	5.0
	0.0	1.0	0.3	1.3
	10.0	0.0	2.0	12.0
	9.1	0.0	0.9	10.0
	13.4	0.6	1.0	15.0
	8.5	3.5	1.0	13.0
	0.0	4.0	1.0	5.0
	0.0	4.0	6.0	20.0
	9.0	0.0	1.0	10.0
Total	$186.1	$28.0	$32.2	$246.3

*Amounts retained in unit of origin.

Exhibit 3
FIRST WACHOVIA CORPORATE FINANCE GROUP
Loan-Sales Status Report, January 13, 1989

Rating	Deal Size ($MM)	Typical Maturities (days)	Last Maturity	LIBOR+ Yield	Status/Comments
P2/A1	5-10	7-30	12/13/88	+ 50	Actively borrowing.
P2/A2/BBB	10-15	14-90	11/02/88	+ 29	Actively borrowing.
NR	10-15	7-60	12/05/88	+ 30	Is investigating commercial paper (CP) program at Goldman.
A-	5-15	14-90	NAv	NAv	Occasional hits. Very competitive.
P1/A1	5-15	14-30	12/01/88	+ 74	Borrowing season winding down.
P1/A1	10-25	14-45	10/11/88	+ 42	Short-term needs in excess of CP. Limited need because of $100MM bond issue.
P2/A2	5-10	14-60	12/02/88	+ 37	Competitive with other banks, occasionally with CP.
P2/A2	10-20	14-60	12/15/88	+ 25	Ratings downgraded to P2/A2.
P2/A2/BBB-	10	30,60,90	12/12/88	+ 56	Usually borrows at LIBOR to sub-LIBOR rates; we quote LIBOR + 6-10; occasionally have hits at 60-90 day range.
A-	5-10	14-30	11/04/88	+ 16	Actively borrowing.
P2/A2/A-	5-15	14-60	NAv	NAv	Now borrowing at LIBOR to LIBOR +5; very aggressive quotes received from 10 other banks.
Ba2	5-10	14-90	12/28/88	+ 20	Ba2 refers to sub. conv. debt; no senior debt. Apparel manufacturer with strong ties to Sears.
A2/F2+	5-10	14-60	NAv	NAv	Competing with Chase, Continental, and CP. CP is typically lowest (LIBOR, all-in) then 1st Wachovia at LIBOR + 3-5.
R	10-20	14-90	12/02/88	+ 30	Company has applied for long-term bond rating; "A" is indicated. Actively borrowing.
NR	5-10	14-90	NAv	NAv	Just beginning to receive quotes: LIBOR + 10-15.
P1/A1	10-25	14-30	12/19/88	+ 84	Excellent investor acceptance; actively borrowing.
NR	5-15	14-90	NAv	NAv	Borrowing need just beginning to build up to double levels and maturities.
P2/A2/A-	5-15	14-90	01/17/89	+ 04	Quotes just beginning. Building investor base. Appears favorable up to $15MM per deal.
NR	10-30	7-14	12/29/88	NAv	Being participated for credit management reasons to Fuji on presold basis.
A3/A-	5-20	30-180	NAv	NAv	Bid-option issues involved. $20MM done 01/12/89 at LIBOR + 16 to mature 02/23/89.
NR	5-15	14-60	NAv	NAv	Just beginning to quote. Small company (revenues $200MM). $5MM done 01/10/89 at LIBOR + 24.
P1/A1	10-25	30,60,90	NAv	NAv	Borrowing again after absence from market. Booked $22MM deal w/$20MM sold in market.
P2/A2	5-10	14,30,60	NAv	NAv	Not borrowing; net investor at present.
P2/A2	5-10	14,30,60	NAv	NAv	Not borrowing.
NR	10	14-30	08/05/88	+ 15	Seasonal borrowings complete.
NR	10-15	14-90	10/31/88	+ 42	Officer now quoting to hold in portfolio taking 35 basis points off posted rates.
NR	5-10	14-30	NAv	NAv	Borrowing overnight.
NR			NAv	NAv	Lending in portfolio at LIBOR + 20-25.
P1/A1	10-30	14-30	NAv	NAv	Considering small acquisition and wants to keep existing $30MM term loan in place. To revisit 1st qtr. 1989.
NR	10-15	14-30	07/19/88	+ 29	Seasonal borrowings complete.

Note: LIBOR = London Interbank Offering Rate.

Notes

Case 14: SIGNET BANKING CORPORATION

In November 1990, Philip Davidson, executive vice president at Signet Bank for planning, information, and financial analysis, was mulling over the challenges the bank would face during the next decade. He had returned from the annual off-site planning meeting, at which Signet's Management Committee had concluded that "business as usual" would not even maintain the status quo in the 1990s. Signet would have to change the way it did business to assure its long-term profitability.

The Management Committee had determined that the best way to counter the increasing competition in the financial services sector was for the bank to transform itself from a traditional commercial bank to a financial service organization. A fundamental component of this plan was a change in the strategic focus of the retail segment. Signet, like all commercial banks, had been losing customer deposits to nontraditional savings and investment products. For example, U.S. bank deposits had grown by 7 percent annually over the past decade; mutual funds had grown by close to 25 percent over the same period. To maintain its position, Signet would have to extract maximum value from its customer franchise by building profitable customer relationships, providing convenient, customer-focused delivery systems, and carefully managing costs.

To become the financial service organization of choice for its customer base, Signet also would have to expand the scope of products and services offered to its customers. Customers would have to view Signet as competitive to both banks and non-banks if Signet was to maintain its present customer base—let alone regain business lost to nontraditional products. One method of attracting customer deposits might be to offer mutual fund accounts similar to those offered by brokerage houses. Signet had already begun offering such products to a select group of customers. Mr. Davidson was now faced with the task of overseeing the introduction of mutual fund accounts to Signet's retail customers in general.

Signet Bank

Signet Banking Corporation was a Southeastern regional bank positioned in the "Golden Crescent" market, which stretched from Baltimore, Maryland, through Washington, D.C., and Richmond, Virginia, to Norfolk, Virginia. Formed by the 1985 merger of three banks, Bank of Virginia, Union Trust Company of Maryland, and Security National Bank in Washington, D.C., Signet Bank had assets in June 1990 totaling $12.7 billion with deposits of $8.1 billion. It had always maintained a strong retail and smaller-business orientation. (Exhibits 1, 2, and 3

Data may have been changed to protect confidental information without altering the nature of the managerial decision.

present recent financial information.) One of Signet's component banks, Bank of Virginia, had started one of the first credit cards in the country, and Signet had aggressively developed VISA and MasterCard portfolios. Signet was one of the larger credit-card processing banks.

Signet had impressed Wall Street analysts with several positive changes that had occurred since the merger. By late 1987, the bank had removed its entire exposure to less-developed countries (LDC), which had been a large one for a regional bank. Profitability had increased to a return on assets of 1.08 percent in 1989 from 1.01 percent in 1988 and 0.97 percent in 1987. Most importantly, Signet undertook a strategic review that resulted in the reorganization of its geographically based structure into five functional lines of business. Analysts agreed that Signet's strategic focus would provide cost-saving opportunities in the short-term as well as longer term cross-selling and revenue-enhancement opportunities.

Retail Banking at Signet

One key conclusion of Signet's strategic study was that, on a full-cost basis, many retail branches and products were unprofitable. Retail management subsequently concentrated on two means of improving profitability: (1) repricing and improving the product mix to enhance product profitability, and (2) lowering operating costs at the branch level. Unfortunately, retail performance from 1988 to mid-1990 did not meet expectations. Net interest margin spreads compressed as the product mix became less favorable. Core deposits in high-margin demand-deposit accounts decreased from 16.2 percent to 14.3 percent, while low-margin certificates of deposit grew from 36.6 percent to 47.4 percent of core deposits. Retail management did, however, make significant strides in reducing costs at the branch level. Controllable expenses decreased by 8 percent in 1989 and another 2 percent in the first half of 1990. Savings from these cost reductions were $8 million in 1989 alone.

Adjusting the product mix and controlling costs were adequate strategies for improving profitability in the short term. Signet's management, however, became increasingly concerned with challenges the retail delivery network would face in the changing financial environment of the 1990s. Bank customers were becoming more sophisticated. Non-bank competitors barraged these customers with solicitations for products that substituted for bank deposit instruments and benefited from the cost advantage of economies of scale due to the competitors' national presence. Customers moved easily to nontraditional products because switching costs were low and traditional banking products had become commodities.

To respond to this environment and meet the challenge to become a financial service organization, the managers of the retail business line developed a set of strategic imperatives. Its primary one was to extract additional value from the existing, strong Signet customer franchise on the theory that high marginal profits and low risks are associated with selling existing products to new customers and new but related products to existing customers.

Signet's 237 branches held over 650,000 accounts. These customers had frequent contact with Signet and a high degree of confidence in the bank. Retail management wanted to reach out to selected segments of these customers with tailored products, including nontraditional banking products such as mutual funds. It also hoped to increase switching costs for these customers to keep them from moving to other financial institutions. Signet wanted to set the pace for innovation by carrying out these strategic actions more quickly than the competition.

The Mutual Fund Industry

The first mutual fund was organized in Boston in 1924. A mutual fund was a company that invested the pooled resources of individual and institutional shareholders with similar financial goals. Mutual funds attracted investors for three reasons. First, by investing in mutual funds, individual investors could hire a professional money manager with an initial investment of as little as $250 to $2,500. The money manager based portfolio decisions on economic and financial research that was often difficult for individuals to gather and use. Second, investors received the benefits of diversification among a variety of industries or types of securities that would not ordinarily have been open to them without a substantial portfolio. The third benefit for investors was the exchange privilege within a family of funds. Shareholders could exchange shares from one fund for another within a group under common management. In changing economic conditions, investors could easily move their money between short- and long-term investments and between investments that were responsive to market changes and those that were not as responsive. Usually the cost of moving among funds sponsored by a single management company was less than moving between one management company and another.

The mutual fund industry reached $1 billion in assets in 1945. Subsequent industry growth was phenomenal, with 400 funds controlling $50 billion in assets in 1970, 564 funds controlling $135 billion in assets in 1980, and 2,900 funds controlling almost $1 trillion in assets in 1990. (Exhibit 4 charts the growth in the types of mutual funds held.)

Historically, mutual funds had consisted primarily of equity funds. By 1990, the Investment Company Institute, a trade association for the mutual fund industry, classified mutual funds into 22 major categories by investment objective, reflecting a proliferation of fund objectives tailored to narrowly focused investor requirements. One of the fastest growing segments of mutual funds was money market funds. Introduced in the early 1970s, money market mutual funds allowed individual investors to participate in high short-term interest rates with the convenience of a checking account. By the end of the 1980s, money market mutual funds had become the first mutual fund investment of 30 percent of all mutual fund investors.

Individual investors seeking high returns coupled with convenience transferred their money from traditional deposit accounts to money market funds because regulatory constraints prevented banks from offering fully competitive products. Although in 1983 banks were finally authorized to offer money market deposit accounts, money market mutual funds paid consistently higher rates, up to a 300 basis point differential in 1989. Money market mutual funds remained the primary competition for bank deposit dollars through the 1980s and equaled about 15 percent of all deposits in commercial banks. (Exhibit 5 shows the shrinkage in the proportion of assets individuals held in bank deposit accounts. Exhibit 6 illustrates how the composition of bank deposits had changed over the 1982-1989 period.)

Mutual Fund Customer Profile

As the total assets in mutual funds grew, so did the number of individuals that invested in them. In 1980, one in twenty people invested in mutual funds, or 6 percent of U.S. households. By 1989, one in four people, or 25 percent of households, invested in mutual funds. Investors in all age groups owned mutual funds, but 45 percent of investors were 25 to 44 years old. Although over 20 percent of all U.S. households in 1989 had a head of household 65 years or older, only 14 percent of mutual fund–owning households were within this age group. Younger investors, who had become familiar with mutual funds, were expected to maintain their investments as they grew older. This was encouraging for the industry, considering the anticipated 28 percent growth rate in the number of individuals aged 35 to 54 by the year 2000.

Mutual funds were owned by households at a wide range of income levels. Almost a quarter of all mutual funds were owned by households with incomes of $25,000 or less, though this figure may have been distorted by the number of retiree households in this income bracket. Sixteen percent of households owning mutual funds in 1989 had annual incomes over $75,000. Sixty-five percent of households with income greater than $75,000 owned mutual funds, compared with 25 percent of the total population.

Mutual Fund Distribution

Many kinds of firms provided a wide range of financial products and services to investors. In 1990, the Investment Company Institute divided mutual fund distribution into six channels: full service brokers, insurance agents, financial planners, captive sales forces of mutual fund underwriters, direct marketers, and deposit institutions or banks. Exhibit 7 compares the use of each channel for mutual fund investment and total investment activity.

The leaders in mutual fund distribution were full-service brokerage houses. Investors who considered such brokerage houses their primary outlet for investment activity made 47 percent of all their mutual fund purchases and 54 percent of their total investment purchases through brokerage houses. By comparison, investors who considered depository institutions their primary outlet for investment activity made 18 percent of all mutual fund purchases and 65 percent of their total investment purchases through banks. These findings challenged a 1989 *Wall Street Journal* study that found that commercial banks were better positioned with investors as a source of investment advice than any other channel. The high usage of brokerage houses for total investment activities may have been due in part to the recent expansion of services provided by brokerage houses such as Fidelity, which offered credit card services, and Merrill Lynch, which offered a full range of deposit services.

Studies by the Investment Company Institute in 1989 showed that 80 percent of investors used one channel for all their investment needs 75 percent of the time. These studies also revealed that 13 percent of mutual fund buyers were "personal guidance oriented" and 19 percent were "comfortable safety oriented." This customer loyalty, coupled with the desire for high levels of personal service and safety, emphasized commercial banks' advantage as the holder of an investor's most basic financial relationship: a transaction or checking account.

When the Basle Committee on Banking Regulations and Supervisory Practices recommended, in 1987, increasing banks' capital requirements, banks began to search for assets that could be managed without additional capital. The potential profitability of mutual fund sales was appealing to commercial banks. The sales fees that the banks received from the mutual fund companies provided noninterest income, a much needed revenue source in times of shrinking net interest margins. Banks eventually realized, however, that they were losing a profit opportunity when they sold others' mutual funds. They received a one-time sales fee but missed the continuing management fees.

Changes in the regulatory and legal environment encouraged commercial banks to begin managing their own mutual funds. Banks had been prohibited from underwriting their own mutual funds since the 1930s. They usually hired a distributor, regulated by the Securities Exchange Act of 1934, to file their fund with the Securities and Exchange Commission. Nevertheless, in 1987, Norwest Bank (an aggressive regional bank headquartered in Minneapolis, Minnesota) successfully tested a limit of the Glass-Steagall Act by allowing one subsidiary to manage a fund that another subsidiary sold.

Another factor that encouraged commercial banks to begin managing their own mutual funds was the Bush administration's 1990 proposal for an overhaul of the U.S. financial system as part of its plan to resolve growing problems within the banking industry. Besides strengthening the deposit insurance fund, Treasury officials wanted to give consumers more choices for managing their money and to open new opportunities for banks to make money. The barriers surrounding banks, erected after the Depression, would be dropped, allowing banks to become stockbrokers, sell insurance, open branches nationwide, and underwrite bonds and mutual funds.

As a result of these and other changes, 79 of the 100 largest U.S. banks, 47 of the top 50 banks, and all the top ten banks offered their own mutual funds by 1990. Analysts, however, had determined that investors did not buy mutual funds from banks because banks had only recently begun to offer the funds. In addition, banks did not offer a wide variety of mutual fund investment alternatives. Commercial bank mutual funds typically lacked the brand recognition, cost savings, and 24-hour service provided by funds such as Dreyfus and Fidelity. Investors were also uncertain about who in the bank they should contact for information about mutual funds.

Mutual Funds at Signet Bank

By the fall of 1990, Signet had introduced the sale of externally managed mutual funds to a select group of customers. A subsidiary of the bank, Signet Investment Corporation, offered over 500 mutual funds to its brokerage customers. Mutual fund sales and fees from 16,000 brokerage accounts made up 60 percent of the subsidiary's revenues in 1990.

In addition, on October 12, 1990, Signet Investment Corporation introduced a family of funds managed in-house by Signet Asset Management, a division of Signet Trust Company. The "SBK Select Series" of funds included an equity fund, an income fund, two tax-free municipal bond funds, and two money market funds. After the introduction of these funds, Signet Asset Management concentrated on transferring trust assets held in individual accounts, formerly managed in "common funds," into the new mutual funds. The division's goal was to convert $300 million of the $4 billion of trust assets under management to mutual funds, thereby allowing the bank to participate in the mutual fund management fees for these assets. Such a transfer also would benefit trust clients because a properly managed fund would increase the yield earned by trust assets in an amount equivalent to the difference between quarterly and monthly compounding of interest.

Although these mutual fund programs had proven successful, Signet's retail analysts believed that the bank was not capturing as much of its customers' investment activity as potentially it could. As seen in Exhibit 8, a 1990 study found that 65 percent of the total financial resources of two lucrative customer segments was allotted to non-bank investments. Fifty-five cents of every dollar these investors put in non-bank products came directly from their bank savings accounts. By shifting its focus from core deposits to financial services, Signet management hoped to recapture some of these lost funds.

Signet Investment planned to introduce the SBK Select Series to retail customers in January 1991. Management believed that its goal of $60 million in sales was reasonable given the existing 650,000 retail accounts. The funds in the SBK Select Series had a sales charge of 4 percent of net asset value for transactions of less than $100,000. Most retail transactions fell into this category. Although the minimum initial investment was $1,000, Asset Management expected an average initial investment of $5,000 per customer. It estimated that it cost $100 on average to open an account, plus about 15 percent of the sales charge to pay for the sales representative's time. Expenses throughout the life of the account were borne by the fund investors.

Marketing and Sales

The challenge facing Mr. Davidson was to determine the best way to introduce the SBK Select Series to Signet's retail customers. The retail branches were Signet's most frequent means of reaching customers, and Signet's 20 licensed mutual-fund sales representatives depended on branch employees for customer referrals. Seminars were to be held with every branch employee to explain how the mutual funds worked and how to identify prospective fund clients. This approach might lead to conflict, however, because Signet Insurance sales representatives had historically looked to the branches for referrals for annuity products. Although mutual funds and annuity products were both investment vehicles, they met different investor goals. Management feared that branch employees would be unable accurately to determine an investor's needs and properly to recommend one product over the other. Both

Signet Investment and Insurance worried that this situation could cause conflicts in the branches and between the two subsidiaries.

If the mutual fund program was to succeed, the bank had to broaden its marketing method beyond referrals. One option was to use Signet's customer information base to make sales calls on targeted customer segments via phone or mail. Customer information was to be reorganized by household to enhance such cross-selling opportunities. Until this reorganization was completed, however, garnering sales information from the system would be difficult.

Mutual fund marketing also could use some techniques that had proven successful in Signet's credit card line of business. This marketing technique used extensive real time testing over targeted customer segments to determine the most effective means of marketing credit cards to an over-solicited public. Solicitations were tested on very small and specific customer segments. If the initial results were positive, the marketers immediately defined and solicited larger segments matching the tested specifics. No matter what method was used, marketing the funds to consumers was challenging.

Another challenge would be marketing to branch employees the notion of selling mutual funds. Branch managers' compensation depended upon branch profitability. The growth of core deposits helped branches remain profitable. Branch managers were aware that over half the money invested in mutual funds came from bank savings accounts, a key component of branch core deposits. The fees that retail branches earned on mutual funds thus had to be large enough to encourage branch employees to offer mutual funds to their customers without fear of losing revenues by cannibalizing their traditional products. Regulatory requirements prohibited the payment of commissions on individual transactions to bank employees. Fees could be credited to branch income, however, and counted in when branch performance was assessed to establish bonuses. Mr. Davidson was considering offering the branches referral fees of 10 percent of net mutual fund sales fees, after expenses associated with starting the accounts.

Even with this added incentive, however, it would be difficult to keep the branch managers' attention on the new mutual funds as 1991 brought other changes to the retail banking line of business. The branches offered more customized packages of products, managed retail expenses, and concentrated on service quality. Unless management successfully communicated Signet's strategy of becoming a financial service organization to the branches, branch employees were bound to concentrate on traditionally profitable products.

Mr. Davidson's Dilemma

Mr. Davidson knew that Signet had to offer mutual funds to achieve the bank's strategy of becoming a financial service organization. He decided to focus his analysis of the situation on the following series of questions:

- Would the SBK Select Series attract customers who had taken money out of Signet accounts to open mutual fund accounts elsewhere? How could Signet effectively compete with traditional brokerage houses and mutual funds offered by other banks in the region? Was the $60 million goal for retail mutual fund sales attainable?

- How should Signet market the mutual funds? What role should the branches play in selling and marketing mutual funds? How would the branches handle the internal competition between mutual funds and other investment instruments such as annuities and certificates of deposit? Was the 10 percent referral fee sufficient to encourage branch managers to pay attention to mutual funds?

- Should Signet reorganize the retail, investment, and insurance groups? (Exhibit 9 presents a summary organization chart.) Would this help Signet become a financial service organization in the eyes of its customers?

Beyond these questions, Mr. Davidson wondered whether Signet's strategy would bring the bank through the regulatory changes of the 1990s into the 21st Century.

Exhibit 1
SIGNET BANKING CORPORATION
Consolidated Balance Sheets, June 1989, December 1989, and June 1990
(figures in millions)

	December	June	
	1989	1989	1990
Assets			
Cash and due from banks	$ 523	$ 501	$ 513
Temporary investments:			
Interest-bearing deposits with other banks	231	218	238
Federal funds sold and securities purchased under resale agreements	419	431	621
Other	160	234	161
Total temporary investments	$ 810	$ 883	$ 1,020
Investment securities	3,392	2,908	3,154
Loans:			
Commercial	2,579	2,480	2,633
Credit card	1,418	1,215	1,468
Other consumer	1,400	1,401	1,333
Real estate—construction	1,199	1,149	1,255
Real estate—commercial mortgage	531	556	622
Real estate—residential mortgage	132	127	175
Foreign	8	3	10
Gross loans	$ 7,267	$ 6,931	$ 7,496
Less unearned income	(52)	(32)	(56)
Less allowance for loan losses	(94)	(87)	(120)
Net loans	$ 7,121	$ 6,812	$ 7,320
Premises and equipment (net)	205	198	207
Interest receivable	122	102	126
Due from customers on acceptances	8	11	7
Other assets	295	348	307
Total assets	$12,476	$11,763	$12,654
Liabilities			
Non-interest-bearing deposits	$ 1,383	$ 1,316	$ 1,214
Interest-bearing deposits:			
Money market and interest checking	597	541	596
Money market savings	1,473	1,455	1,511
Savings accounts	418	438	425
Savings certificates	2,562	2,511	2,960
Large denomination certificates	953	953	1,244
Foreign	210	274	146
Total interest-bearing deposits	$ 6,213	$ 6,172	$ 6,882
Total deposits	$ 7,596	$ 7,488	$ 8,096
Securities sold under repurchase agreements	2,054	1,391	2,364
Federal funds purchased	1,020	1,024	552
Other short-term borrowings	497	546	395
Long-term borrowings	361	362	351
Interest payable	53	44	53
Acceptances outstanding	8	11	8
Other liabilities	136	190	86
Total liabilities	$11,725	$11,056	$11,905
Stockholders' Equity			
Common stock ($5 par value)	$ 133	$ 133	$ 132
Capital surplus	108	104	100
Retained earnings	510	470	517
Total equity	$ 751	$ 707	$ 749
Total liabilities and equity	$12,476	$11,763	$12,654
Common shares outstanding	26,673	26,548	26,361

Exhibit 2
SIGNET BANKING CORPORATION
Statements of Consolidated Income
for Three and Six Months Ended June 30, 1989 and 1990
(dollar amounts, except per-share information, in millions)

	Three Months Ended June 30		Six Months Ended June 30	
	1989	1990	1989	1990
Interest income:				
Loans, including fees				
Commercial	$ 72.7	$ 67.6	$ 141.3	$ 133.6
Credit card	45.6	58.5	90.6	117.3
Other consumer	40.9	37.4	81.6	75.7
Real estate—construction	37.1	35.5	71.4	69.5
Real estate—commercial mortgage	15.3	15.7	30.6	29.5
Real estate—residential mortgage	3.2	4.5	6.4	8.9
Foreign	.2	.2	.7	.4
Total loans, including fees	$ 215.0	$ 219.4	$ 422.6	$ 434.9
Temporary investments	17.3	15.8	30.0	29.4
Investment securities—taxable	50.8	70.8	101.6	142.0
Investment securities—nontaxable	7.4	7.2	14.8	14.5
Total interest income	$ 290.5	$ 313.2	$ 569.0	$ 620.8
Interest expense:				
Money market and interest checking	$ 7.3	$ 7.6	$ 14.5	$ 14.9
Money market savings	26.4	24.9	52.3	49.3
Savings accounts	5.4	5.2	10.8	10.2
Savings certificates	52.3	56.7	101.1	108.3
Large denomination certificates	22.0	23.8	44.2	45.4
Foreign	4.0	4.8	5.9	10.1
Total interest on deposits	$ 117.4	$ 123.0	$ 228.8	$ 238.2
Securities sold under repurchase agreements	29.1	40.9	56.8	80.8
Federal funds purchased	13.9	18.4	26.5	38.9
Other short-term borrowings	13.3	9.9	25.4	20.7
Long-term borrowings	7.0	7.7	12.9	15.6
Total interest expense	$ 180.7	$ 199.9	$ 350.4	$ 394.2
Net interest income	$ 109.8	$ 113.3	$ 218.6	$ 226.6
Provision for loan losses	13.7	50.5	24.4	67.5
Net interest income after provision for loan losses	$ 96.1	$ 62.8	$ 194.2	$ 159.1
Noninterest income:				
Credit card service charges	$ 12.3	$ 14.5	$ 24.8	$ 29.5
Service charges on deposit accounts	13.1	13.9	25.6	28.0
Trust income	3.2	4.1	6.2	7.6
Other	9.5	10.3	19.2	24.4
Noninterest operating income	$ 38.1	$ 42.8	$ 75.8	$ 89.6
Securities gains (losses)	4.1	.1	6.2	.1
Total noninterest income	$ 42.2	$ 42.9	$ 82.0	$ 89.5
Noninterest expense:				
Salaries	$ 41.7	$ 44.6	$ 83.0	$ 88.9
Employee benefits	10.9	11.8	22.6	25.0
Occupancy	7.6	8.8	15.6	17.7
Supplies and equipment	10.6	11.0	21.4	22.2
Travel and communications	6.6	8.6	12.2	13.9
Other	18.4	22.7	35.4	46.4
Total noninterest expense	$ 95.8	$ 107.5	$ 190.2	$ 214.1
Income (loss) before income taxes (benefit)	$ 42.5	$ (1.8)	$ 86.0	$ 34.5
Applicable income taxes (benefit)	11.2	(4.7)	23.2	4.5
Net income	$ 31.3	$ 2.9	$ 62.8	$ 30.0
Earnings per common share	$1.15	$0.11	$2.29	$1.13

Exhibit 3

SIGNET BANKING CORPORATION

Average Deposits
(in millions)

	1985		1986		1987		1988		1989	
	Amount	% of Total	Amount	% of Total	Amount	% of Total	Amount	% of Total	Amount	% of Total
Money market and interest checking	$ 312.8	7.6%	$ 415.5	8.5%	$ 535.6	9.8%	$ 562.0	9.3%	$ 571.5	9.2%
Money market savings	811.7	19.6	1,122.5	23.0	1,422.6	26.1	1,460.6	24.2	1,487.8	24.1
Savings accounts	477.8	11.6	499.9	10.3	545.8	10.0	490.3	8.1	433.6	7.0
Savings certificates	1,586.5	38.4	1,747.5	35.8	1,761.9	32.3	2,322.6	38.4	2,483.0	40.2
Demand deposits	946.9	22.8	1,091.5	22.4	1,182.5	21.8	1,210.9	20.0	1,206.3	19.5
Total	$4,135.7	100.0%	$4,876.9	100.0%	$5,448.4	100.0%	$6,046.4	100.0%	$6,182.2	100.0%

Exhibit 4
SIGNET BANKING CORPORATION
Mutual Funds by Fund Type, 1980-1989

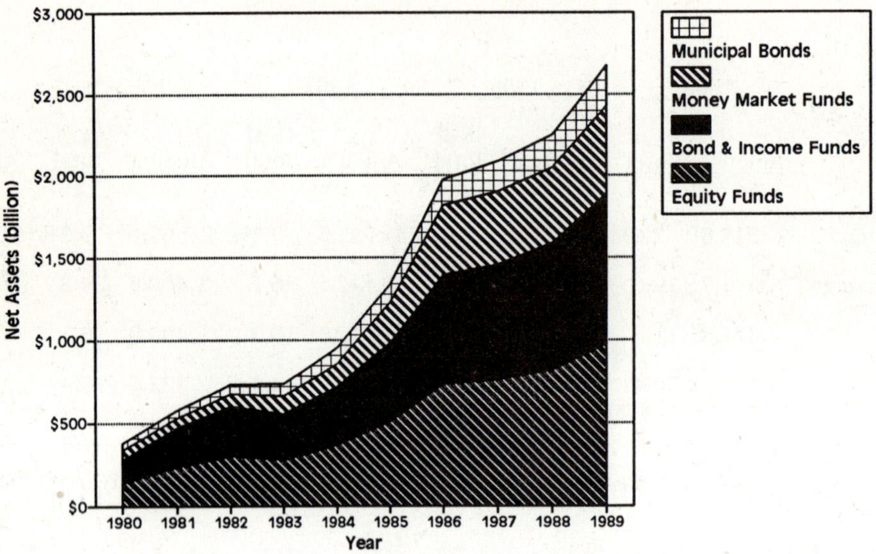

Exhibit 5
SIGNET BANKING CORPORATION
Consumer Investments

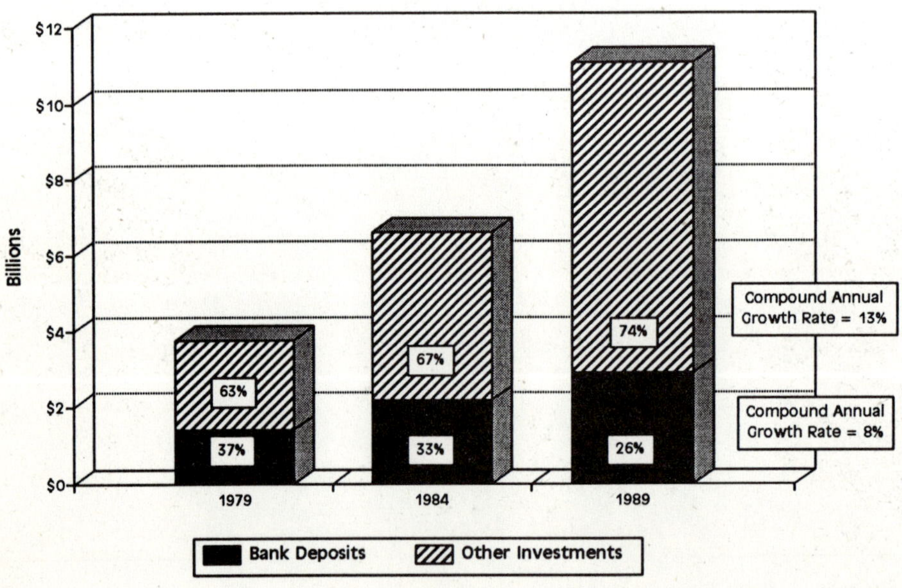

Exhibit 6
SIGNET BANKING CORPORATION
Bank Deposit Composition

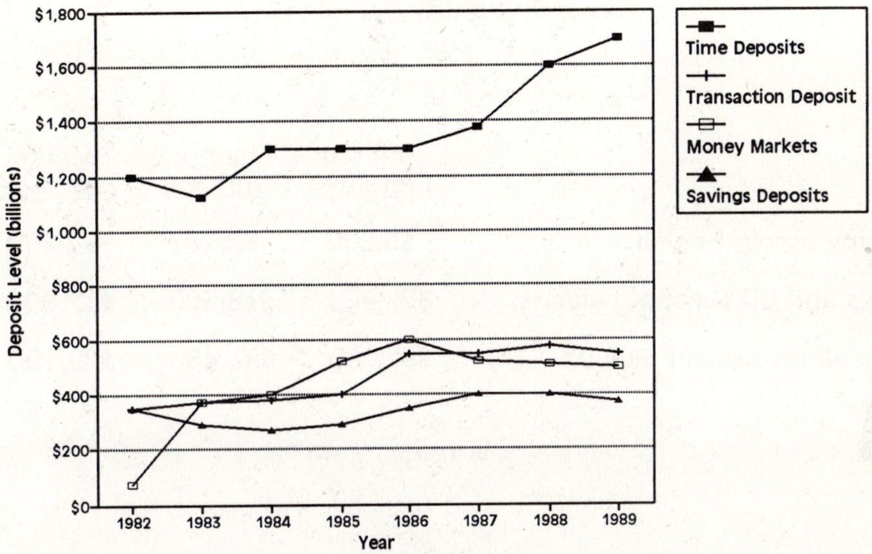

Exhibit 7
SIGNET BANKING CORPORATION
Channels Used for Investment

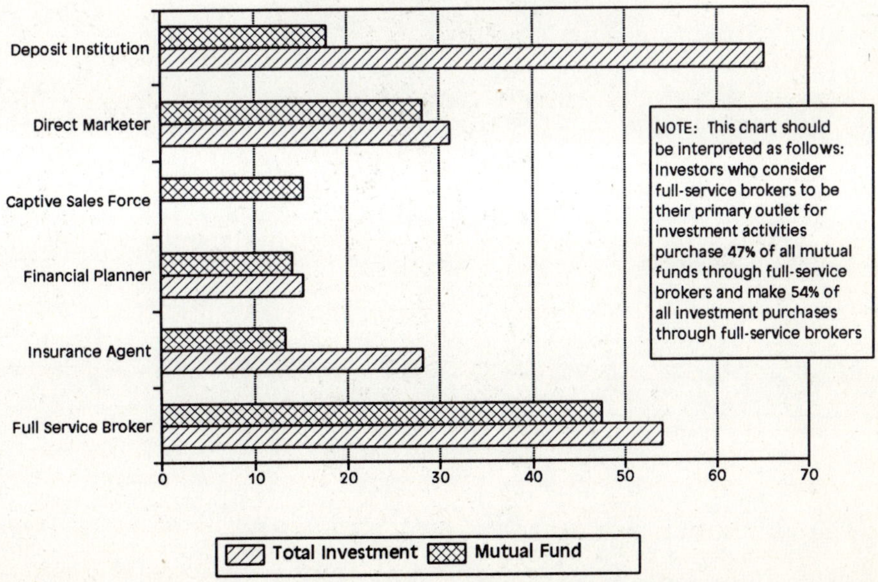

Exhibit 8

SIGNET BANKING CORPORATION

Examples of Two Customer Segments, 1990

	Comfortable Preretiree	Emerging Affluent	Market Average
Average checking account balance	$3,200	$2,200	$2,500
Average savings and CD account balance	$25,900	$18,500	$17,000
Average non-bank investment balance	$52,700	$41,400	$29,100

Exhibit 9
SIGNET BANKING CORPORATION
Organization Chart

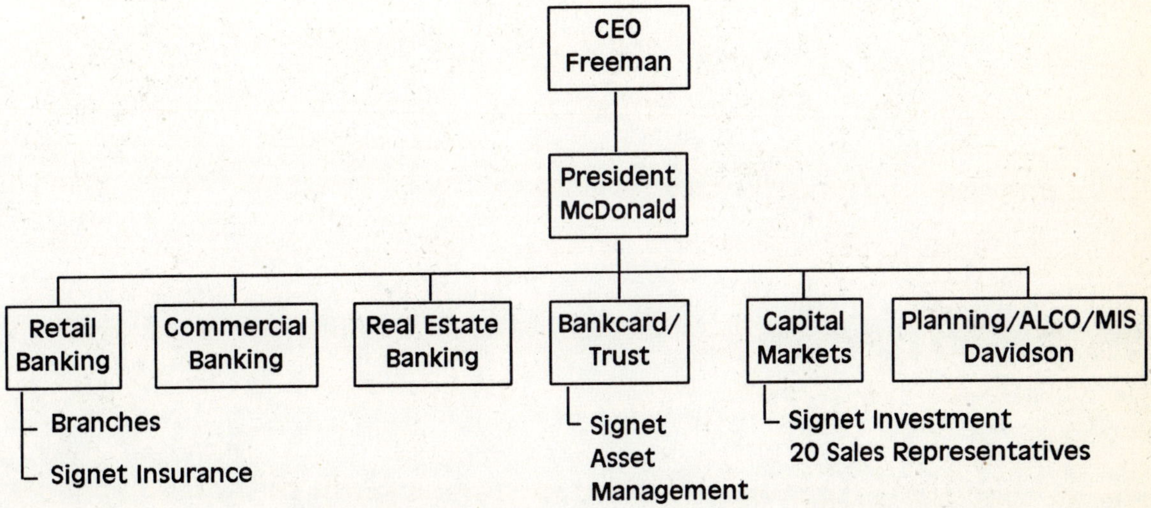

Notes

Case 15: CREDIT SUISSE

Earl Fisher, senior investment officer at a major mutual fund group, completed reading the article in the August 9, 1989, issue of the *Wall Street Journal* about the efforts of Credit Suisse, one of the three major Swiss banks, to develop a global investment banking capability. Credit Suisse had announced it had sold 12 percent of its investment banking subsidiary, CS First Boston, Inc., to a group of Japanese financial institutions. The price was not revealed, but it was probably similar to the price paid when First Boston was taken private in 1988. The article was of more than passing interest to Mr. Fisher because he handled his firm's financial institution investment responsibilities. It also attracted Mr. Fisher's attention because of an investment decision he had made the previous year.

Early in 1988, Mr. Fisher had contemplated the sale of his firm's holdings of First Boston, Inc., then a publicly traded investment banking firm. After studying First Boston and reflecting on the trends in the investment banking industry, Mr. Fisher had decided to maintain his firm's position in the common stock. This proved to be a wise decision. At the time he evaluated First Boston in February 1988, First Boston's stock was trading in the low $20s. In December 1988, Credit Suisse, First Boston management, and other financial institutions bought out the public stockholders at a price of $52.50 a share in cash and some additional deferred compensation. A special holding company of Credit Suisse, CS First Boston, Inc., now owned First Boston in the United States and the Credit Suisse investment banking operations in Europe.

Though Mr. Fisher had thoroughly enjoyed the success of his investment decision, he was also intrigued by the significance of the First Boston and Credit Suisse merger. One of the factors that had led him to consider the sale of First Boston was the apparent trend toward small, specialized investment banking firms on Wall Street as large financial supermarkets stumbled. The Credit Suisse–First Boston deal indicated that some sophisticated players thought large financial institutions might have a significant advantage in the international arena. Mr. Fisher therefore wondered if he should increase his portfolio position in financial institutions with size and international scope.

On the other hand, equally sophisticated financial companies had opted for a completely different approach to international banking. The senior management of Morgan Stanley Group, for example, took pride in having dropped the firm's international department in the late 1970s. They argued that a geographic structure inhibited the development of a global perspective. The financial business should be structured along product lines. Product managers were responsible for developing the firm's product competence in all financial markets where it made sense for Morgan Stanley to compete. Individuals at local offices were responsible for a thorough knowledge of the local market and for devising applications for the firm's products in the local market. The product managers then coordinated the local applications when the solution to a client's financial problems required global scope.

Credit Suisse

Credit Suisse was Switzerland's third largest bank after Union Bank of Switzerland and the Swiss Bank Corporation. It was the oldest of the three, having been chartered as a bank in Zurich in 1856. Though Switzerland was a small country, its major banks were significant participants in the international banking scene because of their overall size and Switzerland's long history as an international financial center. At the end of 1988, Credit Suisse had $76 billion in assets and net profits of $397 million. It was the world's 55th largest bank in assets and 28th in capital. Exhibit 1 lists the largest world banks, and Exhibit 2 presents summary historical financial information for Credit Suisse.

As a "universal" bank, Credit Suisse was allowed by Swiss law to offer a wide range of domestic and international banking services and products, including payment transactions and the acceptance of savings and other deposits; lending to corporations, governments, and individuals; long-term mortgage lending; leasing; factoring; installment credit; and nonrecourse trade financing. Credit Suisse also engaged in a wide range of stock-market, underwriting, and corporate-finance activities as well as investment counseling, management of mutual funds, and the safekeeping of securities. In addition, Credit Suisse was an active trader of foreign exchange, securities, bank notes, and precious metals.

Because of the emphasis on exporting given by Swiss industry and Switzerland's role as a financial service center, Credit Suisse had always actively engaged in international financing transactions. Its first branch outside of Switzerland was established in New York in 1940. Since 1965, Credit Suisse had greatly expanded its international presence. As of December 31, 1987, it had 188 domestic branches and 14 branches and agencies abroad, including New York, Tokyo, London, Miami, Los Angeles, Guernsey, the Cayman Islands, Nassau, Singapore, and Hong Kong. Fifteen major banking and financial subsidiaries and 24 representative offices also belonged to Credit Suisse's international network, ensuring its direct presence in major countries and financial centers throughout the world. The bank had 15,000 staff members worldwide.

Credit Suisse and First Boston, Inc.

The relationship between Credit Suisse and First Boston, Inc. began at the initiative of First Boston, an investment bank established in 1932 and the first in the United States to be publicly owned. First Boston management, in the late 1970s, believed the firm required additional capital to support trading positions and leveraged-buy-out bridge financing. To increase its equity, in 1978 First Boston sold a 30 percent interest to a London investment bank controlled by Credit Suisse.

The resulting corporate structure was convoluted: *The Economist* headlined a story about the firm as "More Names Than A Russian Novel." Corporate entities in New York (First Boston) and London (Financiere Credit Suisse–First Boston) each owned a 40 percent share of the other. The New York and London offices were relatively independent, with the New York office supposed to concentrate on business in the United States and the London office intended to handle the Euromoney markets and investment banking on the continent.

For a decade, the association was very successful. Financiere Credit Suisse–First Boston (Financiere), for example, grew to a dominating position in the Eurobond market and was active in standard investment banking. The group had a unique and broad geographic and currency mix in its international underwriting business. It relied neither on an individual currency nor on issuers from any single country for its capital market business. Financiere also provided investment advisory and portfolio management services to institutional and high-net-worth individual investors worldwide. A subsidiary, Clariden Bank, was a fully licensed Swiss bank with offices in Zurich and Geneva and representative offices in Singapore and Hong Kong. To support its activities, Financiere had about 1,000 employees worldwide, including 120 directors and officers.

First Boston enlarged its share of mainline investment banking and trading businesses in the United States. By 1987, it had the sixth largest capital among U.S. investment banks, offering complete investment-banking services. A relaxed management style allowed aggressive and talented individuals to build a variety of strong departments. Although the relative profitability of various product lines was extremely volatile, the senior executives believed that it was important to have total-market capability rather than build and shrink according to the vagaries of the economy. This strategy resulted in two of the most productive investment bankers' leaving to set up their own firm, Wasserstein and Perella, when First Boston's chairman refused to shut down portions of the (then) money-losing trading functions.

The lack of coordination occasionally resulted in both offices making pitches for the same business, which tended to create ill feelings. As the financial markets became increasingly global, the managerial difficulties of the two firms increased to the point that readjustment was required. The result was CS First Boston, Inc. (CSFB, Inc.).

CS First Boston, Inc.

CSFB, Inc. was the new umbrella holding company through which Credit Suisse conducted its global investment banking operations. The firm had reorganized its activities after the consolidation, forming two principal subsidiaries—First Boston Corporation in New York and Credit Suisse First Boston in London. A new subsidiary, called CS First Boston Pacific, was still in the startup stage, but it was expected to be more important to CSFB, Inc. in the future as the means by which CSFB, Inc. would tap into Asia's explosive growth as a financial center. Though Credit Suisse was the dominant shareholder in CSFB, Inc., with a 44.5% interest (the maximum allowed by the restrictions of the Glass-Steagall Act), there were several other shareholders. Credit Suisse hoped this ownership would help CSFB, Inc. operate globally. Exhibit 3 shows this ownership, which still left CSFB, Inc. a closely held firm. Its market value was about $2 billion at the price it was taken private.

First Boston Corporation

First Boston Corporation was a full-service international investment banking firm serving both suppliers and users of capital around the world. Through its wholly owned subsidiaries, including a broker-dealer in securities, First Boston provided comprehensive financial advisory services and developed innovative financing structures and strategies, raised capital for public and private institutions, and employed its own capital resources to trade and underwrite securities and engage in other principal transactions. Through its subsidiaries, First Boston was a member of the major United States securities and commodities exchanges, as well as foreign exchanges, including the International Stock Exchange in London and the Tokyo Stock Exchange.

To guarantee a comprehensive range of financial advisory, capital raising, and sales and trading services to clients and customers throughout the United States, First Boston had committed major resources to the development of regional investment banking offices. First Boston currently had domestic offices in Atlanta, Boston, Chicago, Dallas, Denver, Houston, Los Angeles, Philadelphia, San Francisco, and San Juan, Puerto Rico. First Boston had foreign offices located in Geneva, Zurich, London, Hong Kong, Melbourne, Sydney, Tokyo, and Toronto.

The business of First Boston was broadly divided into four areas: financial advisory services and underwriting, merchant banking, sales and trading, and research. The Investment Banking Department provided comprehensive financial advisory services, specialized merger, acquisition and divestiture services, underwritings in collaboration with the Capital Markets Department, and other corporate finance activities. Through its merchant banking activities, First Boston facilitated major client transactions and invested in merger and acquisition, recapitalization, leveraged buy-outs, venture capital, and real estate transactions. First Boston's sales and trading area, including the Taxable Fixed Income, Equity, and Municipal Securities Departments, used the firm's own capital to trade in and support the underwriting of securities of corporate and other private issuers as well as government and agency securities. First Boston's Equity Research, Fixed Income Research, and Economic Research Departments performed a wide array of analyses covering all types of securities and domestic as well as international economic conditions.

At October 31, 1988, First Boston had 127 managing directors, 93 directors, 750 vice presidents, and a total of about 5,000 employees worldwide, 3,000 of whom constituted the professional staff. Some 500 investment banking professionals were responsible for developing and maintaining investment banking client relationships and executing investment banking transactions with domestic and foreign clients. Professionals engaged in principal trading and customer sales activities totaled about 1,000, and research professionals numbered 173. In addition, First Boston had about 2,000 operational, administrative, and support personnel.

Credit Suisse First Boston

Credit Suisse First Boston (CSFB) and its subsidiaries were an international financial-services group of companies that had been started in 1978 as a joint venture between Credit Suisse and First Boston, Inc. The services provided by the CSFB group ranged from capital raising and securities trading to investment management and corporate structure services. The principal companies in the CSFB group were Credit Suisse–First Boston Limited, a London-based investment bank that was one of the leading issuing houses in the Eurocapital markets; CSFB (Gilts) Limited, an authorized primary dealer in the United Kingdom gilt-edged market; Credit Suisse First Boston Securities, the group's international bond trading firm in London; and Credit Suisse First Boston Futures Trading S.A., in Zurich, which traded Swiss franc bonds, foreign exchange, precious metals, and related options. These companies were wholly owned by CSFB, which maintained offices in Amsterdam, Frankfurt, Geneva, Zurich, London, Hong Kong, Singapore, and Tokyo. CSFB provided capital-raising and corporate advisory services to its corporate, government, and institutional clients on a worldwide basis and had a leading market role as an underwriter of debt, equity-related, and other securities in the Euromarket.

CSFB was a recognized market leader in the origination and execution of Eurodebt, Euroequity and equity-related, and other financing transactions. Exhibit 4 shows CSFB's position as a Eurobond underwriter at the end of 1988. The CSFB group conducted capital-raising activities principally through operations in London, Frankfurt, and Amsterdam. Credit Suisse First Boston Limited, CSFB's London-based subsidiary, was one of the leading underwriters in the Eurocapital market. CSFB had also established a significant presence in German and Dutch markets.

The CSFB group had a unique and broad geographic and currency mix in its international underwriting business. This placed it in an extremely favorable position to respond to the often unpredictable issuing activity of entities from various countries and, in particular, to the constantly evolving currency preferences of issuers and investors alike. The group relied neither on an individual currency nor on issuers from any single country for its capital markets business.

CSFB managed and participated in public offerings and arranged direct placements of debt and equity securities in the international capital markets for issuers, both public and private, from a wide range of countries. It was active in the following currency capital markets: U.S. dollar, Canadian dollar, Australian dollar, New Zealand dollar, pound sterling, deutsche mark, Dutch guilder, and European currency units. In recent years, a majority of capital market transactions had been directly linked to both interest rate and currency swaps. To strengthen further its overall position in capital markets, CSFB maintained an active agency presence in swap markets and worked closely with both First Boston and Credit Suisse, which participated in these markets as both principal and agent.

The Eurocommercial paper market provided a growing source of financing for sovereign, corporate, and bank borrowers, and the CSFB group had maintained a leading position in this market. It placed Eurocommercial paper as well as other short-term and medium-term securities in the Euromarket, including floating rate notes and syndicated bank loans. CSFB also participated as a dealer in Euro medium-term note programs. Its specialist banking team executed syndicated credit facilities in the international bond market. Borrowing clients were principally corporations domiciled in industrialized countries.

CSFB provided investment advisory and portfolio management services to institutional and high-net-worth individual investors. Investment management activities were conducted by affiliates in Geneva, Zurich, London, and New York. Clariden Bank specialized in providing diversified investment advisory and portfolio management services to substantial private investors worldwide. At October 31, 1988, the total amount of funds under management and under advisory contracts was about SFr. 33 billion.

Credit Suisse's Investment Banking Strategy

Credit Suisse's investment banking strategy, as Mr. Fisher interpreted the firm's actions, was to position itself as the only financial institution with true global investment banking capabilities through major investment banking operations in the three major capital markets of the world: New York, London, and Tokyo. By having major subsidiaries in each of the three major capital markets, the Credit Suisse investment banking activities could gain market share among major corporations by providing access to the best financing available globally through its internal network. The relative significance of the three major capital markets to each other can be seen in Exhibit 5, which shows the amount of financing raised in 1987 in these markets.

Of particular significance to Credit Suisse's strategy was its position in the European capital market. Europe was moving to a single integrated financial market in 1992 with the removal of all restrictions on capital flows in the European Common Market and the possible adoption in the future of a single European currency. This could make Europe the world's most important capital market, given Europe's combined population of 320 million compared to 250 million in the United States and to Japan's 120 million. CSFB's strong position in various parts of the European financial markets put it in a position to benefit from the expected consolidation of the European financial system after 1992.

Unlike Americans, Europeans did not have the freedom to open bank accounts wherever they chose. European banks were not permitted to lend or to borrow without restrictions across national boundaries as U.S. banks were across state lines. This structure partly reflected political considerations and partly the currency controls resulting from the 20th Century European wars. Several centers, particularly London and Switzerland, had structured themselves as hosts of international finance organizations, which were allowed to operate in the international markets with few of the regulations applied to domestic institutions.

The European commercial banking community was two-tiered. Major European institutions that competed with large Japanese and United States banks dominated the international banking business in their countries. The fragmented European domestic retail banking business, however, encompassed more than 1,000 regional banks. Although universal banks were the rule in some countries, such as Germany and Switzerland, that structure was not common in others, such as the United Kingdom.

After 1992, European banks and other financial institutions would probably require only a single banking license to perform a long list of banking activities. Theoretically, under the single-license principle, any European bank could eventually provide a complete range of financial services throughout the Community market. The role of foreign-owned banks in the consumer market was not completely clear.

Positioning for the post-1992 environment was already under way in the industry because survival would require that a bank have international experience, strong capital resources, in-depth management, a good home-market presence, broadly based and efficient operations, and reasonable long-range acquisition strategies. The larger European international financial institutions were expected to be dominant, with smaller institutions forced to seek partners or to sell out. Experience and efficiency would be crucial, so institutions with broader bases of services—German, Swiss, and the United Kingdom banks—would have a distinct advantage over more specialized banking organizations. An increase in friendly mergers, joint ventures, and alliances as means of moving into new markets was expected.

Exhibit 6 shows how European capital markets had been growing in the 1980s, Exhibit 7 provides comparative data on various national equity markets in 1987, and Exhibit 8 compares world banking markets in 1986.

The Management Issue

As Mr. Fisher thought about Credit Suisse's effort to create a global investment bank, he wondered whether the apparent synergies of Credit Suisse's three-legged strategy would be unbalanced by the management problems of running a global operation. Investment banking was an inherently entrepreneurial activity dependent upon the creativity and imagination of strong-willed principals intimately familiar with their own segments of the capital markets. First Boston, Inc. had a long history of internal rivalries, feuding, and top level defections. For a global operation to work, strong teamwork and cooperation were needed. Other commercial banks, most notably Citicorp, which had tried to build global investment banking operations, had had mixed success, with the problem of team building at the core of their difficulties.

In addition to the problems of running a global operation, Mr. Fisher wondered whether the shareholder mix of CSFB, Inc. might create future problems. The history of international consortium commercial banks owned jointly by other financial institutions was full of examples of shareholder conflict because of varied goals, culture, and the changing needs of corporate owners. On the other hand, Mr. Fisher recognized that the strong institutional parents of CSFB, Inc. in all three major capital markets put it in a unique position in international financial markets, particularly with respect to the Japanese. Mr. Fisher recognized that the Credit Suisse approach had both strong advantages and disadvantages.

Exhibit 1
CREDIT SUISSE
Characteristics of the World's 40 Largest Banks, Ranked by Capital, in 1987 and 1988
(dollar figures in millions)

			Capital Strength		Capital Asset Ratio				Profits		Profits on Capital			
			$	Percent	Index		Rank		$	Percent	Percent		Rank	
Capital	Assets	Bank, Location of Head Office	1988	Change	1988	1987	1988	1987	1988	Change	1988	1987	1988	1987
1	17	National Westminster, London	10,907	21.5	6.11	5.70	432	420	2,546	99.9	25.6	14.7	150	441
2	14	Barclays, London	10,545	35.6	5.57	4.89	498	532	2,517	277.0	27.5	9.0	121	551
3	11	Citicorp, New York	9,864	14.9	4.84	4.33	586	604	2,707	n.a.	29.4	-3.3	97	657
4	3	Fuji Bank, Tokyo	9,018	44.5	2.75	2.20	885	866	2,226	33.2	29.2	25.2	98	240
5	8	Credit Agricole, Paris	8,740	7.5	4.08	4.49	712	584	852	33.2	10.1	15.7	610	415
6	2	Sumitomo Bank, Osaka	8,550	33.4	2.55	2.20	906	869	2,389	134.3	31.9	16.9	66	392
7	1	Dai-Ichi Kangyo Bank, Tokyo	8,481	50.4	2.41	1.79	927	899	2,525	58.2	35.8	30.0	44	173
8	4	Mitsubishi Bank, Tokyo	8,200	45.0	2.58	2.14	902	876	2,066	33.0	29.8	29.1	89	178
9	6	Industrial Bank of Japan,Tokyo	8,155	43.3	3.12	2.43	837	847	n.a.	n.a.	n.a.	n.a.	n.a.	n.a.
10	5	Sanwa Bank, Tokyo	7,567	47.9	2.46	1.96	922	888	1,951	36.0	30.8	29.8	79	174
11	31	Union Bank of Switzerland	6,715	3.6	6.06	6.08	436	365	728	0.6	11.0	11.8	589	498
12	22	Bank of China, Peking	6,620	45.3	4.40	3.84	652	675	1,135	9.0	20.3	27.0	263	214
13	19	Deutsche Bank, Frankfurt	6,460	6.0	3.78	4.06	759	649	1,816	97.0	28.9	15.7	101	416
14	67	Japan Development, Tokyo	6,430	3.1	9.90	9.86	126	109	411	-13.7	6.5	15.3	696	422
15	10	Mitsubishi Trust, Tokyo	6,342	49.9	3.08	2.34	815	857	607	15.1	11.5	13.5	573	468
16	35	Swiss Bank Corp, Basel	6,055	4.0	5.91	5.99	458	381	623	1.5	10.5	10.7	601	518
17	18	Bank of Tokyo, Tokyo	5,913	27.3	3.45	3.13	801	775	957	30.1	18.1	16.6	339	400
18	40	Lloyds Bank, London	5,867	35.5	6.25	5.33	410	470	1,723	n.a.	33.8	-9.7	52	666
19	49	J.P. Morgan, New York	5,838	15.0	7.06	6.86	290	268	1,315	265.4	24.1	7.1	178	578
20	12	Banque Nationale de Paris	5,567	9.1	2.83	3.17	880	762	876	16.7	16.4	15.2	414	424
21	37	Midland Bank, London	5,499	17.5	5.45	5.34	511	469	1,254	n.a.	24.6	-21.9	172	676
22	16	Credit Lyonnais, Paris	5,409	38.3	3.02	2.64	854	819	811	0.2	17.4	22.6	365	275
23	28	Paribas, Paris	5,324	2.8	4.38	4.80	659	547	n.a.	n.a.	n.a.	n.a.	n.a.	n.a.
24	9	Tokai Bank, Nagoya	5,088	66.5	2.38	1.62	935	914	1,095	35.7	26.9	52.8	130	51
25	52	Banco do Brasil, Rio de Janeiro	5,063	-99.0	6.31	6.83	401	273	1,212	1,412.0	0.5	0.0	771	644
26	30	Hong Kong Bank, Hong Kong	5,018	8.7	4.43	4.38	645	600	551	19.7	11.4	19.9	575	325
27	26	Societe Generale, Paris	4,874	18.2	3.35	3.23	807	754	863	39.7	19.2	18.2	298	355
28	37	Credit Suisse, Zurich	4,785	8.8	6.35	6.17	395	357	523	5.2	11.4	11 5	577	503
29	21	Long-Term Credit Bank, Tokyo	4,743	32.6	2.93	2.37	866	853	892	23.5	21.5	22.7	234	273
30	51	Rabobank., Utrecht	4,666	10.7	5.77	5.79	475	410	573	13.4	12.9	12.5	545	483
31	13	Mitsui Bank, Tokyo	4,554	35.2	2.32	1.88	937	892	1,413	31.0	35.7	34.2	45	129
32	23	Group Ecurcuil, Paris	4,372	16.2	2.91	2.64	870	820	715	n.a.	17.6	0.0	361	n.a.
33	74	Westpac Banking Corp., Sidney	4,305	84.2	7.17	4.70	277	561	959	44.4	28.9	28.4	102	187
34	27	Dresdner Bank, Frankfurt	4,284	13.9	3.30	3.23	816	752	621	12.5	15.5	14.7	457	439
35	50	Royal Bank of Canada, Montreal	4,170	16.6	5.06	4.60	557	573	1,025	58.6	26.5	17.5	137	374
36	39	Chase Manhattan, New York	4,160	29.4	4.34	3.31	668	744	1,334	n.a.	36.2	-19.2	42	674
37	41	BankAmerica Corp., San Francisco	4,149	27.3	4.45	3.59	644	704	942	8.4	25.4	23.8	154	258
38	68	Banco Bilbao Vizcaya, Bilbao	4,138	57.0	6.53	4.82	365	544	1.077	24.8	31.8	31.7	68	147
39	34	Instituto Bancario S. Paolo, Turin	4,075	14.3	3.95	4.30	730	610	1,048	13.2	27.4	27.9	122	196
40	63	Chemical Banking Corp., NY	3,967	32.1	5.89	3.92	461	664	908	n.a.	26.1	-23.3	141	679

Source: *The Banker*

Exhibit 2

CREDIT SUISSE

Selected Historical Data, 1982-1987
(Swiss francs in millions except for per-share figures)

	Assets Less Contra Accounts①	Equity②	Net Interest Income③	Operating Profit④	Net Income	Market Price Range⑤	Book Value Per Share⑤
1987	106,170	6,613	837	1,151	550	3,840–2,325	2,025
1986	103,003	6,343	829	1,176	566	3,900–2,900	1,716
1985	88,242	5,600	808	1,061	507	3,582–2,251	1,643
1984	83,747	5,242	728	863	417	2,323–1,975	1,537
1983	77,052	4,942	636	761	352	2,236–1,829	1,450
1982	73,225	4,812	536	662	303	1,902–1,486	1,411

①Unconsolidated.
②Equity is paid-up share capital plus published equity reserves.
③Net interest income is interest revenue, including income on money market instruments, minus interest paid.
④Cash flow figure from the annual accounts, generally regarded as the best indication of operating performance (calculated by adding provisions, losses and write-downs to net profit).
⑤Actual.

Source: Salomon Brothers, Inc.

Exhibit 3

CREDIT SUISSE

Ownership of CS First Boston, Inc.
as of August 9, 1989

Owner	Percentage Ownership
Credit Suisse	44.50%
First Boston Management Group	25.00
Metropolitan Life Insurance Company	10.00
Sulliman Olayan*	5.00
Mitsui Trust & Banking Company**	5.00
Dai-Ichi Mutual Life Insurance Company**	2.00
Asahi Mutual Life Insurance Company**	1.00
Daihyaku Mutual Life Insurance Company**	1.00
Meiji Mutual Life Insurance Company**	1.00
Mitsui Mutual Life Insurance Company**	1.00
Nippon Life Insurance Company**	1.00
Sofina S.A.†	1.25
U.S. institutions not identified as of August 9, 1989	2.25
Total	100.00%

*Wealthy, private Middle Eastern investor.
**Japanese financial institutions.
†Belgian finance company.

Source: *Wall Street Journal*, August 9, 1989.

Exhibit 4

CREDIT SUISSE

Major Eurobond Underwriters
Ranked by Number of 1988 Issues as Lead Underwriter
(dollars in billions)

Investment Bank	Issues	Amount	Percent
Nomura International	135	$17.68	10.29%
Credit Suisse/CSFB	82	13.89	8.09
Deutsche Bank	83	11.84	6.89
Daiwa Securities	80	9.43	5.49
Yamaichi	61	7.27	4.23
Nikko Securities	61	6.87	4.00
Merrill Lynch	32	5.95	3.47
Morgan Guaranty Trust	34	5.60	3.26
Industrial Bank of Japan	49	5.59	3.25
Paribas	45	5.52	3.21

Sources: IFR Bondbase

Exhibit 5

CREDIT SUISSE

Volume of 1987 Capital Market Financing
by Regional Corporations in Their Respective Regional Markets
(millions of dollars of proceeds at average exchange rates)

	USA			Europe			Japan*		
	Financial	Non-financial	Total	Financial	Non-financial	Total	Financial	Non-financial	Total
Equities	34,500	33,900	68,400	163,593	73,986	89,607	4,400	23,600	28,000
Bonds	145,600	167,100	312,700	239,019	37,470	301,470	227,900	103,100	331,000
Total	180,100	201,000	381,100	179,712	111,456	291,156	232,300	126,700	359,000
GNP ($billions)		4,700			5,300			2,400	
Financing Per $ GNP	0.038	0.043	0.081	0.042	0.026	0.068	0.097	0.053	0.150

*Includes short-term discount debentures sold by banks.

Source: OECD, EEC, Securities Data Company.

Exhibit 6

CREDIT SUISSE

European Companies' Capital Market Financing, 1985-1988
(expressed in millions of dollars at current exchange rates)

	Debt Issues				Equity Issues				Total Issues			
	Euro	Foreign	Domestic	Total	Euro	Foreign	Domestic	Total	Euro	Foreign	Domestic	Total
1985												
No. of issues	340	93			45	6			385	99		
Volume	33,588	3,478	110,432	147,498	3,253	156	29,233	32,642	36,841	3,634	139,665	180,140
Avg. issue size	99	37			72	26			96	37		
1986												
No. of issues	449	95			107	17			556	112		
Volume	49,465	4,582	142,509	196,556	13,943	2,297	57,570	73,810	63,408	6,879	200,079	270,366
Avg. issue size	110	48			130	135			114	61		
1987												
No. of issues	337	165			109	26			446	191		
Volume	29,239	6,465	165,845	201,549	11,924	3,377	74,306	89,607	41,163	9,842	240,151	291,156
Avg. issue size	87	39			109	130			92	52		
1988												
No. of issues	511	209			43	11			554	219		
Volume	53,931	9,401	n.a.		5,921	740	n.a.		59,852	10,141	n.a.	
Avg. issue size	106	45			138	67			108	46		

Source: Securities Data Co. (Euro and foreign data); OECD (domestic data)

Exhibit 7
CREDIT SUISSE
Major World Equity Market Capitalizations (1987)
(dollar figures in billions)

		1987 Market Capitalization				
	GDP	Amount	Rank	Percent of World	Percent Growth	Percent of GDP
European Economic Community						
Belgium	$ 160	$ 42	14	0.6%	15.2%	26.3%
Denmark	115	19	17	0.3	19.2	16.5
France	987	155	6	2.2	20.5	15.7
Ireland	55	10	20	0.1	19.5	18.2
Italy	842	119	8	1.7	36.8	14.1
Netherlands	244	73	10	1.0	11.7	29.9
Spain	330	72	11	1.0	20.5	21.8
United Kingdom	764	672	3	9.5	20.5	88.0
West Germany	1,274	206	4	2.9	9.1	16.2
Other Europe						
Austria	134	7	21	0.1	11.8	5.2
Switzerland	200	136	7	1.9	10.3	68.0
Finland	98	20	16	0.3	*	20.4
Norway	90	12	19	0.2	27.6	13.3
Sweden	174	49	13	0.7	22.5	28.2
Australasia						
Australia	200	106	9	1.5	21.7	53.0
New Zealand	35	17	18	0.2	*	48.6
Japan	2,830	2,889	1	40.7	21.7	102.1
Hong Kong	46	54	12	0.8	22.9	17.4
Singapore/Malaysia	51	33	15	0.5	15.3	64.7
North America						
Canada	425	199	5	2.8	15.3	46.8
United States	4,461	2,216	2	31.2	10.8	49.7
Total	**$13,515**	**$7,106**				

*Data not available. Information was not available for Greece, Luxembourg, and Portugal

Sources: Salomon Brothers Inc. and MS Capital International

Exhibit 8

CREDIT SUISSE

Geographic Distribution of the 500 Largest Banks (1986)
(dollar figures in billions)

	Number of Banks in Top 500	Pct. of Top 500*	Total Assets	Pct. of Top 500	Total Profit	Pct. of Top 500	ROA**	ROE†
Europe	203	40.6%	$4,047	39.3%	$26.9	40.6%	0.69%	17.6%
Asia	126	25.2	3,345	32.5	15.0	22.7	0.47	17.4
U.S.	110	22.0	2,187	21.2	17.4	26.3	0.80	26.0
Other	61	12.2	717	7.0	6.9	10.4	1.08	10.0
Total	500	100.0%	$10,296	100.0%	$66.2	100.0%		

*Ranked by assets by *The Banker*.
**ROA: Return on assets.
†ROE: Return on equity.

Source: Salomon Brothers Inc. and *The Banker*.

Notes

Case 16: NATIONAL BANK OF LOS ANGELES

John Schultz, chief financial officer of the National Bank of Los Angeles (NBLA), sat down at his desk, putting in front of him the pile of material he had received that morning, August 10, 1988. Even the view over the Hollywood hills from his tenth-floor corner office did not catch his attention. He had returned from a small seminar, hosted by the bank's certified public accounting firm, covering a hot new topic: risk-based capital requirements.

Before going to the seminar, Mr. Schultz had read about the new capital requirements, which were to be implemented by the regulatory authorities over the next few years. Even after the seminar, he was not sure what the implications were for NBLA and how the bank should respond. Many large banks could have trouble meeting the new capital adequacy ratios agreed upon by the Group of Ten countries (Belgium, Canada, France, Germany, Italy, Japan, Netherlands, Sweden, Switzerland, United Kingdom, and the United States) and Luxembourg. NBLA's situation was challenging because it had had many problems in recent years, the most severe having been the write-off of more than $1.4 billion of Latin American debt in 1987. Mr. Schultz felt, however, that the loan portfolio had now been cleared of any significant bad loans. It was time to move forward.

NBLA's chairman of the board wanted a report from Mr. Schultz within the week on the subject of capital adequacy. He asked Mr. Schultz to cover the implications for the major issues facing the bank, such as geographic strategy, rate and form of expansion, product strategy, and pricing. Mr. Schultz was also responsible for determining whether NBLA would meet the new capital adequacy ratios through future profit retention or whether outside capital would be required. If new capital was needed, he also had to recommend the type to issue. "I know it's early to come to any definitive conclusions," the chairman had told Mr. Schultz when he asked for the report, "but the sooner we can get a handle on the implications, the easier it'll be to deal with them. I'd appreciate as concrete recommendations as possible. When we've looked at what you've found, we'll show it to the Management Committee and plan a presentation to the board."

National Bank of Los Angeles

Founded in 1905, NBLA had grown rapidly serving the California market. In particular, it had a loyal base of diverse, middle-market corporate customers. The service given to these companies was among the best in the industry. Although not headquartered in New York, NBLA was considered a money center bank. As of December 31, 1987, it had total assets of

$75.7 billion. (Exhibits 1 and 2 present recent financial statements.) Its size and global presence had made it a significant player in all the financial markets.

As was common among money center banks, NBLA's recent growth had come mainly from global expansion, both in operations and international loans. (Exhibits 3 and 4 summarize the portfolio in 1986 and 1987.) Domestic loan demand had been sluggish; the industry thus jumped at the opportunity to finance developing countries at attractive rates of interest. This ultimately proved to be disastrous; NBLA was not the only bank to write-off billions of dollars in Latin-American debt. NBLA had significantly curtailed its international activity as the result of these problems and was considering expanding its presence in the western retail bank marketplace.

At the end of 1987, the Federal Reserve Board's existing capital adequacy target was a minimum primary capital ratio of 5.50 percent and a total capital ratio of 6.00 percent. (The calculation for NBLA is shown in Exhibit 5.)

The Basle Committee

On December 10, 1987, the Committee on Banking Regulations and Supervisory Practices,* a group composed of the central banks of the Group of Ten countries and Luxembourg, published for comment a framework for assessing the capital adequacy of commercial banks. The need for a consistent worldwide standard to measure banks' capital had arisen as a result of the uncertain economic conditions and a growing perception of the risk presented by off-balance-sheet (OBS) products not previously subject to regulation. Furthermore, the lack of a uniform regulatory environment appeared to give banks an advantage in some markets but put them at disadvantage in others.

In the United States, the Federal Reserve Board was especially concerned with the growing risks from member banks' OBS activities. The ten largest U.S. banks had issued standby letters of credit, interest rate swaps, and foreign exchange contracts, all OBS items, which represented over 130 percent of their total assets. Predictably, because OBS exposure was not included in the calculation of any capital adequacy ratios, banks considered the costs of providing such products much less than the costs of traditional services. The traditional services usually appeared as balance sheet items and thus required capital support. The savings on OBS products were at least in part passed along to the ultimate consumer, but the thin pricing that had developed for many OBS products was considered too small for the risk involved. Low pricing also could encourage excessive use of a product.

---

*This group was generally called The Basle Committee after the location of its meetings at the Bank for International Settlements in Basle, Switzerland. It was not, however, an official organ of that institution but rather an informal group of central bank and regulatory officials.

The regulatory bodies were also concerned with measuring the varying degrees of risk associated with a bank's assets. In the United States, all assets (Treasury bills or international loans) were weighted equally in calculating capital adequacy ratios. This evaluation system had prompted many banks to reduce their liquidity, moving from investments in cash and government securities to loans and other higher risk investments. This change presumably generated higher returns on assets. This possible lack of liquidity was a major concern to federal regulators, especially if a money center bank ran into problems.

A variety of ways of calculating capital adequacy were used elsewhere in the world and, partly as a result, the required level of acceptable capital varied widely. In some systems, banks (especially those owned by the government) appeared to operate with virtually no capital. Consequently, even the narrowest of spreads over the cost of funds and doing business could produce an acceptable return on equity. This condition put the banks headquartered in more stringent regulatory systems at a great competitive disadvantage. They could pass up the business, lower their profitability on equity, or upset their regulatory agencies. Both the banks affected and their regulators began to press for more uniformity.

The search was not an easy one. Not only did regulatory practices and philosophies differ among the major economic powers, but the purpose and function of the financial institutions differed, as did the nature of the ownership. Should a bank owned by a national government, for example, be required to have any capital at all? Should it be required to make a profit if its purpose was to maintain employment? What should be done about doubtful loans in economic systems that do not permit bankruptcy but instead encourage borrowing from government-owned banks? It took extended and complex negotiations to agree on the framework of an approach. Eventually, the United States and the United Kingdom forced the issue by announcing the adoption of a joint approach without waiting for final assent of the other major players. Ultimately, the result was the Basle agreement.

The Basle agreement had three parts. The first, and most critical, was a *common definition of capital*. Because accounting methods varied from country to country, capital was divided into two tiers. The first tier was considered *core* capital. Core capital was defined as reported common shareholders' equity plus cumulative preferred stock up to 25 percent of core capital. By 1992, core capital had to be calculated net of all goodwill. Any new goodwill incurred after the adoption of the rules had to be deducted immediately.

The second tier, called *supplementary* capital, included everything else in the capital structure, such as undisclosed reserves, general loan loss reserves, preferred stock above the core capital limit, and subordinated debt. The second tier was a compromise that allowed countries flexibility in regulating their banks. Some rules that applied were:

- supplementary capital was limited to 50 percent of net capital;
- subordinated debt could not account for more than half of supplementary capital;
- the loan loss reserves to be included in supplementary capital after 1992 were limited to 1.25 percent of weighted risk assets;

- if banks were allowed to include in supplementary capital the unrealized gains on equity securities (as in Japan), the gain would be discounted by 55 percent to reflect market volatility and tax liability.

The second part of the Basle agreement established a *capital ratio standard*. To insure a minimum acceptable standard, the initial first tier capital standard was set equal to each bank's 1987 core ratio. By 1990, core capital had to be at least 3.625 percent of risk-weighted assets (to be discussed below) and 4.00 percent by 1992. Total Tier 1 and Tier 2 had to be double these proportions. The Federal Reserve Board indicated these would be minimum levels, but banks would be encouraged to operate above them.

The final part of the Basle accord established *risk weights* for both on- and off-balance-sheet items. These weights ranged between 0 percent and 100 percent, with 100 percent for the most risky. Each asset was assigned a weight based on the risk category it fell in. For example, cash was assigned a weight of 0 percent; commercial loans a weight of 100 percent. (The categories and weights to be applied to U.S. banks are outlined in Exhibits 6 and 7.) The sum of the weighted assets was the bank's risk-weighted assets, to be used in calculating the capital-adequacy ratio.

Conclusion

The Basle Committee's guidelines for capital adequacy had serious ramifications. NBLA was going to have to develop a new strategy. With continuing bank consolidation likely and with interstate banking being phased in over the next few years, Mr. Schultz knew the chairman wanted to be able to acquire other banks to take advantage of deregulation. The rule eliminating goodwill from the capital adequacy computation would make acquisitions more difficult for NBLA.

Of course, NBLA could always raise additional capital to effect its compliance and allow room for maneuver. NBLA had just issued an additional $500 million in perpetual floating-rate preferred stock. This security offered corporate investors a significant tax advantage over debt of comparable quality. The average cost on NBLA's preferred issues,* all of which were floating-rate-adjusted-quarterly stocks, was 9.07 percent. The preferred stock could be counted as part of Tier 1 capital to a maximum of 25 percent of Tier 1 capital. Any residual amount could be counted as part of Tier 2 capital.

Common stock was another source of potential capital, although not an attractive one. The price of NBLA stock had dropped to a low of $25.62 in the weeks after the October 19, 1987, stock market crisis, less than half the high for the year of $62.00. The price had

---

*The lower yield at which these preferreds could be sold was particularly attractive to companies, such as NBLA, that were paying relatively low taxes. The use of preferred stock in such circumstances was considered to reduce the cost of capital to the issuer.

recovered somewhat in early 1988, however, and by April was trading in the range of $29.00 to $31.50, about 60 percent of the book value of $51.75 as of December 1987. The yield was about 11 percent on the current dividend of $3.40. NBLA's beta was 1.13. Book value had grown at a compound rate of 5 percent to 6 percent over the previous ten years, but some analysts were forecasting a 19 percent to 29 percent growth over the next five years. The loss in 1987 complicated the interpretation of these forecasts, however.

Another alternative was to reduce the size of the bank's assets through sale of loans and loan participations. Sale of assets with high risk weightings could significantly reduce the capital requirements. Not only would this action shrink assets, but NBLA would probably be able to keep some of the spread. Depending on the type of transaction, the profit could either be recorded at the time of sale or over the remaining term of the loan. Mr. Schultz wondered, however, what the reaction of the bank's loyal middle-market customers would be when they discovered that NBLA had sold off their loans. Competition was intense in the California markets, and NBLA had been promoting itself as a reliable provider of business finance.

Finally, the allocation of assets could be altered or riskier products modified to accommodate the capital requirements. Higher pricing would help, but it was possible that some product lines might have to be dropped.

To address these two latter alternatives, Mr. Schultz would have to determine how profitable the various product lines were. Although he did not have the time before he was due to meet with the chairman to prepare a detailed study, he thought he could make a rough estimate of the capital costs of the major components of NBLA's capital. This information would allow him to estimate a weighted cost for each product to compare to that line's earnings rate. It also would point toward the information he would need to come to a more definitive conclusion.

The *real* short-term risk-free rate had been relatively high since 1981 compared to its long-run average. In 1981 and 1982, for example, the 30-day Treasury-bill rate had returned almost 8 percent on a real basis. This figure had fallen to 2 percent by late 1987, but it was again rising in 1988. By midyear, it was back to a real rate of 3 percent and still rising. By comparison, the real rate of return on the 30-day T-bill over the 1926-1987 period had been calculated to be only 0.4 percent.

The historic spread, 1926-1987, between the real short-term risk-free rate and the return on common stocks was 6.6 percent (geometric mean) and 8.8 percent (arithmetic mean).

Mr. Schultz had a challenging task to prepare the briefing for the chairman. To project the bank's capital requirements, he first had an assistant prepare a listing, as of December 31, 1987, (included as Exhibit 8) of all the bank's OBS instruments that would be subject to risk-weighting assessments. His assistant also provided Mr. Schultz with detail on the bank's investment securities shown in Table 1.

Table 1
Investment Securities
(millions of dollars)

	One Year or Less	Greater than One Year
U.S. government and agencies	$ 73	$7,098
State, local, and agencies	226	2,942
Foreign	315	1,758

Although the terms of the Basle agreement were not completely firm and the implementation not yet entirely agreed to by the several U.S. regulatory authorities, Mr. Schultz expected no significant changes following an early August vote of 5–1 by the Federal Reserve Board approving the proposals.

Exhibit 1
NATIONAL BANK OF LOS ANGELES
Balance Sheet as of December 31, 1986-1987
(millions of dollars)

	1986	1987
Assets		
Required reserves with the Federal Reserve Banks	$ 880	$ 1,400
Cash and due from domestic banks	2,564	4,574
Cash and due from foreign banks	3,717	5,407
Federal funds sold to domestic banks	1,358	2,525
U.S. short-term securities under resale agreement	1,192	2,218
Trading account assets (net)		
U.S. and agency issues of one year or less to maturity	1,828	1,095
U.S. and agency issues of greater than one year to maturity	601	455
Investment securities (see Table 1)	9,344	12,412
Loans (see Exhibit 3)	49,281	62,250
Less: Allowance for loan losses	(836)	(2,585)
Net loans	$48,445	$59,665
Premises and equipment	593	1,321
Due from customers on acceptances	2,315	1,901
Accrued interest receivable	823	1,371
Other assets*	2,046	3,392
Total assets	$75,706	$97,736
Liabilities		
Total deposits	$48,818	$69,386**
Short-term debt	16,679	17,089
Acceptances outstanding	2,333	1,906
Accounts payable and accruals	895	1,564
Other liabilities	1,260	1,443
Long-term subordinated debt†	773	1,263
Other long-term debt	1,048	1,334
Total liabilities	$71,806	$93,985
Stockholders' Equity		
Preferred stock	$ 388	$ 880
Common stock	760	875
Capital surplus	476	1,025
Accumulated translation adjustment	(5)	23
Retained earnings	2,299	966
Treasury stock	(18)	(18)
Total stockholders' equity	$ 3,900	$ 3,751
Total liabilities and stockholders' equity	$75,706	$97,736

*Includes $500 million of goodwill.
**Includes $16.3 billion of foreign deposits.
†Qualifies as primary capital under existing regulations.

Exhibit 2
NATIONAL BANK OF LOS ANGELES
Income Statement for the Years Ending December 31, 1985-1987
(millions of dollars except per-share figures.)

	1985	1986	1987
Interest Income			
Loans	$5,068	$4,662	$ 5,221
Investment securities	465	530	879
Trading account assets (net)	161	159	132
Federal funds sold and securities under resale agreements	150	165	323
Deposits in other banks	260	195	336
Total interest income	$6,104	$5,711	$ 6,891
Interest Expense			
Deposits	$2,638	$2,223	$ 2,911
Short-term borrowings	1,347	1,198	1,289
Long-term debt	154	142	176
Total interest expense	$4,139	$3,563	$ 4,376
Net interest income	$1,965	$2,148	$ 2,515
Provision for loan losses	$ 352	$ 549	$ 1,865
Net interest income after provision for loan losses	$1,613	$1,599	$ 650
Noninterest Income			
Trust fees and commissions	$ 105	$ 125	$ 197
Fees for other banking services	511	546	768
Trading account profits	29	59	93
Foreign exchange trading profits	127	129	191
Investment securities gains	161	186	71
Settlement of pension obligation	—	—	158
Other income	28	104	75
Total noninterest income	$ 961	$1,149	$ 1,553
Noninterest Expense			
Salaries	$ 775	$ 870	$ 1,188
Employee benefits	176	210	230
Occupancy expense	248	249	314
Equipment expense	158	167	222
Other expenses	558	638	1,142
Total noninterest expense	$1,915	$2,134	$ 3,096
Income (loss) before taxes	$ 659	$ 614	$(893)
Income taxes	170	111	175
Net income	$ 489	$ 503	$(1,068)
Earnings per share	$9.16	$9.46	$(20.85)
Dividends per share	3.10	3.25	3.40
Market price range per share	41½-58	51-70½	25⅝-62
Price-earnings ratio	4-6×	5-7×	n.matl.
Book value per share	$57.00	$63.80	$51.75

Exhibit 3

NATIONAL BANK OF LOS ANGELES

Loan Portfolio Composition as of December 31, 1986-1987
(millions)

	1986	1987
Domestic Loans		
Commercial and financial	$20,633	$23,786
Real estate:		
Construction	2,564	4,936
Commercial mortgages	2,896	4,350
Residential mortgages	2,696	4,264
Consumer loans	5,266	7,121
Other	255	616
Total	$34,310	$45,073
International Loans		
Commercial and financial	$ 6,283	$ 7,613
Banks and other financial institutions	2,783	3,101
Governments and official institutions	3,493	2,980
Residential mortgages	1,101	2,278
Other	1,311	1,205
Total	$14,971	$17,177

Exhibit 4

NATIONAL BANK OF LOS ANGELES

Geographic Distribution of Earnings
(millions)

	Total Revenue	Income Bef.Taxes	Net Income
1985			
International			
Europe	$ 915	$ 68	$ 50
Latin America	680	104	77
Asia and Pacific	439	(19)	(14)
Middle East and Africa	143	9	7
North America	164	36	27
Total International	$2,341	$ 198	$ 147
United States	$4,724	$ 461	$ 342
Total	$7,065	$ 659	$ 489
1986			
International			
Europe	$ 859	$ 116	$ 96
Latin America	594	62	51
Asia and Pacific	315	—	—
Middle East and Africa	124	(13)	(11)
North America	123	(5)	(4)
Total International	$2,015	$ 160	$ 132
United States	$4,845	$ 454	$ 371
Total	$6,860	$ 614	$ 503
1987			
International			
Europe	$ 965	$ 273	$ 214
Latin America	503	(1,505)	(1,490)
Asia and Pacific	318	(107)	(105)
Middle East and Africa	109	(134)	(130)
North America	120	(2)	(2)
Total International	$2,015	$(1,475)	$(1,513)
United States	$6,429	$ 582	$ 445
Total	$8,444	$ (893)	$(1,068)

Exhibit 5

NATIONAL BANK OF LOS ANGELES

Capital Ratio Calculation, December 31, 1986 and 1987
1987 Federal Reserve Board Guidelines

	1986	1987
Common stockholders equity	$3,512	$2,871
Preferred stock	388	880
Mandatory convertible securities	773	1,263
Allowance for loan losses	836	2,585
Primary capital	$5,509	$7,599
Secondary capital*	980	1,254
Total capital	$6,489	$8,853
Primary capital as a percent of gross assets**	7.20%	7.58%
Total capital as a percent of gross assets**	8.48%	8.82%

*Includes long-term debt meeting certain maturity- and preference-ranking criteria.
**Gross assets are total assets plus the allowance for loan losses.

Note on cost of funds:

1. Secondary capital currently had an average cost of 9.3 percent. Approximately 30 percent was fixed rate; the remainder was floating rate.
2. Mandatory convertible securities had an average current cost of 8.7 percent. About 30 percent was fixed rate; the remainder was floating rate.
3. All of the preferred stock was floating rate–preferred whose rate was reset quarterly. Its current cost was 9.07 percent.

Exhibit 6
NATIONAL BANK OF LOS ANGELES
On-Balance-Sheet Conversion Weights for U.S. Banks

Risk Weight	Instruments
0%	•Cash and currency items •All balances with Federal Reserve Banks •Securities (direct obligations) issued by U.S. government or its agencies with maturities of one year or less
10%	•Securities issued by U.S. government or its agencies with maturities of over one year and all other claims on the U.S. government or its agencies •Securities and other claims guaranteed by the U.S. government or its agencies •Portions of loans and other assets collateralized by securities issued by, or guaranteed by, the U.S. government or its agencies or by cash on deposit in the lending institution •Federal Reserve bank stock
20%	•All claims on domestic depository institutions •Claims on foreign banks with an original maturity of one year or less •Claims guaranteed by, or backed by the full faith and credit of, domestic depository institutions •Local currency claims on foreign central governments to the extent the bank has local currency liabilities in the foreign country •Cash items in the process of collection •Securities and other claims on, or guaranteed, by U.S. government-sponsored agencies •Portions of loans and other assets collateralized by securities issued by, or guaranteed by, government-sponsored agencies •General obligation claims on, and claims guaranteed by, U.S., state, and local governments that are secured by the full faith and credit of the state or local taxing authority •Claims on official multilateral lending institutions or regional development institutions in which the U.S. government is a shareholder or a contributing member
50%	•Revenue bonds or similar obligations, including loans and leases, that are obligations of U.S., state, or local governments, but for which the government entity is committed to repay the debt only out of revenues from the facilities financed •Credit equivalent amounts of interest rate and foreign exchange rate related contracts, except for those assigned to a lower risk category •First mortgages on 1- to 4-family domestic residential property
100%	•All other claims on private obligors •All other assets

Source: Alexander G. Cole, "Risk-Based Capital: A Loan and Credit Officer's Primer," *The Journal of Commercial Bank Lending* (August 1988), pgs. 4-21, adjusted for subsequent decision of the Federal Reserve Board.

Exhibit 7

NATIONAL BANK OF LOS ANGELES

Conversion Weights for Off-Balance-Sheet Instruments

Risk Weight	Instruments
100%	• Direct credit substitutes and acceptances • Sale and repurchase agreements and asset sales with recourse, where the credit risk remains with the bank • Forward agreements to purchase assets, including financing facilities with certain drawdown • Acquisitions of risk participations in bankers acceptances and participations in direct credit substitutes
50%	• Certain transaction-related contingent items, i.e., performance bonds, warranties and standby letters of credit related to particular transactions • Note issuance facilities and revolving underwriting facilities • Unused commitments with a maturity* exceeding one year including commercial credit lines.
20%	• Short-term self-liquidating trade-related contingencies, i.e., documentary credits collateralized by the underlying shipments
5%	• Exchange rate contracts with maturities of one year or more
1%	• Exchange rate contracts with maturities of less than one year
0.5%	• Interest rate contracts with maturities of one year or more
0%	• Interest rate contracts with maturities of less than one year • Unused commitments with maturities* of less than one year, or which can be canceled at any time

*After 1992, the original maturity rather than the remaining maturity will be the determining criterion.

Source: Alexander G. Cole, "Risk-Based Capital: A Loan and Credit Officer's Primer," *The Journal of Commercial Bank Lending* (August 1988), pgs. 4-21, adjusted for subsequent decisions of the Federal Reserve Board.

Exhibit 8

NATIONAL BANK OF LOS ANGELES

Off-Balance Sheet Items as of December 31, 1987
(dollar figures in billions)

Instrument	Amount	Typical Pricing (annualized)
Standby letters of credit	$ 12.2	25 to 50 bp. As low as 10 bp for large, 3A companies.
Long-term unused commercial lines of credit	41.0	Same as standby letters of credit.
Commercial trade letters of credit	1.6	50 to 75 bp.
Long-term exchange rate contracts	85.0	A positive margin if possible; a negative if necessary.
Short-term exchange rate contracts	152.6	Same as long-term exchange rate contracts.
Long-term interest rate contracts*	102.4	20 to 25 bp.

*Such as interest rate and currency swaps, future rate agreements, forward interest rate contracts, and interest rate caps and floors.

Case 17: WINSTON FURNITURE COMPANY, INC.

In mid-August 1987, Michael Easterly, head of the investment banking department at the Thomson McKinnon Securities, Inc. (Thomson) office in Atlanta, was evaluating the details of a proposed $10 million public offering of Winston Furniture Company, Inc. (Winston) common stock. He needed to determine the price at which the stock would be offered to the public. Mr. Brown, the president of Winston who held 35.5 percent of the company's outstanding stock, and a local investment group (which held 51 percent) were naturally interested in receiving the highest price possible. Mr. Brown had personally borrowed to finance part of his stock ownership under terms that provided for sharing the appreciation of the stock with the lenders. Other officers of the company did not own shares but had a nominal amount under option.

Mr. Easterly was slightly uncomfortable because Thomson had little experience with firms in the furniture industry. Bringing in a comanager with a good reputation in this industry could help with the offering but would cut Thomson's management fee in half.

Company Background

Winston designed, manufactured, and sold casual furniture for both outdoor and indoor use. Winston's products were constructed of aluminum, wrought iron, and tubular steel and were offered in numerous style collections. The products featured durable painted finishes and extensive use of fabric cushions and vinyl strapping in various color patterns. The company had combined a cost-efficient manufacturing process, an effective marketing organization, and responsive shipping and customer service programs to become one of the largest sellers in the United States of upper-medium price, quality metal casual furniture.

Winston began business in 1975 as a division of Marathon Corporation, a privately held company. On March 28, 1986, management of Winston and certain investors acquired the aluminum-furniture business of Marathon's division in a leveraged buy-out. On November 29, 1986, Winston bought the wrought iron and tubular steel furniture business (Lyon-Shaw) from the B.B. Walker Company. The acquisition diversified Winston's product lines and expanded its presence in the upper-medium-priced casual furniture segment. Winston's executive offices were located in Birmingham, Alabama. Its manufacturing facilities were in Haleyville, Alabama, and Salisbury, North Carolina.

The development and operations of Winston's business were largely dependent upon the continued active participation of its current management team: William Brown, president; Bobby Tesney, general manager; and Steve Hess, vice president of marketing and sales. This team collectively had over 30 years experience in the furniture industry.

Management's goal was to produce a high-quality product of superior design and style at the lowest possible manufacturing cost and deliver it promptly to dealers and their customers. To this end, Winston had extensively refurbished and modernized the Haleyville facility in 1984 and 1985 at a cost of about $1.5 million. The most significant improvement was the installation of a state-of-the-art powder-coated painting system. As a result of these changes, Winston had reduced the number of plant personnel from 325 to 285, lowering manufacturing costs. These low manufacturing costs, combined with management's philosophy of strict cost controls in other areas, had enabled Winston to increase gross margins without the need of substantial price increases.

In August 1987, the company was modifying the manufacturing systems at the Salisbury plant to implement the policies and procedures used at Haleyville. These changes principally included the addition of another state-of-the-art painting system and would cost about $1 million.

The company was marketing its products through independent sales representatives, primarily to specialty patio, department, and furniture stores and to certain commercial customers. Winston had a total of 3,000 active customer accounts, most which were located east of the Rocky Mountains. The opportunity thus existed to expand to the West Coast.

Winston's consolidated income statements, including pro forma data combining Lyon-Shaw for all of 1986 and analysts' projections for 1987, are shown in Exhibit 1. Recent balance sheets are provided in Exhibit 2.

Winston had been saddled with large debt-servicing requirements over the past several months, which had significantly impaired earnings. The debt had arisen from both the leveraged buy-out and the Lyon-Shaw acquisition in 1986. Thus, management had approached Mr. Easterly about a public equity issuance as a way of reducing the debt service.

Industry Background

The casual-furniture industry was highly competitive and included many manufacturers, none of which dominated the market. Nonetheless, some competitors had greater sales volumes and greater financial resources than Winston. Entry into the upper-medium-priced segment of the metal casual furniture market may have been restricted by the specialized distribution channel used. The significant capital investment required for plant and equipment to achieve sufficient economies of scale also deterred new competitors from entering the market.

Although there was an increasing amount of foreign-produced casual furniture being imported into the United States, Winston's sales had not been adversely affected. The metal furniture produced abroad was generally limited in design, styles, and colors, of lesser quality than the company's products, and was marketed in the lower-end price range.

Management believed that customers purchased based on quality, styling, design, availability, prompt delivery, personal service, and price, as well as on their discretionary incomes. While short-term sales would largely depend on domestic economic performance, demographic trends were expected to give the furniture industry a boost into the 1990s as baby-boomers hit the prime age to buy.

Furniture and home furnishings industry sales were about $5.5 billion in 1986 and were projected to grow at a rate of 5 percent to 7 percent a year for the next decade.

Thomson McKinnon Securities Inc.

Founded in 1885, Thomson McKinnon was the largest privately held retail-oriented investment banking and brokerage firm. It provided a broad array of investment products and services to individuals and institutions and a full range of corporate financial services to middle-market companies. The transactions it concentrated on were in the $5- to $150-million range. Since 1983, the firm had managed or comanaged underwritings for 77 clients raising nearly $2 billion.

The investment banking activity, staffed by over 80 professionals, was headquartered in New York City. A major office for the Southeastern region was located in Atlanta, where six professionals were on the staff. The firm also had 36 other offices in the Southeast and was represented in all 11 states in the region. The strategy was to provide Southeastern clients with the local marketplace familiarity, local accessibility, and market penetration advantages enjoyed by regional firms, along with the resources of a large, national investment bank.

The Public Offering

Mr. Easterly knew that the average price-earnings ratio for the industry was about 13. Betas of companies in the industry were 0.75 in an up market and 1.00 in a down market. According to *Value Line*, profit margins averaged about 4.5 percent; return on equity, 13 percent; return on assets, 7 percent; debt-to-equity ratios, 40 percent; and dividend payout, 25 percent. To make comparison with similar firms in the industry, he had an analyst prepare information on nine other firms, presented here in Exhibit 3.

A variety of factors usually determined the size and price of an offering. Typically, public offerings took place for no less than $10 million, and between 20 percent and 45 percent of a company was sold. This dollar amount suited Winston's needs well, but management wanted to limit the amount of control given up. It also wanted to sell the stock for at least $15 a share. This would represent a fivefold increase in price over management's original cost basis of $3 per share.

In addition to the pricing issue, Mr. Easterly was debating whether to share this deal with a comanager. By bringing in another investment bank with its own distribution network, Thomson would be able to spread its underwriting risk. Thomson had had some recent disappointing experience in placing issues on its own and wanted to avoid such events in the future. Furthermore, the market might receive this issue more favorably from a firm that had recognized expertise in the furniture industry, which Thomson was lacking. Bringing in a qualified furniture comanager would likely achieve a broader distribution of the stock among investors, especially by assuring the participation of institutional investors. This broader distribution could generate higher stock prices and a strong aftermarket.

A comanager would not cost Winston any additional management fees. Thomson, however, would have to split its $250,000 fee (2½ percent) with the comanager. It also ran the additional risk of losing Winston as a client as the comanagers jockeyed for position with the firm.

In considering a comanager, Mr. Easterly wanted a regional firm with a strong reputation in the furniture industry and with some knowledge of Winston. There were two candidates that stood out from the rest of the crowd in meeting these criteria: Robinson Humphrey and Wheat First Securities. Robinson, located in Atlanta, was a well-known name in furniture. Due to its proximity to Winston, it was surely familiar with the company. Wheat, based in Richmond, Virginia, was not in direct competition with Thomson's Atlanta office. Wheat's expertise with furniture companies was widely recognized. It had been invited by Winston a few months earlier to take this issue to market but had turned Winston down.

Underwriting risk was shared proportionally among comanagers, as were fees. Thus, in this transaction, if a comanager was invited to participate, both risk and fees would be shared 50-50.

Underwriting Procedure

Several days before an offering, the underwriter(s) will have contacted potential customers and normally will have taken enough verbal orders or expression of interest (on the basis of a preliminary prospectus) at the yet undetermined offering price to place the entire offering. If possible, the underwriter(s) will have overallotted the offering. Industry practice provided that issuing companies grant the underwriter(s) an option to purchase up to 15 percent additional shares over the amount originally planned for the offering. This allocation was called the "Green Shoe" amount after the issue originating this practice. The arrangement permitted the underwriter(s) to take a short position in the offering to effect stabilization (as described later) without market risk. The Green Shoe also permitted the underwriter(s) to earn 15 percent more in commissions as well as to satisfy unexpected demand on the part of institutional clients.

Five days before the offering date, the underwriter(s) would sign a contract (the Underwriting Agreement) to purchase at a specified price all of the shares to be offered. Should the market take a drastic turn downward in the interim five days, the offering could be canceled, and the underwriter(s) would incur no loss.

Should the market only soften somewhat, however, the offering would probably proceed as planned. In this case, investors would likely attempt to avoid their verbal orders to purchase the stock at the offering price because the stock's value in the open market would be expected to fall after issuance. The underwriter(s) could thus lose orders but would be forced to purchase the stock at the price specified in the Underwriting Agreement. They could therefore be stuck holding a significant number of shares trading in the stock market at a value below the price paid to the company.

During and immediately following the offering, the underwriter(s) would buy and sell shares to stabilize the stock price on the market. This activity, known as "making a market" in the stock, could last from one hour to one month following the offering. The underwriter(s) will lose on these transactions if the offering price is too high or if the market softens. Of course, the Green Shoe overallotment option helps to mitigate the risk by allowing the underwriters to sell short ahead of the issue and cover with the Green Shoe shares if the regular issue sells out.

If the offering price was too low, the stock would go to a large premium above the issue price, and the company would not have received the full value of the offering.

Underwriters make a market in recently issued stock to reinforce a reputation for successful offerings and to provide better service to underwriting clients and investors. Underwriters expected the investor in new issues to hold the stock for a reasonable period and certainly not to sell it during the stabilization period. Investors who sold out too quickly might not be offered shares in subsequent attractive issues.

In August 1987, the market appeared quite strong for Winston's initial public offering. (Price indices and over-the-counter volume are provided in Exhibit 4.) There was another recent furniture company issue on the market, and comparable companies were trading high. Most analysts felt that both underwriters and corporations faced only downside risk by waiting for the market. Mr. Easterly knew he had some decisions to make. Should he bring in a comanager and, if so, whom? How many shares should Winston issue at what price to raise the $10 million?

Exhibit 1
WINSTON FURNITURE COMPANY, INC.
Consolidated Statements of Income, Years Ended December 31, 1982-1985,
Pro Forma for 12 Months Ended December 31, 1986, and March 31, 1987,
and Projected for Year Ending December 31, 1987
(dollars in thousands)

	FY Ended 12/31/82		FY Ended 12/31/83		FY Ended 12/31/84		FY Ended 12/31/85		Pro Forma① FY Ended 12/31/86		Pro Forma① Trailing 12 months 3/31/87		Projected FY Ended 12/31/87	
Net sales②	$14,399	100.0%	$17,643	100.0%	$19,706	100.0%	$20,876	100.0%	$30,463	100.0%	$31,396	100.0%	$34,897	100.0%
Cost of sales	10,096	70.1	11,688	66.2	13,456	68.3	12,157	58.2	19,091	62.7	19,393	61.8	21,348	61.2
Gross margin	$ 4,303	29.9%	$ 5,955	33.8%	$ 6,250	31.7%	$ 8,719	41.8%	$11,372	37.3%	$12,003	38.2%	$13,549	38.8%
Selling, G&A, R&D expenses	2,526	17.5	3,215	18.2	3,463	17.6	4,000	19.2	5,309	17.4	5,303	16.9	6,092	17.5
Operating income	$ 1,777	12.3%	$ 2,740	15.5%	$ 2,787	14.1%	$ 4,719	22.6%	$ 6,063	19.9%	$ 6,700	21.3%	$ 7,457	21.4%
Amortization	19	0.1	18	0.1	18	0.1	18	0.1	1,185	3.9	1,226	3.9	1,361	3.9
Earn. bef. int. & tax	$ 1,758	12.2%	$ 2,722	15.4%	$ 2,769	14.1%	$ 4,701	22.5%	$ 4,878	16.0%	$ 5,474	17.4%	$ 6,096	17.5%
Interest expense	546	3.8	336	1.9	343	1.7	223	1.1	2,816	9.2	2,868	9.1	2,769	7.9
Interest income	—	—	—	—	(31)	−0.2	(59)	−0.3	(75)	−0.2	(66)	−0.2	(51)	−0.1
Earn. bef. tax.	$ 1,212	8.4%	$ 2,386	13.5%	$ 2,457	12.5%	$ 4,537	21.7%	$ 2,137	7.0%	$ 2,672	8.5%	$ 3,378	9.7%
Income tax③	560	3.9	1,091	6.2	1,095	5.6	2,121	10.2	1,061	3.5	1,299	4.1	1,554	4.5
Net income	$ 652	4.5%	$ 1,295	7.3%	$ 1,362	6.9%	$ 2,416	11.6%	$ 1,076	3.5%	$ 1,373	4.4%	$ 1,824	5.2%

	FY Ended 12/31/86	Trailing 12 months 3/31/87	FY Ended 12/31/87
Net Income Per Common Share: As reported Primary④	$1.61	$2.06	$2.73
Fully diluted⑤	$1.08	$1.37	$1.81
Cash flow (net income plus depreciation & amortization)	$2,511		$3,929
EBIT/Interest as reported	1.7×	1.9×	2.2×

Compound Annual Growth Rates (1983-1986): Revenues② = 36.7%; Operating income = 30.3%; EBIT = 21.5%

①Pro forma data prepared as if the acquisitions of Winston and of Lyon-Shaw occurred on January 1, 1986.
②Sales for FY'82, FY'83, and FY'84 include gross sales of a previously owned wrought iron division of $6,554,000, $5,963,000, and $3,639,000, respectively. This division was sold in 1984. Compound annual growth rate for revenues excludes wrought iron sales in 1983.
③Because of state income taxes and the amortization for reporting purpose of goodwill not deductible for tax purposes, the company's tax rate will be a few percentage points higher than the federal statutory tax rate.
④Current shares of common stock outstanding total 667,000.
⑤Includes 359,000 shares of common stock to be issued upon conversion of $500,000 of convertible subordinated notes.

Exhibit 2
WINSTON FURNITURE COMPANY, INC.
Consolidated Balance Sheets
as of March 28, 1986, December 31, 1986, and June 26, 1987
(thousands of dollars)

	March 28, 1986 (division of Marathon)	December 31, 1986	June 26, 1987 (unaudited)
Assets			
Cash	$ 4	$ 280	$ 101
Accounts receivable, net	8,533	10,001	5,735
Inventories	1,403	3,079	2,591
Prepaid expenses	156	363	213
Total current assets	$10,096	$13,723	$ 8,640
Property, plant, & equip.	3,749	5,916	6,083
Accum. depreciation	1,869	395	795
Net prop., plant, & equip.	$ 1,880	$ 5,521	$ 5,288
Other assets, inc. goodwill	41	13,419	12,955
Total assets	$12,017	$32,663	$26,883
Liabilities & Equity			
Notes payable	$ 2,545	$ 5,268	$ 1,337
Accounts payable—trade	342	1,113	1,200
Accounts payable—intraco.	1,915	—	—
Accrued expenses	473	1,344	1,571
Accrued income taxes	—	288	625
Payable on L-S acquisition	—	3,823	—
Total current liabilities	$ 5,275	$11,836	$ 4,733
Long-term debt*	1,737	17,671	18,143
Deferred income taxes	13	37	63
Common stock (666,667 shares outstanding)	—	67	67
Paid-in capital	—	1,933	1,933
Retained earnings	—	1,119	1,944
Corporate investment	4,992	—	—
Total equity	$ 4,992	$ 3,119	$ 3,944
Total liabilities & equity	$12,017	$32,663	$26,883

*See note on next page.

Exhibit 2 (continued)

WINSTON FURNITURE COMPANY, INC.

Note on Long-Term Debt
(dollars in thousands)

Investment	Balance June 26, 1987	Current Interest	Annual Amortization	Repayment Term
7% Industrial Development Bond	$ 435	$ 30.4	$60-$85	1986-1992
14% Subordinated Notes	14,500	2,030.0	1,812	1990-1997
14% Convertible Subordinated Notes*	500	70.0	—	1997
Floating rate term at prime plus 2½% (currently 10¾%)	1,146	123.0	204	1986-1989
Floating rate term at prime plus ¾% (currently 9%)	1,482	133.4	144	1986-1992
Miscellaneous	80	.8	—	—
	$18,143	$2,387.6	$2,220	

*Convertible at any time into the number of shares equal to 35% of the then outstanding shares of common stock. The conversion price is $14,285 for each 1% of outstanding common stock obtained.

Terms and conditions of the subordinated and convertible notes provide that cash dividends cannot be paid until net worth exceeds $5 million and thereafter are limited to 3.5% of net income. Various financial ratios must be maintained, and these notes are secured by substantially all of the current assets of the company and the fixed assets of the Lyon-Shaw division. Prepayment was prohibited before 1991 and at a premium thereafter except that $7.25 million can be prepaid at a penalty of 10% from the proceeds of an issue of common stock.

Exhibit 3
WINSTON FURNITURE COMPANY, INC.
Comparable Publicly Owned Companies in the Furniture Industry

Company Name	BenchCraft	Berkline	Bush Ind.	Dresher	Kincaid	Pulaski	Rowe	Stanley	Universal	MEAN	MEDIAN	Winston
Fiscal Year Ends	12/86	6/86	12/86	6/86	1/87	10/86	11/86	12/86	12/86			
Traded	OTC	OTC	AMEX	OTC	OTC	OTC	OTC	OTC	OTC			
Closing Price 8/14/87	$13.75	$12.50	$29.25	$11.13	$11.25	$21.50	$15.75	$ 9.63	$19.25			
Annual Low	10.33	12.00	15.00	10.25	8.87	16.50	11.25	8.25	14.50			
High	15.25	15.75	33.125	13.13	15.00	22.25	16.50	14.50	20.63			
Trailing 12 month EPS	0.97	0.70	1.43	0.62	0.78	1.70	1.15	0.73	1.12			
P/E	14.2×	17.9×	20.5×	17.9×	14.4×	12.6×	13.7×	13.2×	17.2×	15.7×	14.4×	
Beta①	.50	2.36	4.66	1.96	3.61	.93	2.33	N.A.	2.11			
Estimated FY'87 EPS	$ 1.15	$ 1.10	$ 1.55	$ 0.65	$ 1.02	$ 1.80	$ 1.30	N.A.	1.20			
P/E②	12.0×	11.4×	18.9×	17.1×	11.0×	11.9×	12.1×	16.0×	12.1×	13.8×		
FY'86 Sales (millions)	$126.5	$86.0	$65.4	$39.9	$74.6	$98.4	$81.7	$166.0	191.4	$103.3	$86.0	$30.4
FY'86 Net profit margin	3.9%	2.0%	3.8%	6.1%	3.6%	4.3%	2.6%	1.6%	9.0%	4.1%	3.8%	5.4%
Growth 1982-86												
in sales	28.1	6.6	46.4	21.7	9.2③	19.0	20.8	12.8④	19.5③	20.5	19.5	26.9
in oper. income	18.3③	26.8	47.4	55.5	N.M.	27.0	8.7	N.M.	N.A.	23.0	22.6	31.8
Market capitalization	$77.0	$18.8	$87.8	$46.7	$38.3	$62.4	$31.5	$38.5	$346.5			
L/T debt to total capital	39.5%	7.4%	44.3%	0.0%	27.9%	39.3%	31.0%	66.4%	0.2%	28.4%	31.0%	
Market capital + debt to FY'86 revenues	76.1	23.9	151.5	117.1	63.4	84.1	51.3	58.8	181.2	89.7	76.1	
Market value to book value	2.6×	0.8×	6.2×	3.7×	1.6×	2.0×	1.4×	1.3×	2.6×	2.5×	2.0×	
to total capital⑤	1.6	0.8	3.4	3.7	1.2	1.2	0.9	0.4	2.6	1.8	1.2	

Note: Brief descriptions of these firms are provided on the following pages.
①Obtained from Media General weekly financial reports.
②Earnings estimates are a composite of estimates by furniture industry analysts obtained from the Mead Data Central Lexis/Nexis data service.
③Growth Rates for 1983-86.
④Growth Rates for 1984-86.
⑤Total capital = book value of common stock + long-term debt.

Exhibit 3 (continued)

WINSTON FURNITURE COMPANY, INC.

Bench Craft Inc. Manufactured upholstered furniture and distributed it nationally under its own trade name. Customers were primarily furniture retailers and retail chains. Sales and profits declined significantly in 1982, but they have grown strongly since then. A large increase in debt in 1985 was applied to a major increase in assets. Shares were issued to the public in December 1983. Insiders controlled approximately 27 percent of the stock, and Universal Furniture owned 32 percent.

Berkline Corp. Manufactured upholstered furniture, also offering reclining chairs, coordinated room groupings of chairs, sofas, and accessory pieces. Net sales increased abruptly in 1983 from $66 million the previous year to $81 million, with slower increases thereafter. Assets remained at about $36 million until 1987, when they increased slightly to $38.7 million. Net income was volatile, ranging from break even to $2 million.

Bush Industries One of three leading manufacturers of ready-to-assemble furniture including room dividers and wall systems, cabinets, and carts and desks (including those used for personal computers and audio/visual components). Customers included mass merchandisers, catalog showrooms and catalog sales, appliance dealers, department stores, and independent wholesalers. Revenues increased significantly in 1984 and again in 1986. Net income declined slightly in 1985, but otherwise had grown strongly since 1983. Long-term debt had been steady since 1984. The company was closely held, having been offered to the public in April 1985.

Dresher, Inc. A leading domestic manufacturer and marketer of brass beds and brass accessories. Product line expansion has been directed to beds composed of wicker, rattan, and other metals. Sales and profits have increased steadily since 1982. Long-term debt was virtually nil. Officers and directors held about 19 percent of the stock, with institutions holding 39 percent.

Kincaid Furniture Company, Inc. Manufactured traditional American bedroom and dining room furniture for the middle-price market and thus attempted to appeal to the broadest furniture market. Sales had increased steadily since at least 1981, although profits declined by one-third in 1985 from the prior year's level. A further decline of one-third took place in 1986, but in 1987 profits recovered to above their 1985 levels. Stock was initially issued in May 1986. Management controlled about 13 percent of the stock, with another 13 percent being held by two investment banks for their own portfolios.

Exhibit 3 (continued)

WINSTON FURNITURE COMPANY, INC.

Pulaski Furniture Manufactured medium-priced wooden bedroom, dining room, and occasional furniture in traditional styles. The company's sales increased steadily from 1983 on, following five years of flat revenues. Earnings, which had been quite volatile during the 1978-1983 period, increased in every year thereafter except for 1985. Long-term debt, which had been paid off by 1982, increased first to $10 and then $20 million. Officers and directors owned about 14 percent of the common stock.

Rowe Furniture Manufactured and sold nationally a full line of medium-priced upholstered furniture. The product line included sofas, sleep sofas, chairs, and recliners in contemporary styles. Sales showed a steady increase from 1983 onward, although net income hit its peak in 1984 and then declined through 1986. A slight increase was recorded in 1987. Long-term debt remained constant at about $10 million. In 1986, approximately 20 percent of the common stock was repurchased by the company. Insiders owned 42 percent of the stock.

Stanley Interiors Corp. Designed, manufactured, imported, and marketed upholstered furniture, wood furniture, fabrics, draperies, and wall coverings. Sales declined slightly in 1985 but recovered the next year. Profits followed a similar pattern but were still below their 1984 level. Long-term debt increased significantly in 1986 in order to fund an increase in inventories, although receivables and fixed assets also increased. Common stock was initially issued in August 1986. Insiders owned 8 percent but investment banking firms controlled 50 percent.

Universal Furniture Ltd. Designed, manufactured, and sold medium-priced wooden furniture for the dining room and bedroom as well as occasional furniture. The company's plants were located in Asia. Sales grew rapidly in 1985 and 1986. The increase in profits lagged but was almost 50 percent in 1986. The stock was offered to the public in June 1986, with 50 percent remaining in the control of insiders.

Exhibit 4

WINSTON FURNITURE COMPANY, INC.

Stock Market Statistics, July-August 1987

	Closing Prices			
Date	Dow-Jones Industrials	Standard & Poor 400	Over-the-Counter Industrials	Over-the-Counter Volume
July				
10	2,456	359.9	426.0	131.9
17	2,510	368.3	434.1	152.9
24	2,585	362.0	429.1	147.3
27	2,494	363.4	428.9	112.0
28	2,520	365.4	430.0	125.8
29	2,539	369.4	431.2	136.0
30	2,567	373.2	433.6	154.2
31	2,572	373.6	434.9	142.6
August				
3	2,557	375.5	433.1	133.5
4	2,547	373.0	432.8	140.4
5	2,567	374.5	436.3	151.8
6	2,594	377.4	440.8	149.7
7	2,592	379.7	443.6	165.3
10	2,635	383.9	446.3	130.8
11	2,680	390.0	449.4	185.4
12	2,669	391.2	449.2	172.1
13	2,691	391.8	451.6	160.2
14	2,685	392.0	451.6	147.6

Case 18: DAKOTA MENSKA, INC.

Tuesday morning, March 1, 1988, Seig Markel, principal at the investment banking firm of Morgan Stanley & Co. Incorporated, took an earlier train than usual into Manhattan to have an extra hour for last-minute reflection on the pricing decision he would have to make later that morning. He had worked late Monday night, talking several times to Morgan Stanley's Tokyo office to assess the Japanese market. Then he had slept restlessly, most of his dreams appearing in purple, green, and orange, the house colors that adorned the products of Dakota Menska, Inc.

At about 11:30 a.m., Michael Hamilton, treasurer of Dakota Menska, Inc., would call Mr. Markel with the final details of the debt issue Dakota was planning. Mr. Markel, along with representatives of the other two firms invited to bid, would have about 30 minutes to prepare a final price. Dakota typically awarded its financing business using "talk-offs," a process roughly equivalent to competitive bidding. Mr. Markel therefore wanted to demonstrate that Morgan Stanley knew the market. Confidence in the firm's pricing ability might result ultimately in an invitation to lead a non-competitive issue.

Dakota Menska, Inc.

Dakota Menska, Inc., was founded in the late 1800s as North Dakota Mining and Manufacturing Company by A.B. Menska, a Finnish chemist who had immigrated to the United States to pursue his interest in photography. His insights into the marketing of photographic products and his ability to develop the necessary chemical processes to support these requirements had permitted his company to become one of the world's largest producers of imaging products. Its vibrant packages were evident in retail outlets the world over, and it also had a significant share of the industrial imaging market. Initially a by-product of its imaging business, Dakota's chemical products had developed into a large, separate business. On Mr. Menska's death, the directors renamed the company to simplify its name and pay a tribute to him.

Two additional product lines had been selected for development several years earlier: health care and life sciences. Both industries enjoyed and were expected to continue to enjoy above-average profit margins. Health care, at least, was projected to grow more rapidly than the gross national product. To carry out this strategy, Dakota was internally developing a world-class research nucleus. In addition, acquisitions were being sought of companies with strong development and marketing capabilities in the pharmaceutical industry.

Details have been changed to protect confidential information without changing the nature of the managerial decision.

In late 1987, the Silver Bullet Drug Company became the target of a hostile takeover. Silver Bullet, which manufactured, marketed, and distributed prescription pharmaceuticals (ethical drugs), over-the-counter medicines (proprietary drugs), and household consumer products, fit Dakota's criteria for an acquisition. Acquiring Silver Bullet would be a further important step in diversifying away from Dakota's mature core businesses. Silver Bullet also offered substantial cost efficiencies in research, manufacturing, and distribution, as well as economies in purchasing. Dakota therefore entered the bidding as a "white knight," ultimately winning ownership of Silver Bullet for a cost of $5.1 billion. The acquisition would be one of the largest ever made outside the energy industry, and some security analysts suggested that Dakota had paid too much for Silver Bullet.

Some credence had been given this view early in the previous week when the two major bond-rating agencies downgraded Dakota's debt rating to A2/A in response to the pending transaction. Mr. Markel was not sure the agencies were correct in their assessments, which are summarized in Exhibit 1.

The task facing Dakota's financial officers was to develop and execute a plan to finance the acquisition. A $5 billion temporary bridge loan had been arranged with a consortium of international banks at LIBOR plus 12.5 basis points (bp). This spread included a 5 bp facility fee. Commercial paper totaling $500 million had also been sold. Dakota Menska had filed a shelf registration for $1.5 billion in debt. At least half of this would be issued now, with the rest to be sold at a later date.

In planning for the debt, management decided to maintain a fixed-to-floating-debt ratio of about 50/50, with no more than 40 percent of long-term debt to capitalization. (Exhibits 2, 3, and 4 present summary financial information for Dakota.) If possible, Dakota wished to attain an average long-term borrowing rate of no more than 9.5 percent. Finally, Mr. Hamilton thought the option to repay (call) debt was valuable to the issuer. He believed the market cost (paid in higher interest) to get the feature was significantly less than the theoretical value of the call to the issuer.

In a recent conversation, Mr. Hamilton had said his first objective was for a highly successful issue that held its value in the secondary market. This would establish a bench mark for the issues that would follow. Second, he expected a tight spread, preferably less than 100 bp over Treasuries of comparable maturity. Third, he wanted the flexibility to increase the size of the deal above the $750 million minimum.

Dakota was faced with one minor and one major problem that could adversely affect the market's reception of its securities. The minor problem was a design flaw in a recently introduced product that resulted in a much shorter shelf life than planned and advertised. This product, and all other Dakota products incorporating it into their design, had to be recalled from the dealers. The effect on profitability, however, was apparently not enough to warrant a mention in the 1987 annual report.

The more serious problem was the patent litigation that Dakota had lost to Landcam, the originator of and largest factor in the instant-camera market. In June 1986, Landcam had won its patent-infringement suit against Dakota for an instant camera Dakota had introduced. Landcam was seeking $11 to $12 billion in damages.

Dakota's management had issued a statement on February 19 calling Landcam's claims "ludicrous" and "ridiculously inflated," an exercise in fantastic and fanciful speculation wholly divorced from fact. The claim, for $5.7 billion, was more than twice Dakota's total revenues from its instant-picture business and ten times Landcam's total after-tax net earnings on all its businesses for the period 1976-1985.

Knowledgeable analysts considered an award in the $1 to $2 billion range more likely, and one recent report had forecasted a settlement of only $600 million. Nevertheless, analysts worried about the similarity of the situation to the Pennzoil-Texaco litigation and its subsequent highly adverse effect on Texaco's credit standing. Texaco bonds went from a Baa2 rating to Ca, increasing the company's cost of debt by 400 bp and correspondingly damaging the value of the outstanding securities.

The trial to establish damages had not yet been scheduled but was expected soon. The judge in the case had set March 18 as the date for the next meeting with attorneys.

Market Sentiment and Situation

Mr. Markel, in his conversations with prospective members of the underwriting group and with investors, had responded to their expressions of concern by pointing out that, in contrast with the Texaco situation, this case was being tried by a judge rather than by a jury. It was being litigated in Federal rather than a Texas (or other state) court. He detected that the Dakota name did have market appeal and wondered whether the investors were using the litigation in playing poker with the pricing. His conclusion was that a larger spread than otherwise needed would be required for a successful issue.

Another marketing concern was the size of the issue. At $750 million, it would be among the largest investment-grade, ten-year issues ever put on the market. Under normal conditions, the rough rule of thumb was that an issue of less than $250 million required no size premium. The premium for an issue in the $250 million to $500 million range could be zero if the issue were popular but could be as high as 5 bp. Between $500 and $750 million, another 5 bp had to be offered. Mr. Markel had to assess whether these rules would hold in Dakota's case, given the uncertainties of its situation. Statistics that Mr. Markel's assistant had gathered on trading levels for single-A securities are presented in Exhibit 5. Exhibit 6 provides information on the characteristics of selected large issues of investment-grade corporate debt.

In addition to the pricing decision, Mr. Markel had several other issues to address in developing his marketing plan. For example, there was always the concern that if the bonds were put into "weak hands," they might be offered in the "grey market" before the issue had been completely sold out by the underwriters. This situation would interfere with the orderly marketing process by undercutting the price. How should the bonds be distributed among the various constituencies interested in them? How should they be allocated to the syndicate members for retail sales versus to the "institutional pot"?* What mix of domestic and foreign placements was right?

The Morgan Stanley fixed-income sales force had been testing the market by discussing the forthcoming issue with likely prospects. For discussion purposes, they had been using a 100 bp spread above Treasuries, which were then at 8.125 percent for a ten-year bond. A noncall period of seven years was proposed, with the bond callable thereafter at par. Covenants would be standard: negative pledge, sale-and-leaseback limits, standard legal defeasance, but no cross default.

The sales force reported the following as of Friday afternoon:

Investment advisor	9½% would attract interest
Mutual fund manager	Interested in long paper
Major regional bank	Noncall for life
Investment advisor	4-year maximum
Major insurance co.	115 bp spread
Investment advisor	105 bp spread
Major corp. pension	$30 million
Money center bank	$50 million
Charitable fund	$5 million

The syndicate structure, which had been put in place Friday afternoon, was headed by three managers, each committed to 20 percent of the total issue. The remaining 22 members were committed for 2 percent to 3 percent each, although a number reported getting expressions of interest well in excess of their allocations.

Several of the "major bracket" firms reported a demand at 110 bp over Treasuries. Late Friday evening, the syndication department reported receiving a call from the press asking about a rumor that the size of the issue might be increased.

In conversations with Morgan Stanley's Tokyo office the previous evening, Mr. Markel had learned that Japanese institutions were interested in buying $60 million of the Dakota issue if the spread were 100 bp. He was concerned, however, that some duplication might

*The "pot" was a portion of the deal set aside for large institutional orders that could not efficiently be split among the underwriters. These customers were supplied from a centralized allocation maintained by the lead manager. The purchaser was allowed to direct part of the spread on the purchase from the pot to an investment bank that had rendered services to the purchaser even if the recipient was not a member of the underwriting group.

exist between this amount and the orders put in by the New York offices of Japanese institutions.

At 11:00 a.m., Mr. Markel received a list of expressions of interest from institutional buyers, who would qualify for being supplied from the pot, incorporating information provided by the two other managers of the offering syndicate. These offers were tentative and subject to change or cancelation depending on the final terms of the deal. The total was $521.5 million, with the largest position ($60 million) being spoken for by a New England financial group. The other investors on the list of 40 included large, solid financial institutions as well as corporate and state pension funds.

Prospective members of the underwriting group had also been polled regarding interest from retail customers who would not qualify for allocations from the pot. Morgan Stanley's own sales force reported that $60 million of tentative orders had been received, and the total for all underwriters was $542.5 million.

The Financial Markets

Interest-rate forecasts by the economists of major investment banks, as summarized in Exhibit 7, were unanimous in projecting a decline in rates during the first half of 1988 and an increase later in the year. Major differences of opinion existed, however, about the extent of the decline. One firm forecast June 1988 rates on 30-year Treasuries as low as 7 percent, but another projected trading to remain in an 8½ percent to 9½ percent range. By the end of the year, rates as high as 11 percent were discussed.

Exhibit 8 illustrates the yield curve that existed the previous week, on February 22, 1988. Exhibits 9 and 10 chart, for 10-year and 30-year industrial issues, respectively, a statistical analysis (maximum, minimum, mean, and standard deviation) of the spreads of reoffer yields over bench mark Treasury issues for the 1980-1987 period.

The Treasury market had been somewhat volatile recently, as shown in Table 1:

Table 1
Closing Yields on 10-Year Treasuries
(8⅛s of 1998)

Date	Yield
Monday, February 22	8.23%
Tuesday, February 23	8.17
Wednesday, February 24	8.20
Thursday, February 25	8.24
Friday, February 26	8.17
Monday, February 29	8.15

A glance at the screens on which government bond prices were displayed showed Mr. Markel that a sharp recovery was in progress Tuesday morning. The yield on the 10-year Treasuries so far on March 1 is shown in Table 2:

Table 2
"Pricing Day" Yields for 10-Year Treasuries

Eastern Standard Time	Yield
8:00 AM	8.150%
8:30	8.52
9:00	8.147
9:30	8.143
10:00	8.142
10:30	8.133
11:00	8.128
11:30	8.125

Profits and Risk Management

The profits in the transaction were not entirely unrelated to the risk the underwriters could afford to take. For example, Morgan Stanley's compensation would result from three components:

Management fee: This fee of $1.30 per $1,000 bond would be shared equally among the managers. Assuming an issue of $750 million, Morgan Stanley would earn $325,000 ($1.30 × 750,000 × 1/3) from this fee.

Underwriting fee: This fee would be $1.20 per $1,000 bond underwritten. From experience, however, Mr. Markel knew that only some 40 percent of Morgan Stanley's fees could be counted on to contribute to overhead and profits. The other 60 percent would be spent on the indirect out-of-pocket costs of the issue. A contribution of $72,000 ($1.20 × 150,000 × 40%) could be expected on a $750 million issue if Morgan Stanley underwrote $150 million.

Selling Concession: This fee was the commission, of $4.00 a bond, earned on the bonds actually sold. Mr. Markel estimated that Morgan Stanley itself would actually place about half of the issue. If this proved to be the case, the firm would earn $1.4 million ($4.00 × 350,000) of selling-concession fees.

Considering these contribution figures, Mr. Markel had to decide how far he should be prepared to go to help the distribution; whether a stabilization bid should be developed; and whether he should try to hedge against the chance of a loss. He wondered how much money Morgan Stanley would lose if the market turned down a point against the issue.

Mr. Hamilton's Call

Promptly at 11:30, Mr. Hamilton was on the telephone. "As you know, Seig," Mr. Hamilton said, "we've cut the field from six to three. We are asking each of the three to give us a quote on the following basis:

> Ten-year fixed-rate, noncallable for seven years;
> a quote for $750 million and $1 billion.

Please give me a call before noon with your bid."

In addition to the issues already noted, Mr. Markel now had to determine the coupon, the reoffering price, the investors' yield to maturity, the gross spread, and the net interest cost. (The Appendix provides tabulations to aid in this analysis.)

Mr. Markel's secretary slipped him a note that the two other managers of the syndicate had called to discuss how to handle the final bid. Mr. Markel also noted the president of Morgan Stanley walking toward his desk, no doubt to learn what decisions he had reached.

Exhibit 1

DAKOTA MENSKA, INC.

Summary of Rating Agency Press Releases
Announcing the Lower Bond Ratings

January 25, 1988

Moody's Investors Service, Inc. reported it might downgrade Dakota Menska, Inc.'s $2.5 billion of debt because of its plan to pay more than $5 billion for Silver Bullet Drug. Moody's noted also that Silver Bullet's debt, currently rated at Aa2, was under review for possible downgrading depending on the effect of the financing plans on Dakota's financial structure and profitability as well as on how Silver Bullet would be integrated into the Dakota operation.

February 22, 1988

Moody's Investors Service, Inc. announced it had downgraded the debt ratings of Dakota Menska, Inc., and Silver Bullet Drug Company because of Dakota's pending $5.1 billion acquisition of the drug company and because of the potential damage of the Landcam award. The Dakota debt was reduced from Aa1 to A2. Moody's noted that the transaction would significantly increase Dakota's debt leverage. The levels would subsequently decline only gradually because of the likelihood that Dakota would continue its aggressive use of capital to expand. In addition, the adjustment in rating reflected the risk inherent in the Landcam litigation, although Moody's took no position about the size of the potential damage award.

Standard & Poor's Corp. reported it had reduced the debt ratings of Dakota Menska, Inc., and Silver Bullet Drug Company to single A because of the $5.1 billion acquisition of Silver Bullet and the potential Landcam settlement. While endorsing the acquisition from a strategic point of view, the S&P announcement pointed to the probable increase in debt leverage to 50 percent from the previous level of 35 percent, with funds flow falling from 79 percent of debt to 30 percent, as adverse factors. The press release also noted that Dakota's expansion into office information management systems, consumer batteries, and computer diskettes exposed it to increased competitive pressures. Finally, S&P called attention to the Landcam litigation. Though no further large acquisitions were expected, the settlement (likely to be in excess of $1 billion) could hurt Dakota's financial flexibility.

Exhibit 2

DAKOTA MENSKA, INC.

Summary Consolidated Statement of Earnings
for Years Ending December 31, 1985-1987
(millions of dollars except per-share figures)

	1985	1986	1987
Sales	$10,631	$11,550	$13,305
Costs			
Cost of goods sold	7,129	7,613	8,004
Selling, general, and admin. expense	2,378	2,693	3,190
Extraordinary expenses	563	520	—
Total costs	$10,070	$10,826	$11,194
Operating earnings	$ 561	$ 724	$ 2,111
Plus: Investment income	129	129	83
Less: Interest expense	183	200	181
Other income (expense)	23	(55)	(29)
Earnings before income taxes	$ 530	$ 598	$ 1,984
Provisions for taxes	198	224	806
Net earnings	$ 332	$ 374	$ 1,178
Average number of shares outstanding (millions)	341	339	335
Net earnings per share	$ .97	$1.10	$3.52
Market price per share			
High	$35½	$46⅝	$70⅝
Low	27⅜	30⅝	42

Exhibit 3

DAKOTA MENSKA, INC.

Summary Consolidated Statement of Financial Condition
as of December 31, 1986 and 1987
(millions)

	1986	1987
Assets		
Current assets		
Cash and marketable securities	$ 613	$ 954
Receivables	2,563	3,086
Inventories	2,973	2,178
Deferred income taxes	348	326
Prepayments	215	151
Total current assets	$ 5,811	$ 6,695
Net properties	6,276	6,663
Other long-term assets	815	1,093
Total assets	$12,902	$14,451
Liabilities and Shareholders' Equity		
Current liabilities		
Payables	$ 3,440	$ 3,549
Taxes, income and other	209	380
Dividends payable	142	146
Total current liabilities	$ 3,791	$ 4,075
Long-term debt	991	2,212
Other long-term liabilities	603	743
Deferred income taxes	1,209	1,408
Total long-term and other liabilities	$ 2,723	$ 4,363
Shareholders' equity		
Common stock and paid-in capital	936	933
Retained earnings	6,533	7,139
Less: Treasury stock at cost	(1,081)	(2,059)
Total shareholders' equity	$ 6,388	$ 6,013
Total liabilities and shareholders' equity	$12,902	$14,451

Exhibit 4

DAKOTA MENSKA, INC.

Summary Consolidated Statement of Changes in Financial Position
Years Ended December 31, 1985-1987
(millions)

	1985	1986	1987
Funds provided by operations			
Net earnings	$ 332	$ 374	$1,178
Charges to earnings not involving an expenditure of cash:			
Depreciation and amortization	838	975	995
Provision (credit) for def. tax.	(80)	101	193
Retirement of properties	76	183	303
Total	$1,166	$1,633	$2,669
Funds used for acquisition of assets			
Additions to properties	1,495	1,438	1,652
Increase in:			
Receivables	263	217	523
Inventories	182	132	106
Other items, net	99	269	222
Total	$2,072	$2,056	$2,503
Funds provided or (decreased) by financial transactions			
Dividends to shareholders	(553)	(551)	(572)
Treasury stock purchases	(353)	—	(978)
Increase in other liabilities	1,035	851	424
Inc. (dec.) in long-term debt	708	223	1,301
Total	$ 129	$ 300	$ 175
Inc. (dec.) in cash and marketable securities	($ 198)	($ 200)	$ 341
Cash and marketable securities			
Beginning of year	1,001	813	613
End of year	$ 813	$ 613	$ 954

Exhibit 5
DAKOTA MENSKA, INC.
Trading Levels for Selected Issues
(dollar figures in millions)

				Trading Levels								
				2/24			2/25			2/26		
Issuer	Issue	Ratings	Size	Price	Yield	Spread*	Price	Yield	Spread*	Price	Yield	Spread*
10-Year Issues												
RJR Nabisco**	8⅞% Notes due 3/01/98	A1/A	$200.0	IN SYNDICATE			98¼	9.14	+90	98½	9.10	+88
Union Pacific***	8⅞% Notes due 3/01/98	A1/A+	200.0	IN SYNDICATE			–	–	–	98⅜	9.12	+90
Johnson Controls	8⅞% Notes due 2/15/98	A2/A	150.0	98½	9.10	+90	98¼	9.14	+90	98⅜	9.12	+90
Times Mirror	8⅞% Notes due 2/01/98	A1/A+	100.0	98⅞	9.05	+85	98⅝	9.09	+85	98¾	9.07	+85
J.C. Penney	9⅜% Notes due 2/01/98	A1/A+	200.0	101½	9.15	+95	101⅛	9.19	+95	101¼	9.18	+96
Ryder System	9⅜% Notes due 1/15/98	A2/A	100.0	101	9.23	+103	100⅝	9.27	+103	101	9.22	+100
Weyerhaeuser Co.	9⅜% Notes due 1/01/98	A1/A+	150.0	101¾	9.10	+90	101½	9.14	+90	101⅝	9.12	+90
30-Year Issues												
Eastman Kodak	8⅝% S.F.Debs.due 6/15/16	A2/A-	$300.0	89	9.78	+140	88	9.90	+150	88	9.90	+150
McDonald's Corp.	9¾% Bonds due 11/01/17	Aa2/AA	100.0	103⅛	9.43	+105	103	9.45	+105	102⅜	9.50	+110
Kimberly Clark	9½% S.F.Debs.due 2/01/18	Aa2/AA	100.0	100⅝	9.43	+105	100½	9.45	+105	100	9.50	+110
BP America	9⅞% S.F.Debs.due 1/15/18	A1/AA	250.0	100⅞	9.78	+140	100⅝	9.80	+140	100⅝	9.80	+140
Kmart Corporation	10½% S.F.Debs.due 12/01/17	A1/A	200.0	105⅞	9.88	+150	105⅝	9.90	+150	105⅛	9.95	+155
Georgia Pacific	9¾% S.F.Debs.due 1/15/18	A2/A–	200.0	99¼	9.83	+145	99	9.85	+145	98½	9.90	+150
Georgia Pacific	9½% S.F.Debs.due 2/15/18	A2/A–	200.0	96⅞	9.83	+145	96⅝	9.85	+145	96⅛	9.90	+150
Quantum Chemical	10½% Bonds due 1/15/18	Baa2/BBB–	300.0	100⅛	10.48	+210	100	10.50	+210	100	10.50	+210

*Spreads in basis points over 10- and 30-year U.S. Treasury:

8⅛% of 1998	8⅞% of 2017
2/22: 8.23	2/22: 8.42
2/23: 8.17	2/23: 8.35
2/24: 8.20	2/24: 8.38
2/25: 8.24	2/25: 8.40
2/26: 8.22	2/26: 8.40

**Freed to trade 2/25.
***Freed to trade 2/26.

Exhibit 6

DAKOTA MENSKA, INC.
Selected Large Investment-Grade Corporate Debt Issues

Date	Issuer	Rating (millions)	Size	Issue	Call Provision*	Gross Spread
8/14/84	Chevron Capital USA	Aa3/AA	$1,000	Notes due 8/01/87	NC-L	$ 5.00
3/26/85	Eastman Kodak Company	Aaa/AAA	400	Debentures due 4/01/15	NRF-10	8.75
7/09/85	IBM Corporation	Aa2/AA	500	Notes due 7/15/15	NRF-10	8.75
7/10/85	Atlantic Richfield	Aa3/AA–	500	Notes due 7/15/95	NC-L	6.75
7/10/85	Atlantic Richfield	Aa3/AA–	500	Debentures due 7/15/05	NC-L	8.75
2/25/86	ARCO	A2/AA–	450	Debentures due 3/01/16	NC-L	8.75
3/21/86	Occidental Petroleum	Baa1/BBB+	600	Senior Notes due 3/15/96	NC-7	17.50
3/21/86	Occidental Petroleum	Baa1/BBB+	600	Senior Notes due 3/15/91	NC-4	13.75
3/21/86	Occidental Petroleum	Baa1/BBB+	300	Senior Notes due 3/15/93	NC-5	15.00
3/31/86	General Electric Co.**	Aaa/AAA	500	Notes due 4/01/89	NC-L	2.95
4/09/86	General Motors	Aa1/AA+	500	Debentures due 4/15/16	NRF-10	8.75
8/19/86	General Motors	Aa1/AA+	400	Notes due 8/15/93	NC-5	6.71
1/22/87	RJR Nabisco Corp.	A1/A	500	S.F. Debentures due 2/01/17	NRF-10	8.75
3/13/87	RJR Nabisco Corp.	A1/A	500	S.F. Debentures due 3/15/17	NRF-10	8.75
1/27/88	Mobil Oil Canada Ltd.	Aa3/AA–	500	Notes due 2/15/93	NC-L	4.00
3/02/88	GE Capital Corp.**	Aaa/AAA	500	Reset Notes due 3/15/18	NC-L	3.25

*Noncallable (NC) for number of years indicated or for the life of bond (L); nonrefundable (NRF) at a lower rate for the number of years specified.
**Competitive bid.

Exhibit 7

DAKOTA MENSKA, INC.

Interest Rate Outlook of Selected Investment Banks
(Source and dates of forecasts indicated in parentheses following outlook)

Morgan Stanley

Although rates on the long bond may fall to 8½ percent by mid-year, overconsumption in the U.S., a drop in the dollar, and the specter of higher inflation may push yields as high as 11 percent by late 1988. If inflationary expectations remain quiescent throughout 1988, despite the falling dollar, the upsurge in interest rates will be postponed until 1989. (Paulus, 1/8)

Merrill Lynch

Rates on the 30-year Treasury bonds may fall as low as 8.6 percent in early 1988 as inventory levels decline and consumer spending is reduced. Increased inflation and a lower dollar late in 1988 will push yields on the long bond to approximately 9.4 percent. (Steinberg, 1/27)

First Boston

Rates on 30-year Treasury bonds may fall as low at 7 percent by June because of decreased inventory levels and reduced consumer spending. The economy is expected to accelerate in the second half of 1988, testing capacity constraints in various industries and pushing yields on the long bond to 11 percent. (Francis, 1/28)

Salomon Brothers

Slowed economic growth in early 1988 may cause rates on 30-year Treasury bonds to fall as low at 8 percent by June. By late 1988, increased consumer spending, greater capital expenditures, and a higher inflation rate will push yields on the long bond to between 9½ and 10 percent. (DiClemente, 1/27)

Goldman, Sachs

Improved trade figures, a relatively stable dollar, and slowed economic growth in the first few months of 1988 will cause 30-year Treasury bonds to maintain a trading range of 8½–9½%. By late 1988, however, large trade and budget deficits, a weaker dollar, and the possibility of higher inflation rates may force rates on the long bond to over 10 percent. (Dudley, 1/27)

Shearson Lehman

Weak consumer spending and the possibility of a recession will cause rates on 30-year Treasury bonds to fall to 8¼ percent during the first few months of 1988. If a recession is avoided, rates may climb to 9 percent by year-end. If, however, a recession does occur, yields on the long bond may fall to 7½ percent late in 1988 or early in 1989. (Sherman, 1/28)

Exhibit 8
DAKOTA MENSKA, INC.
Treasury Yield Curve, February 22, 1988

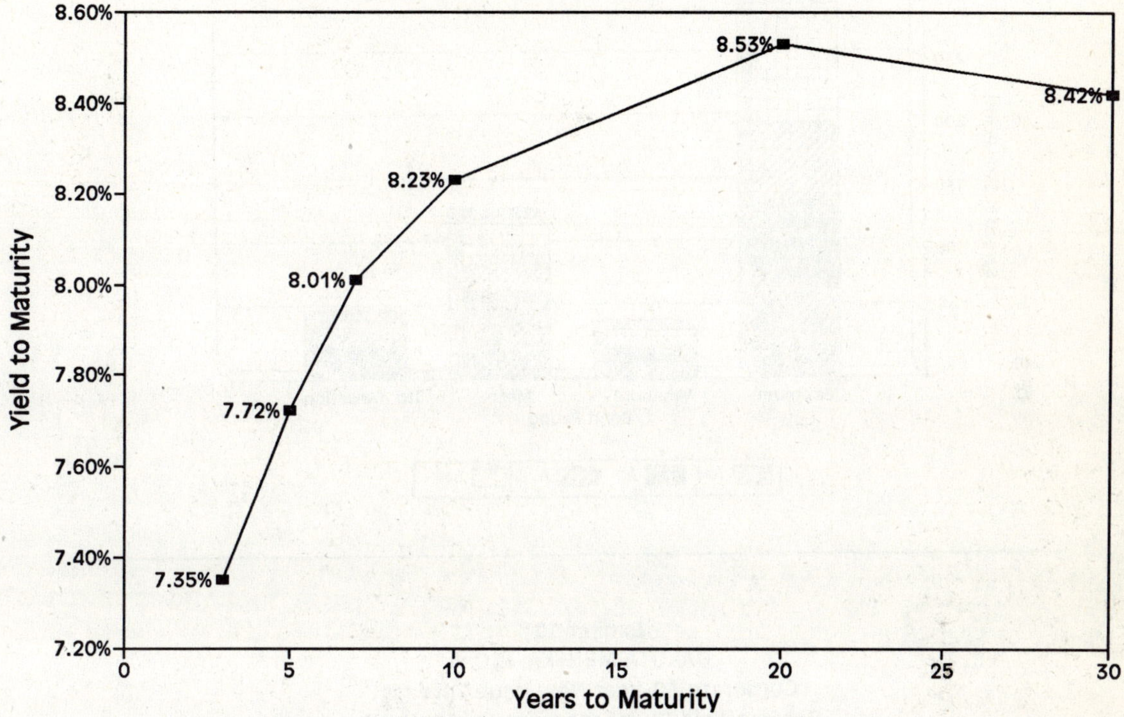

Exhibit 9
DAKOTA MENSKA, INC.
Corporate 10-Year New Issue Spreads
Reoffer Yield Over Treasuries (1980-1987)

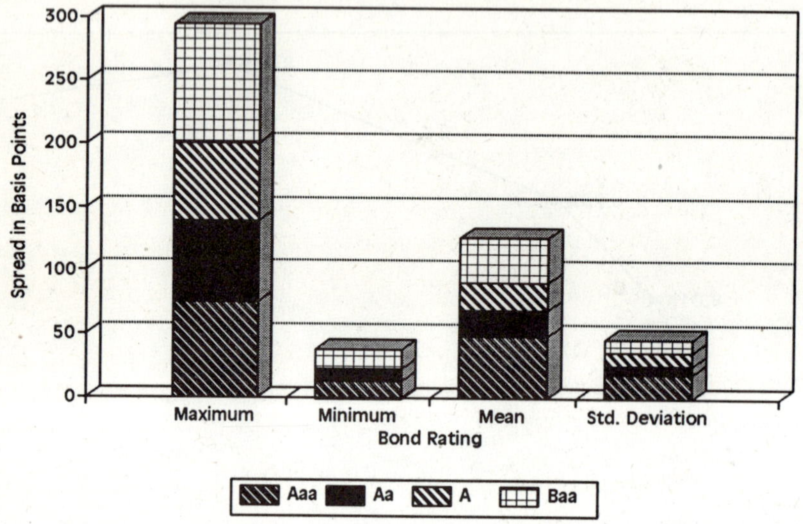

Exhibit 10
DAKOTA MENSKA, INC.
Corporate 30-Year New Issue Spreads
Reoffer Yield Over Treasuries (1980-1987)

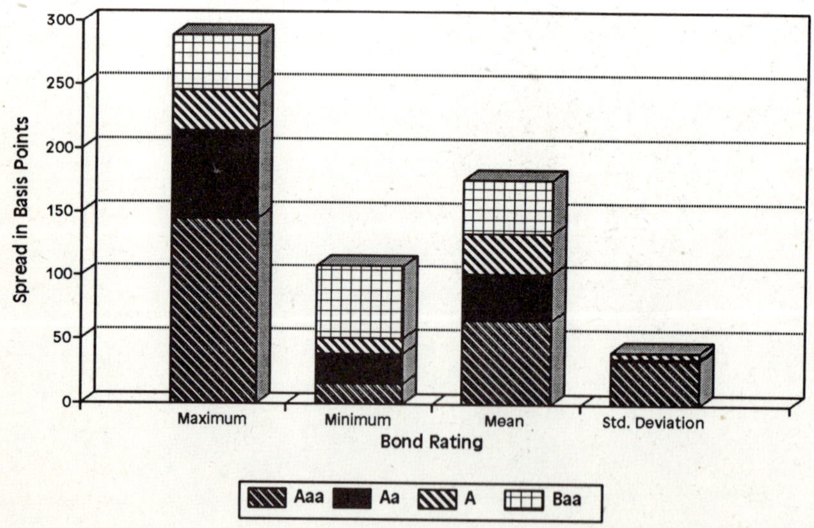

Appendix

DAKOTA MENSKA, INC.

Cost of Borrowing After Expenses at Coupon Rate Specified

The attached tables are provided for convenience in calculating the yield to the purchaser and the cost to the issuer given the coupon, the offering price, and the issuing costs.

Table 1, in which the costs are set at zero, allows calculation of the yield to maturity to the purchaser. For example, if the bond has a coupon of 9.250 percent (the fourth column of Coupon Rates) and is sold at 99.500 percent of par (as shown in the first column), the yield is 9.328 percent. The difference between the coupon rate and the yield reflects the pickup in year 10 of the 50 basis point discount.

Tables 2, 3, and 4 permit calculation of the cost to the borrower net of the costs indicated at the top of the table. For example, as shown in Table 3, if the issue has a cost of 1 percent, has a coupon of 9.250 percent, and is to be sold at 99.500 percent of par, the cost to the issuer will be 9.485.

The tables can also be used in reverse. For example, from the data in Table 1, the various combinations of coupon and price that yield a desired return can be estimated. For example, a return of approximately 9.125 percent to the investor can be obtained either with a coupon of 9.000 and a price of 99.200, or with a combination of 9.125 and 100.0. According to Table 3 (1 percent cost), the cost of borrowing under these two alternatives would be 9.279 percent (9.0, 99.2) and 9.281 (9.125, 100).

From the borrower's perspective, given costs of 1 percent as in Table 3, two combinations (of those presented in the Table) set the bounds on the alternatives if the target maximum cost is 9.5 percent. At a coupon of 9.125 percent, a price of no less than 98.600 must be offered; at a coupon of 9.250 percent, the price must be 99.400. These combinations offer yields to the purchaser of 9.343 percent and 9.344 percent, virtually the same subject to rounding.

Table 1
Appendix (continued)
DAKOTA MENSKA, INC.
Cost of Borrowing After Expenses at Coupon Rate Specified
Ten-year Bond; Two Payments per year; Gross Spread: 0.000; Two Payments per Year

Assumed Offering Price	Net Proceeds to Issuer	Coupon Rate 8.875	9.000	9.125	9.250	9.375	9.500	9.625	9.750	9.875
98.500	98.500	9.107	9.233	9.359	9.486	9.612	9.738	9.864	9.991	10.177
98.525	98.525	9.103	9.229	9.355	9.482	9.608	9.734	9.860	9.987	10.113
98.550	98.550	9.099	9.225	9.351	9.478	9.604	9.730	9.856	9.983	10.109
98.575	98.575	9.095	9.221	9.347	9.474	9.600	9.726	9.852	9.978	10.105
98.600	98.600	9.091	9.217	9.343	9.470	9.596	9.722	9.848	9.974	10.101
98.625	98.625	9.087	9.213	9.340	9.466	9.592	9.718	9.844	9.970	10.097
98.650	98.650	9.083	9.209	9.336	9.462	9.588	9.714	9.840	9.966	10.093
98.675	98.675	9.079	9.206	9.332	9.458	9.584	9.710	9.836	9.962	10.088
98.700	98.700	9.076	9.202	9.328	9.454	9.580	9.706	9.832	9.958	10.084
98.725	98.725	9.072	9.198	9.324	9.450	9.576	9.702	9.828	9.954	10.080
98.750	98.750	9.068	9.194	9.320	9.446	9.572	9.698	9.824	9.950	10.076
98.775	98.775	9.064	9.190	9.316	9.442	9.568	9.694	9.820	9.946	10.072
98.800	98.800	9.060	9.186	9.312	9.438	9.564	9.690	9.816	9.942	10.068
98.825	98.825	9.056	9.182	9.308	9.434	9.560	9.686	9.812	9.938	10.064
98.850	98.850	9.052	9.178	9.304	9.430	9.556	9.682	9.808	9.934	10.060
98.875	98.875	9.048	9.174	9.300	9.426	9.552	9.678	9.804	9.930	10.056
98.900	98.900	9.044	9.170	9.296	9.422	9.548	9.674	9.800	9.926	10.052
98.925	98.925	9.041	9.166	9.292	9.418	9.544	9.670	9.796	9.922	10.048
98.950	98.950	9.037	9.163	9.288	9.414	9.540	9.666	9.792	9.918	10.044
98.975	98.975	9.033	9.159	9.285	9.410	9.536	9.662	9.788	9.914	10.040
99.000	99.000	9.029	9.155	9.281	9.406	9.532	9.658	9.784	9.910	10.036
99.025	99.025	9.025	9.151	9.277	9.403	9.528	9.654	9.780	9.906	10.032
99.050	99.050	9.021	9.147	9.273	9.399	9.524	9.650	9.776	9.902	10.028
99.075	99.075	9.017	9.143	9.269	9.395	9.520	9.646	9.772	9.898	10.024
99.100	99.100	9.013	9.139	9.265	9.391	9.516	9.642	9.768	9.894	10.020
99.125	99.125	9.010	9.135	9.261	9.387	9.513	9.638	9.764	9.890	10.016
99.150	99.150	9.006	9.131	9.257	9.383	9.509	9.634	9.760	9.886	10.011
99.175	99.175	9.002	9.128	9.253	9.379	9.505	9.630	9.756	9.882	10.007
99.200	99.200	8.998	9.124	9.249	9.375	9.501	9.626	9.752	9.878	10.003
99.225	99.225	8.994	9.120	9.245	9.371	9.497	9.622	9.748	9.874	9.999
99.250	99.250	8.990	9.116	9.242	9.367	9.493	9.618	9.744	9.870	9.995
99.275	99.275	8.986	9.112	9.238	9.363	9.489	9.614	9.740	9.866	9.991
99.300	99.300	8.983	9.108	9.234	9.359	9.485	9.610	9.736	9.862	9.987
99.325	99.325	8.979	9.104	9.230	9.355	9.481	9.607	9.732	9.858	9.983
99.350	99.350	8.975	9.100	9.226	9.351	9.477	9.603	9.728	9.854	9.979
99.375	99.375	8.971	9.096	9.222	9.348	9.473	9.599	9.724	9.850	9.975
99.400	99.400	8.967	9.093	9.218	9.344	9.469	9.595	9.720	9.846	9.971
99.425	99.425	8.963	9.089	9.214	9.340	9.465	9.591	9.716	9.842	9.967
99.450	99.450	8.959	9.085	9.210	9.336	9.461	9.587	9.712	9.838	9.963
99.475	99.475	8.956	9.081	9.206	9.332	9.457	9.583	9.708	9.834	9.959
99.500	99.500	8.952	9.077	9.203	9.328	9.453	9.579	9.704	9.830	9.955
99.525	99.525	8.948	9.073	9.199	9.324	9.449	9.575	9.700	9.826	9.951
99.550	99.550	8.944	9.069	9.195	9.320	9.446	9.571	9.696	9.822	9.947
99.575	99.575	8.940	9.066	9.191	9.316	9.442	9.567	9.692	9.818	9.943
99.600	99.600	8.936	9.062	9.187	9.312	9.438	9.563	9.688	9.814	9.939
99.625	99.625	8.932	9.058	9.183	9.308	9.434	9.559	9.684	9.810	9.935
99.650	99.650	8.929	9.054	9.179	9.305	9.430	9.555	9.680	9.806	9.931
99.675	99.675	8.925	9.050	9.175	9.301	9.426	9.551	9.676	9.802	9.927
99.700	99.700	8.921	9.046	9.171	9.297	9.422	9.547	9.672	9.798	9.923
99.725	99.725	8.917	9.042	9.168	9.293	9.418	9.543	9.669	9.794	9.919
99.750	99.750	8.913	9.039	9.164	9.289	9.414	9.539	9.665	9.790	9.915
99.775	99.775	8.909	9.035	9.160	9.285	9.410	9.535	9.661	9.786	9.911
99.800	99.800	8.906	9.031	9.156	9.281	9.406	9.531	9.657	9.782	9.907
99.825	99.825	8.902	9.027	9.152	9.277	9.402	9.528	9.653	9.778	9.903
99.850	99.850	8.898	9.023	9.148	9.273	9.398	9.524	9.649	9.774	9.899
99.875	99.875	8.894	9.019	9.144	9.269	9.395	9.520	9.645	9.770	9.895
99.900	99.900	8.890	9.015	9.140	9.266	9.391	9.516	9.641	9.766	9.891
99.925	99.925	8.886	9.012	9.137	9.262	9.387	9.512	9.637	9.762	9.887
99.950	99.950	8.883	9.008	9.133	9.258	9.383	9.508	9.633	9.758	9.883
99.975	99.975	8.879	9.004	9.129	9.254	9.379	9.504	9.629	9.754	9.879
100.000	100.000	8.875	9.000	9.125	9.250	9.375	9.500	9.625	9.750	9.875

Table 2
Appendix (continued)
DAKOTA MENSKA, INC.
Cost of Borrowing After Expenses at Coupon Rate Specified
Ten-year Bond; Two Payments per year; Gross Spread: 0.500; Misc. Expenses: 0.000

Assumed Offering Price	Net Proceeds to Issuer	Coupon Rate								
		8.875	9.000	9.125	9.250	9.375	9.500	9.625	9.750	9.875
98.500	98.008	9.184	9.310	9.437	9.564	9.691	9.817	9.944	10.071	10.197
98.525	98.032	9.180	9.307	9.433	9.560	9.687	9.813	9.940	10.067	10.193
98.550	98.057	9.176	9.303	9.429	9.556	9.683	9.809	9.936	10.063	10.189
98.575	98.082	9.172	9.299	9.425	9.552	9.679	9.805	9.932	10.059	10.185
98.600	98.107	9.168	9.295	9.421	9.548	9.675	9.801	9.928	10.055	10.181
98.625	98.132	9.164	9.291	9.417	9.544	9.671	9.797	9.924	10.050	10.177
98.650	98.157	9.160	9.287	9.414	9.540	9.667	9.793	9.920	10.046	10.173
98.675	98.182	9.156	9.283	9.410	9.536	9.663	9.789	9.916	10.042	10.169
98.700	98.207	9.153	9.279	9.406	9.532	9.659	9.785	9.912	10.038	10.165
98.725	98.231	9.149	9.275	9.402	9.528	9.655	9.781	9.908	10.034	10.161
98.750	98.256	9.145	9.271	9.398	9.524	9.651	9.777	9.904	10.030	10.157
98.775	98.281	9.141	9.267	9.394	9.520	9.647	9.773	9.900	10.026	10.153
98.800	98.306	9.137	9.263	9.390	9.516	9.643	9.769	9.896	10.022	10.149
98.825	98.331	9.133	9.260	9.386	9.512	9.639	9.765	9.892	10.018	10.145
98.850	98.356	9.129	9.256	9.382	9.508	9.635	9.761	9.888	10.014	10.140
98.875	98.381	9.125	9.252	9.378	9.504	9.631	9.757	9.884	10.010	10.136
98.900	98.406	9.121	9.248	9.374	9.501	9.627	9.753	9.880	10.006	10.132
98.925	98.430	9.118	9.244	9.370	9.497	9.623	9.749	9.876	10.002	10.128
98.950	98.455	9.114	9.240	9.366	9.493	9.619	9.745	9.872	9.998	10.124
98.975	98.480	9.110	9.236	9.362	9.489	9.615	9.741	9.868	9.994	10.120
99.000	98.505	9.106	9.232	9.358	9.485	9.611	9.737	9.864	9.990	10.116
99.025	98.530	9.102	9.228	9.355	9.481	9.607	9.733	9.860	9.986	10.112
99.050	98.555	9.098	9.224	9.351	9.477	9.603	9.729	9.856	9.982	10.108
99.075	98.580	9.094	9.220	9.347	9.473	9.599	9.725	9.852	9.978	10.104
99.100	98.605	9.090	9.217	9.343	9.469	9.595	9.721	9.848	9.974	10.100
99.125	98.629	9.087	9.213	9.339	9.465	9.591	9.717	9.844	9.970	10.096
99.150	98.654	9.083	9.209	9.335	9.461	9.587	9.713	9.840	9.966	10.092
99.175	98.679	9.079	9.205	9.331	9.457	9.583	9.709	9.836	9.962	10.088
99.200	98.704	9.075	9.201	9.327	9.453	9.579	9.705	9.832	9.958	10.084
99.225	98.729	9.071	9.197	9.323	9.449	9.575	9.701	9.828	9.954	10.080
99.250	98.754	9.067	9.193	9.319	9.445	9.571	9.697	9.824	9.950	10.076
99.275	98.779	9.063	9.189	9.315	9.441	9.567	9.693	9.820	9.946	10.072
99.300	98.804	9.059	9.185	9.311	9.437	9.563	9.690	9.816	9.942	10.068
99.325	98.828	9.056	9.182	9.308	9.434	9.560	9.686	9.812	9.938	10.064
99.350	98.853	9.052	9.178	9.304	9.430	9.556	9.682	9.808	9.934	10.060
99.375	98.878	9.048	9.174	9.300	9.426	9.552	9.678	9.804	9.930	10.055
99.400	98.903	9.044	9.170	9.296	9.422	9.548	9.674	9.800	9.925	10.051
99.425	98.928	9.040	9.166	9.292	9.418	9.544	9.670	9.796	9.921	10.047
99.450	98.953	9.036	9.162	9.288	9.414	9.540	9.666	9.792	9.917	10.043
99.475	98.978	9.032	9.158	9.284	9.410	9.536	9.662	9.788	9.913	10.039
99.500	99.003	9.029	9.154	9.280	9.406	9.532	9.658	9.784	9.909	10.035
99.525	99.027	9.025	9.151	9.276	9.402	9.528	9.654	9.780	9.905	10.031
99.550	99.052	9.021	9.147	9.272	9.398	9.524	9.650	9.776	9.901	10.027
99.575	99.077	9.017	9.143	9.269	9.394	9.520	9.646	9.772	9.897	10.023
99.600	99.102	9.013	9.139	9.265	9.390	9.516	9.642	9.768	9.893	10.019
99.625	99.127	9.009	9.135	9.261	9.387	9.512	9.638	9.764	9.889	10.015
99.650	99.152	9.005	9.131	9.257	9.383	9.508	9.634	9.760	9.885	10.011
99.675	99.177	9.002	9.127	9.253	9.379	9.504	9.630	9.756	9.881	10.007
99.700	99.202	8.998	9.123	9.249	9.375	9.500	9.626	9.752	9.877	10.003
99.725	99.226	8.994	9.120	9.245	9.371	9.497	9.622	9.748	9.873	9.999
99.750	99.251	8.990	9.116	9.241	9.367	9.493	9.618	9.744	9.869	9.995
99.775	99.276	8.986	9.112	9.237	9.363	9.489	9.614	9.740	9.866	9.991
99.800	99.301	8.982	9.108	9.234	9.359	9.485	9.610	9.736	9.862	9.987
99.825	99.326	8.979	9.104	9.230	9.355	9.481	9.606	9.732	9.858	9.983
99.850	99.351	8.975	9.100	9.226	9.351	9.477	9.602	9.728	9.854	9.979
99.875	99.376	8.971	9.096	9.222	9.347	9.473	9.599	9.724	9.850	9.975
99.900	99.401	8.967	9.093	9.218	9.344	9.469	9.595	9.720	9.846	9.971
99.925	99.425	8.963	9.089	9.214	9.340	9.465	9.591	9.716	9.842	9.967
99.950	99.450	8.959	9.085	9.210	9.336	9.461	9.587	9.712	9.838	9.963
99.975	99.475	8.956	9.081	9.206	9.332	9.457	9.583	9.708	9.834	9.959
100.000	99.500	8.952	9.077	9.203	9.328	9.453	9.579	9.704	9.830	9.955

Table 3
Appendix (continued)
DAKOTA MENSKA, INC.
Cost of Borrowing After Expenses at Coupon Rate Specified
Ten-year Bond; Two Payments per Year; Gross Spread: 1.000; Misc. Expenses: 0.000

Assumed Offering Price	Net Proceeds to Issuer	Coupon Rate 8.875	9.000	9.125	9.250	9.375	9.500	9.625	9.750	9.875
98.500	97.515	9.261	9.389	9.516	9.643	9.770	9.897	10.024	10.151	10.279
98.525	97.540	9.258	9.385	9.512	9.639	9.766	9.893	10.020	10.147	10.274
98.550	97.565	9.254	9.381	9.508	9.635	9.762	9.889	10.016	10.143	10.270
98.575	97.589	9.250	9.377	9.504	9.631	9.758	9.885	10.012	10.139	10.266
98.600	97.614	9.246	9.373	9.500	9.627	9.754	9.881	10.008	10.135	10.262
98.625	97.639	9.242	9.369	9.496	9.623	9.750	9.877	10.004	10.131	10.258
98.650	97.664	9.238	9.365	9.492	9.619	9.746	9.873	10.000	10.127	10.254
98.675	97.688	9.234	9.361	9.488	9.615	9.742	9.869	9.996	10.123	10.250
98.700	97.713	9.230	9.357	9.484	9.611	9.738	9.865	9.992	10.119	10.246
98.725	97.738	9.226	9.353	9.480	9.607	9.734	9.861	9.988	10.115	10.242
98.750	97.763	9.222	9.349	9.476	9.603	9.730	9.857	9.984	10.111	10.238
98.775	97.787	9.218	9.345	9.472	9.599	9.726	9.853	9.980	10.107	10.234
98.800	97.812	9.215	9.341	9.468	9.595	9.722	9.849	9.976	10.103	10.230
98.825	97.837	9.211	9.337	9.464	9.591	9.718	9.845	9.972	10.099	10.225
98.850	97.862	9.207	9.334	9.460	9.587	9.714	9.841	9.968	10.095	10.221
98.875	97.886	9.203	9.330	9.456	9.583	9.710	9.837	9.964	10.091	10.217
98.900	97.911	9.199	9.326	9.453	9.579	9.706	9.833	9.960	10.086	10.213
98.925	97.936	9.195	9.322	9.449	9.575	9.702	9.829	9.956	10.082	10.209
98.950	97.961	9.191	9.318	9.445	9.571	9.698	9.825	9.952	10.078	10.205
98.975	97.985	9.187	9.314	9.441	9.567	9.694	9.821	9.948	10.074	10.201
99.000	98.010	9.183	9.310	9.437	9.563	9.690	9.817	9.944	10.070	10.197
99.025	98.035	9.180	9.306	9.433	9.560	9.686	9.813	9.940	10.066	10.193
99.050	98.060	9.176	9.302	9.429	9.556	9.682	9.809	9.936	10.062	10.189
99.075	98.084	9.172	9.298	9.425	9.552	9.678	9.805	9.932	10.058	10.185
99.100	98.109	9.168	9.294	9.421	9.548	9.674	9.801	9.928	10.054	10.181
99.125	98.134	9.164	9.291	9.417	9.544	9.670	9.797	9.924	10.050	10.177
99.150	98.159	9.160	9.287	9.413	9.540	9.666	9.793	9.920	10.046	10.173
99.175	98.183	9.156	9.283	9.409	9.536	9.662	9.789	9.916	10.042	10.169
99.200	98.208	9.152	9.279	9.405	9.532	9.658	9.785	9.912	10.038	10.165
99.225	98.233	9.148	9.275	9.401	9.528	9.654	9.781	9.908	10.034	10.161
99.250	98.258	9.145	9.271	9.398	9.524	9.651	9.777	9.904	10.030	10.157
99.275	98.282	9.141	9.267	9.394	9.520	9.647	9.773	9.900	10.026	10.152
99.300	98.307	9.137	9.263	9.390	9.516	9.643	9.769	9.895	10.022	10.148
99.325	98.332	9.133	9.259	9.386	9.512	9.639	9.765	9.891	10.018	10.144
99.350	98.357	9.129	9.255	9.382	9.508	9.635	9.761	9.888	10.014	10.140
99.375	98.381	9.125	9.252	9.378	9.504	9.631	9.757	9.884	10.010	10.136
99.400	98.406	9.121	9.248	9.374	9.500	9.627	9.753	9.880	10.006	10.132
99.425	98.431	9.118	9.244	9.370	9.496	9.623	9.749	9.876	10.002	10.128
99.450	98.456	9.114	9.240	9.366	9.493	9.619	9.745	9.872	9.998	10.124
99.475	98.480	9.110	9.236	9.362	9.489	9.615	9.741	9.868	9.994	10.120
99.500	98.505	9.106	9.232	9.358	9.485	9.611	9.737	9.864	9.990	10.116
99.525	98.530	9.102	9.228	9.355	9.481	9.607	9.733	9.860	9.986	10.112
99.550	98.555	9.098	9.224	9.351	9.477	9.603	9.729	9.856	9.982	10.108
99.575	98.579	9.094	9.221	9.347	9.473	9.599	9.725	9.852	9.978	10.104
99.600	98.604	9.090	9.217	9.343	9.469	9.595	9.721	9.848	9.974	10.100
99.625	98.629	9.087	9.213	9.339	9.465	9.591	9.717	9.844	9.970	10.096
99.650	98.654	9.083	9.209	9.335	9.461	9.587	9.713	9.840	9.966	10.092
99.675	98.678	9.079	9.205	9.331	9.457	9.583	9.710	9.836	9.962	10.088
99.700	98.703	9.075	9.201	9.327	9.453	9.579	9.706	9.832	9.958	10.084
99.725	98.728	9.071	9.197	9.323	9.449	9.576	9.702	9.828	9.954	10.080
99.750	98.753	9.067	9.193	9.319	9.446	9.572	9.698	9.824	9.950	10.076
99.775	98.777	9.064	9.190	9.316	9.442	9.568	9.694	9.820	9.946	10.072
99.800	98.802	9.060	9.186	9.312	9.438	9.564	9.690	9.816	9.942	10.068
99.825	98.827	9.056	9.182	9.308	9.434	9.560	9.686	9.812	9.938	10.064
99.850	98.852	9.052	9.178	9.304	9.430	9.556	9.682	9.808	9.934	10.060
99.875	98.876	9.048	9.174	9.300	9.426	9.552	9.678	9.804	9.930	10.056
99.900	98.901	9.044	9.170	9.296	9.422	9.548	9.674	9.800	9.926	10.052
99.925	98.926	9.040	9.166	9.292	9.418	9.544	9.670	9.796	9.922	10.048
99.950	98.951	9.037	9.163	9.288	9.414	9.540	9.666	9.792	9.918	10.044
99.975	98.975	9.033	9.159	9.285	9.410	9.536	9.662	9.788	9.914	10.040
100.000	99.000	9.029	9.155	9.281	9.406	9.532	9.658	9.784	9.910	10.036

Table 4
Appendix (continued)
DAKOTA MENSKA, INC.
Cost of Borrowing After Expenses at Coupon Rate Specified
Ten-year Bond; Two Payments per Year; Gross Spread: 1.000; Misc. Expenses: 0.500

Assumed Offering Price	Net Proceeds to Issuer	Coupon Rate								
		8.875	9.000	9.125	9.250	9.375	9.500	9.625	9.750	9.875
98.500	97.023	9.340	9.467	9.595	9.722	9.850	9.977	10.105	10.233	10.360
98.525	97.047	9.336	9.463	9.591	9.718	9.846	9.973	10.101	10.228	10.356
98.550	97.072	9.332	9.459	9.587	9.714	9.842	9.969	10.097	10.224	10.352
98.575	97.096	9.328	9.455	9.583	9.710	9.838	9.965	10.093	10.220	10.348
98.600	97.121	9.324	9.451	9.579	9.706	9.834	9.961	10.089	10.216	10.344
98.625	97.146	9.320	9.447	9.575	9.702	9.830	9.957	10.085	10.212	10.340
98.650	97.170	9.316	9.443	9.571	9.698	9.826	9.953	10.081	10.208	10.336
98.675	97.195	9.312	9.440	9.567	9.694	9.822	9.949	10.077	10.204	10.332
98.700	97.220	9.308	9.436	9.563	9.690	9.818	9.945	10.073	10.200	10.327
98.725	97.244	9.304	9.432	9.559	9.686	9.814	9.941	10.069	10.196	10.323
98.750	97.269	9.300	9.428	9.555	9.682	9.810	9.937	10.065	10.192	10.319
98.775	97.293	9.297	9.424	9.551	9.678	9.806	9.933	10.060	10.188	10.315
98.800	97.318	9.293	9.420	9.547	9.675	9.802	9.929	10.056	10.184	10.311
98.825	97.343	9.289	9.416	9.543	9.671	9.798	9.925	10.052	10.180	10.307
98.850	97.367	9.285	9.412	9.539	9.667	9.794	9.921	10.048	10.176	10.303
98.875	97.392	9.281	9.408	9.535	9.663	9.790	9.917	10.044	10.172	10.299
98.900	97.417	9.277	9.404	9.531	9.659	9.786	9.913	10.040	10.168	10.295
98.925	97.441	9.273	9.400	9.527	9.655	9.782	9.909	10.036	10.164	10.291
98.950	97.466	9.269	9.396	9.524	9.651	9.778	9.905	10.032	10.159	10.287
98.975	97.490	9.265	9.392	9.520	9.647	9.774	9.901	10.028	10.155	10.283
99.000	97.515	9.261	9.389	9.516	9.643	9.770	9.897	10.024	10.151	10.279
99.025	97.540	9.258	9.385	9.512	9.639	9.766	9.893	10.020	10.147	10.274
99.050	97.564	9.254	9.381	9.508	9.635	9.762	9.889	10.016	10.143	10.270
99.075	97.589	9.250	9.377	9.504	9.631	9.758	9.885	10.012	10.139	10.266
99.100	97.614	9.246	9.373	9.500	9.627	9.754	9.881	10.008	10.135	10.262
99.125	97.638	9.242	9.369	9.496	9.623	9.750	9.877	10.004	10.131	10.258
99.150	97.663	9.238	9.365	9.492	9.619	9.746	9.873	10.000	10.127	10.254
99.175	97.687	9.234	9.361	9.488	9.615	9.742	9.869	9.996	10.123	10.250
99.200	97.712	9.230	9.357	9.484	9.611	9.738	9.865	9.992	10.119	10.246
99.225	97.737	9.226	9.353	9.480	9.607	9.734	9.861	9.988	10.115	10.242
99.250	97.761	9.223	9.349	9.476	9.603	9.730	9.857	9.984	10.111	10.238
99.275	97.786	9.219	9.346	9.472	9.599	9.726	9.853	9.980	10.107	10.234
99.300	97.811	9.215	9.342	9.469	9.595	9.722	9.849	9.976	10.103	10.230
99.325	97.835	9.211	9.338	9.465	9.591	9.718	9.845	9.972	10.099	10.226
99.350	97.860	9.207	9.334	9.461	9.587	9.714	9.841	9.968	10.095	10.222
99.375	97.884	9.203	9.330	9.457	9.584	9.710	9.837	9.964	10.091	10.218
99.400	97.909	9.199	9.326	9.453	9.580	9.706	9.833	9.960	10.087	10.214
99.425	97.934	9.195	9.322	9.449	9.576	9.702	9.829	9.956	10.083	10.210
99.450	97.958	9.192	9.318	9.445	9.572	9.698	9.825	9.952	10.079	10.206
99.475	97.983	9.188	9.314	9.441	9.568	9.695	9.821	9.948	10.075	10.201
99.500	98.008	9.184	9.310	9.437	9.564	9.691	9.817	9.944	10.071	10.197
99.525	98.032	9.180	9.307	9.433	9.560	9.687	9.813	9.940	10.067	10.193
99.550	98.057	9.176	9.303	9.429	9.556	9.683	9.809	9.936	10.063	10.189
99.575	98.081	9.172	9.299	9.425	9.552	9.679	9.805	9.932	10.059	10.185
99.600	98.106	9.168	9.295	9.422	9.548	9.675	9.801	9.928	10.055	10.181
99.625	98.131	9.164	9.291	9.418	9.544	9.671	9.797	9.924	10.051	10.177
99.650	98.155	9.161	9.287	9.414	9.540	9.667	9.793	9.920	10.047	10.173
99.675	98.180	9.157	9.283	9.410	9.536	9.663	9.790	9.916	10.043	10.169
99.700	98.205	9.153	9.279	9.406	9.532	9.659	9.786	9.912	10.039	10.165
99.725	98.229	9.149	9.276	9.402	9.529	9.655	9.782	9.908	10.035	10.161
99.750	98.254	9.145	9.272	9.398	9.525	9.651	9.778	9.904	10.031	10.157
99.775	98.278	9.141	9.268	9.394	9.521	9.647	9.774	9.900	10.027	10.153
99.800	98.303	9.137	9.264	9.390	9.517	9.643	9.770	9.896	10.023	10.149
99.825	98.328	9.134	9.260	9.386	9.513	9.639	9.766	9.892	10.019	10.145
99.850	98.352	9.130	9.256	9.383	9.509	9.635	9.762	9.888	10.015	10.141
99.875	98.377	9.126	9.252	9.379	9.505	9.631	9.758	9.884	10.011	10.137
99.900	98.402	9.122	9.248	9.375	9.501	9.627	9.754	9.880	10.007	10.133
99.925	98.426	9.118	9.245	9.371	9.497	9.624	9.750	9.876	10.003	10.129
99.950	98.451	9.114	9.241	9.367	9.493	9.620	9.746	9.872	9.999	10.125
99.975	98.475	9.111	9.237	9.363	9.489	9.616	9.742	9.868	9.995	10.121
100.000	98.500	9.107	9.233	9.359	9.486	9.612	9.738	9.864	9.991	10.117

Notes

Case 19: HOOSIER HOSE COMPANY

On February 28, 1991, E. Miller Garfield, loan officer at Booth National Bank of Indianapolis, was reviewing the credit file of Hoosier Hose Company (HHC). He had just received a telephone call from Hatcher H. Oates, treasurer of HHC, requesting a third increase in HHC's seasonal loan, from $5.5 million to $7.0 million. The management of HHC had asked for a decision by March 10.

Hoosier Hose Company, with sales of $22.9 million in the fiscal year ending September 30, 1990, manufactured plastic hose for garden, farm, and light industrial use. The plant and corporate offices were located in Indianapolis. Raw plastic was purchased from domestic and foreign sources and mixed with other raw materials. The compound was then extruded onto cores of various types, some of which were purchased and some of which HHC made itself. The semifinished hose was then heated and converted to an elastic state through a process known as vulcanization. HHC employed 300 unionized workers at its plant.

Nonindustrial lines accounted for 95 percent of HHC's sales, with 75 percent going to the lawn and garden market. HHC's share of regional industry sales for its major product lines ranged from 20 to 50 percent. Competition included fully integrated major plastics and rubber companies as well as small local companies. The plastic and rubber hose business was primarily regional in nature.

HHC had difficulty attracting large customers because of capacity constraints. A $5.0 million expansion program was therefore undertaken and had been completed in September 1990. Of the total, $4.5 million had been supplied by long-term debt; the other $0.5 million was generated from operations. Plant capacity was increased from 24 million pounds to 60 million pounds per year, and more warehouse space was provided. The 1990 projected production level was 35.64 million pounds per year.

The Adams Company, a large hardware chain, was HHC's largest customer, usually accounting for 15 percent of total sales. Adams purchased on "dating" basis, whereby invoices were due on May 10 for all shipments made between May 1 of the previous year and the current April 30. Similar terms might be required for any new large accounts. Terms for general sales were 1/2 percent/10 net 30 days.

HHC had been a customer of Booth National since 1915. The relationship had been satisfactory, and Booth currently provided all of HHC's seasonal working capital. The current line was for $5.5 million at 10 percent. HHC was expected to liquidate the loan by June of each year and be out of the bank for at least 120 days. Although the Sycamore National Bank had expressed interest in doing business with HHC, the latter's management preferred restricting HHC's seasonal borrowing to Booth if Booth would provide for its working capital needs.

The Harrison Mutual Life Insurance Company was the only other lender to HHC. In May 1989, Harrison entered into a note purchase agreement that provided for HHC to borrow $4.5 million at 8.75 percent, to be used for the plant expansion project. Principal payments of $350,000 were due annually January 1, 1992 through 2002, with a $650,000 balloon due January 1, 2003. Interest payments were due monthly.

The note purchase agreement specified that HHC must maintain working capital equal to $3.0 million or 50 percent of its consolidated current liabilities, whichever was greater. Unless the acquiring company was in the continuing corporation, the incurrence of further long-term debt, the disposal of a substantial portion of assets, and mergers were prohibited. In addition, HHC could not declare dividends or redeem or acquire any of its capital stock unless the aggregate of these dividends, redemptions, and acquisitions did not exceed 50 percent of net income made after September 30, 1988, plus $1.0 million. Under these terms HHC had a total of $1.4 million available for dividends at the end of the 1990 fiscal year.

HHC was a very closely held company. The two major stockholders were president and vice-president of the company, respectively. Dividend payments were a significant part of their income.

HHC's management had originally estimated HHC's fiscal year 1991 seasonal loan needs at $1.8 million. (Projected monthly financial statements prepared in July 1990 are presented in Exhibits 1 through 4.) Mr. Garfield had approved the line almost as a matter of routine.

Mr. Oates came to Mr. Garfield in September 1990 to request a $2.4 million increase in HHC's seasonal loan to a new level of $4.2 million. Mr. Oates predicted a shortage of low-cost plastic by February 1991 because of the Iraqi invasion of Kuwait. He also anticipated further increases in the price of oil and consequently in the price of petrochemical products. During the oil shortage of 1974–1979, HHC had suffered serious problems in obtaining raw materials, and Mr. Oates thought a repeat of this situation was highly likely.

He therefore proposed that HHC purchase 13.31 million pounds of plastic during the first four months of the fiscal year. The other 4.51 million pounds required would be purchased in approximately equal amounts over the subsequent eight months, as shown in Exhibit 7. (He did not anticipate problems in obtaining other raw materials.) Mr. Oates submitted the statements included as Exhibits 5, 6, and 7 in support of the request. Mr. Garfield contacted representatives of two large domestic petrochemical companies that supplied HHC. They agreed with Mr. Oates' prediction of continuing difficulty in obtaining low-cost plastic. Mr. Garfield therefore increased HHC's line to $4.2 million.

In early January 1991, Mr. Oates requested an additional $1.3 million increase in HHC's line. Mr. Oates cited increased plastics costs as the cause of this need for additional working capital. Through the first quarter of fiscal 1991, HHC had purchased 3.714 million pounds of domestic plastic at the market rate of 35 cents per pound. However, the scarcity of domestic plastic and rapid increases in petroleum prices had necessitated that the company enter into a contract to purchase 9.6 million pounds of plastic from foreign sources at 20 cents per pound more than anticipated. Twenty-eight percent (2.709 million pounds) of the agreed-upon purchases had not yet been delivered but would arrive in January. At the end of December, inventories were $1,760,000 higher than estimated in the revised projections made in September 1990. (Actual financial statements for October 1990 through February 1991, the first five months of the 1991 fiscal year, are presented in Exhibits 8 through 11.)

HHC's management predicted a strong February/April "summer" order cycle from its customers of at least the forecasted sales levels, despite economists' predictions of a prolonged recession. Mr. Oates thought this another justification for the requested $1.3 million increase in HHC's line of credit.

Booth's past experience with HHC had been that its sales forecasts were often inaccurate. Mr. Garfield called the purchasing vice president of Adams Company to determine his outlook for the plastic hose market. Mr. Garfield was told that demand was very strong. Purchasing executives for two other large hardware chains expressed the same opinion. Booth therefore extended HHC's line to $5.5 million.

By the end of February, sales had not materialized as forecasted. Mr. Oates requested yet an additional $1.5 million on February 28. (His letter to Mr. Garfield is reproduced in Exhibit 12.) HHC's need was critical because its cash balance had dropped to less than 50 percent of the minimum HHC's management thought was needed to carry on operations.

In considering HHC's request for an additional $1.5 million, Mr. Garfield remained aware of Sycamore National Bank's interest in HHC. Money was currently tight, with interest rates for short-term debt over 12 percent. Interest rates were expected to decline in the near future; however, continuing signs of a recession necessitated caution in the bank's lending policy. In addition, funds were tight due to the recent crisis in the nation's financial sector. Booth's senior management was working to bring capital up to required levels and was emphasizing profitability over growth. Mr. Garfield believed that Sycamore National was employing a similar capital accumulation policy. HHC's management requested a decision by March 10.

Exhibit 1

HOOSIER HOSE COMPANY

Projected Monthly Statements of Income and Retained Earnings
for the Fiscal Year Ending September 30, 1991
(dollar amounts in thousands)

	Fiscal Year 1990 Actual	Fiscal Year 1991 Projections: 1990 October	Novem.	Decem.	1991 January	February	March	April	May	June	July	August	September	Fiscal Year 1991 Total
General sales	$19,500	$1,670	$1,410	$1,300	$2,300	$2,200	$2,100	$2,290	$2,300	$2,300	$2,070	$1,490	$1,280	$22,710
Sales to Adams Co.	3,440	100	100	200	500	600	600	800	400	400	100	100	100	4,000
Total sales	$22,940	$1,770	$1,510	$1,500	$2,800	$2,800	$2,700	$3,090	$2,700	$2,700	$2,170	$1,590	$1,380	$26,710
Cost of sales*	17,160	1,340	1,150	1,140	2,130	2,130	2,060	2,350	2,040	2,040	1,650	1,210	1,040	20,280
Gross profit	$ 5,780	$ 430	$ 360	$ 360	$ 670	$ 670	$ 640	$ 740	$ 660	$ 660	$ 520	$ 380	$ 340	$ 6,430
Selling & admin. exp.**	3,970	370	348	348	458	458	450	483	450	450	404	355	337	4,910
Interest expense	370	33	33	38	46	46	46	48	33	33	33	33	33	452
Profit before tax	$ 1,440	$ 27	$ (21)	$ (25)	$ 167	$ 166	$ 144	$ 210	$ 178	$ 178	$ 83	$ (8)	$ (30)	$ 1,068
Tax	490	9	(7)	(9)	57	57	49	71	60	60	28	(3)	(10)	363
Profit after tax	$ 950	$ 18	$ (14)	$ (17)	$ 110	$ 110	$ 95	$ 138	$ 117	$ 117	$ 55	$ (5)	$ (20)	$ 705
Beg. retained earn.	3,300	3,930	3,948	3,934	3,837	3,947	4,057	4,072	4,211	4,328	4,365	4,420	4,415	3,930
	$ 4,250	$3,948	$3,934	$3,917	$3,947	$4,057	$4,152	$4,211	$4,328	$4,445	$4,420	$4,415	$4,395	$ 4,635
Less dividends	320	0	0	80	0	0	80	0	0	80	0	0	80	320
End. retained earn.	$ 3,930	$3,948	$3,934	$3,837	$3,947	$4,057	$4,072	$4,211	$4,328	$4,365	$4,420	$4,415	$4,315	$ 4,315

*Depreciation is charged out of inventory at 2 cents per pound.
**Equals 8.5 percent of total sales plus $220.

Note: Forecast prepared July 1990. Actual results for fiscal year 1990 added later for analytical convenience.

Exhibit 2

HOOSIER HOSE COMPANY

Projected Monthly Balance Sheets for the Fiscal Year
Ending September 30, 1991
(dollar amounts in thousands)

	Fiscal Year 1990 Actual	Fiscal Year 1991 Projections											
		1990 October	Novem.	Decem.	1991 January	February	March	April	May	June	July	August	September
Assets													
Minimum cash bal.	$ 500	$ 500	$ 500	$ 500	$ 500	$ 500	$ 500	$ 500	$ 500	$ 500	$ 500	$ 500	$ 500
Marketable securities	715	211	97	0	0	0	0	0	2,076	2,134	2,161	2,124	1,546
Accounts receivable①	2,540	2,910	2,790	2,840	4,320	4,990	5,470	6,440	3,080	3,480	3,350	2,840	2,630
Inventories②	3,240	3,590	4,130	4,680	4,240	3,800	3,430	2,770	2,420	2,070	2,110	2,590	3,240
Total current assets	$ 6,995	$ 7,211	$ 7,517	$ 8,020	$ 9,060	$ 9,290	$ 9,400	$ 9,710	$ 8,076	$ 8,184	$ 8,121	$ 8,054	$ 7,916
Prop P&E (net)	8,570	8,580	8,590	8,600	8,600	8,610	8,600	8,610	8,600	8,590	8,600	8,600	8,610
Other assets	320	320	330	330	340	350	350	360	360	360	360	370	370
Total assets	$15,885	$16,111	$16,437	$16,950	$18,000	$18,250	$18,350	$18,680	$17,036	$17,134	$17,081	$17,024	$16,896
Liabilities and Owner's Equity													
Accounts payable③	$ 720	$ 1,170	$ 1,170	$ 1,170	$ 1,170	$ 1,170	$ 1,170	$ 1,170	$ 1,170	$ 1,170	$ 1,170	$ 1,170	$ 1,170
Accrued expenses④	610	244	591	595	713	714	706	740	692	692	647	598	580
Accrued taxes⑤	385	9	2	(7)	(41)	16	65	45	106	166	104	101	91
Notes payable	0	0	0	614	1,470	1,553	1,597	1,773	0	0	0	0	0
Cur. por. of LT debt	0	0	0	0	350	350	350	350	350	350	350	350	350
Total current liabs.	$ 1,715	$ 1,423	$ 1,763	$ 2,373	$ 3,662	$ 3,803	$ 3,888	$ 4,079	$ 2,318	$ 2,379	$ 2,271	$ 2,219	$ 2,191
Long-term debt	4,000	4,500	4,500	4,500	4,150	4,150	4,150	4,150	4,150	4,150	4,150	4,150	4,150
Total liabilities	$ 5,715	$ 5,923	$ 6,263	$ 6,873	$ 7,812	$ 7,953	$ 8,038	$ 8,229	$ 6,468	$ 6,529	$ 6,421	$ 6,369	$ 6,341
Capital stock	$ 6,240	$ 6,240	$ 6,240	$ 6,240	$ 6,240	$ 6,240	$ 6,240	$ 6,240	$ 6,240	$ 6,240	$ 6,240	$ 6,240	$ 6,240
Retained earnings	3,930	3,948	3,934	3,837	3,947	4,057	4,072	4,211	4,328	4,365	4,420	4,415	4,315
Total owner's eq.	$10,170	$10,188	$10,174	$10,077	$10,187	$10,297	$10,312	$10,451	$10,568	$10,605	$10,660	$10,655	$10,555
Total liabs. & eq.	$15,885	$16,111	$16,437	$16,950	$18,000	$18,250	$18,350	$18,680	$17,036	$17,134	$17,081	$17,024	$16,896

①See Exhibit 3.
②See Exhibit 4.
③Includes 30 days raw material purchase.
④Includes 30 days selling and administrative expenses, 30 days interest expense, and 15 days direct labor ($210).
⑤One fourth of estimated yearly tax will be paid January 15, April 15, and July 15. The balance of taxes due from previous year will be paid on October 15. Paid installments in excess of outstanding obligations create a negative balance in the Accrued Taxes account.

Note: Forecast prepared July 1990. Actual results for fiscal year 1990 added later for analytical convenience.

Exhibit 3

HOOSIER HOSE COMPANY

Projected Monthly Accounts Receivable Balances for the Fiscal Year
Ending September 30, 1991
(dollar amounts in thouusands)

	1990 October	November	December	1991 January	February	March	April	May	June	July	August	September	Total
General sales	$1,670	$1,410	$1,300	$2,300	$2,200	$2,100	$2,290	$2,300	$2,300	$2,070	$1,490	$1,280	$22,710
Sales to Adams Co.	100	100	200	500	600	600	800	400	400	100	100	100	4,000
Total sales	$1,770	$1,510	$1,500	$2,800	$2,800	$2,700	$3,090	$2,700	$2,700	$2,170	$1,590	$1,380	$26,710
Plus begin. A/R*	2,540	2,910	2,790	2,840	4,320	4,990	5,470	6,440	3,080	3,480	3,350	2,840	2,540
Less collections**	1,400	1,630	1,450	1,320	2,130	2,220	2,120	6,060	2,300	2,300	2,100	1,590	26,620
Ending A/R	$2,910	$2,790	$2,840	$4,320	$4,990	$5,470	$6,440	$3,080	$3,480	$3,350	$2,840	$2,630	$ 2,630

*October balance includes $900,000 owed by Adams on sales to them since May 1990.
**35 days sales outstanding.

Note: Forecast prepared July 1990.

Exhibit 4

HOOSIER HOSE COMPANY

Projected Monthly Inventory Balances for the Fiscal Year
Ending September 30, 1991
(dollar amounts in thousands)

	1990 October	Novem.	Decem.	1991 January	February	March	April	May	June	July	August	September
Raw Materials and Supplies:												
Opening balance①	$1,230	$1,230	$1,230	$1,230	$1,230	$1,230	$1,230	$1,230	$1,230	$1,230	$1,230	$1,230
Plus purchases②	1,170	1,170	1,170	1,170	1,170	1,170	1,170	1,170	1,170	1,170	1,170	1,170
Less transfers to work in process	1,170	1,170	1,170	1,170	1,170	1,170	1,170	1,170	1,170	1,170	1,170	1,170
Closing balance	$1,230	$1,230	$1,230	$1,230	$1,230	$1,230	$1,230	$1,230	$1,230	$1,230	$1,230	$1,230
Work in Process:												
Opening balance③	$ 610	$ 610	$ 610	$ 610	$ 610	$ 610	$ 610	$ 610	$ 610	$ 610	$ 610	$ 610
Plus raw material additions	1,170	1,170	1,170	1,170	1,170	1,170	1,170	1,170	1,170	1,170	1,170	1,170
Plus cost of production④	520	520	520	520	520	520	520	520	520	520	520	520
Less transfers to finished goods	1,690	1,690	1,690	1,690	1,690	1,690	1,690	1,690	1,690	1,690	1,690	1,690
Closing balance	$ 610	$ 610	$ 610	$ 610	$ 610	$ 610	$ 610	$ 610	$ 610	$ 610	$ 610	$ 610
Finished Goods:												
Opening balance⑤	$1,400	$1,750	$2,290	$2,840	$2,400	$1,960	$1,590	$ 930	$ 580	$ 230	$ 270	$ 750
Plus additions from work in process	1,690	1,690	1,690	1,690	1,690	1,690	1,690	1,690	1,690	1,690	1,690	1,690
Less cost of sales	1,340	1,150	1,140	2,130	2,130	2,060	2,350	2,040	2,040	1,650	1,210	1,040
Closing balance	$1,750	$2,290	$2,840	$2,400	$1,960	$1,590	$ 930	$ 580	$ 230	$ 270	$ 750	$1,400
Total Closing Inventory	$3,590	$4,130	$4,680	$4,240	$3,800	$3,430	$2,770	$2,420	$2,070	$2,110	$2,590	$3,240

①October balance includes 1.56 million pounds of plastic and $684,000 of nonplastic raw materials.
②Monthly purchases include $520,000 of plastic and $650,000 of nonplastic raw materials.
③October balance includes 774,500 pounds of plastic.
④Includes $60,000 depreciation charged each month to production costs (2 cents per pound).
⑤October balance includes 1.23 million pounds of plastic.

Note: Forecast prepared July 1990.

Exhibit 5

HOOSIER HOSE COMPANY

Revised Projected Monthly Statements of Income and Retained Earnings
for the Fiscal Year Ending September 30, 1991
(dollar amounts in thousands)

	Fiscal Year 1990 Actual	1990 October	Novem.	Decem.	1991 January	February	March	April	May	June	July	August	September	Fiscal Year 1991 Total
		Fiscal Year 1991 Projections												
General sales	$19,500	$1,670	$1,410	$1,300	$2,300	$2,200	$2,100	$2,290	$2,300	$2,300	$2,070	$1,490	$1,280	$22,710
Sales to Adams Co.	3,440	100	100	200	500	600	600	800	400	400	100	100	100	4,000
Total sales	$22,940	$1,770	$1,510	$1,500	$2,800	$2,800	$2,700	$3,090	$2,700	$2,700	$2,170	$1,590	$1,380	$26,710
Cost of sales*	17,160	1,340	1,150	1,140	2,130	2,130	2,060	2,350	2,040	2,040	1,650	1,210	1,040	20,280
Gross profit	$ 5,780	$ 430	$ 360	$ 360	$ 670	$ 670	$ 640	$ 740	$ 660	$ 660	$ 520	$ 380	$ 340	$ 6,430
Selling & admin. exp.**	3,970	370	348	348	458	458	450	483	450	450	404	355	337	4,910
Interest expense	370	33	36	48	62	67	65	64	33	33	33	33	33	540
Profit before tax	$ 1,440	$ 27	$ (24)	$ (35)	$ 150	$ 145	$ 125	$ 193	$ 178	$ 178	$ 83	$ (8)	$ (30)	$ 980
Tax	490	9	(8)	(12)	51	49	43	66	60	60	28	(3)	(10)	333
Profit after tax	$ 950	$ 18	$ (16)	$ (23)	$ 99	$ 95	$ 83	$ 127	$ 117	$ 117	$ 55	$ (5)	$ (20)	$ 647
Beg. retained earn.	3,300	3,930	3,948	3,932	3,829	3,928	4,023	4,026	4,153	4,270	4,308	4,362	4,357	3,930
	$ 4,250	$3,948	$3,932	$3,909	$3,928	$4,023	$4,106	$4,153	$4,270	$4,388	$4,362	$4,357	$4,337	$ 4,577
Less dividends	320	0	0	80	0	0	80	0	0	80	0	0	80	320
End. retained earn.	$ 3,930	$3,948	$3,932	$3,829	$3,928	$4,023	$4,026	$4,153	$4,270	$4,308	$4,362	$4,357	$4,257	$ 4,257

*Includes depreciation of 2 cents per pound.
**Equals 8.5 percent of total sales plus $220.

Note: Prepared September 1990.

Exhibit 6
HOOSIER HOSE COMPANY

Revised Projected Monthly Balance Sheets for the Fiscal Year
Ending September 30, 1991
(dollar amounts in thousands)

	Fiscal Year 1990 Actual	Fiscal Year 1991 Projections: 1990 October	Novem.	Decem.	1991 January	February	March	April	May	June	July	August	September
Assets													
Minimum cash bal.	$ 500	$ 500	$ 500	$ 500	$ 500	$ 500	$ 500	$ 500	$ 500	$ 500	$ 500	$ 500	$ 500
Marketable securities	715	211	0	0	0	0	0	0	390	769	1,127	1,413	1,158
Accounts receivable①	2,540	2,910	2,790	2,840	4,320	4,990	5,470	6,440	3,080	3,480	3,350	2,840	2,630
Inventories②	3,240	4,060	5,320	6,720	6,820	6,058	5,366	4,384	3,712	3,039	2,756	2,913	3,240
Total current assets	$ 6,995	$ 7,681	$ 8,610	$10,060	$11,640	$11,548	$11,336	$11,324	$ 7,682	$ 7,788	$ 7,733	$ 7,666	$ 7,528
Prop P&E (net)	8,570	8,580	8,590	8,600	8,600	8,610	8,600	8,610	8,600	8,590	8,600	8,600	8,610
Other assets	320	320	320	330	340	350	350	360	360	360	360	370	370
Total assets	$15,885	$16,581	$17,520	$18,990	$20,580	$20,508	$20,286	$20,294	$16,642	$16,738	$16,693	$16,636	$16,508
Liabilities and Owner's Equity													
Accounts payable③	$ 720	$ 1,640	$ 1,890	$ 2,020	$ 1,710	$ 848	$ 848	$ 848	$ 848	$ 847	$ 847	$ 847	$ 847
Accrued expenses④	610	244	594	605	730	735	725	757	692	692	647	598	580
Accrued taxes⑤	385	9	1	(11)	(43)	6	48	31	91	151	96	94	83
Notes payable	0	0	363	1,807	3,516	4,156	3,899	3,765	0	0	0	0	0
Cur. por. of LT debt	0	0	0	0	350	350	350	350	350	350	350	350	350
Total current liabs.	$ 1,715	$ 1,893	$ 2,848	$ 4,421	$ 6,263	$ 6,095	$ 5,870	$ 5,750	$ 1,981	$ 2,041	$ 1,941	$ 1,889	$ 1,860
Long-term debt	4,000	4,500	4,500	4,500	4,150	4,150	4,150	4,150	4,150	4,150	4,150	4,150	4,150
Total liabilities	$ 5,715	$ 6,393	$ 7,348	$ 8,921	$10,413	$10,245	$10,020	$ 9,900	$ 6,131	$ 6,191	$ 6,091	$ 6,039	$ 6,010
Capital stock	$ 6,240	$ 6,240	$ 6,240	$ 6,240	$ 6,240	$ 6,240	$ 6,240	$ 6,240	$ 6,240	$ 6,240	$ 6,240	$ 6,240	$ 6,240
Retained earnings	3,930	3,948	3,932	3,829	3,928	4,023	4,026	4,153	4,270	4,308	4,362	4,357	4,257
Total owner's eq.	$10,170	$10,188	$10,172	$10,069	$10,168	$10,263	$10,266	$10,393	$10,510	$10,548	$10,602	$10,597	$10,497
Total liabs. & eq.	$15,885	$16,581	$17,520	$18,990	$20,580	$20,508	$20,286	$20,294	$16,642	$16,738	$16,693	$16,636	$16,508

①See Exhibit 3.
②See Exhibit 7.
③Includes 30 days raw material purchase.
④Includes 30 days selling and administrative expenses, 30 days interest expense, and 15 days direct labor ($210).
⑤One fourth of estimated yearly tax will be paid January 15, April 15, and July 15. The balance of taxes due from previous year will be paid on October 15. Paid installments in excess of outstanding obligations create a negative balance in the Accrued Taxes account.

Note: Forecast prepared September 1990.

Exhibit 7

HOOSIER HOSE COMPANY

Revised Projected Monthly Inventory Balances for the Fiscal Year
Ending September 30, 1991
(dollar amounts in thousands)

	1990 October	Novem.	Decem.	1991 January	February	March	April	May	June	July	August	September
Raw Materials and Supplies:												
Opening balance①	$1,230	$1,700	$2,420	$3,270	$3,810	$3,488	$3,166	$2,844	$2,522	$2,199	$1,876	$1,553
Plus purchases②	1,640	1,890	2,020	1,710	848	848	848	848	847	847	847	847
Less transfers to work in process	1,170	1,170	1,170	1,170	1,170	1,170	1,170	1,170	1,170	1,170	1,170	1,170
Closing balance	$1,700	$2,420	$3,270	$3,810	$3,488	$3,166	$2,844	$2,522	$2,199	$1,876	$1,553	$1,230
Work in Process:												
Opening balance③	$ 610	$ 610	$ 610	$ 610	$ 610	$ 610	$ 610	$ 610	$ 610	$ 610	$ 610	$ 610
Plus raw material additions	1,170	1,170	1,170	1,170	1,170	1,170	1,170	1,170	1,170	1,170	1,170	1,170
Plus cost of production④	520	520	520	520	520	520	520	520	520	520	520	520
Less transfers to finished goods	1,690	1,690	1,690	1,690	1,690	1,690	1,690	1,690	1,690	1,690	1,690	1,690
Closing balance	$ 610	$ 610	$ 610	$ 610	$ 610	$ 610	$ 610	$ 610	$ 610	$ 610	$ 610	$ 610
Finished Goods:												
Opening balance⑤	$1,400	$1,750	$2,290	$2,840	$2,400	$1,960	$1,590	$ 930	$ 580	$ 230	$ 270	$ 750
Plus additions from work in process	1,690	1,690	1,690	1,690	1,690	1,690	1,690	1,690	1,690	1,690	1,690	1,690
Less cost of sales	1,340	1,150	1,140	2,130	2,130	2,060	2,350	2,040	2,040	1,650	1,210	1,040
Closing balance	$1,750	$2,290	$2,840	$2,400	$1,960	$1,590	$ 930	$ 580	$ 230	$ 270	$ 750	$1,400
Total Closing Inventory	$4,060	$5,320	$6,720	$6,820	$6,058	$5,366	$4,384	$3,712	$3,039	$2,756	$2,913	$3,240

①October balance includes 1.56 million pounds of plastic and $684,000 of nonplastic raw materials.
②Monthly purchases include $650,000 of nonplastic raw materials.
③October balance includes 774,500 pounds of plastic.
④Includes $60,000 depreciation charged each month to production costs (2 cents per pound).
⑤October balance includes 1.23 million pounds of plastic.

Note: Forecast prepared September 1990.

Exhibit 8

HOOSIER HOSE COMPANY

Actual Statements of Income and Retained Earnings for the Five Months
Ending February 28, 1991
(dollar amounts in thousands)

	1990 October	November	December	1991 January	February	Actual Total Oct-Feb	Revised Projected Total Oct-Feb
General sales	$1,580	$1,260	$1,290	$1,910	$1,700	$ 7,740	$ 8,880
Sales to Adams Company	70	70	160	400	480	1,180	1,500
Total sales	$1,650	$1,330	$1,450	$2,310	$2,180	$ 8,920	$10,380
Cost of sales*	1,250	1,010	1,100	1,990	1,870	7,220	7,890
Gross profit	$ 400	$ 320	$ 350	$ 320	$ 310	$ 1,700	$ 2,490
Selling & admin. exp.	378	346	349	411	390	1,874	1,982
Interest expense	33	39	58	71	76	278	246
Profit before tax	$ (11)	$ (65)	$ (57)	$ (162)	$ (156)	$ (452)	$ 262
Tax	(4)	(22)	(19)	(55)	(53)	(154)	89
Profit after tax	$ (7)	$ (43)	$ (37)	$ (107)	$ (103)	$ (298)	$ 173
Beg. retained earnings	3,930	3,923	3,880	3,762	3,655	3,930	3,930
	$3,923	$3,880	$3,842	$3,655	$3,552	$ 3,632	$ 4,103
Less dividends	0	0	80	0	0	80	80
End. retained earnings	$3,923	$3,880	$3,762	$3,655	$3,552	$ 3,552	$ 4,023

*Includes depreciation of 2 cents per pound.

Exhibit 9

HOOSIER HOSE COMPANY

Actual Monthly Balance Sheets
October 1990 to February 1991
(dollar amounts in thousands)

	Fiscal Year 1990 Actual	October	November	December	January	February	Revised Projected February 1991
Assets							
Cash	$ 500	$ 500	$ 490	$ 490	$ 470	$ 220	$ 500
Marketable securities	715	590	0	0	0	0	0
Accounts receivable①	2,540	2,790	2,550	2,750	3,780	4,060	4,990
Inventories②	3,240	4,530	6,460	8,480	9,150	8,648	6,058
Total current assets	$ 6,995	$ 8,410	$ 9,500	$11,720	$13,400	$12,928	$11,548
Prop P&E (net)	8,570	8,570	8,580	8,600	8,600	8,590	8,610
Other assets	320	320	320	330	330	340	350
Total Assets	$15,885	$17,300	$18,400	$20,650	$22,330	$21,858	$20,508
Liabilities and Owner's Equity							
Accounts payable	$ 720	$ 2,020	$ 2,420	$ 2,600	$ 2,790	$ 1,890	$ 848
Accrued expenses	610	621	595	617	692	676	735
Accrued taxes③	385	(4)	(26)	(45)	(184)	(237)	6
Notes payable	0	0	791	2,976	4,636	5,237	4,156
Cur. por. of long-term debt	0	0	0	0	350	350	350
Total current liabilities	$ 1,715	$ 2,637	$ 3,780	$ 6,147	$ 8,285	$ 7,917	$ 6,095
Long-term debt	4,000	4,500	4,500	4,500	4,150	4,150	4,150
Total liabilities	$ 5,715	$ 7,137	$ 8,280	$10,647	$12,435	$12,067	$10,245
Capital stock	$ 6,240	$ 6,240	$ 6,240	$ 6,240	$ 6,240	$ 6,240	$ 6,240
Retained earnings	3,930	3,923	3,880	3,762	3,655	3,552	4,023
Total owner's equity	$10,170	$10,163	$10,120	$10,002	$ 9,895	$ 9,792	$10,263
Total liabilities & equity	$15,885	$17,300	$18,400	$20,650	$22,330	$21,858	$20,508

①See Exhibit 10.
②See Exhibit 11.
③The balance of taxes due from previous year was paid October 15. One fourth of estimated yearly tax ($83.25) was paid January 15. Paid installments in excess of outstanding obligations created a negative balance in the Accrued Taxes account.

Exhibit 10

HOOSIER HOSE COMPANY

Actual Accounts Receivable Balances for the Five Months
Ending February 28, 1991
(dollar amounts in thousands)

	1990 October	November	December	1991 January	February	Total
General sales	$1,580	$1,260	$1,290	$1,910	$1,700	$7,740
Sales to Adams Co.	70	70	160	400	480	$1,180
Total sales	$1,650	$1,330	$1,450	$2,310	$2,180	$8,920
Plus begin. A/R*	2,540	2,790	2,550	2,750	3,780	2,540
Less collections	1,400	1,570	1,250	1,280	1,900	7,400
Ending A/R	$2,790	$2,550	$2,750	$3,780	$4,060	$4,060

*October balance includes $900,000 owed by Adams on sales to them since May 1990.

Exhibit 11

HOOSIER HOSE COMPANY

Actual Inventory Balances for the Five Months
Ending February 28, 1991
(dollar amounts in thousands)

	1990 October	November	December	1991 January	February	Actual Total Oct-Feb	Revised Projected Total Oct-Feb
Raw Materials and Supplies:							
Opening balance①	$1,230	$2,080	$3,130	$4,340	$5,090	$1,230	$1,230
Plus purchases②	2,020	2,420	2,600	2,140	848	10,028	8,108
Less transfers to w-i-p.	1,170	1,370	1,390	1,390	1,390	6,710	5,850
Closing balance	$2,080	$3,130	$4,340	$5,090	$4,548	$4,548	$3,488
Work in Process:							
Opening balance③	$ 610	$ 610	$ 680	$ 690	$ 690	$ 610	$ 610
Plus raw material additions	1,170	1,370	1,390	1,390	1,390	6,710	5,850
Plus cost of production④	520	520	520	520	520	2,600	2,600
Less transfers to fin. goods	1,690	1,820	1,900	1,910	1,910	9,230	8,450
Closing balance	$ 610	$ 680	$ 690	$ 690	$ 690	$ 690	$ 610
Finished Goods:							
Opening balance⑤	$1,400	$1,840	$2,650	$3,450	$3,370	$1,400	$1,400
Plus additions from w-i-p	1,690	1,820	1,900	1,910	1,910	9,230	8,450
Less cost of sales	1,250	1,010	1,100	1,990	1,870	7,220	7,890
Closing balance	$1,840	$2,650	$3,450	$3,370	$3,410	$3,410	$1,960
Total Closing Inventory	$4,530	$6,460	$8,480	$9,150	$8,648	$8,648	$6,058

①October balance includes 1.56 million pounds of plastic and $684,000 of nonplastic raw materials.
②Monthly purchases include $650,000 of nonplastic raw materials.
③October balance includes 774,500 pounds of plastic.
④Includes $60,000 depreciation charged each month to production costs (2 cents per pound).
⑤October balance includes 1.23 million pounds of plastic.

Exhibit 12

HOOSIER HOSE COMPANY
1846 Mad Anthony Wayne Boulevard
Indianapolis, Indiana 46291

February 28, 1991

Mr. E. Miller Garfield
Loan Officer, National Banking Group
Booth National Bank
777 Dauphine Avenue
Indianapolis, Indiana 46291

Dear Mr. Garfield:

This letter confirms our telephone conversation in which I requested an increase in our company's line of credit from $5.5 million to $7.0 million. This money will be used to finance increased inventories and to raise the cash balance. HHC's cash balance has fallen to $220,000 from the $500,000 which we believe is needed to carry on operations.

According to the revised plan, 13.31 million pounds of plastic were purchased during the first four months of fiscal 1991. Unfortunately, we could not locate the entire quantity from our usual sources. The purchase from foreign sources of 9.6 million pounds of plastic at 55 cents per pound, as opposed to the anticipated 35 cents per pound, has raised the inventory requirements by $1,920,000. In addition, sales have been only 80 percent of forecast in January and February.

Considering our current backlog of orders, we anticipate March sales at $2.4 million: $1.88 million general and $.52 million to Adams Company. After March, sales are uncertain, but we hope this upward trend will continue throughout the 1991 fiscal year. Sales of $26.7 million are expected in fiscal 1992, when we anticipate sales will recover to about the level we originally expected for fiscal 1991. Selling prices for garden hose have remained firm, with the average for HHC's several product lines being 75 cents per pound.

Currently, HHC produces 2.97 million pounds of finished goods per month. The average price of plastic in raw material inventory is currently 49.84 cents per pound. The inventory also includes $684,000 of non-plastic raw materials. One half-pound each of plastic and non-plastic raw materials are required per pound of finished goods. We use 21.89 cents of nonplastic raw material per pound of finished goods. These costs vary directly with production.

The cost of production (excluding raw materials) is 17.51 cents per pound of finished goods. Approximately 60 percent of this cost is fixed over the short-term. The variable portion of the cost of production is directly proportional to the pounds of finished goods produced. The high fixed percentage is due mainly to a union agreement which requires salary payments to employees laid off at 75 percent of normal pay for up to one year. HHC has a good relationship with labor, and we wish to maintain our policy of level production and even employment.

HHC's cost of sales should average 86 percent until all the foreign plastic is sold. We expect this to occur when cumulative sales from October 1, 1990, have reached $25 million. Cost of sales should average 76 percent afterwards. The FIFO method of inventory valuation is used. The contracts outstanding for the purchase of plastic at 35 cents per pound, the price at which plastic is now readily available, are cancelable upon 30 days notice.

Sincerely,

Hatch

Hatcher H. Oates
Treasurer
Hoosier Hose Company

Case 20: PADGETT BLANK BOOK COMPANY

Negotiations with Padgett Blank Book Company had been going on for almost a year. Mr. Francis Libris hoped the time had come when they could be pushed to a mutually satisfactory conclusion. If not, Padgett might seek another bank as its source of funds. Alternatively, Mr. Libris would be subject to criticism by his superiors for failing to deliver on his commitment to manage and structure the relationship properly. Mr. Libris was vice president of the Windsor Trust Company of New York, one of the largest banks in the United States. He was responsible for the Midtown commercial lending center of the bank, to which Padgett's account was assigned because its small executive offices were on an upper floor of the same building in which the center was located. It was a significant account for the center and an important one to its profitability.

Padgett had borrowed small amounts off and on from Windsor since it had first established an account with the bank in 1939. Even the acquisition of several small companies (for less than $1 million each) in the late 1970s and early 1980s did not require high levels of debt. The acquisition of a long-coveted competitor at an attractive price on short notice in early 1988 brought Padgett suddenly to the bank, asking for an additional $3.6 million loan. Combined with the $3.6 million already outstanding at that time, Windsor's total exposure could rise to $7.2 million, well in excess of the $5 million advised credit line that had been approved for the company. The request was granted nevertheless, under an internal guidance line of $8 million, and the rate was continued at prime. Mr. Libris had been working since then to structure the arrangements on a more orderly basis than 90-day notes with no protective covenants.

It was now January 1989. Mr. Libris hoped to have the new terms worked out so they could be reflected on the financial statements for the 1989 fiscal year that would end April 30. Although he knew there was a chance that a negotiation completed before the auditors finished their field work could be shown in the report, he preferred to have the arrangements made without this complication.

Mr. Libris wondered whether he should take a fresh look at the situation. He had originally tried to persuade Padgett's management to finance part of the company's requirements in the form of long-term debt from a life insurance company. When the financial vice president declined this idea, Mr. Libris decided to see how the loan could be repaid to the bank within the period initially suggested by the credit committee. As time had gone on, he began to think that these constraints might not be appropriate to the situation and that a more creative solution might prove acceptable both to the credit committee and to Padgett's management. Because Mr. Libris knew he would have to get the approval of his superiors before he undertook a different initiative with Padgett's management, time was getting exceedingly short. He had to develop both the implications of the credit committee's original decision and of any alternatives that appeared to be superior.

Padgett Blank Book Company

The Padgett Blank Book Company, a closely held, publicly traded (over-the-counter) company, manufactured a variety of stationery products including notebooks, loose-leaf binders, forms, and filler paper for students and record-keeping purposes. The company was over 100 years old. Its ownership remained primarily with the descendants of the founders, now a large and widely spread group. Few family members were active in the company's management, and the major connection with most of the owners came in the form of the quarterly dividend check. A few members of the family depended on the dividends for most of their income. Most of the shareholders considered Padgett just another investment and an illiquid one at that because the market for the company's stock was extremely thin. A significant payout was considered important by management.

Management, which was largely professional, appeared competent, responsible, and reasonably effective. Its expertise was largely in operations, which were carried on at several plants in the New England and mid-Atlantic areas, and in marketing, which was controlled out of the executive office in New York. Management was not financially oriented, Mr. Libris had observed.

Padgett's customers were some 5,000 wholesalers and retailers in the U.S. and Canada. No single customer or small group of customers accounted for a substantial share of Padgett's sales. Terms were 2/10 net 30, but few customers took the discount. Many stretched payment for an additional 30 days. The business had a slight seasonal peak in the late summer when big back-to-school sales took place. Because the company tried to maintain level production to reduce unit cost in the highly competitive market, a seasonal variation of about $2 million occurred in its borrowing pattern. The peak occurred in the summer.

A consolidation had been taking place in the business since the early 1970s, initially caused by the high inflation rate of the period that made it difficult for small firms to finance their current assets. Financial difficulties and inventory problems resulting from the subsequent mid-seventies recession further reduced the level of the competition. Changes in the tax rules effective in 1986 provided new impetus for the smaller companies to sell. Finally, the sharp drop in the stock market in October 1987 combined with a resurgence of paper price increases and shortages of supply had frightened some owners, such as those at Tri-State Tablet, enough that they put their firms on the market. It had not been possible to pass all the price increases through to the customers because of strong competition from large, integrated paper companies. In Padgett's case, the drop in the corporate tax rate helped compensate for smaller margins.

Many competitors had been acquired by national corporations with strong marketing skills and good financial resources. The response of Padgett's management had been to acquire smaller companies that fit into its product or marketing needs. The acquisition of its competitor, Tri-State Tablet Company, in April 1988 was the culmination of these efforts.

Padgett's financial statements for fiscal year 1988 had been given an unqualified opinion by the national C.P.A. firm that audited them. Straight-line depreciation was used for reporting purposes with accelerated depreciation used for taxes. Inventory had been valued on a lower of cost (FIFO) or market basis. Financial statements for the 1985-1988 fiscal years are presented in Exhibits 1 and 2. Exhibit 3 is a standard computerized spread used by Windsor's credit department to organize a company's financial statements for analysis.

Padgett's Relationship with Windsor Trust

Windsor Trust had historically been Padgett's only lending bank and was the only lending bank in early 1989. Among other benefits of this relationship, Padgett used Windsor Trust as the depository for its substantial New York state and Federal tax payments. So far during the 1989 fiscal year, Padgett's average collected balance with Windsor had been $524,000. Affiliated companies and subsidiaries had balances that had averaged $231,000. The loan balances outstanding had ranged from $3.3 to $7.2 million, with an average of $5.05 million. The loan had last been cleaned up for an extended period from March 31, 1985, to January 8, 1986.

Padgett maintained a small deposit relationship with the Phoenix Bank of Manhattan, a major bank that had long been soliciting a more important role in the company's financial arrangements. In addition, several out-of-town banks were used to service the various plant locations.

The speed with which the Tri-State Tablet acquisition had been made had not allowed for careful planning of the financial arrangements. Mr. Libris' superiors had been reluctant to double the loan to Padgett without a carefully structured financial program as well as appropriate protective covenants. With Mr. Libris' assurance that these questions could be quickly resolved, the divisional senior vice president had authorized the loan and established a new temporary credit limit of $8 million. It had been expected, however, that the loan would be formally structured long before January 1989, which was a source of embarrassment to Mr. Libris. He knew he also would be embarrassed and his profit plan damaged if he should lose the account to Phoenix or if it were taken over completely by an insurance company.

Once the dust created by the acquisition had settled, Mr. Libris met with John Ruhl, Padgett's financial vice president, to discuss the company's plans. Based on these conversations, Mr. Libris and Windsor's credit department prepared a preliminary financial forecast for Padgett's 1989-1992 fiscal years. Summary figures from this forecast are presented in Exhibit 4.

Mr. Libris was distressed to note that, even under what he thought were assumptions that minimized the need for funds, Padgett would still have $4.4 million in short-term debt on the books at the end of 1992 fiscal year. Assuming the company could generate about $1 million in "undedicated" cash each subsequent year, a total of eight years would be required to retire the debt. This was considerably longer than the typical bank five-year term loan that a company of Padgett's size might expect. Windsor was willing to stretch to six years for important relationships, but a seven-year term loan would be considered a bit long for a company like Padgett, which did not enjoy the financial flexibility afforded firms having easy entry to the public capital markets.

Mr. Libris decided that a need of this duration appropriately called for insurance company financing. After he had met with officers of several companies, he wrote Mr. Ruhl to propose a 12- to 15-year loan and to quote terms an insurance company might offer. (Mr. Libris' letter is reproduced as Exhibit 5.) He also pointed out that Windsor might be able to structure an arrangement that would allow the bank to take the seasonal needs while the insurance company would take the long-term core requirements of $5 million.

Mr. Ruhl's response was emphatically negative. While he appreciated the information, he reported that management did not like the high, fixed rates that were currently being charged. Furthermore, management did not like the idea of an elaborate set of covenants. Mr. Ruhl said that he particularly disliked the type of covenant that could throw the company in default without management's explicit action. "Violation of a debt-capital ratio, for instance," explained Mr. Ruhl, "could occur as the result of an adverse year rather than anything we do. I don't mind agreeing not to borrow or pay dividends if certain conditions would result, but I just don't see agreeing to a lot of things that are out of my control. I can't see getting tied up in all these technicalities." Mr. Ruhl indicated that he did not see anything wrong with the present, friendly, informal loan. "After all," he said, "if you don't like what we're doing—anything at all—you can call your entire loan at the end of any 90-day period. Isn't this better protection for you than fancy agreements?"

In the months that followed this disappointing outcome, Mr. Libris met frequently with Mr. Ruhl to get a thorough understanding of the business. He planned to prepare a forecast of future needs that would accurately reflect Padgett management's thinking and his own insights into the company. By late in 1988, preliminary estimates for the 1989 fiscal year were becoming available so Mr. Libris could incorporate them into his forecasts. The forecasts, which were prepared showing the effects of 5 percent, 10 percent, and 15 percent growth in sales over the 1990-1992 fiscal years, are included as Exhibit 6.

Mr. Ruhl thought that this effort was most helpful, although he noted that two last-minute changes should be incorporated in the planning. First, he expected to shift to LIFO inventory valuation for the 1989 fiscal year, which would result in a tax benefit of $500,000. Second, management had decided to dispose of a redundant warehouse that had been part of the Tri-State acquisition. Management expected to receive $700,000 from the cash sale and tax refunds on the book loss.

Alternatives

Mr. Libris still thought that splitting the loan—maybe with the bank's own real estate department—had promise. For instance, Padgett owned outright a large, general-purpose warehouse. Its appraisal value of $3 million was more than the amount at which it was carried on the books. Although Mr. Libris was not an experienced real-estate lending officer, he believed the property would be attractive collateral for a mortgage loan. Another alternative might be to wait until the loan had been partly retired and then invite another bank to share the remainder for the duration of the repayment. Part of the loan could be rotated between banks to allow each a cleanup period of several months. Finally, he had discovered that Padgett's small Canadian operation was self-contained with a negligible amount of intercompany transfers and charges. With net current assets of $1.8 to $2.0 million to offer as collateral and no direct debt, the Canadian subsidiary could probably raise $1.0 million from Canadian banks. The Canadian banks would require a "floating charge," a form of security agreement, against all current assets of the subsidiary.

Although U.S. banking law and practice was not identical to Canadian and British practice with respect to "floating liens," asset-based finance might offer useful alternatives. It would be expensive to take effective security against Padgett's receivables because the company had so many customers and the average account was small. A factoring arrangement might be suitable, in which Padgett could sell its accounts on a nonrecourse basis to a commercial finance company. Windsor Bank itself did not operate a factoring function, however. It would be necessary to find one that had experience in the paper distribution business, or the costs of the factoring, which were usually about 2 percent of accounts purchased, would be too high. On the other hand, if Padgett factored its accounts, it could eliminate its credit department and would have no bad debts.

Windsor could always grant credit against the security of the accounts receivable even though the bank would not monitor the accounts as closely as a factor would. The loan would be limited to a percentage of receivables to provide some protection against losses. A security interest in the inventory also could be required, although the granting of this security could upset some major paper companies who were Padgett's sources of supply.

Money Market Consideration and Pricing Aspects

Funds were readily available in the financial markets in January 1989, although the prime rate had risen rapidly during 1988 and now stood at 10½ percent. The prime's low in recent years had been 7½ percent from September 1986 to March 1987. By January 1988, prime had risen to 8¾ percent. Thirty-day commercial paper was currently yielding 9.30 percent, up from 8.82 percent the first week in December 1988. The Treasury yield curve was relatively flat, with one-year notes trading at 9.07 percent, five-year notes at 9.18 percent, 10-year bonds at 9.17 percent, and 30-year bonds at 9.0 percent.

These increases in the interest rates were an issue that Mr. Libris would have to address in preparing a proposal for Mr. Ruhl. First, should the loan (or loans) be priced at a fixed rate or at a floating rate? Fixed-rate loans were generally offered at a premium of ½ to 1 percent above the floating rate.

In adjusting the prime rate to the conditions of the borrower, Windsor bank officers often used what they termed a "risk premium" system. This approach added or subtracted 25 basis points (¼ percent) to the price for such factors as the size of the company's sales (add points for small size and lack of access to public markets), purpose, term, escalating versus level payments, debt profile, liquidity posture, and (subtract points for) relationship benefits (for example, balances, tax payments and corporate trust). Of course, the final rate had to be checked against the market, which in Padgett's case was highly competitive as the result of Phoenix's interest.

Second, Mr. Libris was considering whether to offer Padgett a "cash cap" on the loan, if Mr. Ruhl decided to put a significant portion of it on a floating rate. A *cash-cap loan* was one which established a maximum rate of interest due currently in cash as well as an index rate by which the total interest due would be determined. If the index rose above the cash-cap rate, the difference between total interest and the cash-cap amount due would be set up as a separate loan on the respective books. Interest on this loan also would be calculated under the index-cash-cap arrangement. When the index interest rate again declined below the cash-cap rate, the borrower would continue to pay at the cash-cap rate, with the difference being used to amortize the separate cash-cap loan. When that loan had been repaid, the interest rate would fall to the index level.

Because of the complications that had already been experienced and that were likely to arise while completing the negotiations, Mr. Libris knew that he had no more time to collect information. He had to work quickly toward a satisfactory resolution of the loan structure with Padgett's management.

Exhibit 1

PADGETT BLANK BOOK COMPANY

Income Statements for the Fiscal Years Ended
April 30, 1985-1988
(thousands of dollars except per-share figures)

	1985	1986	1987	1988
Net sales	$26,331	$27,219	$36,897	$41,308
Cost of goods sold	15,728	16,077	21,937	24,555
Depreciation and amortization	*	510	667	739
	$10,603	$10,632	$14,293	$16,014
General and admin. expense	5,814	5,087	7,139	7,821
Selling expense	**	1,878	2,603	3,147
Operating expenses	$ 5,814	$ 6,965	$ 9,742	$10,968
Operating profit	$ 4,789	$ 3,667	$ 4,551	$ 5,046
Interest expense	—	32	220	379
Other expenses (income)	83	(42)	(39)	(71)
Profit before taxes	$ 4,706	$ 3,677	$ 4,370	$ 4,738
Income taxes	2,702	1,893	2,216	2,132
Profit after taxes	$ 2,004	$ 1,784	$ 2,154	$ 2,606
Number of shares (000)	1,000	1,115	1,116	1,118
Earnings per share	$2.00	$1.60	$1.93	$2.33
Dividends per share	1.00	1.00	1.00	1.00

*Included in cost of goods sold in 1985.
**Included in general and administrative expenses in 1985.

Exhibit 2

PADGETT BLANK BOOK COMPANY

Balance Sheets as of April 30, 1985-1988
(thousands of dollars)

	1985	1986	1987	1988
Assets				
Current Assets				
Cash and securities	$ 1,691	$ 266	$ 658	$ 834
Accounts receivable	4,734	5,542	6,350	7,754
Inventory	7,276	7,743	10,959	14,360
Prepayments and other	233	194	153	563
Total current assets	$13,934	$13,745	$18,120	$23,511
Property, plant, equip.	–	8,718	11,265	12,468
Less: Accumulated depn.	–	3,384	4,912	5,209
Net prop., plant, equip.	$ 4,797	$ 5,334	$ 6,353	$ 7,259
Other assets	59	257	386	224
Total assets	$18,790	$19,336	$24,859	$30,994
Liabilities and Owners' Equity				
Current Liabilities				
Short-term notes	$ –	$ –	$ 3,118	$ 7,221
Accounts payable	1,127	1,619	2,158	1,958
Accruals	395	397	703	1,014
Other current liabilities	271	251	418	824
Current portion, long-term debt	615	117	51	52
Total current liabilities	$ 2,408	$ 2,384	$ 6,448	$11,069
Long-term debt	338	221	507	455
Deferred taxes	538	568	714	756
Other liabilities	136	126	116	151
Total liabilities	$ 3,420	$ 3,299	$ 7,785	$12,431
Owners' Equity				
Common stock	5,587	5,587	5,587	5,587
Retained earnings	9,783	10,450	11,487	12,976
Total owners' equity	$15,370	$16,037	$17,074	$18,563
Total liabilities and net worth	$18,790	$19,336	$24,859	$30,994

Exhibit 3

PADGETT BLANK BOOK COMPANY

Cash Flow and Ratio Analysis, Fiscal Years
Ended April 30, 1985-1988
(dollar figures in thousands)

	1985	1986	1987	1988
Sources				
Profit after taxes plus depn. and amort.*		$ 2,294	$ 2,821	$ 3,345
Deferred taxes		30	146	42
New long-term debt		–	337	–
New short-term debt		–	3,118	4,103
Accounts payable		492	539	(200)
Accruals		2	306	311
Other current liabilities		(20)	167	406
Other liabilities		(10)	(10)	35
Total Sources		$ 2,788	$ 7,424	$ 8,042
Uses				
Dividends paid in cash		$ 1,117	$ 1,117	$ 1,117
Capital expenditure		979	1,575	1,530
Repayment of long-term debt		615	117	51
Accounts receivable		808	808	1,404
Inventory		467	3,216	3,401
Prepayments and other current assets		(39)	(41)	410
Other assets		198	129	(162)
Intangibles*		68	111	115
Total Uses		$ 4,213	$ 7,032	$ 7,866
Change in cash and securities		$(1,425)	$ 392	$ 176
Working capital	$11,526	$11,361	$11,672	$12,442

*Intangibles amortized as purchased.

Exhibit 3 (continued)

PADGETT BLANK BOOK COMPANY

	1985	1986	1987	1988
Profitability				
Sales growth	n.a.%	3.4%	35.6%	12.0%
Gross profit margin	40.3	39.1	38.7	38.8
Operating expenses÷sales	22.1	25.6	26.4	26.5
Pretax margin	17.9	13.5	11.8	11.5
After-tax margin	7.6	6.6	5.8	6.3
Return on aver. owners' equity	n.a.	11.4	13.0	14.6
Return on total assets	10.7	9.2	8.7	8.4
EBIT÷Total assets	25.0	19.2	18.5	16.5
Dividend payout	50.2	62.6	51.9	42.9
Turnover on Sales				
Receivables	5.6×	4.9×	5.8×	5.3×
Inventory	3.6	3.5	3.4	2.9
Accounts payable	23.4	16.8	17.1	21.1
Working capital	2.3	2.4	3.2	3.3
Fixed asset	5.5	5.1	5.8	5.7
Net worth	1.7	1.7	2.2	2.2
Leverage				
Total debt÷owners' equity	22.3%	20.6%	45.6%	67.0%
Long-term debt÷owners' equity	2.2	1.4	2.9	2.4
Interest coverage	n.a.×	115.9×	20.9×	13.5×
Liquidity				
Quick ratio	2.7×	2.4×	1.1×	.8×
Current ratio	5.8	5.8	2.8	2.1

Exhibit 4

PADGETT BLANK BOOK COMPANY

Summary Figures from Preliminary Projection
of Financial Position, Fiscal Years Ending
April 30, 1989-1992
(millions of dollars)

	1989	1990	1991	1992
Sources of Funds				
Net sales	$55.2	$60.7	$66.8	$73.5
Profit after taxes	3.3	3.6	4.2	4.8
Noncash charges	.9	.9	1.0	1.1
Cash generated from operations	$ 4.2	$ 4.5	$ 5.2	$ 5.9
Disposition of assets	.2	—	—	—
Total sources	$ 4.4	$ 4.5	$ 5.2	$ 5.9
Uses of Funds				
Dividends	$ 1.1	$ 1.1	$ 1.1	$ 1.1
Increase in working capital*	2.4	2.4	3.1	3.6
Capital expenditures	1.0	1.0	1.0	1.0
	$ 4.5	$ 4.5	$ 5.2	$ 5.7
Effect on Short-Term Debt				
*Including retirement of short-term debt:	.7	.2	.8	1.1
Leaving a balance in short-term debt of	$ 6.5	$ 6.3	$ 5.5	$ 4.4

Assumptions:

1. 10% sales growth
2. 6 to 6½% after-tax margin
3. Accounts receivable turnover 5.7 (17.5% of sales)
4. Inventory turnover 3.6 (27.8% of sales)
5. Accounts payable turnover 21.3 (4.7% of sales)

Exhibit 5
PADGETT BLANK BOOK COMPANY
Mr. Libris' Letter Outlining Proposed Term Loan Arrangement

Windsor Trust Company
Midtown Commercial Lending Center
Avenue of the Americas at 47th Street
New York, New York

Francis X. Libris
Vice President and Manager

May 15, 1988

Mr. John Ruhl
Vice President-Finance
Padgett Blank Book Company
New York, NY

Dear John:

Thank you for the opportunity last week to review the financial plans you have for Padgett. This letter sets forth our thoughts relating to the need for properly incorporating your bank loan into these plans.

Currently, Padgett has $6,853,000 outstanding in short term 90-day notes, and we understand that an additional $1.0 to $1.5 million is likely to be borrowed to support new receivables of your new acquisition. This is in contrast with the circumstance of May 1986 when we financed your previous acquisition, and our loan outstanding increased from $500,000 to $1,850,000. At that time, an anticipated restructuring of the loan was postponed until a clearer definition of longer term corporate cash need could be ascertained.

In late 1987, we expressed an interest in discussing with you a restructuring of the then loan outstanding so that legitimately long-term funds could be sourced on a proper long-term basis. Our subsequent conversations and cash flow study were complicated by the anticipated major acquisition and its impact.

Enclosed is a copy of our most recent Padgett forecast, the results of which we have jointly reviewed. On balance, our feeling is that the forecast may tend to understate the cash requirement in that it assumes moderate sales growth, the upholding of traditional margins, and tight control over capital expenditures and dividends. The forecast does seem to indicate a long term need of at least $5 million which cannot be properly funded through the bank on anything resembling a full-payout term-loan basis.

Given what appears to be the clear nature of the need, it seems appropriate that financing discussions with an insurance company be initiated. This suggestion is rooted in our firm feeling that it is strategically unwise from the standpoint of the company, as well as that of the bank, to fulfill substantial long-term financial need through the continued use of 90-day notes.

On a confidential basis and without revealing your name, we have talked with three insurance companies within the last week. Discussions included the following generalized parameters for life insurance company lending:

amount:	no problem
term:	12-15 years
rate:	fixed, 9½% minimum
payback:	level payments desired but flexibility offered, e.g., three years of grace
prepayment:	all want protection designed to discourage it; however, there are provisions for prepayment without penalty if they were to turn you down for a requested increase in amount and you were able to obtain a commitment from another source
availability of money:	good

There is the possibility of bank participation in the first five years of an insurance company loan, but (as you can well understand) it is the lender taking the longest maturities who controls the negotiation of loan agreement covenants from the lenders' point of view. Inclusion of the Bank whose interest rates are geared to a floating prime rate offers a partial hedge, without guarantee, against known fixed interest cost. Bank pricing would probably look like the prime rate plus ¼ percent for the first three years and prime plus ½ percent for years four and five. While an insurance company loan requires no deposit balances to be maintained, we would expect balances of 5 percent against the average loan outstanding. A 5 percent balance increment is roughly equivalent to ¼ percent in interest rate.

We all recognize the fact that interest rates have again risen; however, the Economics Department of this Bank does not feel that long-term interest rates will see reduced levels in the foreseeable future. Financing demands on the capital markets are expected to continue strong, inflation psychology seems to be rising, the deficits are not yet under control, and any advantage to be gained in avoiding the long-term market is, at best, marginal. It might, in fact, be dangerous.

For any needs consistent with prudent bank lending, Windsor Trust stands ready to finance your business. Our desire to assist in every way we can is complete and sincere.

Sincerely,

Frank

Francis X. Libris
Vice President

Exhibit 6

PADGETT BLANK BOOK COMPANY

Projected Financial Statements for Fiscal Years Ending April 30, 1990-1992
Assuming 5, 10, and 15 Percent Sales Growth
(dollar figures in millions except per-share figures)

	1988	1989	5% Growth			10% Growth			15% Growth		
	Actual	Est.	1990	1991	1992	1990	1991	1992	1990	1991	1992
A. Income Statements											
Sales, net	$41.32	$57.80	$60.69	$63.72	$66.91	$63.58	$69.94	$76.93	$66.47	$76.44	$87.91
Cost of sales	24.56	36.08	37.27	38.86	40.81	39.05	42.65	46.93	40.82	46.61	53.61
Depn. & amort.	0.74	0.94	0.91	1.00	1.10	0.91	1.00	1.10	0.91	1.00	1.10
General & admin.	7.82	10.23	10.75	11.29	11.87	11.26	12.40	13.65	11.77	13.55	15.59
Selling expense	3.15	4.61	4.84	5.09	5.35	5.08	5.60	6.15	5.30	6.11	7.03
Operating profit	$ 5.05	$ 5.94	$ 6.92	$ 7.48	$ 7.78	$ 7.28	$ 8.29	$ 9.10	$ 7.67	$ 9.17	$10.58
Interest expenses*	0.38	0.95	0.80	0.72	0.61	0.90	0.86	0.81	1.01	1.10	1.18
Other exp. (income)	(.07)	(.71)	0.07	0.07	0.07	0.07	0.07	0.07	0.07	0.07	0.07
Pretax earnings	$ 4.74	$ 5.70	$ 6.05	$ 6.69	$ 7.10	$ 6.31	$ 7.36	$ 8.22	$ 6.59	$ 8.00	$ 9.33
After-tax earnings	2.61	3.42	3.63	4.01	4.26	3.79	4.42	4.93	3.95	4.80	5.60
Earnings per share on 1,118,000 shares	$ 2.33	$ 3.06	$ 3.25	$ 3.59	$ 3.81	$ 3.39	$ 3.95	$ 4.41	$ 3.54	$ 4.29	$ 5.01
Dividends per share	1.00	1.03	1.08	1.19	1.27	1.13	1.31	1.47	1.18	1.43	1.66

*Includes interest calculated on the cash deficit at 11%.

Note: Figures may not add because of rounding.

Exhibit 6 (continued)
PADGETT BLANK BOOK COMPANY

B. Balance Sheets	1988 Actual	1989 Est.	5% Growth 1990	1991	1992	10% Growth 1990	1991	1992	15% Growth 1990	1991	1992
Assets											
Cash (minimum)	$ .83	$ 1.17	$ 1.23	$ 1.29	$ 1.36	$ 1.29	$ 1.42	$ 1.56	$ 1.35	$ 1.55	$ 1.78
Excess cash	—	—	.01	.73	1.24	—	—	—	—	—	—
Acc. receivable	7.75	10.12	10.62	11.15	11.71	11.13	12.24	13.46	11.63	13.38	15.38
Inventory	14.36	16.18	16.99	17.84	18.74	17.80	19.58	21.54	18.61	21.40	24.61
Prepayments, etc.	.56	.23	.24	.26	.27	.26	.28	.31	.27	.31	.36
Total current assets	$23.51	$27.71	$29.10	$31.27	$33.32	$30.48	$33.52	$36.87	$31.86	$36.64	$42.14
Plant & equip.	12.47	13.27	14.27	15.27	16.27	14.27	15.27	16.27	14.27	15.27	16.27
Less: accum. depn.	5.21	6.04	6.95	7.95	9.05	6.95	7.95	9.05	6.95	7.95	9.05
Net plant & equip.	$ 7.26	$ 7.23	$ 7.32	$ 7.32	$ 7.22	$ 7.32	$ 7.32	$ 7.22	$ 7.32	$ 7.32	$ 7.22
Other	.22	.11	.11	.11	.11	.11	.11	.11	.11	.11	.11
Total assets	$30.99	$35.05	$36.54	$38.71	$40.65	$37.91	$40.95	$44.20	$39.29	$44.07	$49.47
Liabilities and Owner's Equity											
Short-term notes	$ 7.22	$ 7.45	$ 6.29	$ 5.50	$ 4.35	$ 6.29	$ 5.50	$ 4.35	$ 6.29	$ 5.50	$ 4.35
Acc. payable	1.96	2.72	2.85	3.00	3.14	2.99	3.29	3.62	3.12	3.59	4.13
Accruals	1.01	1.44	1.52	1.59	1.67	1.59	1.75	1.92	1.66	1.91	2.20
Other	.82	1.15	1.21	1.33	1.40	1.27	1.39	1.53	1.33	1.61	1.85
Current portion, LTD	.05	.05	.05	.05	.05	.05	.05	.05	.05	.05	.05
Total current liabs.	$11.06	$12.82	$11.93	$11.48	$10.61	$12.19	$11.98	$11.47	$12.46	$12.66	$12.58
Long-term debt	.46	.40	.35	.30	.25	.35	.30	.25	.35	.30	.25
Deferred taxes	.76	.80	.80	.80	.80	.80	.80	.80	.80	.80	.80
Other	.15	.20	.20	.20	.20	.20	.20	.20	.20	.20	.20
Cash deficit*	—	—	—	—	—	1.02	1.37	1.89	2.01	3.44	5.23
Total liabilities	$12.43	$14.22	$13.28	$12.78	$11.86	$14.56	$14.65	$14.61	$15.82	$17.40	$19.06
Common stock	5.59	5.59	5.59	5.59	5.59	5.59	5.59	5.59	5.59	5.59	5.59
Retained earnings	12.98	15.24	17.67	20.34	23.18	17.76	20.71	24.00	17.88	21.09	24.82
Total owner's equity	$18.56	$20.83	$23.25	$25.93	$28.77	$23.35	$26.30	$29.59	$23.47	$26.68	$30.41
Total liability & owner's equity	$30.99	$35.05	$36.53	$38.71	$40.63	$37.91	$40.95	$44.20	$39.29	$44.07	$49.47

*Includes interest calculated on the cash deficit at 11%.

Exhibit 6 (continued)

PADGETT BLANK BOOK COMPANY

	1989 Est.	5% Growth 1990	5% Growth 1991	5% Growth 1992	10% Growth 1990	10% Growth 1991	10% Growth 1992	15% Growth 1990	15% Growth 1991	15% Growth 1992
C. Cash Flow										
Sources										
After-tax earnings	$3.42	$3.63	$4.01	$4.26	$3.79	$4.42	$4.93	$3.95	$4.80	$5.59
Noncash charges	.94	.91	1.00	1.10	.91	1.00	1.10	.91	1.00	1.10
Funds from operations	$4.36	$ 4.54	$5.01	$5.36	$4.70	$5.42	$6.03	$4.86	$5.80	$6.69
Deferred taxes	.04	—	—	—	—	—	—	—	—	—
Accounts payable	.76	.14	.14	.14	.27	.30	.33	.41	.47	.54
Accruals	.43	.07	.07	.08	.14	.16	.17	.22	.25	.29
Other and miscellaneous current liabilities	.33	.06	.12	.07	.12	.12	.14	.17	.27	.24
Other liabilities	.05	—	—	—	—	—	—	—	—	—
Other assets	.11	—	—	—	—	—	—	—	—	—
Total sources	$6.08	$4.81	$5.34	$5.65	$5.22	$6.00	$6.67	$5.66	$6.79	$7.76
Uses										
Dividends	$1.16	$1.21	$1.34	$1.42	$1.26	$1.47	$1.64	$1.31	$1.59	$1.86
Capital expenditures	.80	1.00	1.00	1.00	1.00	1.00	1.00	1.00	1.00	1.00
Short-term debt	(.23)	1.16	.79	1.15	1.16	.79	1.15	1.16	.79	1.15
Long-term debt	.05	.05	.05	.05	.05	.05	.05	.05	.05	.05
Minimum cash	.34	.06	.06	.06	.12	.13	.14	.18	.20	.23
Accounts receivable	2.36	.50	.53	.56	1.01	1.11	1.22	1.52	1.74	2.01
Inventory	1.82	.81	.85	.89	1.62	1.78	1.96	2.43	2.79	3.21
Prepay & def. charge	(.33)	.01	.01	.01	.02	.02	.03	.04	.04	.05
Intangibles	.11	—	—	—	—	—	—	—	—	—
Total uses	$6.08	$4.80	$4.63	$5.14	$6.24	$6.35	$7.19	$7.69	$8.20	$9.56
Net cash flow	—	.02	.71	.51	(1.01)	(.35)	(.52)	(2.03)	(1.41)	(1.80)
Cumulative	—	.02	.73	1.24	(1.01)	(1.36)	(1.88)	(2.02)	(3.43)	(5.23)

Exhibit 6 (continued)
PADGETT BLANK BOOK COMPANY

	1988	1989	5% Growth			10% Growth			15% Growth		
	Actual	Est.	1990	1991	1992	1990	1991	1992	1990	1991	1992
D. Analytical Ratios											
Profitability											
Sales growth	12.0%	39.9%	5.0%	5.0%	5.0%	10.0%	10.0%	10.0%	15.0%	15.0%	15.0%
E.P.S. growth	20.7	31.4	6.2	10.3	6.3	10.8	16.5	11.2	15.5	21.4	16.5
Gross profit margin	38.8	35.9	38.6	39.0	39.0	38.6	39.0	39.0	38.6	39.0	39.0
Operating exp. ÷ Sales	26.5	25.7	25.7	25.7	25.3	25.7	25.7	25.7	25.7	25.7	25.7
Pretax margin	11.5	10.3	10.0	10.5	10.6	9.9	10.5	10.7	9.9	10.5	10.6
After-tax margin	6.3	5.9	6.0	6.3	6.4	6.0	6.3	6.4	5.9	6.3	6.4
Return on average owner's equity	14.6	17.4	16.5	16.3	15.6	17.1	17.8	17.6	17.9	19.1	19.6
Return on total assets	8.4	9.8	9.9	10.4	10.5	10.0	10.8	11.2	10.1	10.9	11.3
EBIT ÷ Total assets	16.5	19.0	18.7	19.1	19.0	19.0	20.1	20.4	19.4	20.7	21.2
Dividend payout	42.9	33.8	33.3	33.3	33.3	33.3	33.3	33.3	33.2	33.2	33.2
Turnover											
Receivables	5.3×	5.7×	5.7×	5.7×	5.7×	5.7×	5.7×	5.7×	5.7×	5.7×	5.7×
Inventory	2.9	3.6	3.6	3.6	3.6	3.6	3.6	3.6	3.6	3.6	3.6
Accounts payable	21.1	21.3	21.3	21.3	21.3	21.3	21.3	21.3	21.3	21.3	21.3
Working capital	3.3	3.6	3.5	3.2	2.9	3.5	3.3	3.0	3.4	3.2	3.0
Fixed asset	5.7	8.0	8.3	8.7	9.3	8.7	9.6	10.6	9.1	10.4	12.2
Net worth	2.2	2.8	2.6	2.4	2.3	2.7	2.6	2.6	2.8	2.9	2.9
Leverage											
Total debt ÷ owners' equity	67.0%	68.3%	57.1%	49.3%	41.3%	62.3%	55.7%	49.3%	67.4%	65.2%	62.7%
Long-term debt ÷ owners' equity	2.4	1.9	1.5	1.1	0.9	1.5	1.1	0.8	1.5	1.1	0.8
Interest coverage	13.5	7.0	8.7	10.3	12.6	8.0	9.6	11.1	7.5	8.3	8.9
Liquidity											
Quick ratio	.8×	1.0×	1.0×	1.1×	1.3×	1.0×	1.1×	1.3×	1.1×	1.2×	1.4×
Current ratio	2.1	2.2	2.4	2.7	3.1	2.5	2.8	3.2	2.6	2.9	3.3
Working capital	$12.44	$14.89	$19.40	$29.98	$29.55	$18.29	$21.46	$25.23	$19.40	$23.98	$29.55

Notes

Case 21:
FINANCIAL SERVICES SECURITIES LIMITED PARTNERSHIP

In the spring of 1992, Janet Anderson, a commercial loan officer for First Business Bank of North Carolina, returned to her office to prepare a response to a request for a $500,000 loan by Financial Services Securities Limited Partnership (FSSLP). FSSLP was a small company, in its sixth year of operation, located near her branch in Chapel Hill, North Carolina. It was growing very fast and was seeking a bank loan of $500,000 to support continued expansion of its business as well as for a potential acquisition.

Ms. Anderson's specialty was lending to small companies. She had called on FSSLP when it moved to Chapel Hill in 1987 and had visited occasionally with management to keep in touch with developments. The branch manager had been successful in getting the company's corporate accounts, which the company had managed responsibly. FSSLP's president, John Small, maintained his personal accounts with a competing bank. The limited partners, who had provided the start-up financing, lived elsewhere and had no present or prospective relationships with First Business Bank.

FSSLP had financed its development to date with equity funds provided by the partners and operating funds generated by the business. Mr. Small's request for a loan was thus the first opportunity Ms. Anderson had had to propose a loan. She had spent the morning with Mr. Small reviewing the company's history and collecting financial information. (Summaries of the financial data are included as Exhibits 1 and 2.)

Financial Services Securities Limited Partnership

Financial Services Securities Limited Partnership was a leading data base and publishing company specializing in the financial services industries. FSSLP maintained comprehensive data bases on 1,200 publicly traded financial service companies including banks, thrifts, investment banks, mortgage bankers, investment managers, and real estate investment trusts. The banks and thrifts covered collectively included over three quarters of the assets of all insured depository institutions. FSSLP served as a clearinghouse of information, collecting corporate, market and financial data on these companies and sending it to securities analysts, investors, executives, and others.

The customer base for FSSLP products was principally the investment community, including the securities analysts of Wall Street firms, the managers and analysts of money management firms, and the top management and strategic planners of financial services firms. The data bases were very valuable to FSSLP's customers. The purchase of a $10,000 data base replaced the work of the two to three full-time research assistants who would be needed if the data-gathering effort was performed in-house. FSSLP data was also widely used by banking publications such as the *American Banker, National Mortgage News, U.S. Banker*, and *Bankers Monthly* and was often cited in national and regional newspapers and periodicals. The success of FSSLP in building its clientele was attributed to the timeliness, accuracy, integrity, and responsiveness of its data products.

Since its founding in 1986, FSSLP had grown very rapidly. Sales had increased from $310,000 in 1986 to $3,100,000 in 1991. Over the same period, the total staff of FSSLP had grown from 8 to 37 as its original product line had expanded and new products had been successfully offered. Profitability had improved from a loss in 1986 to a profit of $300,000 in 1991. Management projected a record year in 1992 for the company, with sales estimated at $4,000,000 and profits at $500,000. Recently, the company had been honored as one of 500 fastest growing small private companies in the United States in *Inc.* magazine's annual *Inc.* 500 list.

Because of the nature of its business, FSSLP was very computer intensive. Every employee had a personal computer on their desk and used it extensively in their work during the day. All the computers were tied together in a local area computer network. All the terminals could access all of the company's extensive system of computer data bases.

FSSLP's Products

The data bases were the most important of FSSLP's products, both because of the revenue they directly generated and because they were the foundation for the other products such as the investment publications and fax newsletters. FSSLP's data bases included data bases relating to bank and thrift historical financial performance and bank merger activity. These data bases provided detailed GAAP and regulatory information in an easy-to-use menu-driven computer program. It was simple to produce "comp" groups, find undervalued investment opportunities, or do any number of tasks that require sorting quickly through a large volume of financial information. Companies could be selected using over 500 criteria such as price-earnings ratios, price to book value, region, return on average equity, and equity to assets.

FSSLP had developed a wide range of additional products within its market niche. Included were investment publications, fax newsletters, compensation guides, monthly newsletters, and comparative analyses. Revenue for the company was evenly split between the sale of data bases and other products. Quarterly statistical publications were the most important of the other products.

FSSLP was continually active in the development of new products. Generally, these new products built on the company's growing expertise in data base management and financial institution reporting. Recently, it had entered into an agreement with the Saudi Arabian Monetary Authority (the central bank of Saudi Arabia) to develop a system of regulatory financial reports for Saudi financial institutions that would be similar to bank call reports in the United States. Some of FSSLP's top management were beginning to spend a significant amount of time traveling to Saudi Arabia to work on the project.

FSSLP's Management

FSSLP's management team was young and bright. John Small, the president and the original founder, was 41. He held a Ph.D. in Economics from Duke University and had spent 10 years in the management of a medium-sized commercial bank and in the research arm of a major Wall Street investment bank before founding FSSLP in 1986. Bob Jones, executive vice president of the company, was 33. He had joined the company six months after its founding and had been with the company ever since. Mr. Jones was a Phi Beta Kappa graduate of Williams College and was instrumental in the development of new product lines for the company.

Four second-level managers were responsible for the functional areas of the company, including sales, company analysis and data base maintenance, computer systems, and publications. These four managers had also been with the company for several years, all having joined the company within its first two years of operation. All four of the second-level managers were graduates of well regarded Eastern colleges and universities, and all four had ranked in the top 10 percent of their college classes. The age of the second-tier managers ranged between 26 and 35. All six managers had equity stakes in the company.

Because of the youth of the company's management and the firm's location in a college town, the company environment was informal, with many employees wearing blue jeans. This informal environment, coupled with FSSLP's fast growth and college town location, had attracted a high quality group of recent college graduates as its primary employee base. FSSLP recruited on the campuses of several colleges including Duke and the University of North Carolina, both of which were located nearby. The young staff members that FSSLP hired were as diverse as the student bodies of campuses at which it recruited. New employees were equally balanced between male and female, and all races were represented.

Once hired, FSSLP's new employees were put through a two-week company-wide orientation program. There was also an ongoing company training program with classes conducted twice a month on topics relating to the financial services industry. These classes ranged from accounting for financial institutions to the strategic outlook for the financial services industry. They were taught by a combination of the management of FSSLP and instructors hired from several nearby graduate business schools. In addition to formal training, new hires received informal training in their daily jobs from their supervisors and experienced employees. Every week there was a regular company meeting with John Small and other top managers where all the employees discussed company plans and policies and a wide range of issues about the company.

Starting salaries at FSSLP were at the low end of the market range for new college graduates, and benefits were primarily a basic health care plan. However, new employees could rapidly advance because of the growth of the company. Two outstanding performers had been made partners after only two years with the company. Because of the age and ambitions of FSSLP's employees and FSSLP's relatively low wages, turnover was high among first-line employees, averaging 30 percent per year. Many left the company to attend graduate or professional schools in subjects such as business or law.

The Proposed Acquisition

The acquisition that FSSLP was planning was a small newsletter company located in the Washington, D.C., area. The company specialized in newsletters to community banks focusing on how to improve the quality of bank operations and the management of bank balance sheets. The company had been very successful in its three years of operations, reporting current revenue of $400,000 and an annual pretax profit of $100,000. It had a subscriber base of 500 community banks around the United States, and this was increasing as a result of the growing reputation of its newsletters. The company had a staff of eight, but its president was the sole owner and the key figure in the company's success.

FSSLP's management saw opportunities to improve substantially the profitability of the venture by combining it with its Chapel Hill operation. In addition, FSSLP management saw further opportunities to expand the product line offered to the proposed acquisition's customer base of community banks. If this acquisition worked the way that FSSLP management hoped, they planned to seek other acquisitions that were complimentary to FSSLP's product lines and that would build on its growing data base and publishing expertise.

Recently, FSSLP itself had been the target of an acquisition offer by a larger company. The offer had been turned down by FSSLP's management who thought the offer too low and who wished to retain their entrepreneurial independence. Industry rumors speculated that the larger company might try to start a de novo operation that would compete with FSSLP's principal product lines.

The Loan Request

Ms. Anderson wanted to make the loan that FSSLP desired. She did not have many small companies in her portfolio that had the growth potential and management that FSSLP enjoyed. She realized that over time that FSSLP could be a major relationship for both her loan portfolio and First Business Bank of North Carolina. To date, FSSLP had only been a depository customer. Now that it wanted to borrow to finance the acquisition of the newsletter company, there were a variety of issues to be addressed.

The nature of the company created some problems for her under the traditional lending approaches of the bank. FSSLP had an unusual balance sheet. Though the company had strong cash flow, it showed a negative equity on its balance sheet. FSSLP's profits did not result in substantial increases in the stated assets of the company or in the tangible net worth of the company.

This was a result of two factors. The first was that as a private company organized as a limited partnership (which was not taxed at the company level), FSSLP had a policy of distributing 50 percent of its profits to its shareholders. FSSLP did this so shareholders could have the cash to pay tax liability resulting from the profits of the company (under IRS rules the profits of the company were treated as income to the partners). The second factor was FSSLP's policy of reinvesting its remaining profits in the future growth of the company. Because this investment took the form of the creation of new data bases and the training of its growing group of employees, it did not show up on the balance sheet as additional assets or additional equity. Accounting rules required FSSLP to expense the cost of creating these data bases and the training of its employees. Because FSSLP leased its office space, office equipment, and computers, it had no plant and equipment.

As Ms. Anderson thought about FSSLP, she wondered how she might structure a loan that would provide the money that FSSLP wanted and that would also provide the security that the bank wanted in the absence of the tangible collateral the bank normally required for small business loans. Though the data bases had a major value, because they were intangible, they were not included as an asset on the balance sheet. Their development expenses resulted in reported losses for the company. Ms. Anderson wondered how to analyze the company given its unusual nature.

She wondered whether she should assign a value to the data bases. If so, how should she value them? What kind of security interest might be possible in them? She also wondered how to deal with the growth of the company and its young management in preparing her credit evaluation of the company and developing a loan structure. Finally, she wondered whether the limited partnership provided any security benefits to her. All the significant investors in the company were limited partners, which limited their liability. Mr. Small, the president of FSSLP, was the company's only general partner. His principal asset was his 70 percent interest in the company.

Exhibit 1
Financial Services Securities Limited Partnership
Balance Sheets as of December 31, 1986-1991 and
Projected Balance Sheet as of December 31, 1992
(thousands)

	1986	1987	1988	1989	1990	1991	1992*
Assets							
Cash	$ 50	$ 75	$100	$125	$125	$150	$200
Accts. receivable	50	100	150	175	200	250	300
Miscellaneous assets	25	25	35	50	65	75	100
Total	$125	$200	$285	$350	$390	$495	$600
Liabilities							
Accounts payable	$ 50	$100	$125	$150	$175	$200	$100
Subscription liabs.	300	400	435	425	365	295	250
Miscellaneous liabs.	25	25	25	25	25	25	25
Equity	(250)	(325)	(300)	(250)	(175)	(25)	210
Total	$125	$200	$285	$350	$390	$495	$600

*Projected

Note: FSSLP's subscription liability resulted from the common industry practice of selling subscriptions for cash but only recognizing the revenue for accounting purposes as each issue was mailed.

Exhibit 2
Financial Services Securities Limited Partnership
Summary Income Statements for the Years Ended December 31, 1986-1991
and Projected for the Year Ending December 31, 1992
(thousands)

	1986	1987	1988	1989	1990	1991	1992*
Sales	$300	$650	$950	$1,800	$2,300	$3,000	$4,000
Expenses	700	750	900	1,700	2,150	2,700	3,500
Net income	(400)	(100)	50	100	150	300	500
Distributions	—	—	25	50	75	150	250
Operating cash flow	(350)	(25)	125	300	450	590	920

*Projected

Case 22: PATRIOTS HALL

June Brown, vice president of the mortgage subsidiary of Monumental Insurance Corporation, was reviewing a loan proposal submitted by two of her subordinates in July 1988. The proposed borrower, Diamond Ventures, was a current customer of Monumental with a good 20-year track record as owners, developers, and managers. Its owners and managers were active in regional politics and were in good standing with the various land planning and regulation bodies in the area. Diamond had developed three million square feet (sf) of commercial space and numerous residential projects throughout Northern Virginia. Diamond was now developing an additional one million sf of office space. The size of the loan ($26.5 million) needed to finance this project required that a careful evaluation should be made of the risks associated with the development. As Ms. Brown studied the loan request package, she wanted to be sure to assess all potential problems.

The Project

Patriots Hall Building One was a proposed commercial condominium unit consisting of a five-story, 200,000-sf office building and 675-car parking garage on 10.9 acres of land located in Fairfax County, Virginia. The project was the first of three office buildings proposed for the 63-acre mixed-use development called Patriots Hall Corporate Center. When completed, the three office buildings would total 500,000 sf and occupy 27.9 of the 63 acres. The balance of Patriots Hall Corporate Center would consist of 82 town houses and a historical visitor's center to complement the 250-year-old Patriots Hall Presbyterian meetinghouse that existed on the site. The total estimated cost of Patriots Hall Corporate Center when fully built was $100 million.

As a commercial condominium unit, Patriots Hall Building One represented a new concept in real estate development. Historically, an office building was owned in total by a single entity, which rented space to one or more tenants. In a commercial condominium unit, individual office suites were owned by their occupants, who also held an ownership interest in common areas such as building lobbies and garages. In the Patriots Hall Corporate Center, the three buildings themselves would each be individually owned. The condominium element would be the common ownership of parts of the 27.9 acre site. For instance, Patriots Hall Building One would have a 40 percent ownership of the common areas. The parking garage included in the Patriots Hall Building One phase was part of the common area to be owned by all three of the office buildings.

The Patriots Hall project was located in an unincorporated area of Fairfax County near Vienna and Fairfax, Virginia, at the intersection of residential and commercial sections of Fairfax County. The location had good access to Washington's Metro System and was close to Interstate 66. Dulles International Airport was about 10 miles away. The area had been developing rapidly. To the northeast and southeast of the site were well established residential neighborhoods with older, smaller homes. To the northwest adjoining the site was a 45-acre industrial/commercial complex owned and occupied by a major pharmaceutical company. Directly opposite to the southwest was the campus of a local community college.

Because of the lack of other office buildings at its location, the Patriots Hall project was considered a "pioneering-speculative" office development. The speculative nature of Patriot Hall Building One had been significantly reduced, however, because Diamond had preleased 160,000 sf to a major tenant, Capital Gas and Electric Company. Capital Gas was the dominant gas and electric supplier in Northern Virginia and enjoyed an excellent credit rating. Its lease in Building One was for 20 years at a base rent of $15.93 per sf. The base rent would increase at the end of every five-year period by 13.14 percent of the previous base rent. Additional rent would be charged for a pro-rated share of all operating expenses (excluding management fees) and real estate taxes. The remaining 40,000 sf in the project were to be leased at average gross effective rents of no less than $20 a sf. Base terms were projected to be five years for 50 percent of the unleased space and ten years for the remaining 50 percent.

The Market

Fairfax County was the fastest growing county in the metropolitan Washington area, with its strong and stable economy built around the Federal government. It was both the center for a growing high-tech community and a bedroom community for the government- and service-based economy of Washington, D.C. Projections for the 25-year period 1985-2010 showed Fairfax County jobs increasing almost 100 percent from 380,000 jobs in 1985 to 716,000 jobs in 2010. Fairfax County ranked sixth among U.S. counties in per capita income, reflecting Northern Virginia's status as one of the most affluent regions of the United States.

Fairfax County's industrial base included research and development companies, trade and professional associations, diversified computer, engineering and professional services, distribution facilities, and light manufacturing firms. These companies accounted for one out of every four jobs in the county in 1985. (Exhibit 1 provides a summary of Fairfax County employment and space use in 1985.) There were also an increasing number of foreign firms located in Fairfax County, attracted by its proximity to the nation's capital and the excellent air service available from both Washington's Dulles and National Airports.

Fairfax County had one of the most highly educated skilled labor forces in the nation. Over 41 percent of its residents were college educated and almost 90 percent were high-school graduates. These very capable workers performed hundreds of jobs ranging in diversity from corporate executives to data processors, from senior computer systems engineers to electronic assemblers, from banking presidents to tellers, and from skilled artists and craftpersons to nonskilled workers.

The work force was primarily white collar. Over 76 percent of the jobs were professional-managerial, administrative support, and sales positions. The 1980 U.S. Bureau of the Census data showed that 25.1 percent of Fairfax residents were engaged in professional or technical work as engineers, scientists, technicians, and technical support. Another 20 percent were working in management and administration; 10.5 percent in sales; and 21 percent in clerical positions.

Eleven percent of the total jobs in the metropolitan area in 1985 were in Fairfax County, and Fairfax County expected to increase its share of regional employment to 15 percent by the year 2000. Women accounted for a large portion of this employment; 61 percent of the women in the county held jobs.

Fairfax County's strong and growing economy resulted in both low unemployment rates and rising property values. During much of the 1980s, Fairfax County unemployment rate was below 3 percent and in 1988 was 2.1 percent. Property values were steadily rising and were projected to continuing to rise. In the five years from 1979 to 1984, the value of residential and business property in Fairfax County more than doubled (from $13.3 billion in 1979 to $29.1 billion in 1984). Over the five-year period 1979-1984, more than 800 new firms had located in the county. A substantial number of these firms were high technology companies. By 1985, over 505 high-tech firms were located in Fairfax County, employing over 42,000 people in fields ranging from biotechnology to telecommunications.

Total supply of office space in the immediate area of the county near the project was 4.9 million sf, of which 850,000 sf (17 percent) were vacant. Most of this market was made up of older or smaller properties. Net absorption for the last three years had averaged 300,000 sf. Completed new supply of office space had averaged 600,000 sf, of which 50 percent was vacant upon completion. New buildings under construction had been substantially vacant in 1985. In 1987, 88 percent of new space was preleased. Rental rates for the county ranged from $16.50 to $24.00 per square foot (psf). Asking rents in newer properties were $22.00 to $24.00 psf compared with $16.00 to $19.00 psf for older properties.

One other project of similar scale, Dulles Acres Corporate Center (350,000 sf), was now under construction in the immediate area of Fairfax County near Patriots Hall. This project was scheduled for completion in about two years but was in an inferior location to Patriots Hall. Diamond Ventures also planned to redevelop Business Drive Center (150,000 sf) in the immediate area beginning later in 1989.

Data on comparable land sales, office building sales, rents, and expenses are contained in Exhibits 2 through 5.

The Loan

The proposed loan was for a face amount of $26,500,000 for a term of ten years at an annual interest rate of 9.65 percent. The loan amortization schedule called for constant monthly payments of principal and interest based on a 30-year, fully amortized loan schedule. A $4 million letter of credit issued by a bank satisfactory to Monumental would provide additional security for the loan. Release from the letter of credit would be contingent upon the project achieving certain occupancy rates.

The purpose of the loan was to provide permanent financing for the project and to take out the construction loan of $26,000,000 being provided to the project by Fairfax County National Bank. Exhibit 6 shows a statement of sources and uses of funds for the project. Exhibit 7 shows the expected performance of the project as it leased up and the expected debt service coverage.

Potential Problems

Despite the strong growth of Fairfax County, Ms. Brown knew that no real-estate-development project was riskless; potentially, something could always go wrong. In thinking about Patriots Hall, she knew that she should both evaluate the risks that applied to all real estate development and define and evaluate risks unique to the Patriots Hall project.

Exhibit 1

PATRIOTS HALL

Summary of Nonretail Employment;
1985 Economic Development Survey
Fairfax County, Virginia

Classification	Firms	Space Used (sf)	Employment
Research & development, technical manufacturing, & technical services	665	13,987,622	51,050
National & international trade & professional associations	111	1,161,211	3,399
Wholesale distribution	223	3,655,343	5,043
Contract construction	247	1,331,325	8,583
Other manufacturing	148	2,303,059	4,381
Transportation & warehousing	37	864,450	1,170
Corporate headquarters	33	2,724,734	6,836
Marketing office	136	1,182,383	4,438
Regional office	26	296,590	1,137
Administrative office	23	415,699	1,088
Manufacturer's representative	26	80,185	432
Business service	307	1,356,556	4,781
Industrial service	45	198,820	481
Major utility installations	5	1,457,009	2,320
TOTAL	2,032	31,013,986	95,139

Exhibit 2

PATRIOTS HALL
Comparable Land Sales

Sale No.	Date	Location	Size Sq. Ft.	Sale Price PFS	Comments
(1)	12/85	W/S North Ave., West near intersection of Martin St. Block 115 Lot 1, Fairfax, VA	219,890 (5.048 acres)	$5.00	•to be developed as an auto dealership •zoned office industrial, research
(2)	12/85	W/S North Ave., West near intersection of Martin St. Block 537, Lot 1, Fairfax, VA	227,165 (5.215 acres)	$3.56	•to be developed as a mini-warehouse •zoned office industrial, research
(3)	1986	Henry Ave., adjacent to Patriots Hall Block 101, Lot 3	924,517 (21.224 acres)	$6.66	•most closely comparable to Patriots Hall •purchased by pharmaceutical company that owns a total of 45 acres neighboring subject property. Land was previously leased and no new development has occurred as the improvements are existing.

Exhibit 3
PATRIOTS HALL
Comparable Office Building Sales

Property	Date of Sale	Year Built	Price (000)	Rentable Area (sf)	Price per SF	Estimated Cap. Rate	Comments
1. George Plaza George Center Vienna, VA	7/87	1981	$22,659 net of rent supports	177,330 13.5 acre site	$127	8.25%	•average annual gross rental of $18.40 psf •located in market with 20% vacancy rate •lower effective rental rates •property has high leasing risk over next 2 years •17% vacancy rate for property
2. Fairfax Center 400 Fairfax Avenue Fairfax, VA	6/87	1985	$41,500	271,000	$153	8.2%	•fully leased estimated net income 12.56 psf •asking rent $23.00 psf gross •90% of tenants are large, blue chips
3. Dulles Center Dulles Access Rd. Fairfax, VA	late 1987	1985	$36,000	163,000	$221	7.8%	•better office market, more prestigious location •90% leased @ $24 psf with cash flow guarantees to 95% •purchased by Japanese investor •90% of tenants are large, blue chips
4. Tysons Corners Route 7 Fairfax County, VA	1986	1986	$22,500	113,510 20 acre site	$198	8.10%	•fully leased for 10 years @ 16.00 escalating to 21.25 •net income estimated $16.00 psf
5. Virginia Life Building Reston Business Center Reston, VA	1986	1969	$14,950	107,000	$140	8.75%	•older property 1st year net; $1.341M ($12.23 psf)

Exhibit 4
PATRIOTS HALL
Rent Comparables

Location	Tenant	Commence Date	Term	Rent PSF	Escalation	Miscellaneous
A. Dulles Access Road/Reston Market						
1000 Cameron Ave. Reston, VA (Reston Park)	B/A Management Corporation	1/28/88	5 yrs, 5 mos.	$25.00 + tenant electric	Pro rata share above 1988 base	•5 months free rent (effective rent = $22.76 psf) •right of 1st refusal on contiguous space •option to cancel: -if tenant takes 8000 sf in another Reston Park building @ prevailing rates -by paying unamortized costs of improvements leasing, commissions + 2 months free rent •building is 2 years old
1000 Cameron Ave. Reston, VA (Reston Park)	Capital Gas & Electric	6/1/87	5 yrs.	$23.00 + tenant electric excluding HVAC	Pro rata share above 1986 base	•2 months free rent (effective rent = $22.22) •building is 2 years old
Dulles Access Park I Herndon, VA	Virginia Design	12/87	5 yrs.	$23.50 + tenant electric		•building is 1 year old
Airport Corporate Center Reston, VA	VPI Communications	1/88	5 yrs	$23.50 + tenant electric		•building is 2 years old
B. Vienna/Tysons Corner Market						
2 Tysons Center Vienna, VA	Business Publishers	3/21/88	5 yrs.	$27.00 + tenant electric		•building is 1 year old

Exhibit 4 (continued)
PATRIOTS HALL

Tysons Business Center Vienna, VA	James Securities, Inc.	5/1/88	5 yrs.	$30.00 + tenant electric		•operating expense stop = $4.00 psf •real estate tax stop = $2.55 psf •building is 1 year old
C. Fairfax Market						
1270 Lee Highway Fairfax, VA	Jones, Brown, & Smith	1/1/88	5 yrs.	$19.00 + tenant electric	Pro rata share above 1987 base	•tenant work letter of $8.00 psf on 1,746 sf •total rent credit of $31,758 to be applied over 1st 6 months of lease •building is 5 years old
D. Fairfax County Market						
15 Commerce Drive Fairfax County, VA	Southeast Administrators Inc.	5/1/88	5 yrs.	$18.28 + tenant electric	Pro rata shares over 1988 base	•Right to cancel lease based on scheduled penalties •building is 8 years old
8 Commerce Drive Fairfax County, VA	Southern Rixca Inc.	1/1/88	5 yrs.	$17.50 + tenant electric	Pro rata share over 1987 base	•3 months free rent (effective rent = $16.54 psf) •right to terminate after 11/90 based on payment of 6 months rent penalty •building is 15 years old
8 Commerce Drive Fairfax County, VA	Virginia State Safety Council	2/15/88	5 yrs.	Year 1 $15.25 2 $15.50 3 $15.75 4 $16.00 + tenant electric	Pro rata share over 1988 base	•landlord to provide small storage area of 4'×7' complete with shelving and door @ landlord's expense.

Note: All of these properties are in established office markets. Fairfax County buildings are characterized by difficult highway access.

Exhibit 5

PATRIOTS HALL

Expense Comparables in Dollars per Square Foot

	1000 Commerce Ave. Reston, VA		Soldiers Ridge McLean, VA		Business II Fairfax County, VA		Patriots Hall One Fairfax County, VA
	Actual 1987	Proj. 1989	Actual 1987	Proj. 1989	Actual 1987	Proj. 1989	Projected 1989
Operating Expenses							
Cleaning	.63	.68	.59	.64.	.76	.82	.84
Utilities	1.64	1.77	1.53	1.66	1.23	1.33	2.04
Repairs & maintenance	.55	.59	.25	.27	.79	.85	.26
Reserve for replacement			.04	.04	.02	.02	.05
Landscaping & snow removal	.11	.12	.10	.11	.22	.24	.15
Security	.22	.24	.06	.06	.19	.21	.12
Office & administration			.16	.17	.40	.43	.07
Total payroll and fringe			.38	.41	.09	.10	.45
Management fees	.62	.67	.51	.55	.72	.78	.90
Operating expenses subtotal	3.77	4.07	3.62	3.91	4.42	4.78	4.88
Fixed Expenses							
Real estate taxes	N.A.	N.A.	1.85	2.00	1.25	1.35	1.85
Insurance	.24	.26	.23	.25	.20	.22	.19
Fixed expenses subtotal	.24	.27	2.08	2.25	1.45	1.57	2.04
Total fixed & operating expenses	4.01	4.34	5.70	6.16	5.87	6.35	6.93

Exhibit 6
PATRIOTS HALL
Sources and Uses of Financing for Patriots Hall Building One

Sources:	$26,500,000	Monumental loan
	1,569,000	Borrower equity
	$28,069,000	Total
Uses:	$ 3,500,000	Land
	1,737,000*	Off-site improvements
	1,585,000**	Site improvements
	14,521,000***	Construction
	600,000	Tenant improvements
	2,743,000	Soft costs (including leasing commissions)
	3,012,000	Interest reserve
	371,000	Owner's contingency
	$28,069,000	

*Total estimated cost of widening Adams Avenue.
**This total includes approximately $950,000 for improvements to the entire 27.9-acre site.
***Includes construction cost for parking garage estimated at $4,000,000.

Exhibit 7
PATRIOTS HALL
Projected Performance of Patriots Hall Building One

Fiscal Year Ending July*	Average Annual Year End Occupancy**	Average Annual Gross Rental Per Sq. Ft.	Net Income Before Deprec., Debt Service, & Income Taxes	Debt Service × Earned Before Deprec. & Income Taxes
1990	85%	18.13	2,235,000	.83***
1991	99%	22.21	2,970,000	1.10
1992	99%	22.47	2,968,000	1.10
1993	99%	22.74	2,966,000	1.09
1994	99%	23.03	2,946,000	1.09
1995	99%	$24.83	$3,253,000	1.20

*Disbursement estimated in August 1989; therefore fiscal year analysis used.
**Assumes 100% occupancy by Capital Gas Company and 95% occupancy of the balance of the space.
***Vacancy of 15% covered by a $4,000,000 letter of credit whose release is contingent upon leasing of vacant space.

Notes

Case 23: OMEGA CABLE SYSTEM

In the fall of 1989, one of Prudential Capital's lending officers referred a potential customer to Lucinda Cochrane, head of Prudential Capital's Risk Management Group. Omega Cable System, the potential customer, was a cable television company located in the southeastern United States. It was currently financed by the Palmetto Bank, a southeastern regional bank, through several floating-rate credit facilities. The Prudential Capital lending officer thought Omega might be a candidate for the interest-rate risk management services offered by Ms. Cochrane's unit because the Palmetto loan agreement stipulated that Omega had to acquire interest-rate risk protection within six months of loan closing.

Omega Cable System

Omega Cable System, a limited partnership, was a general partner in two cable-TV (CATV) enterprises in the Atlanta, Georgia, metropolitan area. Omega's own general partners were James Smith and Alvin Jones. Mr. Smith, the financial expert for Omega, was a graduate of a well-known southeastern business school and had over 20 years' experience in the CATV business. Mr. Jones was the marketing expert for Omega, having been in the CATV business for over ten years. He had engineered the successful purchase and sale of several CATV systems.

Omega had recently purchased one CATV system outright—Alpha System, with 60,000 subscribers—which it expected to expand. Omega had also contracted to buy and complete the development of a second system, Beta System, which had 28,000 subscribers. The two systems were located in neighboring suburbs of the Atlanta metropolitan area for which rapid growth was projected. The Alpha and Beta Systems each had its own group of loans at Palmetto. Ms. Cochrane was being asked to provide interest-rate protection for the Alpha system loans. Exhibit 1 summarizes key provisions of the Alpha loans.

The primary source of repayment for the systems' bank loans was cash flow from operations: subscriber revenue less expenses such as programming, marketing, and overhead. Cash flow growth was predicated both from expansion of the subscriber base and from the ability to raise the average monthly revenue per subscriber over time. The average monthly revenue for the Omega systems was currently below that of the industry. For example, the existing basic monthly subscription rate in Omega's suburbs was $10.60. Other Atlanta area cable systems averaged $14 to $18. Omega planned to raise its rate gradually to avoid provoking significant opposition in the community or experiencing subscriber runoff. Omega projected average monthly revenue per subscriber (basic plus extras such as pay-channels and remote controls) to increase from a present level of $30 to $50 by 1995. Exhibit 2 provides summary financial projections for the Alpha system.

The Cable Television Industry

In 1988 nearly 50 million U.S. households were paying an average of about $15 a month for basic cable service. Cable systems paid copyright fees for broadcasts of commercial TV stations. They paid on a per-subscriber basis for other ad-supported channels that viewers could only receive through a cable hook-up or a satellite dish. USA Network, for example, charged about 13 cents a month per subscriber, while ESPN charged about 27 cents. In addition to the fees from cable systems, the largely cable-only channels generated ad revenue of close to $1.5 billion in 1988. Exhibit 3 provides basic statistics for the CATV and related industries.

Another cable service was pay-channels, which were available to basic subscribers as add-ons for roughly $8 to $12 a month per channel. The pay services offered movies that had opened in theaters only one year before. Prior to pay-TV airing, most films would have been made available on videocassettes. Time's HBO channel had the widest potential audience of about 17 million subscribers.

The larger cable channels, with access to more than 45 percent of U.S. homes, had enormous untapped potential. Their collective average viewership was only about 10 percent of the overall TV audience, substantially less than that of any of the traditional networks, but programming costs had been low enough for some large channels to be profitable. The restricted delivery capability of most cable systems was limiting development of new cable channels. Until fiber optic cable, or some other delivery system capable of carrying many more signals at once, replaced coaxial cable, system operators would be restricted in the number of services they could offer. Turner Broadcasting System, however, was able to launch its new TNT channel—which mostly ran old MGM movies—in October 1988. And a new business and news channel, owned by NBC and system operator Cablevision Systems, was expected to debut in April 1989.

With the power of the networks eroding and cable systems having large potential audiences of their own, both basic and pay-cable channels were bidding for more programming, particularly sports events, which viewers had seen for free in the past. ESPN shared in the broadcasting rights to NFL games and recently had received a large major league baseball contract. HBO had aired several championship boxing bouts. But despite the sales of movies and former network shows to pay-services, the cable-only channels were not yet a major source of revenue for suppliers of filmed entertainment.

This condition was likely to change in the future. Some cable-only stations increasingly resembled independent TV stations, and the next breakthrough in their programming would be a cable channel's winning the rights to a recent half-hour network comedy hit. To date, all such shows had been syndicated to individual TV stations.

In the future, consumers were likely to pay more for television programming. Driving factors behind the increases included inflation and higher subscription fees. As cable companies made larger investments in original programming to win more viewers, they would seek higher fees from the systems that carried their signals. The systems, in turn, would raise subscriptions to cover their costs. It was also likely that some basic channels would convert to pay services in their quest for revenues. To this growing market presence was added pay-per-view, which would gain from NBC's decision to offer some of the 1992 summer Olympics on a pay channel.

Regulation and the Cable Industry

The cable industry was influenced by a variety of regulatory restrictions, largely from the Federal Communications Commission (FCC). Regulation of the broadcast and programming industries was primarily intended to keep companies from gaining unfair competitive advantages.

Telephone companies, for example, were generally prohibited from owning CATV systems in their phone service areas. This reflected concern that phone companies would be able unfairly to subsidize TV businesses with the profits from their telephone operations. Nevertheless, the possibility of branching into the cable industry was being investigated by Pacific Telesis, one of the Baby Bells. Such a development would challenge the virtual monopolies of cable system companies in local markets and enable people to have more viewing choices, given the phone companies' potential application of fiber-optic cable.

The three major television networks were prohibited from owning cable systems, but they could invest in cable channels. Networks also faced restrictions on how much programming they could produce themselves and were not allowed to have a financial interest in the syndication of products that they initially aired. In addition, ownership of commercial TV stations by any one entity was restricted to 12 stations whose local broadcasts (excluding cable) collectively reached no more than 25 percent of U.S. viewers.

The largest network affiliate stations were generally limited to airing no more than three hours of network programming per night (including reruns of former network shows), which had contributed to the demand for first-run syndication product. Also, local stations would soon benefit from restoration of a syndication-exclusivity rule. This rule prohibited cable channels (such as Ted Turner's superstation, WTBS) from airing a syndicated program in markets for which a local station held exclusive broadcast rights. The cable systems would have to black out such superstation programming on a market-by-market basis.

Cable systems, on the other hand, had gained flexibility from the repeal of a "must-carry" rule that had required them to broadcast certain numbers of local TV stations. Repeal was likely to hurt some independent TV stations, which would be dropped from cable systems, and discourage the start-up of new independent stations. Also, foreign ownership of U.S. broadcast interests was prohibited, which had required Rupert Murdoch to become an American citizen so his NEWS Corporation could own a sizable group of TV stations.

Prudential Capital's Risk Management Group

Prudential Capital Corporation was a merchant banking subsidiary of The Prudential Insurance Company of America, the largest insurance company in the United States. Prudential Capital specialized in providing medium-term and long-term financing to corporations. Prudential Capital's Risk Management Group (RMG) was organized in 1983 and had become increasingly active in the marketplace as time had passed. Between June 1987 and December 1988, the RMG had handled over $600 million in notional transactions.

Products offered by the RMG included interest-rate and currency swaps, interest-rate caps and floors, treasury hedges, options on caps and swaps, participating interest-rate agreements, and general risk-management advisory services. These products could be applied to managing floating-rate and fixed-rate risks, reducing costs on fixed-rate debt, protecting the value of assets, and in various accounting, tax, and asset/liability-matching applications. The RMG preferred to work with loans of $5 million or more. Terms on an interest-rate protection product usually had maturities up to ten years and could be applied to the whole loan or part of the loan. Prudential Capital or other Prudential affiliates acted as the counterparty to interest-rate management products. The interest-rate-management product agreements were separate from any Prudential Capital loan agreement the customer might have and could be sold back to Prudential Capital at anytime at the market price. (Appendix A describes the RMG products in more detail.)

The Alternatives

There were several different approaches Ms. Cochrane could suggest to provide Omega with protection. Protection could be provided for Omega's construction debt by an average or straight cap, an interest-rate collar, or a forward-rate agreement. Protection could be provided for Omega's long-term debt by an interest-rate swap, an interest-rate cap, an interest-rate collar, fixed-rate financing, or by some combination of these alternatives.

As Ms. Cochrane thought about the various possibilities, she decided that three alternatives made the most sense for the Alpha System loans designated as "A," "B," and "C." The first alternative was to hedge the rates on Alpha's loans during the construction period, to 1991, using one (or more) of three alternatives and then fix the term-loan rate via a swap agreement. This swap would allow Omega to call the loan in 1993, with a penalty to unwind the swap, if it wished to refinance at a lower rate or otherwise change the terms of the deal. The second alternative was to hedge Alpha's loans until 1991 and then fix the rate on the term debt by substituting a noncallable term loan from Prudential. The third alternative was to hedge Alpha's loan until 1993, the call date on the existing debt. Exhibit 4 provides information on the cost of the three alternatives, and Exhibit 5 is a schedule of current interest rates. Appendix B presents selections from the rate charts Ms. Cochran's department had prepared.

Ms. Cochrane wondered what form of protection she should recommend to the loan officer and Omega that would best meet Omega's needs. As shown in Exhibit 6, intermediate-term rates had fallen dramatically since their peaks in 1981 and 1984. They had risen again following the lows of 1987, and it was unclear whether the recent rise was a reversal of the decline that had begun again earlier in 1989. As indicated by the LIBOR rates shown in Exhibit 7, short-term rates showed a pattern similar to long-term rates. The yield curve, having been flat or upward sloping for several years, had recently inverted.

If Omega wished to terminate the interest rate protection (as, for example, might be required if the Alpha System was sold before the end of the interest-rate protection agreement), it could do so. The cost of the termination could not be established in advance because it would depend on the interest rates at the time Omega wished to unwind the agreement. If rates had fallen, Omega would have to pay Prudential the present value, calculated for the remainder of the term, of the difference between the contract and the rate current at the time of repayment. If rates had risen, Prudential would pay Omega.

Exhibit 1
OMEGA CABLE SYSTEM
Key Provisions of Alpha System Loan Agreement with Palmetto Bank

FACILITIES:

A) $33,000,000 1st Tier Senior Debt at LIBOR plus 1.25%.
B) $11,000,000 2nd Tier Senior Debt at LIBOR plus 2.25%. Additional deferred interest of $965,000 due in month 60 (1.5% interest accrual).
C) $20,000,000 CATV Construction Loan at LIBOR plus 1.25%.
D) $6,000,000 Land Acquisition and Construction Loan of LIBOR plus 1%.

AVAILABILITY:

A) At closing.
B) At closing.
C) 8/89 through 12/90 on a 1:1 basis with capital expenditures.
D) 75% of appraised value. Construction period to be determined.

MATURITY:

Facilities (A), (B), & (C) roll together at 12/90 and amortize as follows:

Year 1	1991	3.0%	Year 5	1995	18.0
Year 2	1992	6.5	Year 6	1996	23.0
Year 3	1993	10.0	Year 7	1997	26.0
Year 4	1994	13.5			100.0%

D) 20-year amortization, 5-year call.
Facilities (A), (B), and (C) are interest-only from 8/89 to 12/90, and have a call in month 60 (8/93).

FINANCIAL COVENANTS:

1) Cash flow/Debt service (including principal and interest).
1989 – Not applicable
12/1990 – .90
12/1991 – 1.20
12/1992 and thereafter – 1.50

2) Total debt/cash flow.
1989 – Not applicable
12/1990 – 10:1
12/1991 – 7:1
12/1992 – 6:1
12/1993 – 5:1
12/1994 – 4:1
12/1995 and thereafter – 3:1

3) $800,000 semi-annual cash balance requirement.

4) Minimum net working capital of $800,000 required at each draw.

Exhibit 2

OMEGA CABLE SYSTEM

Selected Projections for Alpha System
(dollars in millions)

	1990	1991	1992	1993	1994	1995
Revenues	$22,409	$25,531	$28,932	$32,334	$35,255	38,219
Cash flow	10,145	12,317	13,743	17,283	19,394	21,517
Senior debt	38,800	60,000	57,600	53,200	44,800	34,800
Debt service	6,152	7,184	8,648	10,344	13,776	14,440
CF/Debt service (coverage)	1.65×	1.71×	1.73×	1.67×	1.41×	1.49×
New subscribers	7,720	6,616	4,584	4,192	4,352	4,520
Ending subscribers	63,232	69,848	74,432	78,624	82,976	87,496

Exhibit 3

OMEGA CABLE SYSTEM

Selected Statistics of the U.S. CATV and Related Industries

Number of:

TV households	90.4 million	Network affiliate stations	650
Cable TV households	51.6 million	Independent TV stations	350
		National cable-only channels	50

Millions of households receiving leading cable channels:

Basic service		**Pay service**	
ESPN	50.1	HBO	17.0
Cable News Network	49.6	Showtime	6.6
WTBS	47.9	Cinemax	6.0
USA Network	46.4	Disney Channel	4.3
MTV	44.4	The Movie Channel	2.7

Approximate audience share (late 1988):

Network (NBC, ABC, CBS) stations	63%
Independent TV stations	22
Basic cable channels	11
Pay TV channels	2
Public Broadcasting	3

Volume and Growth (1980–1988) Statistics

	Value	Compound Annual Growth Rate
Movie box office ($billions)	$4.5	6.2%
Prerecorded music	6.2	6.2
Consumer spending on CATV	13.0	23.3
TV advertising sales		
Networks	9.6	8.1
TV stations	14.7	11.3
Gross national product ($trillions)	4.9	7.5
Personal consumption expenditures	3.2	8.1
Consumer price index	118.3	4.6
Admissions to movie theaters (billions)	1.1	0.8
Basic cable households (millions)	48.6	12.0
Pay cable subscriptions (millions)	37.2	19.6

Exhibit 4

OMEGA CABLE SYSTEM

Cost of Three Alternative Solutions Being Considered

Alternative I

A. Hedge floating-rate loans (A), (B), and (C) between August 1989 and end of 1990 with one (or a combination) of the following:

Product	Cost* for 16 mos.
1. Cap on 3 mos. LIBOR @ 10.5%	$108,000
2. Collar on 3 mos. LIBOR @ 10.5%/7.5%	36,000
3. Swap	Company pays 8.97% (BEY**), receives 3-month LIBOR

B. Hedge term loan (A), (B), and (C) using a forward swap to lock in a fixed rate between January 1, 1991, and December 31, 1997:

Company pays 9.11% and receives 3 months LIBOR (fees included in the quotation).

Alternative II

A. Cost of hedging floating-rate loans (A), (B), and (C) between summer 1989 and end of 1990: same as Alternative I.A.1, I.A.2, and I.A.3.

B. Refinance floating-rate term loans (A), (B), and (C) with a new 7-year fixed-rate term loan at January 1, 1991:

Interest	Delay Fee	Coupon
10.60%	0.50%	11.10%

Alternative III

A. Hedge floating-rate loans (A), (B), and (C) between now and 1993 call date with one of the following for the entire amount:

Product	Product Cost*
1. Cap on 3 mos. LIBOR @ 10.5%	$1,830,850
2. Collar on 3 mos. LIBOR @ 10.5% / 7.5%	315,150
3. Swap vs. 3 mos. LIBOR	9.05%

*Cost quotation assumes that the entire amount is financed with the alternative. Use of smaller amounts in combination would result in somewhat higher fees.

**Bond-equivalent yield (semi-annual compounding).

Exhibit 5

OMEGA CABLE SYSTEM

Interest Rates in August 1989

Maturity	Treasuries (Bond Equivalent Yield)
1 year	8.26%
2 years	8.30
3 years	8.27
4 years	8.23
5 years	8.17
7 years	8.20
10 years	8.17
30 years	8.13
	LIBOR
3 months	8.94%
6 months	8.94

Exhibit 6
OMEGA CABLE SYSTEMS
Chart of Five-Year Treasury Rates, 1979-1988

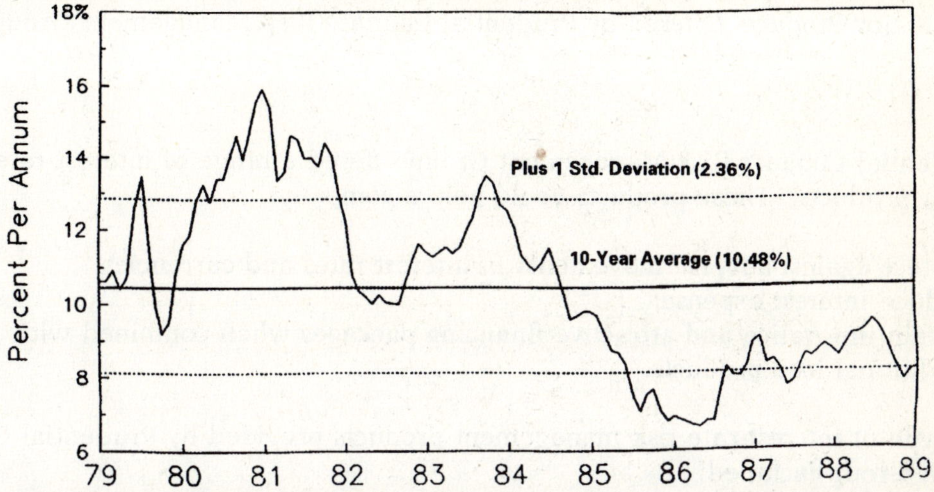

Exhibit 7
OMEGA CABLE SYSTEMS
Chart of 90-Day LIBOR Rates, 1979-1988

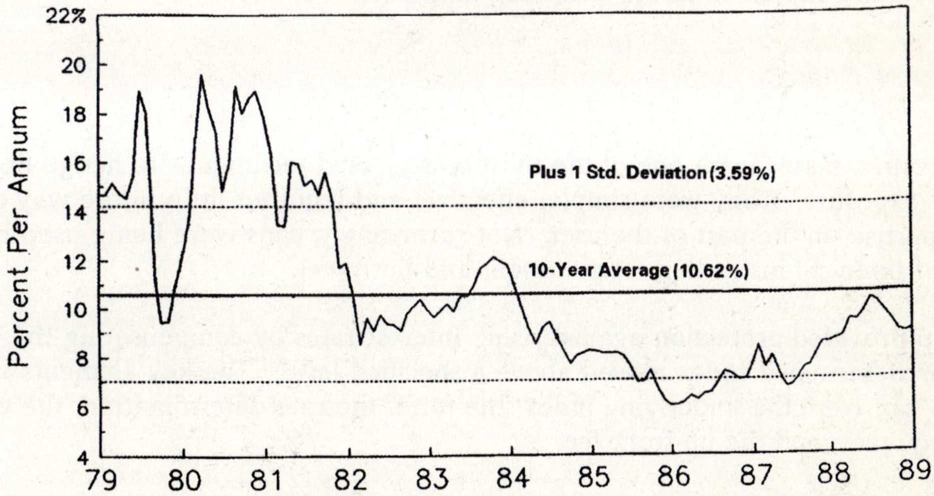

Appendix A

OMEGA CABLE SYSTEM

Major Products Offered by Prudential Capital's Risk Management Group

Prudential Capital's Risk Management Group offered a range of interest-rate risk management products. These products could help a company:

- Protect against adverse movements in interest rates and currencies;
- Reduce interest expense;
- Obtain innovative and attractive financing packages when combined with traditional loan products.

The major type of interest-rate risk management products provided by Prudential Capital's Risk Management Group included:

Caps
Collars
High/low floaters
Forward Rate Agreements (FRAs)
Swaps
Swaptions
Participating Interest-Rate Swaps

These products are explained in the following material.

CAPS

Interest-rate caps were one of the most widely used techniques to hedge floating interest-rate exposure. They were simple, effective, and required little in the way of time or financial expertise on the part of the user. Not surprisingly, caps were being used by virtually every type of financial institution, corporation, and borrower.

A cap provided protection against rising interest rates by compensating the borrower if rates on a predetermined index moved above a specified level. The key elements in an interest-rate cap were the underlying index, the term, the rate determination, the cap level, the payment frequency, and the up-front fee.

Note: All rates mentioned in the examples are for illustrative purposes and do not necessarily reflect rates that were currently available.

Caps were sold based on a variety of interest-rate indexes and maturity ranges. They could be set on the London Interbank Offering Rate (LIBOR), commercial paper, average daily prime rate, Treasury bills, and certificates of deposit. Although normally caps were thought of as medium-term hedging instruments, they could be structured for a period as short as three months or as long as 12 years.

For instance, a borrower paying floating-rate interest might buy a cap that had a strike level of 8 percent, was tied to LIBOR, had a three-year term, and was paid quarterly. On a debt of $100 million, the cap might cost 1.85 percent of the principal, or $1.85 million. If interest rates moved to 9 percent, the borrower would be paid $253,475 for that quarter.

The payment on an interest-rate cap was usually equal to the amount of interest that would be paid on the agreed principal sum at the prevailing market rate (as determined by the index) minus the amount of interest that would be paid on the underlying amount at the strike rate. If the market rate was at or below the strike rate, no payment would be made.

The borrower benefited most when interest rates remained below the strike rate and the cap did not pay off. In that respect, the cap was much like an option: the borrower paid an up-front premium to protect against adverse market moves. If the market was stable or moved in his favor, the borrower lost the cost of the premium.

Similarly, there was a trade-off between the strike level and the premium paid for a cap. A cap with a high strike rate cost less, but it would not provide as much protection as a cap at a lower strike price. As with any hedge, the borrower had to consider the market outlook and the borrower's own tolerance for risk in determining the parameters of a cap.

Although caps were used by a variety of borrowers, they were particularly attractive to real estate developers who financed their construction through short-term, floating-rate loans. Because adverse interest rate moves could make a project unprofitable, real estate developers needed a hedging vehicle that provided total assurance of the cost of financing. Caps met the requirements nicely.

Collars

A collar combined the simultaneous purchase of a cap and the sale of a floor on a floating rate index such as LIBOR. The purchase of a cap limited the potential base cost (that is, ignoring the loan spread) of floating rate debt at a predetermined maximum level, or cap rate. The sale of a floor limited the extent to which the hedger could take advantage of declining rates to a predetermined minimum level, or floor rate. As a result, a collar bracketed a range within which the interest rate index could move.

In a normal yield curve environment, the buyer of a collar usually paid a single up-front fee because the cap cost more than the receipt from the sale of the floor. When the yield curve was flat or inverted, collars became cheaper because the floor became more valuable relative to the cap. When the floor rate was set at or near current rates, it was often possible for the buyer to receive an up-front fee.

For example, a buyer of a five-year, three-month, LIBOR-based collar on $20 million with a cap at 11.5 percent and a floor at 9.5 percent (given rates prevailing at the time this example was constructed) received an up-front fee of $260,000. When spread over the life of the collar, this gain represented about 33 basis points per annum.

Under the above structure, there were three possible scenarios during the life of the collar:

1) Rates rise above 11.5%. Prudential Capital would reimburse the buyer for the difference between the actual three-month LIBOR rate and 11.5%. The buyer's maximum base cost would be 11.5% minus the coupon effect of the fee of 0.33%, or 11.17%.

2) Rates fall between 11.5% and 9.5%. The buyer's base cost would be equal to the actual LIBOR rate minus 0.33%.

3) Rates fall below 9.5%. The buyer would pay Prudential Capital the difference between 9.5% and the actual rate. The buyer's minimum base cost would be 9.5% minus 0.33%, or 9.17%.

In short, the base cost would always be within the 9.17%–11.17% range.

High/Low Floaters

A high/low floater was similar to a cap in that it limited the potential cost of floating rate debt and still allowed the borrower to retain benefits from falling rates. Unlike a cap, a high/low floater did not require an up-front fee because the cost was spread over the life of the hedge.

The periodic exchange of payments between the buyer and the seller made a high/low floater look like a complicated swap, but it effectively functioned as a cap.

For example, if a company with $50 million of LIBOR-based floating-rate debt wanted to cap its base cost at around 11 percent for three years, it could enter into a high/low floater agreement to receive LIBOR from Prudential Capital and to pay Prudential Capital a formula rate on half of the notional amount, or $25 million. The formula rate might be the lesser of (23% − LIBOR) or (LIBOR + 1%). When rates were at or below 11 percent, the company paid (LIBOR + 1%) and received LIBOR on $25 million. When rates were above 11 percent, the company paid (23% − LIBOR) and received LIBOR on $25 million. The net effect was that the base rate the company paid on $50 million was (LIBOR + 0.5%) up to a maximum level of 11.5 percent.

In short, high/low floaters were appropriate for companies that wanted to buy protection on floating-rate debt without giving up the benefit of any rate decreases or paying an up-front fee.

Forward Rate Agreements (FRAs)

A FRA was an agreement between two parties to compensate each other for short-term interest-rate movement over a predetermined period. It was based on a floating-rate index, usually LIBOR. The buyer of a FRA locked in a fixed rate whereas the seller created a floating rate. On the maturity date, the actual floating rate would be compared to the contract rate. This difference was then paid to or received from the customer.

FRAs enabled borrowers to hedge their short-term interest-rate risk exposure without up-front fees. FRAs could be tailor-made to match almost any index and maturity up to three years. Unlike financial futures, FRAs did not involve basis risk, daily margining, or continuous market monitoring.

For example, a project developer expecting to draw down $50 million of its three-month LIBOR-based construction loan two months hence might want to take advantage of currently attractive rate levels. To lock in the cost of financing before the first reset, the developer could buy a two-month FRA from Prudential Capital at a rate of 8.50 percent against three-month LIBOR.

There were three possible outcomes two months from the purchase date:

1) LIBOR rises above 8.50%. Prudential Capital would reimburse the developer the difference between the actual three-month LIBOR rate and 8.50%.

2) LIBOR falls below 8.50%. The buyer would pay Prudential Capital the difference between three-month LIBOR and 8.50%.

3) LIBOR equals 8.50%. No cash would be exchanged.

Regardless of interest-rate movements over the successive two months, the developer had fixed its three-month borrowing rate on the $50 million at 8.50 percent.

FRAs were very useful for borrowers who had a short-term view on rates because they allowed frequent changes in hedging strategies. They were very appropriate for hedging seasonal borrowings. FRAs were priced off of the Eurodollar futures curve. When this curve was inverted, FRAs were an attractive hedging vehicle for floating-rate borrowers.

Swaps

Interest rate swaps were a highly versatile, widely used financial instrument. They could be used to get low-cost funds or to hedge interest rate exposure. Essentially, swaps were an instance of "comparative advantage," in which borrowers each raised funds at their lowest cost of financing and then swapped obligations with another party to obtain their optimal interest-rate structure.

A typical swap transaction might involve a corporation with a low credit rating that wanted long-term, fixed-rate funds and a bank with a high credit rating that wanted floating-rate dollars to finance its short-term loan portfolio. The bank, due to its higher credit rating, might be able to obtain fixed-rate funds at a rate 2 percent lower than the corporation could obtain but could get floating-rate funds at only a 0.5 percent differential from the corporation. The differences between the two sets of rates created a comparative advantage that could be exploited through a swap even though the bank's cost of funds was less at all maturities.

To take advantage of the situation, the bank might issue a seven-year, fixed-rate, 12 percent Eurobond while the corporation would take out a floating-rate loan at LIBOR plus 1 percent. The bank and the corporation would then swap interest rate payments. The corporation paid the 12 percent bond obligation while the bank paid the LIBOR portion of the corporation's floating-rate loan. The corporation, however, would pay the remaining 1 percent on its original loan.

As a result of the swap, both parties reduced their borrowing costs and obtained their desired interest rate structures. The bank financed its floating-rate loan portfolio through floating-rate funds at a 0.5 percent better rate than it could get by itself. Similarly, the corporation had obtained fixed rate financing at a rate 1 percent lower than it could otherwise have achieved. Transaction costs with a swap intermediary would have reduced the savings marginally.

Treasurers could use swaps to manage the balance sheet actively. Swap users had complete freedom to unwind or offset swap positions without altering the underlying assets or liabilities. They could change the nature of their assets or liabilities from fixed-rate to floating-rate.

For example, if a company issued $50 million of 10-year notes at a fixed rate of 10 percent and simultaneously entered into a swap in which it received 9.5 percent and paid six-month LIBOR, it would have created synthetic floating-rate debt with an effective cost of LIBOR + 0.5%. The company could benefit from declining interest rates and, at the same time, have complete flexibility in "fixing" the rate on the loan. Early end of the swap could be achieved by selling (unwinding) the swap or entering into a new swap with the opposite structure.

There were two possible outcomes of this example:

1) Rates fall: Swap is unwound at a profit.

Assuming two years have passed and rates have fallen 1.0% (parallel shift), the company would receive a payment of about $2.9 million, which could be used to lower its effective rate on the underlying fixed-rate loan by approximately 1.0%.

It is possible that this gain could be taxable when realized. To achieve the same economic result without the tax consequences, the company could arrange a new swap to pay fixed at 8.5%.

2) Rates rise: Swap is unwound at a loss.

Assuming two years have passed and rates have increased 1.0% (parallel shift), the company would make a payment of about $2.7 million, which would increase its effective borrowing cost by about 1.0%.

When interest rates were low, floating-rate borrowers often used swaps to lock in attractive rates. Borrowers who were not required to fix for a particular period could reduce their effective interest costs by selling the right to cancel the swap at a predetermined time.

Suppose a commercial paper issuer wanted to lock in a fixed rate on $50 million for four to five years. The company entered into a five-year swap with Prudential Capital and simultaneously sold Prudential Capital the option to cancel the swap four years later. As a result, the company paid 8.50 percent and received the one month commercial paper rate, and Prudential Capital had the option to cancel the swap in four years. By contrast, the company would have had to pay 8.60 percent and 8.65 percent on a conventional four- and five-year swap, respectively.

Under the above structure, there were two possible outcomes four years from the time of the agreement:

1) One-year swap rate rises above 8.50%: Prudential Capital would cancel the swap and the company would again pay a floating rate.

2) One-year swap rate at or below 8.50%: Prudential Capital would not cancel the swap, and the company continues to pay 8.50% for one more year.

By selling an option to cancel the swap, the company created a synthetic putable issue with a lower-than-market fixed rate for four years. On the other hand, the company was exposed to the risk of paying higher rates in the last year. Therefore, this strategy would be most appropriate for floating-rate borrowers with flexible funding horizons, such as finance companies.

Cancelable swaps tended to be attractively priced in maturity segments of the yield curve that were positively sloped. The positive slope increased the value of the put option, which reduced the all-in rate. Cancellation features could be applied to any swap, even existing ones.

Currency swaps enabled global and U.S. borrowers to obtain funding in a particular currency that might otherwise be more expensive or even inaccessible. With currency swaps, borrowers could borrow in one currency and then swap their interest payments into their desired currencies.

Assume a U.S. company wanted to raise $50 million Canadian dollars to finance its Canadian operations. The company could obtain a five-year Canadian financing in two steps:

Step 1: The company issues fixed-rate notes at a rate of the current five-year U.S. Treasury rate plus a loan spread.

Step 2: At the same time, the company enters into a currency swap to exchange its U.S. borrowings for Canadian dollars at the current exchange rate. At maturity, the same amount of cash will be reexchanged. In addition, the company agrees to receive the same fixed rate it pays in Step 1 and pays a fixed rate quoted as a spread over the five-year Canadian Treasury rate. Thus, the company locks in its borrowing costs for the entire issue.

Suppose the company could issue fixed notes in the United States at 9.5 percent (1.1 percent above the five-year Treasury rate); given the current exchange rate at 1.195, the company needed to borrow US$42 million. In addition, the company was able to receive U.S. 9.5 percent and pay Canadian 11.30 percent (1.67 percent above the five-year Canadian Treasury rate) on a currency swap. The economics of the transaction were as follows:

U.S. dollars borrowed	$42 million
Canadian dollars received on swap	$50 million
Pay on loan	(U.S. 9.50%)
Receive on swap	(U.S. 9.50%)
Pay on swap	(Canadian 11.30%)
Net cost	(Canadian 11.30%)

As a result, the all-in-cost of funding was a Canadian fixed rate of 11.30 percent.

Currency swaps were available in most major currencies and in a variety of maturities and payment structures (fixed-fixed, fixed-floating, or floating-floating). Final maturities under ten years were readily available. In most currencies, swaps could be structured to match any principal flows (compounding, amortizing, or roller-coaster).

Swaptions

Fixed-rate borrowers with callable issues suffered an opportunity cost when interest rates fell before the call date. Borrowers could reduce their effective borrowing costs by selling options on swaps (swaptions) to realize the value of call features embedded in their debt.

Suppose a company had $50 million of 12 percent debt maturing May 1, 1996, callable at par on May 1, 1993. The company sold Prudential Capital a call option on a three-year swap (time remaining to maturity on call date) with a strike level of 11.5 percent. The strike was set at a level equal to the all-in cost of refunding.

The option could be exercised by Prudential Capital only on May 1, 1993 (bond call date). In return, the company received an up-front payment of $1.25 million.

Under the above structure, there were two possible outcomes on May 1, 1993:

1) Three-year swap rates below 11.5%: Prudential Capital exercises the option. The company pays fixed at 11.5% and receives LIBOR. At the same time, it calls its 12% debt and refunds in the floating rate market. If the company refunds at LIBOR+0.5%, its effective borrowing costs (internal rate of return) will be 11.47% from today to May 1, 1996. Alternatively, the company can refund with fixed-rate debt and unwind the swap at a loss.

2) Three-year swap rates at or above 11.5%: Swaption expires worthless. The company continues to fund with its 12% debt. Its effective borrowing cost is 11.47% between today and May 1, 1996.

As a result, the sale of the 11.5 percent swaption reduced the company's borrowing costs by 53 basis points per annum regardless of interest rate movement.

In sum, swaptions could be used by borrowers to take advantage of declines in interest rates before the call date of their debt. These options were very attractively priced on occasions when the yield curve was inverted. While this strategy was very popular in the new issue market, it also could be applied to existing callable debt.

Participating Swaps

A participating swap is a product that provides good protection against rising rates and a share in the benefit of declining rates even if rates were to fall to zero. Unlike a cap, the borrower is not required to pay an up-front fee. In return, the borrower gives up a percentage of the benefits from falling interest rates but does not accept an explicit floor.

For example, a company with $50 million of LIBOR-based floating-rate debt would like to cap its base cost at 10.5 percent for three years. The company is able to execute a participating swap with a 75 percent participation rate. During the next three years, the company would receive three-month LIBOR and pay a formula rate on $50 million. The formula rate is set and capped at 10.5 percent. When LIBOR is below 10.5 percent, the rate that the company pays is reduced. The reduction is calculated as 75 percent of the difference between 10.5 percent and LIBOR. When LIBOR is at or above 10.5 percent, the company pays 10.5 percent.

The cap level could be adjusted to increase or decrease the participation rate. Participating swaps were available in all final maturities up to ten years. They also could be structured to match any principal flows. LIBOR, commercial paper, and Prime could be hedged with three-month LIBOR as the most common index.

Summary Comparison

Table 1 is a comparison of the major floating-rate hedge products.

Table 1
Comparison of Hedge Products

Product	Up-front Fees	Protection Against Rates Moving Up	Participation in Rates Moving Down	Maturity Range Up To
Caps	Yes	Yes	Yes	10 years
Collars	Sometimes	Yes	Yes, to floor level	10 years
High/Low Floaters	No	Yes	Yes	10 years
Forward Rate Agreements	No	Yes	No	3 years
Swaps	No	Yes	No	10 years
Participating Swaps	No	Yes	Partial	10 years

There was no single correct hedge for all companies. Each company's interest rate view and cash flow constraints must be considered. Selecting an appropriate hedge program required taking a view on interest rates. Not hedging was also taking a view, whether or not there was a conscious decision not to hedge. Therefore, the best strategy was to monitor the interest rate environment closely and actively manage the underlying interest rate risks accordingly.

Swaps and FRAs would be the least expensive protection against very high rates, especially if the company could not bear much risk of higher rates. Caps would result in higher costs than swaps if interest rates increased significantly but in lower costs if rates fell. Collars may result in lower costs than swaps if rates remain stable or fall. High/low floaters and participating swaps were appropriate for borrowers who wanted the same protection caps provided but wanted to avoid paying up-front fees.

Appendix A

Exhibit A1
OMEGA CABLE SYSTEM
Distribution of LIBOR Rates, 1979-1989

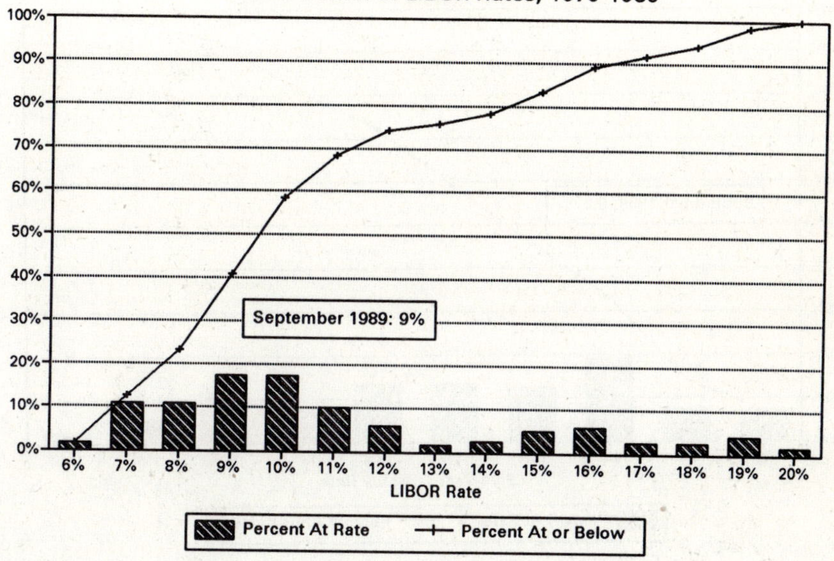

Exhibit A2
OMEGA CABLE SYSTEM
Distribution of Prime Rates, 1979-1989

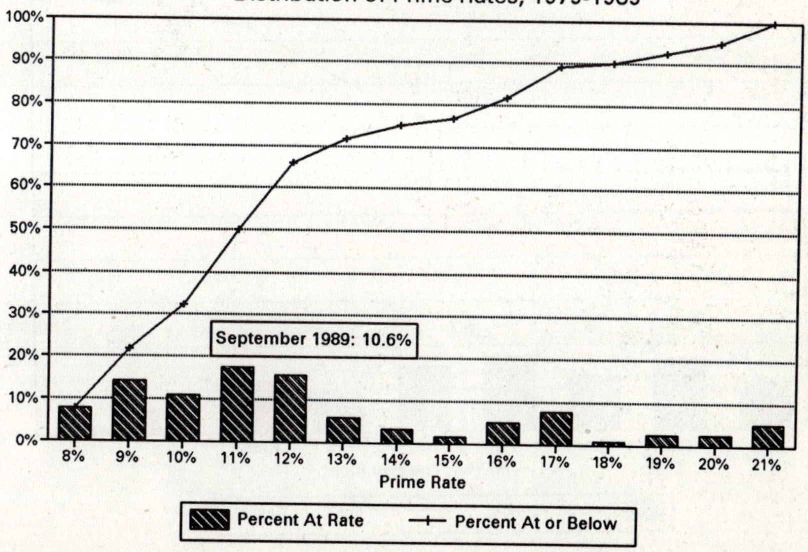

Appendix A (continued)

Exhibit A3
OMEGA CABLE SYSTEM
Distribution of Five-Year Treasury Rates, 1979-1989

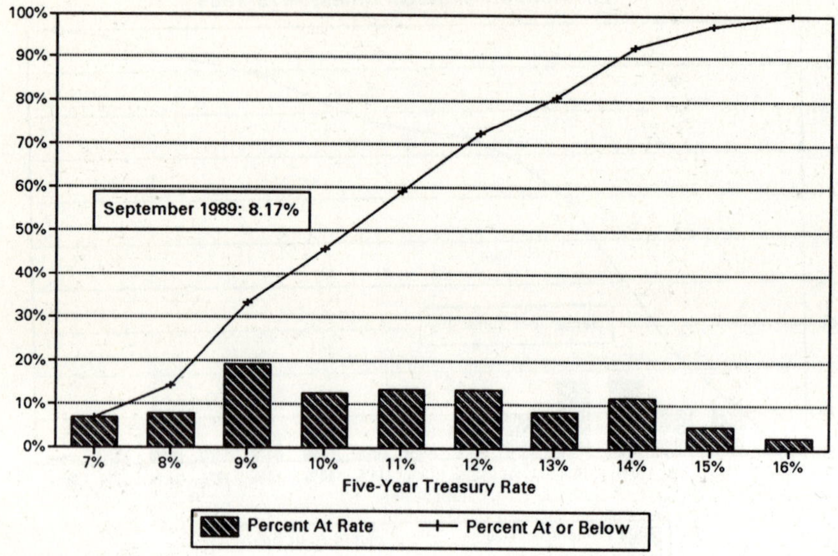

Exhibit A4
OMEGA CABLE SYSTEM
Distribution of Ten-Year Treasury Rates, 1979-1989

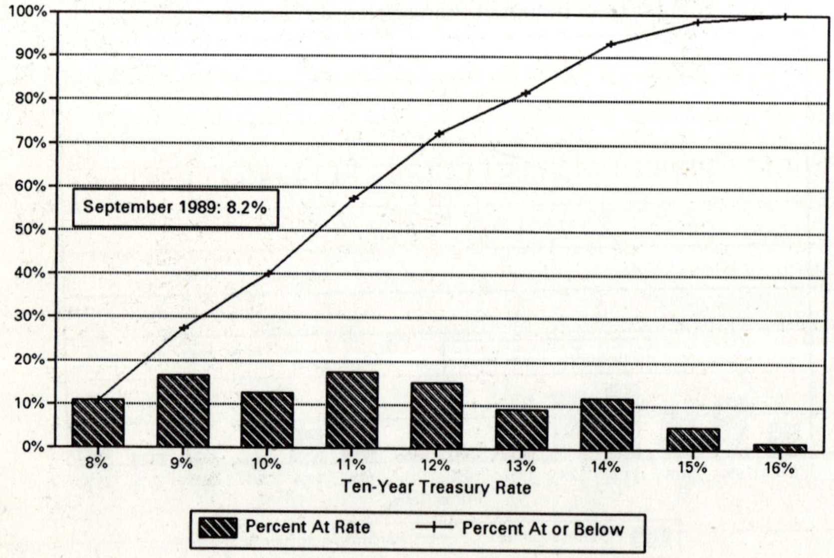

Appendix A (continued)

Exhibit A5
OMEGA CABLE SYSTEM
Cumulative Rate Distribution, 1979-1989

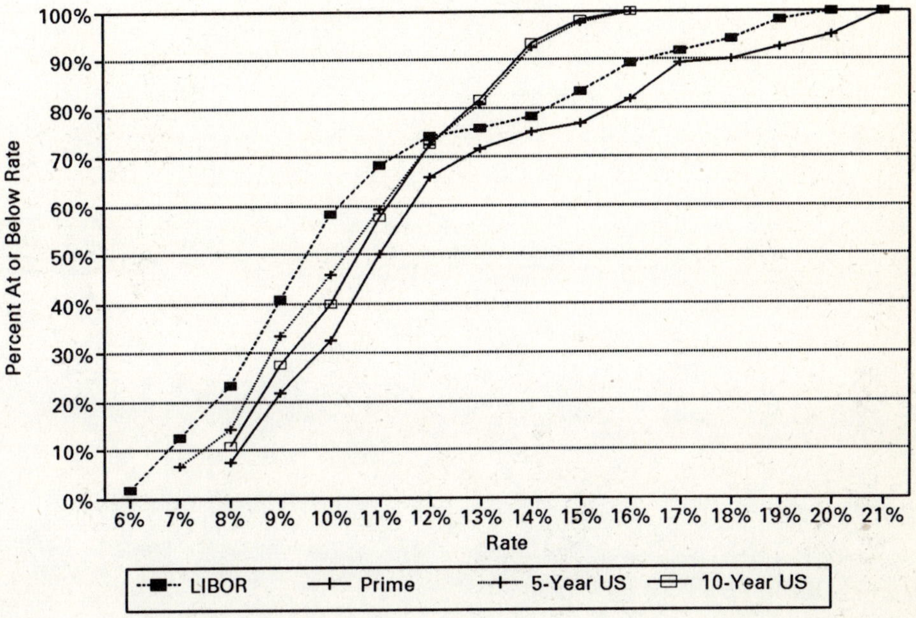

Exhibit A6
OMEGA CABLE SYSTEMS
Money Market Rate Variability, 1979-1989

	Minimum	Maximum	Average	Std. Deviation
30-day commercial paper	5.77%	19.25%	9.95%	3.27%
Three-month LIBOR	5.98%	19.60%	10.62%	3.59%
Three-month Treasury	5.32%	17.71%	9.38%	3.15%
Prime rate	7.50%	20.50%	11.98%	3.56%
One-year Treasury	5.72%	16.72%	9.87%	2.85%
Five-year Treasury	6.64%	15.93%	10.48%	2.36%
Ten-year Treasury	7.08%	15.32%	10.65%	2.13%
Spread, ten-year less one-year Treasury (basis points)	-307	245	81	124

Notes

FIRST SOUTHEAST FINANCIAL SERVICES CORP.

Sitting in traffic during the commute to his home in Charlotte, North Carolina, in February 1992, Phil Brown, senior vice president for risk management of First Southeast Financial Services Corp., thought about the immense changes that had occurred in the financial services business in the previous decade and the problems that this posed for risk management in financial institutions. Risk management had been much simpler when he started in the banking industry 25 years before. In particular, it was so much more complex to manage risk in a business like the options unit at First Southeast Financial Services Corp. than it was to manage the credit risk in traditional bank lending.

This changed risk situation had been highlighted in a speech made on January 30, 1992, by G. Gerald Corrigan, President of Federal Reserve Bank of New York. Speaking to the New York State Bankers Association, Mr. Corrigan had warned:

> You had all better take a very, very hard look at off-balance sheet activities, including the payments, clearance, and settlement risk associated with many of those activities. The growth and complexity of off-balance sheet activities and the nature of the credit, price, and settlement risk they entail should give us all cause for concern, especially when it seems so easy to accept the view that what counts is net, not gross exposures. That distinction between gross and net may be relevant in some cases, and it may be fine when all else is well, but in the event of a major disruption, I assure you that it will be the gross, not the net, that will really matter in most segments of the financial marketplace both nationally and internationally....Off-balance sheet activities have a role, but they must be managed and controlled carefully, and they must be understood by top management as well as by traders and rocket scientists. They must also be understood by supervisors. In that regard, I can assure you that at both the national and the international level we are redoubling our efforts to ensure that supervisory policies for these activities are sensitive to the full range of risks they present to individual institutions and markets generally.

Mr. Brown had read Mr. Corrigan's speech the previous day as he was catching up on his reading. He shared many of Mr. Corrigan's concerns and knew that First Southeast was not immune from the risks that Mr. Corrigan warned about.

Details of the case have been changed to protect confidential information without altering the nature of the managerial decision.

First Southeast Financial Services Corp.

First Southeast Financial Services Corp. was the merchant banking subsidiary of First Southeast Bancorp, the eighth largest bank holding company in the United States at the end of 1991. First Southeast had created the third largest retail banking organization in the United States, consisting of 1,070 offices in eight states and the District of Columbia. First Southeast's retail base included four million households in the United States, 5 percent of the total. First Southeast Bancorp's 1991 income statement and balance sheet are shown in Exhibits 1 and 2.

Formed in May 1987 as a result of a reorganization of First Southeast Bancorp, First Southeast Financial Services Corp. (Servco) was First Southeast Bancorp's focal point for providing wholesale, corporate, and merchant banking services on a global basis to large corporations, financial institutions, and governments. Servco's broad experience and reservoir of expertise also supported First Southeast Bancorp's other banks, thereby helping to create incremental value for the entire First Southeast system. Servco's major lines of business included international banking, corporate banking, cash management, institutional trust and investments, securities sales and trading, derivative products such as futures, swaps, options, and various capital markets, corporate finance, and structuring activities. At the end of December 1991, Servco's balance sheet included $6.5 billion of assets and $2.6 billion in loans. Servco's net income for 1991 was $92 million.

The Changing Financial Services Environment

During the decade of the 1980s, the financial services environment changed dramatically. As a result of deregulation, bank product portfolios went from a mix of relatively few, conceptually simple, standardized, long-lived products to a mix of many, conceptually complex, individually tailored, short-lived products. At the same time, the production and distribution of bank products shifted from exclusively in-house production and distribution through focused channels and knowledgeable sales forces to include purchase from third parties and distribution through a wide range of channels without sales forces thoroughly experienced in each product. These two trends, coupled with a more competitive, broader market for bank services, made the process of risk management for many banks increasingly difficult.

The changing financial services environment had several effects on bank risk management. Routine regulatory and audit review processes became more complex and required that management have more knowledge of its businesses. Traditional measures of risk, such as the portfolio risk-adjusted interest margin, the noninterest revenue margin, and the net operating earnings of business units no longer provided sufficient information for risk management. At the same time, computer systems could not provide the required integration of accounting and management information for new products. It was also becoming difficult to assign responsibility for risk assessment and management because of the increasing product flow across many organizational units, the growing geographic dispersion of banking organizations, and the increasing complexity of products.

The First Southeast Financial Services Corp. Risk Management Process

In this environment, Mr. Brown and his colleagues had been charged with the responsibility for finding new and effective ways to measure and control the institution's risk exposure. Servco's risk management process had three basic goals. The first goal was to manage the bank's three major risks (interest rate risk, liquidity risk, and credit risk) in a balanced fashion. The second goal was to avoid surprises or catastrophic losses, always a potential in a rapidly changing environment. The third goal was to manage risk in a way that maximized profitability.

The process that Servco used to manage its risk was built around information and control systems. The system's objectives were to provide sufficient information to allow management a high comfort level with environmental uncertainty and to balance levels of risk effectively against levels of potential profits.

Servco's risk management process had four basic elements: the process for managing ongoing exposures, the process for assessing new risk, the assignment of the risk control responsibility, and the development of management information to monitor risk.

Servco managed ongoing exposure by monitoring individual activities and products. Exposure levels were controlled to insure that the bank was not subject to high concentrations of risk in specific activities or products. This process also arranged for efficient risk protection through risk diversification, hedges, credit limits, insurance, and adequate bank capital.

To evaluate new risks, Servco had developed a risk assessment process that covered the elements (such as regulation, service, image, tax, contingent liability, and profit) associated with new products. This risk assessment process was applied to new activities and products under consideration for introduction.

Specific risk control responsibilities had been assigned, including responsibility for developing a risk assessment and management process, risk policies, and new activity approval and for monitoring ongoing activities. Activity centers having some responsibility for risk management within Servco included Corporate, Marketing, Treasury, Finance, Legal, Operations, Systems, Planning, and Risk Management.

The fourth and final element of Servco's risk management process involved developing adequate management information for monitoring risks. These reports were prepared by responsibility, activity, and exposure, and by risk type (financial, operational, and strategic). Risk was monitored by defining measures of exposure, quantifying risk goals, and reporting exposure levels against risk goals.

The Option Market

In the early 1980s, there was virtually no organized bank proprietary option trading. Of course, bank trust departments used listed stock options in managing customer portfolios, but the strategies and perceived exposure were limited. The profit potential and risk were the customer's.

Though options were not formally recognized as a product, banks nevertheless dealt in assets and liabilities that would subsequently be regarded as including imbedded options because their existence, duration, or yield was discretionary on the part of the bank or its counterparty to a transaction. A mortgage with a prepayment provision was the classic example of such an asset. In addition, option terms worked their way into a wide variety of other bank transactions. Until the late 1980s, most banks treated these options as ancillary products to a bank's main business. No options expertise was developed, no effort was made to market or price options as detachable products, no strategies were developed to deal in these products and manage their risk.

This environment changed dramatically by the late 1980s. Worldwide, several hundred banks were dealing in options. Virtually every major international bank managed an options book with significant risk and perceived profit potential. Among the driving forces behind this "new" industry were:

- customer demands for nonlinear* asset and liability exposure;
- banks perceived need to provide competitive option quotes as part of a complete line of customer services;
- trading profit opportunities;
- fear of being left behind in an expanding and trendy industry;
- and disenchantment with the loan business.

Bank option dealers traded with every kind of market participant including nonfinancial corporations, investment institutions, financial institutions, and other trading banks.

Corporations usually viewed themselves as using options to buy insurance on the price risk in an asset or liability. Sometimes they were locking in a range of exposure. Options were especially useful if the exposure was unknown—for example, the foreign exchange (FX) risk in a venture that might or might not take place. Common transactions for corporate customers included buying interest rate caps and buying FX options to protect foreign receivables and payables. For example, mining companies sometimes wanted to "fence" the price of gold for

---

*That is, the worth of an outcome does not change in a linear manner to a change in a related variable. An option at expiration has no value if the value of the item optioned is less than the exercise price. An option's value may increase nonlinearly with the value of the optioned item if the value is greater than the exercise price. Risk-averse individuals may be willing to give up chances for some gain in exchange for less chances of loss.

their production two to three years hence. In this case, a put/call combination might assure them that the price would be no less than $400 an ounce but not more than $500 an ounce at a specific future date. A bank loan officer might encourage or even require such a transaction to eliminate certain risk of a venture when making a bank lending decision.

Investors frequently used options for hedging investments such as stocks, bonds, and mortgage backed securities. Usually, this involved writing calls for "income enhancement" (in exchange for giving up profit potential) or buying puts for "disaster insurance." Mutual funds especially liked to write calls against bonds and notes already in their portfolios because their shares were often sold on a current-yield basis. Regional banks and thrifts often perceived the needs of both corporations and investment institutions. They had nonlinear corporate interest rate exposure that needed managing, and they also had investment portfolios.

Major banks often found themselves on the opposite side of the open interest in an option. This could happen consciously in the interbank market or invisibly through listed options. Sometimes, banks were simply passing on the exposure they had acquired by making markets. Other times they were consciously taking a risk position for an expected profit.

Because of the explosive growth of bank option trading, most traders were new to the business. A typical trader had one or two years of experience. Someone with four years of experience in 1992 was an "old timer." However, because most bank option traders were intelligent and energetic and were exposed to a high volume of trading in a short period, there was not an industry-wide expertise problem. On the other hand, lack of experience at the supervisory level and above was an industry-wide problem. Options were so different from other trading vehicles that managers simply had to learn to think differently. This was not easy for someone for whom options was not a full-time preoccupation.

Corporate customers were usually inexperienced and naive. Also, because they usually had a variety of responsibilities and made relatively few trades, their traders frequently did not learn as fast as bank traders. Similarly, though many investment institutions had used options for ten years or more, their experience had not produced much expertise. Legal and marketing constraints on strategies and the distraction of short-term performance pressures prevented them from developing a broader strategic view. As a result of these factors, in 1992 bank traders enjoyed a distinct edge of expertise and experience over most of their counterparts at both corporate and investment institutions.

Bank Option Policy

When banks were first exposed to options to satisfy customer demand, they often began with a direct layoff of every option traded. The exposure to adverse market movement was thus minimal. This form of arbitrage was quite profitable in the early days of option trading when even large customers were very naive and inefficiencies were common. By 1992, however, option markets were too efficient for a bank to hope it could operate a significant options profit center by making "look-alike" trades. Major option-trading banks had to take inventory onto their books and actively manage it. This strategy required more risk management because of its complexity, but it also provided more opportunities.

Most banks began option trading as an extension of cash trading. Foreign exchange desks would give option-trading authority to an FX spot trader. Similar arrangements would be made at bond desks and money market desks for their option-like products. In part, these arrangements were the result of the misapprehension that options were "little spot contracts." It also recognized the marketing realities and the need to hedge option trades in the underlying markets.

In the second half of the 1980s, there had been a steady trend toward viewing options trading as a separate business. Option traders were less likely to be former spot traders, and they frequently were organizationally separate from spot desks. This approach helped banks avoid "doubling up" on spot positions. It also provided opportunities for the management of diversification and for collective expertise development. Furthermore, it reduced the pressure on an options trader to "force" trades when no good opportunities were available.

Each bank had to make several policy decisions that shaped its overall options strategy. The most important issues that had to be addressed included:

- market orientation (trading versus customer orientation, market-making versus selective positioning, layoff versus running a book, marketing versus price competition)
- product design (standard or custom)
- trading control (centralization versus local decision-making)
- dealing strategy (separate business versus extension of cash trading).

Some bank treasurers believed that their primary job was to find profitable positions. To them, customers were a distraction from the business at hand. Others believed that consistent profitability from pure trading was impossible. They believed that customer order flow was the key to consistent profits. A few banks tried both approaches with different groups of traders.

Some banks believed that, to make money in options, they needed to make deep, tight markets in all options in every possible underlying instrument. They were willing to wind up with a few undesirable positions to get the order flow. Other banks liked to "pick their spots" by making good markets in certain segments where they believed they had an advantage or by not trading until option prices looked attractive.

If a bank decided that customer order flow was important, it needed a marketing strategy. Some banks competed on price alone. They would quote tight prices and hope to attract enough volume to overcome the problems of low margins and high risk. They attracted business from banks that had chosen trading over corporate order flow and from some large corporations in major financial markets whose treasury operations competed as profit/loss centers.

Most major banks had tried broader marketing approaches, and many believed that they still had not found the right answer. There was no apparent reason why traditional marketing concepts of market segmentation, training, advisory services, product differentiation, and old-fashioned relationship-building would not be appropriate in options. These approaches, however, had not been completely effective. Common bank complaints included:

- "It's hard to find and keep good marketing people who understand options."
- "Missionary work is a big investment."
- "Price consciousness overcomes customer loyalty."

Product Design

In recent years there had been public discussion, and some action, among major banks regarding emulating the investment banks' approach. The investment banks had hired high-powered "quants" or "rocket scientists" to design risk management products for customers, to price them, and to manage their risk. This move recognized the increasing complexity of corporate financial risk, the increasing customer sophistication, and the inability of traditional risk management vehicles to satisfy customer needs. Bank FX and interest-rate corporate desks began using terms like "investment banking" and "financial engineering." Non-bank specialty boutiques also appeared to cater to complex financial risk concerns.

This approach afforded the institution the opportunity for product/service differentiation, for building ongoing customer relationships, and for avoiding destructive price competition. But it was expensive, and it seldom produced the low-cost, low-risk result the customer was hoping for. Those who opted for standardized products pointed to their simplicity, their efficiency, and to the fact that they were getting better over time. They viewed the "investment banking" approach as a costly attempt to solve problems that could not be solved.

Trading Control

At one extreme, a bank could centralize all quotes, trading decisions, and risk management in a single office. This approach permitted better risk and strategy monitoring, facilitated the development of collective expertise, and usually minimized expenses. At the other extreme, a bank could set up independent centers around the world, recognizing a need to participate in different time zones, to be close to the customers and competition, and to diversify strategies and book exposure. Most major banks tried a combination of the two. Typically, three major trading centers were maintained along with a few customer-service offices. No two banks were alike in the extent of centralization of strategic decision making, pricing decisions, personnel development, and risk management.

Option Trading Strategies

There were at least as many option trading strategies as there were traders, although many traders were vague in defining the strategies they used. Many used more than one strategy, and all strategies evolved over time. Weak traders wandered from one strategy to another without a plan or defined criteria. Most strategies could be classified in three broad categories: scalping, implied volatility trading, and underwriting.

In its narrowest form, a *scalper* was a market maker who tried to make money by buying on the bid and selling on the offer. This trader did not want to build inventory but was looking for turnover. If the turnover was not high compared to inventory, the trader was not scalping. In bank option trading, a strategy of scalping an individual option was not usually feasible because trades did not take place frequently enough. To scalp profitably an individual option, inventory had to turn over so rapidly that the likely impact on the option's price from underlying price movement was small compared to the bid/offer spread.

Major elements of a successful scalping program included:

- plenty of order flow
- good, efficient access to spot markets in which bid/ask spreads were narrower than in the option market
- good option market information and a feel for where the option market "really is"
- mental quickness
- discipline, especially in controlling size and taking losses.

The biggest potential problem in this strategy was forgetting the strategy. A manager needed to monitor the book to make sure that both profits and losses were small and that positions turned over fast enough that they did not become bets on changes in implied volatility. The second biggest problem was forcing trades when trading was light. Sometimes weak management would encourage a trader to "find a way" to meet profit goals. This usually meant taking unreasonable risk for small expected profits.

A more common and popular approach was to scalp *implied volatility*. A trader would buy options on the bid or sell on the offer and temporarily spread off the position on a neutral basis in the spot market. Since the position was incrementally neutral, it was usually insensitive to underlying price movement, at least for price changes that normally occurred in a few hours or a day. If market volatility changed, however, the option price could change even if spot prices did not. Increased expected volatility in the price of the spot instrument would increase the price of the option, to the trader's profit. Decreased expected volatility in the spot price of the instrument would reduce the price of the option to the trader's loss. If the trader had managed to avoid positions with large short-term time sensitivity, the main concern was to turn the position over before suffering an adverse implied volatility change.

There were wide ranges of popular techniques for forecasting these changes. As in scalping, it was important to establish a position in which there would not be much "noise." Traders wanted most of the action to be due to implied volatility change. This meant the position must be easy to get into and out of. The spread had to be much more sensitive to implied volatility changes than to time and price changes. Also the position needed to turn over reasonably quickly—usually in less than 25 percent of the options' life. If the position was kept for a long time, the dynamics of time decay and underlying price movement would begin to dominate the position's profitability.

Key success elements included:

- the ability to forecast the change in implied volatility in reasonable time horizons
- a good understanding of option spread dynamics
- discipline to reduce the position when the implied volatility forecast was no longer appropriate or when the spread's characteristics changed.

The biggest problem with this strategy was the chance that the trader would build up a large position without thinking through the results of unfavorable scenarios. An implied volatility trader was going to have losing streaks and potentially could be a big loser if the downside risk was not properly controlled.

Underwriting was a term lifted from the insurance industry. An insurance underwriter sold a policy because the price looked attractive compared to the statistical distribution of events that might occur. The underwriter took a position and lived with the result. Similarly, a trader might put on a neutral spread if its implied volatility seemed too high or too low compared to expectations for the actual volatility of the underlying option. With a large universe of option classes available, this strategy was consistently profitable on a year-to-year basis but not on a quarter-to-quarter basis. In a typical year, most of the profits usually occurred in the best two or three months.

This was a strategy for responding to option price aberrations. It produced profits when option prices "corrected themselves," but it did not rely on that phenomenon. It was based on the assumptions that actual volatility could be forecasted with tolerable expected error. Implied volatilities would occasionally be inefficient enough to offer opportunities. In other words, volatility could prove to be very high or low compared to the forecast and expected error of actual volatility.

For a successful underwriting strategy, a trader needed:

- a forecasting methodology
- perspective on expected error and changes in implied volatility
- a very good understanding of option dynamics
- a broad universe of option markets
- the discipline to initiate and keep positions only if implied volatility aberrations were substantial
- the discipline to stay reasonably neutral.

A common error in using this strategy was forgetting the importance of substantial price aberrations and taking positions that were "comfortable" or "had been working." This was similar to an insurance company's underwriting a life insurance policy at a statistically unprofitable price. Another error was ignoring the remote unfavorable scenarios, a problem also in implied volatility-positioning strategy.

Framework for Option Risk Management

The term "risk" had almost too many meanings in the options world. Banks offered options to customers as part of a line of "risk management" products and services. Most large international banks wanted their customers to think of them as risk management experts, offering a broad range of transactions, advice, and other services to help their customers manage business risk.

For most bankers, however, the more important risks associated with options were the bank's own risks. These could have many forms:

- A counterparty might default on its option obligation
- Delivery procedures might fail upon the exercise of an option
- The market system might fail, suspending normal trading and liquidity
- Credit line limitations might be too restrictive
- The bank's information system might fail, and the bank might lose track of its positions
- A trader might make a transaction error (a misunderstanding with a counterparty with respect to option terms, price, or quantity, or an accidental trade at a totally inappropriate price or quantity)
- A trader might "go berserk" and quickly make large, inappropriate trades
- A trader might defraud the bank
- The bank's accounting procedure might be inadequate to track the department's exposure and profits accurately and promptly
- The bank's overall trading strategy might not be profitable
- There might not be enough good trading opportunities
- The bank might lose money because of price changes in the options and related positions in its book
- Traders might misrepresent their exposure, either accidentally or purposely
- Exposure limits might be too restrictive to allow profitable trading or too broad to provide adequate control

Because of options complexity, simple units of risk or one-dimensional risk management mechanisms (such as the trading limits that were applied to spot positions) were not useful control mechanisms. In most businesses, risk analysis involves simple units of risk:

- How many dollars were committed to a position? (e.g., an investment in stocks or bonds)
- What was the maximum possible loss? (e.g., an investment protected by a put)
- What was the chance of losing some money on this transaction? (e.g., an auto loan with a predictable default rate)

- How much of a commodity was the trader long or short? (e.g., a spot FX position)

None of these questions were very important in options-risk analysis because the risk profile of an options position was usually too complex. Risk had to be described in terms of the dollar losses that a position *might* suffer as a result of changes in either individual- or multiple-option pricing variables. Risk management required:

1. definition of a few variable change scenarios to be monitored.
2. establishment of exposure limits for each scenario. No position would be permissible if, hypothetically, a defined scenario would produce a loss more than the appropriate exposure limit.
3. a reporting system that frequently described the current exposure to each scenario.
4. timely management review of exposure reports.
5. immediate action when exposure limits were violated.

It was most important to manage risk *by scenario* and *prospectively*. Worst-case analysis was not useful because frequently there was no typical worst case. Truly horrifying scenarios (such as long-term interest rates tripling over night) were probably not worth looking at. Risk managers had to decide which scenarios were worth considering, and these scenarios had to be fully defined in option-variable terms. Then, exposure had to be calculated. It would be irresponsible simply to trust the traders until a remote event actually occurred.

Different kinds of risk issues had to be addressed through a multidimensional approach to analysis. Important questions included:

- Was the bank too exposed to the possibility of losing a significant portion of the bank's annual earnings?
- Was the bank too exposed to the possibility of losing a significant portion of the bank's annual option trading profit?
- Was the bank too exposed to the possibility of having a bad month?
- Was the bank too exposed to any risks, given the quality of our position? (Was its opportunity for expected profit commensurate with its risk?)

The First Southeast Financial Services Corp. Risk Control System

First Southeast's option desk was part of Servco's Option Products and Swaps Department headed by a senior vice president. The department handled a variety of nontraditional investment banking and derivative products including interest rate swaps, interest rate caps and floors, foreign exchange options and domestic OTC options. Ten professionals handled interest rate swaps. Nine others were divided between interest rate caps and floors (3), foreign exchange options (2), and domestic OTC options (4).

In the domestic over-the-counter market, Servco was both a market maker and a direct investor. Unlike market makers in other parts of the bank, such as government securities, Servco's option traders were not always in the market. They would move into and out of the market on both the buy and sell side depending on their positions. Servco's domestic OTC options business was confined to options on government securities and mortgage-backed securities because government regulation restricted banks to writing options on securities in which they could make direct investments. Because government regulations prohibited First Southeast from investing in equity securities directly, Servco was also prohibited from making equity option investments.

Because on a day-to-day basis it did not make sense for Servco's Management Committee to be equally concerned with all aspects of option risk management, risk management responsibilities were distributed within the organization. The Management Committee, however, kept responsibility for setting policy and monitoring catastrophic risk.

There were three levels of risk management responsibility:

- Management Committee level
- Managerial level
- Trading Room level.

The risk management activity was divided into five functions, which are described in the following paragraphs. This structure helped Servco's credit management and senior executives to assess the risk both to Servco and to its customers from a variety of adverse developments on the products in which Servco was dealing. The actions with respect to the first, second, and third functions were policy decisions that were not frequently changed. There was an annual meeting at which risk levels, scenarios, and exposure limits were formally agreed upon between the Credit Policy and the Management committees.

■ The first function was to define levels of risk concern based on the likelihood of events occurring. The Management Committee had this task and had set three levels of risk:

LEVEL A:	Scenarios so remote that each would be expected only once every 50 years.
LEVEL B:	Remote scenarios that could be expected once every three to five years.
LEVEL C:	Common scenarios that could be expected about once each year.

■ The second function was to develop specific scenarios to be monitored for each LEVEL of remoteness. This task was divided between the Management Committee and the managerial level. Three to six scenarios would be developed for LEVEL A and five to ten for LEVEL B. Assignment of scenarios for LEVEL A and LEVEL B was the responsibility of the Management Committee. This involved considerable senior management judgment because these events were so remote that statistical analysis was of help only at the broadest conceptual level. Assignment of scenarios for LEVEL C was a Managerial level responsibility.

■ The third function was to determine absolute exposure limits for each scenario for LEVEL A and LEVEL B and a single limit for all LEVEL C scenarios. The Management Committee was responsible for this function. Exposure limits for LEVEL A were expected to reflect potential loss levels that would seriously impact annual holding company earnings and that would threaten the operation of the options trading group. For LEVEL B, exposure limits were to reflect a loss that the bank would consider "serious but understandable." LEVEL C limits were to be about as severe as a "bad month."

■ The fourth function was to adjust exposure limits in response to changing opportunities. The exposure limits established by the Management Committee were liberal enough to be appropriate even in times of extraordinarily good opportunity. Less exposure was proper if opportunities were average or poor. It would be a Managerial level responsibility to establish temporary lower LEVEL B exposure limits and adjust them as opportunity required. It would be a Trading Room responsibility to establish temporary lower LEVEL C limits and adjust them. In both cases, an assessment of the opportunities available would consider not only market opportunities but also the competence and experience of trading personnel.

■ The fifth function was to monitor risk reports. At each level, risk reports were promptly prepared and approved unless limits were violated. Preparation of all reports was a Trading Room responsibility. LEVEL A reports were prepared weekly and were monitored by the Management Committee within three working days of the report data. LEVEL B reports were prepared daily. Monitoring was a Managerial responsibility and included a weekly written decision about the fourth function. A copy of this decision was sent to the Management Committee. LEVEL C reports were prepared daily. Monitoring was a Trading Room responsibility with written weekly updates for the fourth function.

Because the new derivative products were different from traditional loans, Servco's management had recognized that a different approach was required to set exposure limits. Servco's exposure was a result of two different types of risks. The first was the risk of failure by a counterparty in a transaction. The counterparty was in a position equivalent to a loan customer because the bank was essentially extending credit to it. If the counterparty failed to perform, Servco (and its parent, First Southeast, in case of a large problem) would probably have to bear the cost of closing the position.

A second risk was inherent in the nature of the products involved in the transactions, such as interest rate swaps and options. The volatility and risk of some products varied more than others, such as the duration and price sensitivity of long-term compared with short-term government securities. The risks of other products varied over time. Interest rate swaps, for example, had little risk at the beginning and the end but higher risk levels during the interim.

To deal with these combinations of risks, Servco used a sophisticated statistical approach in setting exposure limits to any one customer. Servco had established two basic dimensions to the limits. The first was an absolute limit of 10 percent of First Southeast's capital. The bank did not want to be subject to any greater loss from a single customer. The second was a lower limit reflecting the chance of loss associated with the risk of a particular customer. This limit was determined by the combination of the risks associated with the individual customer's credit worth and the risk associated with the particular products that Servco was trading with the institution. The total exposure to a customer summed across product lines could not at any time exceed the absolute total limit established for that customer.

Each customer had a unique risk profile translated into a customer-specific limit, and each product had a product unique risk profile translated into a product-specific limit. Customer risk profiles were established using standard tools and techniques of credit analysis. For example, because most of the counterparties in option transactions were other financial institutions, Servco looked carefully at relative capital levels in determining credit worthiness. Other characteristics being equal, an institution with a high level of capital to total assets was deemed more credit worthy than one with a low level and would therefore be given a higher exposure limit.

If the counterparty wanted to trade government securities (for daily settlement), Servco's risk would be that the customer would be unable to deliver (or pay for) the bonds it had sold to (or bought from) Servco. In that case, Servco would be caught short without the bonds it had probably already sold to another party (or be caught with bonds in its portfolio it had not planned to hold). Servco would then have to purchase (or sell) bonds from (to) another source to complete the transaction. Its risk would be any adverse price movement of the bonds compared to the transaction its traders had made.

The volatility of price changes in government bonds, for instance, was a combination of the rate of change in interest rates and the maturity of bonds being traded. A 10-basis-point change in interest rates during the day would have a greater impact on the market price of a 30-year Treasury bond than it would on a one-year bond. An analysis of the changes in bond prices indicated that short-term bill prices virtually never moved more than 1 percent in a day. Daily long-term bond prices rarely moved by as much as 3 percent.

If the maximum credit exposure Servco would accept with a particular customer was $1 million and the potential loss that could be suffered if the customer failed to pay was 1 percent of the face value of the bonds, Servco would restrict the outstanding transactions in those bonds to that customer to $100 million in face value. If the potential loss was 3 percent, Servco would restrict its outstanding trades awaiting payment to $33 million.

Servco followed a similar procedure in establishing limits for the options desk. Servco would calculate the credit exposure it wished to have for a particular customer. Then, considering events of Level A, B, and C, it would determine the maximum notional value of option trading that might result in a loss the size of the credit exposure limit. The level of option trading would not exceed the maximum potential loss allowed by Level A risk events, the most conservative calculation. Trading limits were established in a similar way for every customer and every product handled by Servco.

The Recommendation

As Mr. Brown reviewed the problems and risks associated with option trading, he wondered how well Servco would handle the problem of risk management with its option desk in the event of a major upheaval in the options market. The option risk management system had worked well to date, but it had not been tested in a major market upheaval. Mr. Corrigan's concerns were timely, and careful attention should be paid to the way that risk was managed in options trading. Moreover, Mr. Corrigan's remarks undoubtedly indicated that bank examiners and regulatory authorities would be looking carefully at the way these risks were managed.

Mr. Brown knew that he would be expected to report to his superiors in the next month about the soundness of Servco's option risk management system. He wondered whether he should leave the system as it was, recommend adoption of a modified version of this system, or recommend a totally different system. To help him in his analysis, Mr. Brown began mentally to list the benefits and drawbacks of the existing system.

Exhibit 1
FIRST SOUTHEAST FINANCIAL SERVICES CORP.
Balance Sheets as of December 31, 1990 and 1991
(millions of dollars)

	1990	1991
Assets		
Cash and due from banks	$ 6,707	$ 5,050
Time deposits, due from banks	1,348	1,411
Investment securities (approximate market value: 1991—$5,848; 1990—$5,206)	5,052	5,904
Trading account securities	2,107	1,061
Repurchase agreements	2,470	2,638
Loans	35,265	33,590
Less: Unearned income	741	813
Allowance for loan losses	536	1,220
Net Loans	$33,988	$31,557
Bank premises and equipment	959	963
Customers' liability for acceptances	600	454
Other assets	2,191	1,889
Total assets	$55,422	$50,926
Liabilities and Stockholders' Equity		
Deposits:		
Noninterest bearing	$13,539	11,412
Interest bearing	25,918	26,158
Total deposits	$39,457	$37,570
Short-term borrowings	7,854	8,349
Acceptances outstanding	602	454
Accounts payable and accrued liabilities	1,322	1,250
Long-term debt	3,427	3,138
Total liabilities	$52,662	$48,761
Stockholders' equity		
Preferred stock	2	152
Common stock, par value $2 a share: issued and outstanding: 1991—47,131; 1990—47,015 shares	94	94
Capital surplus	672	674
Retained earnings	1,991	1,315
Total equity	$ 2,760	$ 2,236
Less 1,772 shares of common stock in treasury, at cost	—	(70)
Total stockholders' equity	$ 2,760	$ 2,166
Total liabilities and stockholders' equity	$55,422	$50,928

Exhibit 2
FIRST SOUTHEAST FINANCIAL SERVICES CORP.
Income Statement for Years Ended December 31, 1989-1991
(millions of dollars except per-share figures)

	1989	1990	1991
Interest Income			
Loans, including fees	$3,813	$3,706	$3,486
Investment securities	380	355	391
Trading account	84	13	111
Repurchase agreements	118	110	174
Time deposits, due from banks	129	60	75
Total interest income	$4,525	$4,364	$4,239
Interest Expense			
Deposits	1,866	1,615	1,429
Short-term borrowings	452	408	452
Long-term debt	272	321	284
Total interest expense	$2,590	$2,344	$2,166
Net interest income	$1,935	$2,019	$2,073
Provision for loan losses	376	475	1,254
Net interest income after provision for loan losses	$1,560	$1,544	$ 819
Other Income			
Trust fees	100	116	136
Service charges on deposit accounts	265	292	324
Other charges and fees	132	141	162
Other trading account income	47	60	37
Investment securities gains	18	9	11
Gain on settlement of pension obligations	—	52	—
Other income	148	255	171
Total other income	$ 710	$ 926	$ 841
Other Expenses			
Salaries	827	924	979
Pensions and other employee benefits	175	159	181
Net occupancy of bank premises	152	177	194
Furniture and equipment	146	161	175
Other real estate	50	38	120
Provision for restructuring	—	—	95
Other expenses	539	586	634
Total other expenses	$1,890	$2,045	$2,379
Income (Loss) before Income Taxes	$ 379	$ 425	$ (720)
Applicable income taxes (tax benefit)	66	87	(164)
Net Income (Loss)	$ 313	$ 338	$ (556)
Earnings (Loss) per common share:			
Primary	$6.84	$7.19	$(11.99)
Fully diluted	$6.64	$7.13	$(11.99)

Notes